Rock Climbing
Desert Rock Ⅲ
Moab to Colorado National Monument

Eric Bjørnstad
All topos drawn by Chris Becker, unless otherwise noted

CHOCKSTONE

FALCON®

HELENA, MONTANA

A FALCON GUIDE®

Falcon® Publishing is continually expanding its list of recreational guidebooks. All books include detailed descriptions, accurate maps, and all information necessary for enjoyable trips. You can order extra copies of this book and get information and prices for other Falcon books by writing Falcon, P.O. Box 1718, Helena, MT 59624 or calling toll free 1-800-582-2665. Also, please ask for a free copy of our current catalog. Visit our website at www.FalconOutdoors.com or contact us by e-mail at falcon@falconguide.com.

Please send any corrections or new route information to Eric Bjørnstad at P.O. Box 790, Moab, UT 84532, or call 435-259-7516.

Printed in Canada.

05 04 03 02 01 00 99 TP 10 9 8 7 6 5 4 3 2 1

Falcon and FalconGuide are registered trademarks of Falcon Publishing, Inc.

Cover: Tony Sartin and Kevin Daniels on *Sundevil Chimney,* the Titan, Fisher Towers, by Greg Epperson.

Cataloging-in-Publication Data

Bjørnstad, Eric.
    Rock climbing desert rock III : Moab to Colorado National Monument
    / Eric Bjørnstad ; topos drawn by Chris Becker, unless otherwise
    noted.
            p.   cm. – (A Falcon guide)
        Includes index.
        ISBN 1-56044-754-0 (paperback)
        1. Rock climbing–Utah–Moab Region–Guidebooks. 2. Rock
    climbing–Colorado–Colorado National Monument Area–Guidebooks.
    3. Colorado National Monument (Colo.) 4. Moab (Utah) I. Title.
    II. Series.
    GV199.42.U82M634 1999
    917.88–dc21
                                                                    99-13538
                                                                        CIP

CAUTION
Outdoor recreational activities are by their very nature potentially hazardous. All participants in such activities must assume responsibility for their own actions and safety. The information contained in this guidebook cannot replace sound judgment and good decision-making skills, which help reduce risk exposure, nor does the scope of this book allow for disclosure of all the potential hazards and risks involved in such activities.

Learn as much as possible about the outdoor recreational activities in which you participate, prepare for the unexpected, and be cautious. The reward will be a safer and more enjoyable experience.

 Text pages printed on recycled paper.

WARNING: CLIMBING IS A SPORT WHERE YOU MAY BE SERIOUSLY INJURED OR DIE. READ THIS BEFORE YOU USE THIS BOOK.

This guidebook is a compilation of unverified information gathered from many different climbers. The author cannot assure the accuracy of any of the information in this book. The topos, route descriptions, difficulty ratings, and protection ratings may be incorrect or misleading; it is impossible for any one author to climb every route to confirm the information. Also, ratings of climbing difficulty and danger are always subjective and depend on the physical characteristics (height, for example), experience, technical ability, confidence and physical fitness of the climber who supplied the rating. Additionally, climbers who achieve first ascents sometimes underrate the difficulty or danger of the climbing route out of fear of being ridiculed if a climb is down-rated after subsequent ascents. Therefore, be warned that you must exercise your own judgment on where a climbing route goes, its difficulty, and your ability to safely protect yourself from the risks of rock climbing. Examples of some of these risks are: falling due to technical difficulty or natural hazards, such as holds breaking, falling rock, climbing equipment dropped by other climbers, hazards of weather and lightning, your own equipment failure, or failure or absence of fixed protection.

You should not depend on any information gleaned from this book for your personal safety; your safety depends on your own good judgment, based on experience and a realistic assessment of your climbing ability. If you have any doubt as to your ability to safely climb a route described in this book, do not attempt it.

The following are some ways to make your use of this book safer:

1. **Consultation:** You should consult with other climbers about the difficulty and danger of a particular climb prior to attempting it. Most local climbers are glad to give advice on routes in their area, and we suggest that you contact locals to confirm ratings and safety of particular routes and to obtain firsthand information about a route chosen from this book.

2. **Instruction:** Most climbing areas have local climbing instructors and guides available. We recommend that you engage an instructor or guide to learn safety techniques and to become familiar with the routes and hazards of the areas described in this book. Even after you are proficient in climbing safely, occasional use of a guide is a safe way to raise your climbing standard and learn advanced techniques.

3. **Fixed Protection:** Many of the routes in this book use bolts and pitons which are permanently placed in the rock. Because of variances in the manner of placement, weathering, metal fatigue, the quality of the metal used, and many other factors, these fixed protection pieces should always be considered suspect and should always be backed up by equipment that you place yourself. Never depend for your safety on a single piece of fixed protection because you never can tell whether it will hold weight. In some cases, fixed protection mentioned in this book may have been removed.

Be aware of the following specific potential hazards which could arise in using this book:

1. **Incorrect Descriptions of Routes:** If you climb a route and you have a doubt as to where the route may go, you should not go on unless you are sure that you can go that way safely. Route descriptions and topos in this book may be inaccurate or misleading.

2. **Incorrect Difficulty Rating:** A route may, in fact, be more difficult than the rating indicates. Do not be lulled into a false sense of security by the difficulty rating.

3. **Incorrect Protection Rating:** If you climb a route where you are unable to arrange adequate protection from the risk of falling through the use of fixed pitons or bolts, or by placing your own protection devices, do not assume that there is adequate protection available farther up the route just because the route protection rating indicates the route is not an X or an R rating. Every route is potentially an X (a fall may be deadly), due to the inherent hazards of climbing—including, for example, failure or absence of fixed protection, your own equipment failure, or improper use of climbing equipment.

THERE ARE NO WARRANTIES, WHETHER EXPRESS OR IMPLIED, THAT THIS GUIDE-BOOK IS ACCURATE OR THAT THE INFORMATION CONTAINED IN IT IS RELIABLE. THERE ARE NO WARRANTIES OF FITNESS FOR A PARTICULAR PURPOSE OR THAT THIS GUIDE IS MERCHANTABLE. YOUR USE OF THIS BOOK INDICATES YOUR ASSUMPTION OF THE RISK THAT IT MAY CONTAIN ERRORS AND IS AN ACKNOWL-EDGMENT OF YOUR OWN SOLE RESPONSIBILITY FOR YOUR CLIMBING SAFETY.

TABLE OF CONTENTS

DEDICATION

Dedicated to my climbing partner and longtime friend, the legendary Jimmy Dunn. He is well known to most of us who have pursued the sport of rock climbing; for us he needs no further introduction. The new generation should know, however, that Jimmy is an iconoclast and even today epitomizes the committed climber's lifestyle. He begins his day with one-arm pull-ups, lives in his VW van, does not smoke or consume alcohol, eats no food with eyes, and talks seldom of anything but climbing (and chess). He continues to climb 5.12 and is known for his single-mindedness, his one-shoe-on-and-one-off climbs in New Hampshire (to take advantage of a toe jam), his modest downgrading of many of his climbs, and his one-day ascents of previous multiday routes in the Black Canyon of the Gunnison (Colorado). Perhaps he is best known for *Cosmos* (VI, 5.10, A4), established in 1972. *Cosmos* was El Capitan's 11th established route and first new solo route. Jimmy returned 18 years later with John Middendorf to reclimb the giant overhanging wall, establishing a direct variation on the last six pitches. Jimmy is known to do practice climbs in tennis shoes—thus saving his rock shoes for important climbs—and he always begins a climbing day with a 6- to 8-mile run. He has done numerous new routes on Wall Street (near Moab) and has climbed many routes there using only his left or right hand. In Zion National Park, Jimmy climbed *Angel Hair* (a.k.a. *Dunn Route*, V, 5.11, A3) on Angels Landing without placing bolts or fixed anchors. Many of Jimmy's 5.12 desert offwidths are unrepeated.

Jimmy often rates difficult climbs 5.11++, which could be anything from 5.11+ to 5.13. He is noted for remarking: "We climbed it with a rope and rack and the shirt on our backs." He is credited with discovering the climbing potential at Indian Creek and was the first to find *Supercrack*.

On Castleton Tower, Jimmy made the sixth ascent of the *Kor-Ingalls*, the second ascent (seventh overall) of North Chimney, the first ascent of the West Face (eighth overall), and the first ascent (ninth overall) of the North Face. In the Fisher Towers, he made the sixth ascent of the *Finger of Fate* on the Titan.

In Canyonlands National Park, Jimmy made the first ascent of Candlestick Tower; the third ascent of Standing Rock; the second ascent of Moses, where he established the *Dunn Route*, and the second ascent of Zeus, where he put up *Sisyphus*. In Moab Valley, he made the second ascent of *Disappearing Angel*.

Jimmy studied botany in college, then went from being a beekeeper in Texas to the head of Eastern Mountain Sports Climbing School in New Hampshire, then turned to construction projects to finance a climbing lifestyle, then back to dedicated climbing. He is currently mining Red Cloud Wulfenite in Arizona. He says he is going to take a hiatus from climbing until the year 2000. We look forward to his return.

FOREWORD

Coming round a curve following the banks of the Colorado River heading south toward Moab, the mystery of the canyonlands unfolds with a sudden and unforgettable starkness. The first glimpse appears as a mirage–impossible, unknowable, untrue–of unearthly red rock towers lingering through the millennia, soaring into the hot dusty-blue air. Sandstone spires with spaceship summits orbiting above spiky yucca and prickly pear cactus, lizards lounging in cool shadows away from the blazing sun. You can't help but lift your eyes and strain, inspecting these towering, rust-colored obelisks. You are a climber, you are a seeker, you want to stand on top of these lofty pinnacles that erosion has graciously left behind, to know the secrets of their geologic improbability. You wish to orbit the earth in a spaceship, to defy the laws of gravity. Gazing into the hidden corners of your soul from your desert tower temple in the sky, you see your true self revealed, covered in red dust from head to toe, hands shredded, knuckles bleeding, arms wilted, exhausted, parched, grinning, joyously alive after a great climb.

Rock climbing in the canyonlands of Utah, on the Wingate Sandstone walls and spires near Moab, has been a shared vision quest for several generations of climbers. Intense experience has been shared by partners united by these demanding routes and the bond of goldline and perlon ropes. Desert climbing history has been made slowly and only occasionally written down. For many years these wondrous climbs were a relatively well-kept secret, but ultimately the legendary cracks and spires were too precious–and easily accessible–to withhold. Now that climbers from all corners of the earth are adventuring in canyonlands, we must strive to preserve the vision quest, that untrammeled desert realm, both physical and spiritual, of open and wild spaces, so much a part of canyonlands rock climbing. Our freedom to access the Wingate cliffs we cherish is tied to our preservation of canyonlands. As individuals and as a group, we can tread softly, be polite and courteous to all we meet, and minimize any potential negative impact we might have on the fragile desert soil, the rocks we love, the struggling plants, and the sensitive, shy animals. Give your support to groups that are actively representing climbers and helping to preserve desert rock climbing: The American Mountain Foundation, The Access Fund, and The Nature Conservancy.

Castleton Tower, the Priest, the Fisher Towers, and the pinnacles of Colorado National Monument were all memorable tests of strength and character in my climbing youth. These towering sandstone spires and their stupendous routes remain vivid memories from my desert "hard years" when high-spirited friends and I survived challenging rites of passage up Wingate Sandstone cracks. On vertical, rope-solo aid sojourns, I sought out rarefied summits, to know myself by being alone. With this exciting new volume of the Desert Rock series by local author and canyonlands climbing pioneer Eric Bjørnstad, you can also discover your own paths to the rocks, and find enjoyment on both classic and remote climbs in the sacred spaces of the Colorado Plateau and the canyonlands of Utah.

Ed Webster

ACKNOWLEDGMENTS

The monumental task of collecting, sorting, and researching the countless details of sandstone climbs on the Colorado Plateau–a vast area nearly the size of California–has been possible only through collaboration with hundreds of climbers. Many contributed not only topos and details of their climbs but also gave slides and reviewed information on other areas they had climbed.

Those providing slides are credited with their photographs. Size limitations for these new *Desert Rock* volumes have prevented the use of many photos I would like to have included.

The following are gratefully thanked for their time, support, and contributions:

Jeff Achey, Tom Addison, Jon Allen, Dave Anderson, Jay Anderson, Steve Anderton, Chris Andrews, Steve Angelini, Jim Angione, Joel Arellano, Mark Austin, Jonathan Auerbach, Christie Babalis, Benny Bach, Fran Bagenal, Jed Ballas, Brad Barlage, Fran Barnes, Dave Barnett, Alan Bartlett, John Bates, Dan Batwanis, Fred Beckey, Christine Beekman, Chris Begue, George Bell, Mark Bennett, Bobbie Bensman, Mary Laurence Bevington, Millie Birdwell, Josh Blumental, Jim Bodenhamer, Brad Bond, Jake Bos, Titoune Bouchard, George Bracksieck, Paul Brien, Don Briggs, Dawn Burke, John Burnham, Ralph Burns, Jon Butler, Keen Butterworth, Doug Byerly, John Byrnes, Tony Calderone, Kitty Calhoun, Chip Chace, Les Choy, Erick Christianson, Ben Clower, Tim Coats, Drizzt Cook, Darren Cope, Tom Cotter, Paul Cowan, Jeff Crystal, John Culbertson, Carolyn Dailey, Perry Davis, Steph Davis, Eric Decaria, Carl Diedrich, Topher Donahue, Rick Donnelly, Bill Duncan, Glenn Dunmire, Laura Duran, Teri Ebel, Warren Egbert, Al Engelbach, Brad England, Greg Epperson, Blain Erickson, Dave Evans, Paul Evans, Scott Evans, Michael "Esty" Estenson, Jeff Fassett, Randy Falk, Ralph Ferrara, Matt Fetbrod, Dan Fischer, Joe Fitschan, Bill Flemming, Bill Forrest, Craig Francois, Mike Fredrichs, Elaine Frederick, Ben Folsom, Graham Fontella, Charlie French, Doug Frost, Andrew Fry, James Funsten, Cindy Furman, Paul Gagner, Peter Gallagher, Bego Gerhart, Julie Gilje, John Glaze, David Gloudemans, Jim Goldberg, David Goldstein, Wilson Goodrich, Paul Gonzales, Todd Gordon, Tony Grenko, Patience Gribble, Ken Guza, Chris Haaland, Jesse Harvey, Lisa Hathaway, Jorma Hayes, Calvin Hebert, Leslie Henderson, Mark Henderson, Mark Hesse, Stanley Hill, Kris Hjelle, Ryan Hokanson, Peter Holcombe, Jeff Hollenbaugh, Steve Hong, Russell Hooper, Paul Horton, Jim Howe, Tommie Howe, Galen Howell, Roger "Strappo" Hughes, Al Hunt, Bruce Hunter, Ray Huntzinger, Wendy Hurlbert, George Hurley, Dave Insley, Eric Johnson, Dennis Jump, Chris Kalous, Teri Kane, Pete Keane, Todd Kearns, Jason Keith, Tobin Kelley, Max Kendall, Craig Kenyon, Aaron Kitscher, Sonia Knapp, Stephen Koch, Eric Kohl, Joe Kohl, Jon Krakauer, Eric Kraut, Chuck Kroger, Luke Laeser, Matt Laggis, Rollie Lamberson, Jim Langdon, Mark Lassiter, Dave Levine, John Lewis, Davin Lindy, Young Lowrie, Craig Luebben, the late Keith Maas, Douglas MacDonald, Todd Madaux, Glen Mann, Dan Mannix, John Merkel, Mel Macdonell, Krishen Mangat, Andrew Marquardt, Scott Martin, Bonnie McElhinny, Rob McKeracher, Betsi Mckittrick, Patrick A. Mcloney, Kelly McMenamen, Doug McQueen, Dan McRoberts, Steve Mesdough, Chris "Renegade" Meyer, Dan Michaels, Paul Midkiff, David Mondeau, Sasha Montagu, Matt Moore, Melisa Morrow, Sherry Needich, Dave Nessia, Karen Newman, Bob Novellino, Mike O'Donnell, Tom and Laurie O'Keefe, Jim Olsen, Michele Olsen, Greg Olson, Ron Osborn, Lin Ottinger, Bob Palais, Dava Parr, Sonja Paspal, Simon Oeck, Mike Pennings, Rich Perch, Andy Petefish, Jason Pietryga, Andy Pitas, Wendy Pitas, Linus Platt, Ferdl Ploerer, Hanni Ploerer, David Pollari, Jack Pope, Steve Porcella, Dean Potter, Jason Predock, Joe Prescott, Brad Quinn, Steve Quinlan, Duane Raleigh, Glenn Randall, Alf Frandell, Eric Rasmussen, Angela Renner, Keith Reynolds, Fred Rice, Scott Riley, Stu Ritchie, Mike Ritter, Andy Roberts, Christopher Roberts, Jack Roberts, Ann Robertson, Bill Rothstein, Bill Russel, Tom Russell, Chuck Santagati, Antoine Savelli, Joede Schoeberlein, Sallie Shatz, Joseph Sheader, John Sherman, Walt Shipley, John Shireman,

Rick Showalter, Paul Sibley, Paul Seibert, Eric Siefer, Matt Simpson, Ken Sims, Jeff Singer, Doug Sinor, Geoff Sluyter, Jo Smith, Rick Smith, Doug Snively, Kirby Spangler, Merlin Spiller, Carrie Sood, Alan "Heavy Duty" Stevenson, Tracy Sternburg, Andrea Stoughton, Brett Sutteer, Mary Sutton, Steve Swanke, John Sweeley, Pete Takeda, Brian Takei, Eve Tallman, Drake Taylor, Ramsey Thomas, Tom Thomas, Mel Thorsen, Reed Tindall, Tim Toula, Jake Tratiak, Joe Tuhy, Paul Turecki, Mark Vogel, Ray Vought, Barry Ward, Robert Warren, Darren Watson, Cristie Wayment, Randall Weekley, Ed Webster, Frosty Weller, David Whidden, Mark Whiton, Earl Wiggins, Chad Wiggle, Ron Wiggle, Joel Williams, Chip Wilson, Nate Wilson, Tony Wilson, Mike Wood.

Bill Godshaix has given freely of time and expense in developing and enlarging my shots into an 8- by 10-inch format. These volumes would lack much in quality without his generous contribution.

Stewart Green, Martha Morris, and Jimmy Dunn have been generous with their help in reading and making suggestions of parts of this guide.

I have been very fortunate in being given permission to use the photos of nationally acclaimed photographer Ed Cooper (my climbing partner in the early 1960s).

Chris Becker's meticulously drawn topos have set a standard for detail, accuracy, and artistic excellence. I am profoundly indebted to him. He took time from teaching and house building to accompany me on weekends to Colorado National Monument with K.C. Baum.

James Garrett and his wife, Dr. Franziska Garrett, were tireless in their collaboration on routes in the Fisher Towers and the Moab area.

Mike Baker camped, hiked, and photographed with me, editing and researching all of the areas covered in this guide. He has contributed hundreds of hours and numerous trips to Moab from his home in Aspen. Many thanks to him for his momentous contribution.

Cameron Burns gave numerous photos and topos and many hours of discussion during various trips to Moab from his home near Aspen.

KC Baum also contributed tireless hours to editing, hiking the Colorado National Monument with me, and opening up his files to the area. Thanks also for his history of the monument.

Bret Ruckman, Marco Cornacchione, and Fred Knapp reviewed much of the guide and contributed photos and route descriptions for many of the areas covered herein.

Thanks to Ed Webster for the foreword, and for route information for the Fisher Towers and Colorado National Monument.

Steve "Crusher" Bartlett edited the entire volume, made available numerous photos, and was invaluable in his contributions, especially to the Fisher Towers.

Jay Smith hiked his routes with me and was generous with his time.

Jeff Widen wrote the Environmental Considerations and biography and gave freely of his slides and topos.

The Latitude 40-Degree Company, which produces the excellent Moab East and West maps, continues to add climbing designations and landform names to its popular four-wheel drive and mountain bike maps, making them as valuable for climbers as for other recreationists.

Jim Beyer reviewed his routes with me and contributed the explanation of his rating system.

Kevin Chase, of Moab Climbing Shop, contributed the size comparison chart.

Kyle Copeland, Charlie Fowler, Peter Verchick, Dave Medara, and Tom Gilje gave their time generously and made available information on numerous routes included in this guide.

Finally, the keystone to bringing this volume to fruition, Cris Coffey, who contributed the majority of the editing on the original *Desert Rock* (Chockstone 1988) has, with her critical eye, sharpened and helped clarify these new *Desert Rock* volumes, bringing them from the dark ages to literacy.

Eric Bjørnstad
Moab, 1999

Moon over the Titan

INTRODUCTION TO THE DESERT ROCK SERIES

The sandstone canyon walls, mesas, buttes and spires of the Colorado Plateau are the focus of this new *Desert Rock* series. The geographical boundaries of the series are as follows: Colorado National Monument to Zion National Park (east to west); and Valley of the Gods/Indian Creek to Moab and the San Rafael Swell (south to north). The original *Desert Rock* (Chockstone Press, 1988) attempted to document known climbs established throughout the sandstone formations of the Colorado Plateau. Not included were hundreds of ascents up the buttes, towers, and walls of the Grand Canyon and Zion National Parks. *Rock Climbs in the National Parks* includes a subjective selection of the best of Zion but leaves the 280-mile-long Grand Canyon to future writers.

A technical rock climbing guide is, by necessity, an assemblage of material from a great many sources. This is especially true regarding the vast deserts of the Colorado Plateau. Unlike most areas, where routes are established mainly by resident climbers and route detail is easily accessible, here resident climbers are comparatively few and the majority of sources for route information are scattered across the country and overseas. Although the three years and 8,000 hours of research that went into *Desert Rock* (1988) have provided a solid foundation for the present series of guides, the past couple of years have brought additional contacts with hundreds of climbers, and I have racked up an astonishing number of research hours. I have climbed in the desert for more than 30 years; for 20 years I have made Moab my home. This series of guides is the product of a long love affair with the desert.

The Colorado Plateau is the physiographic province that lies north and east of the Basin and Range province and south and west of the Rocky Mountain province. It covers about 160,000 square miles (nearly the size of California) in Utah, Arizona, New Mexico, and Colorado. Within its vast reaches of sedimentary sandstone lies the greatest potential for crack climbing in the world. It is a sector of North America with thousands of miles of vertically fractured Wingate Sandstone walls. Although hundreds of climbs have been established, this is only a fraction of the potential on the plateau. The majority of routes lie within the higher register of difficulty, but there is a large selection of excellent climbs below the 5.10 level, all within the incomparable canyon country of the high Southwest desert.

In *The Bright Edge*, Stephen Trimble writes, "Time ticks slowly for the Canyon Country. A year means nothing, a human lifetime sees arroyos deepened a bit, the collapse of an arch or cliff here and there, the creation of a new window or two. A millennium scarcely changes the landscape. Only in tens of thousands of years does the land see much change. And even then, a hundred thousand years is a fraction of an instant in the millions and billions of years of the earth's history. On this time scale the Plateau itself becomes a temporary phenomenon, a passing fancy of an earth with a restless skin of drifting, dynamic continents."

The plateau contains eight national parks–Zion, Bryce, Capitol Reef, Arches, and Canyon-lands in Utah; Mesa Verde in Colorado; and Grand Canyon and Petrified Forest in Arizona. The plateau also contains 19 other regions managed by the National Park Service–the greatest concentration of national parks and wilderness areas outside Alaska.

The Colorado River is the principle artery of the plateau, giving it its name and draining 90 percent of canyon country. Each year the river transports about 3 cubic miles of sandstone sediment to the impounded waters behind Glen Canyon Dam. Like the branches of a tree, the

Colorado is fed by a network of tributaries, with countless arroyos further contributing during storms. It is a land of haunting beauty, a region without parallel on earth, and its fragile ecosystem is in grave danger.

What has changed in the years since *Desert Rock* was first published, early in 1988, is the escalating number of people who are discovering and frequenting the desert. Each season attendance records are broken at Canyonlands National Park, Natural Bridges National Monument, and Dead Horse Point State Park. Annual visitation at Zion National Park exceeds 2 million, and Arches National Park is approaching 1 million per year. Recreationists of every disposition now make the desert their vacation destination. The gamut runs from mountain bikers, river runners, climbers, and four-wheel drivers, to hikers, campers, artists, photographers, mystics, and nature enthusiasts. The challenge becomes balancing their enjoyment with preserving what they have come to enjoy.

It has long been assumed that the desert is a tough, indestructible land, indifferent to human impact. In other regions of the country, moisture promotes a bacterial breakdown. Trees rot, litter (with time) dissolves, new growth covers scars. But the desert is so dry and growth so slow that the land is like another planet, where time has stopped. Our appearance has been dramatic and caustic. The dry air mummifies our castaways. Orange peels, eggshells, and other material tossed to the land do not biodegrade. Discards become permanent monuments to our sloth.

Cryptobiotic soil is essential to the health of the desert. Without this vulnerable crust, the majority of indigenous flowers and other shrubs would simply not exist. Once the soil is impacted by tire or foot, such prints remain visible for decades. Recovery is estimated to take up to 250 years. If we are to preserve this island of earth, it is most important that we walk only on slickrock (rock devoid of soil or vegetation), in drainages, or on established trails. Direct cross-country travel is unconscionable.

The indelible print of our seemingly benign inroads into the desert is not readily apparent from our state-of-the-art vehicles, which are equipped with the emblems of our sybaritic society. With us we bring not only quickdraws, spaceship alloy light cams, freeze-dried foods, and satellite maps, but also an invincible confidence in our superiority as a species. We have a long history of annihilating the land as we reshape it to suit us. I implore all who visit the unique canyon country to be responsible not only for our present love of the desert, but for the generations yet to be thrilled by this magical place.

Perhaps now with the kindling of a new consciousness we are on the threshold of a new direction not previously traveled. We may now value and protect the wild regions of the planet not for the short-term plunder of the past, but as the very root of our survival.

Please visit with prudence, responsibility, and love.

Eric Bjørnstad
January, 1996
Moab, Utah

Series Summary

Desert Rock: Rock Climbs in the National Parks includes a subjective selection of routes in Arches and Zion National Parks and the known routes of Capitol Reef and Canyonlands National Parks. It also includes the adjacent Glen Canyon National Recreation Area and Green River area just outside the park boundary of Canyonlands.

Desert Rock: Wall Street to the San Rafael Swell covers the region west of the Colorado River in the Moab area, and includes Wall Street, Day Canyon, Long Canyon, and the majority of routes established in the San Rafael Swell.

Desert Rock: Moab to Colorado National Monument covers climbs east of the Colorado River in the Moab area. Included are Kane Creek, Moab Valley, Sand Flats, the River Road (Scenic Byway 128), Castle Valley, Fisher Towers, Onion Creek, Mystery Towers, and Colorado National Monument.

Desert Rock: Indian Creek Climbs will offer definitive coverage of Indian Creek and Cottonwood Canyon areas.

Desert Rock: Remote Areas of the Colorado Plateau will include sandstone climbs of Valley of the Gods, Tooth Rock, Arch and Texas canyons, and numerous other isolated regions of the Colorado Plateau.

Though the Navajoland was documented in *Desert Rock* (1988) from a historic point of view (equipment lists and other pertinent ascent information excluded), the present volumes do not include the climbs located on the reservation. There is still a climbing ban imposed by the Navajo Tribal Council, although there have been new routes clandestinely established since *Desert Rock*. There have been reports of windshields being broken on unattended Anglo-owned vehicles, as well as climbing equipment being confiscated and stiff fines imposed on those disregarding the climbing ban. On the other hand, reports have also surfaced regarding climbs accomplished on the reservation with the permission of the neighboring Navajo residents. If permission cannot be obtained, please respect tribal limits. After all, there are more legal and spectacular buttes, towers, spires, and canyon walls to climb on the Colorado Plateau than a person could do in a lifetime.

Environmental Considerations of Desert Rock Climbing, by Jeff Widen

The Colorado Plateau is a stunning and magical arena in which to climb. After experiencing the desert world, many climbers have written about the need to slow down, take in the desert's aura and walk more slowly. Indeed, just being within this incredible landscape is a major part of any climbing trip. The starkness of the earth's bare bones, along with the extremes of heat, cold, wind, and weather, are all part of the desert climbing experience. As harsh as the desert may be in many ways, though, it is also an extremely fragile place. Plants and animals carry out a tentative existence and are easily disturbed. The visual scars left by careless activity are extremely slow to heal. The desert needs extra care, a lighter touch.

There is another compelling reason to tread lightly in the desert. The extractive industries of mining, timber cutting, ranching, and water development have long been criticized for their abuse of public lands. Damaging climbing practices threaten to put some climbers in the same

photo: Lin Ottinger

Hindu, Onion Creek Towers

category, at least in the eyes of environmental organizations if not the general public. Land management agencies increasingly view climbing as an activity with real impacts—one that can be dealt with fairly easily, meaning increased regulation. One has only to look at recent attempts at bolt bans by various agencies to understand the seriousness of the threat. Climbers can go a long way toward staving off overly harsh regulations by acting responsibly. Although the debates over climbing styles rage endlessly, nearly all climbers agree on the importance of protecting the climbing environment. The desert contains some of the most radical and outrageous crack climbs on Earth. It's up to everyone climbing there to help protect access to these climbs, and to protect the rock and land itself.

Climbing impacts in the desert center around all aspects of a climb, from multiple trails to rock damage to trash. The desert environment requires extra care at each turn.

Approaches: Check out approach routes in advance. For the driving portion of the approach—a major part of many desert climbs—stay on established roads. If you are unlike most desert climbers and own some beefy four-wheel drive with real clearance, resist the urge to get a few hundred yards closer to the route by driving off road. On foot, follow established approach paths wherever possible. Take an extra minute to see if there is a common route up to a climb. Take special care not to walk over areas of cryptobiotic soil (you can recognize this unique desert plant assemblage by its appearance as black, crusty soil). It is critical for prevention of erosion in the desert, takes hundreds of years to form, and is destroyed instantly when crushed. To avoid cryptobiotic soil and other plants and animals, walk in washes and over slickrock and boulders whenever possible. Approaching climbs in this way will also prevent the all-too-visible trashing of the desert's surface.

Protection: Using clean pro is perhaps the most important part of low-impact climbing in the desert–the rock simply can't take the abuse of piton placement. Free routes don't present much of a problem, since desert cracks are tailor-made for camming devices. On aid routes, however, there are too many examples where cracks have been nailed that could have been climbed with clean hardware (see "Pitons" section below). It's true that you need a huge stock of cam devices to climb desert routes, but that's part of the game. People often go in groups and pool their gear to do these routes. When retreating or rapping off, leave gear, webbing, etc., of neutral colors–brown, black, or tan are best.

Bolts: Nothing raises the ire of land managers more than over-bolting, whether real or perceived. If there is one thing climbers can do to prevent excessive regulation, it is to minimize bolt use. This doesn't mean bolt placement elimination, for indeed the nature of desert climbing–vertical walls and towers without natural rappel anchors–makes bolt placement a necessity. But climbers should keep the number to a minimum. The days of long bolt ladders in the desert are long gone. Short ladders are sometimes necessary to reach the crackless summits of towers, but when the route is a predominately bolt-clipping ascent, the formation is better left unclimbed.

Bolts placed next to cracks would seem anathema to most climbers, yet a disturbing number of bolts can be found next to bomber cam placements. If you don't have the gear, go hit up your friends and come back later. When bolts are placed, they should be placed well, whether to give you the extra courage to do a few more free moves or to prevent the eventual formation of an ugly and unusable hole when the bolt comes out.

The standard desert bolt has long been an angle piton pounded into a 3/8-inch hole and drilled at a slight downward angle. Some of the newer expansion bolts are now being used–check out recent reviews in various climbing publications to see which ones are best for soft rock.

Power drills have no place in the desert. Not only can holes be quickly hand-drilled in sandstone, but a major part of the desert climbing experience is the feeling of quiet and vast open spaces, and the sense of high adventure. The use of power drills not only runs counter to this sense, but leads quickly to over-bolting.

Pitons: Climbers should adopt a minimalist attitude when nailing in the desert. Pin scars are more visible in sandstone, and nailing routes get beat out here faster than on any other rock type. Minimizing piton damage includes reducing the number of pin placements as much as possible, looking for alternative routes, and perhaps stopping to ask yourself whether a formation with existing routes really needs a new nail-up. Devices such as Lowe ball nuts and Tri-cams, Rock and Rollers, and small camming devices can often substitute for pins down to Lost Arrow size. Using clean gear can also have the desirable effect of upping the fear factor of an aid route.

If you must nail, use constructive scarring techniques. This involves favoring upward blows to the pin when cleaning so the eventual hole will accept a nut or other clean pro.

Chipping/Gluing: These are destructive practices that are indefensible anywhere, especially in the desert.

Chalk: Many desert pioneers and early locals climbed without it, but most modern climbers use chalk. White chalk is especially visible and obnoxious on red rock. If you use chalk, use colored chalk–dark brown or dark red are the best colors. Most of the national parks already require colored chalk.

Archaeological Sites: The Colorado Plateau is rich in Native American archaeological resources. Special care must be taken to avoid these areas, whether ruins, rock art panels, or areas with pot shards, tool fragments, or other ancient artifacts. Stealing artifacts is a federal crime. Avoid climbing near any archaeological sites–you can bet there is another perfect crack around the corner.

Human Waste: Desert areas are booming in popularity, and human waste is becoming an increasing problem. It is critical to take the extra couple of minutes to do it right. Go at least 300 feet (91 m) from major washes and other watercourses. Although land managers are looking at the viability of surface disposal, the currently accepted method for dealing with excrement is still to dig a small hole 6- to 8-inches deep and bury the waste. Used toilet paper should be packed out in zip-locked bags and disposed of. There are also reports of increasing human waste near the bases of popular towers–climbers should treat the base of towers as a stream and go several hundred feet away to do their business. It goes without saying that all other trash, tape, old slings, etc., should be carried out.

Wildlife: It is important to respect wildlife closures, usually imposed to protect nesting raptors or other species. Closures are posted at visitor centers or land managers' headquarters.

Attitude: No climbing is totally without impact. But in this desert land–with its special qualities of fragility, beauty, and silence–it is essential that we reduce our impact. We must walk and climb a bit more lightly. The self-interest issue of preventing over-regulation is crucial. But there is also a much bigger issue–it is the right thing to do and makes the incredible experience of climbing in this place all the richer.

INTRODUCTION TO THIS VOLUME

MOAB TO COLORADO NATIONAL MONUMENT

Desert Rock: Moab to Colorado National Monument is a definitive guide that explores the diversity of sandstone ascents established along the Kane Creek drainage, east of the Colorado River; Moab Valley; Sand Flats; the Navajo and Wingate Walls along River Road, upriver from Moab; Castle Valley with Castleton Tower and its neighbors; the incredible Fisher, Onion Creek, and Mystery Towers; and the extraordinary Colorado National Monument at the northeastern edge of the Colorado Plateau.

Visitor Information

Moab Information Center: The multi-agency Moab Information Center is located at the corner of Main and Center Streets. The center houses representatives of the USDA Forest Service, Bureau of Land Management, Travel Council, National Park Service, and Canyonlands Natural History Association. Public restrooms, drinking water, a local events bulletin board, and hundreds of free brochures relating to the nearby rivers, mountains, parks, and canyon country are available at the center. Its 72-seat auditorium is a cool and comfortable haven where educational videos on the area may be viewed.

Canyonlands Natural History Association: There are 64 nonprofit natural history associations working in partnership with National Park Service areas throughout the United States. In the Moab area, the Canyonlands Natural History Association is the concessionaire at the Moab Information Center and nearby Arches National Park, Canyonlands National Park, and Natural Bridges National Monument. The association offers an excellent selection of books, maps, slides, and postcards. The organization's professional staff publishes brochures, books, and maps (many are free), as well as produces numerous educational programs.

Campgrounds

Moab provides a dozen or more fully equipped campgrounds, or you can camp at Bureau of Land Management (public land) sites along the river corridor. On River Road, camping is permitted only at improved recreation sites and at designated undeveloped campsites. Camping at all locations is limited to 14 days within a 30-day period. After 14 days, the next camp must be more than 30 miles (48 km) from the previous camp. Improved campsites contain tables, fire rings, and toilets; sites are obtained on a first-come, first-served basis. Designated, undeveloped campsites are identified by posts with a tent symbol and require a portable toilet system. Ground fires are permitted in existing campfire rings, but you must burn only driftwood or wood obtained from outside the river corridor. Making ground fires and new fire rings at undeveloped sites is not permitted. Vehicles (including mountain bikes) are allowed only on existing roads. Please be responsible.

Cultural History

The Fremont Indian culture lived generally west of the Colorado River and the Anasazi east of the river (650–1,250 years ago). In the Moab area, they established no permanent dwellings, but are thought to have traveled through the region trading with one another while hunting and foraging. The region east of the river has many panels of rock art, although they are not as numerous as those found west of the Colorado.

Flora and Fauna

The common plant life in canyon country includes willow and cottonwood trees, tamarisk, scrub oak, mountain mahogany, desert holly, black brush, Mormon tea, several species of sage and buckwheat, greasewood, cliff rose, rabbitbrush, prickly pear, fish hook and claret cup cacti, narrow-leaf yucca, exotic grasses, and a rich array of wildflowers (their blooms most abundant from the end of April through the first week of May). Be able to identify poison ivy and always be watchful when bushwhacking through side canyons.

Canyonlands wildlife includes elk, mule deer, desert bighorn sheep, mountain lions, and bears in the La Sal Mountains; and coyote, fox, badgers, skunks, squirrels, chipmunks, rabbits, and a variety of rodents found everywhere else. Be on the lookout for black widow spiders hidden in rock crevices, and scorpions (the arachnid that gives birth to live young, rather than laying eggs) living in the bark of trees or hiding beneath clumps of dry wood (or sleeping bags!).

When hiking the high deserts east of the Colorado River, be wary of the faded pygmy rattlesnake. Also found in the area are harmless bull snakes and racers. Less common are great basin rattlers, sidewinders, and the largest rattlesnakes in the Southwest, the 7-foot (15 m) diamondbacks. Lizards are ubiquitous, especially western fences, whiptails, and the amazing collared lizards (members of the iguana family), distinguished by a prominent black band around their necks, and on females in estrus, bright red and orange streaks on their sides until eggs are laid. The collared lizard has been clocked at 17 miles per hour, ranking it among the fastest reptiles. It runs on all four legs until reaching maximum speed, at which point it stands upright and continues running on its hind legs, looking much like a miniature dinosaur.

Cryptobiotic Soil

On the Colorado Plateau, the vulnerable ecosystem of the desert is being dramatically impacted by an exponential surge in visitation. Cryptobiotic soil crust is the critically fragile skin upon which the health of this unique ecosystem depends. It is the product of a symbiotic relationship between mosses, lichens, microfungi, and algae. The soil traps nutrients; fixes nitrogen; adds phosphorous, potassium, and calcium; and recycles dead organic material back into the soil. It is crucial to the development of vascular plants. The subsurface fibrous network of crypto soil plays a major role in controlling wind and water erosion, but once damaged by tire or foot, the whole cryptobiotic community often disintegrates. In addition, tire- or footprints aesthetically degrade the land. Not only is the black, crusty cryptobiotic soil to be avoided, but also avoid its fledgling form, a reddish or light brown crust known as cyanobacteria soil. It may be identified by a crunchy feeling as one walks across it. The soil is nearly invisible in the early stages of its development, but it must be preserved to ensure the good health of the desert. (See "Environmental Considerations of Desert Rock Climbing," by Jeff Widen, page 3.)

Potholes

Whether dry or filled with rainwater, potholes are vulnerable to degradation by the unknowing visitor. Although they appear to be inviting pools maintained for the hot, weary traveler, they are actually home to a variety of organisms which may be destroyed by pollution from human contact (sunscreen, sweat, insect repellents, pets, and other foreign materials). Numerous creatures have adapted to the desert's wet and dry cycle including crustaceans, insects, tadpoles, frogs, and snails. Many are dormant during dry periods and awaken to intense life when moisture returns. It is important for the health of the desert that we do not disturb these fragile islands of life. Unless it is a medical emergency, it is crucial we do not bathe in, swim in, or trample wet or dry potholes. Please be a responsible visitor in this very special land.

Climate

Throughout the Colorado Plateau, spring and autumn are the most pleasant months to visit. In the spring, however, relentless winds are common. Although summer temperatures during June, July, and August are often in the 100-degree range, days are much less unpleasant than in humid areas. Thundershowers can be expected spring, summer, and fall, and are especially dangerous. There have been a number of deaths from lightning strikes throughout the years, including a climber on Castleton Tower in 1995. A few precautions: If lightning occurs, avoid high ground, tall trees, and moist regions such as alcoves or drainages. If possible, stay in your vehicle until the storm passes, or crouch on the ground, preferably on something dry to insulate the body. Do not become a lightning rod by bunching together with your comrades. Mountain bikes and climbing hardware can also be natural lightning rods.

photo: Eric Bjørnstad

Waterfalls along River Road

Rock Strata Sequence Chart

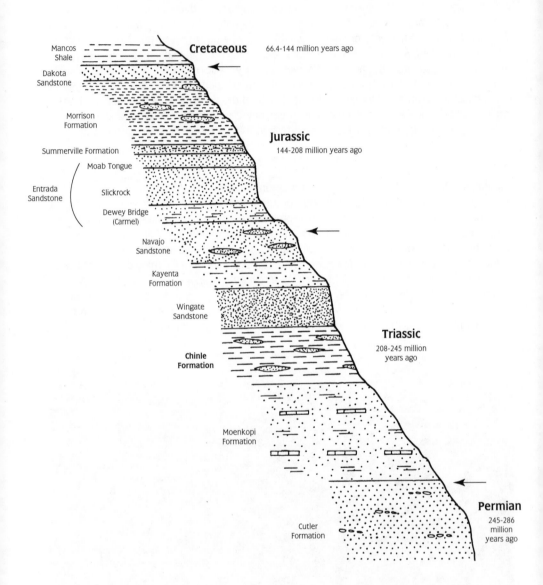

Mancos Shale

Dakota Sandstone

Morrison Formation

Summerville Formation

Moab Tongue

Entrada Sandstone

Slickrock

Dewey Bridge (Carmel)

Navajo Sandstone

Kayenta Formation

Wingate Sandstone

Chinle Formation

Moenkopi Formation

Cutler Formation

Cretaceous   66.4-144 million years ago

Jurassic   144-208 million years ago

Triassic   208-245 million years ago

Permian   245-286 million years ago

Flash floods are another real hazard. They can appear from nowhere and are frequently powerful enough to dislodge large boulders, uproot trees, and tumble vehicles like weightless toys. Avoid washes and dry arroyos, even when a storm seems distant. On the positive side, summer thunderstorms produce spectacular waterfalls cascading from slickrock canyon rims. Locals frequently jam River Road (Scenic Byway 128 east of Moab) during cloudbursts to view more than a dozen major waterfalls within the first mile (1.6 km). Numerous waterfalls also add drama along Potash Road, east of the Colorado River from Moab.

Geology (presented in descending order of age)

Climbs east of the Colorado River are, with very few exceptions, up the aeolian (windblown) Wingate Sandstone which has made desert climbing famous. The Fisher Towers, Onion Creek, Mystery Towers, and River Tower are Cutler Sandstone with a caprock of Moenkopi. River Road to Negro Bill Canyon (mile marker 3) is bordered by Navajo Sandstone. Routes on the BLM Takeout Buttress near mile marker 10 on the River Road climb the Chinle Formation.

Mancos Shale, Dakota Sandstone, the Morrison Formation, and the Summerville Formation are the youngest layers of rock in the region but are not typically found on climbing formations. Entrada Sandstone, the next youngest layer, is found on some formations in Arches National Park, which is included in the first Desert Rock book, Rock Climbs in the National Parks.

Navajo Sandstone, the next layer, is a relatively soft rock found in Zion National Park and along Wall Street. Like the Wingate, it is of aeolian (wind) deposition, fine grained, and often of whitish to buff color. It dominates River Road to Anasazi Buttress at mile marker 3.

Kayenta Sandstone forms a bench between the two cliff-forming layers of Navajo and Wingate. It is the stream-deposited base rock of Dead Horse Point, Island-in-the-Sky, Colorado National Monument, and the protective caprock of most desert towers.

Wingate Sandstone is the predominant rock upon which climbs are established east of the Colorado River. It is also the stratum that comprises the well-known Castleton Tower, Moses, the walls of Indian Creek, and the climbs of Colorado National Monument. Wingate is unique in that it erodes slowly, fracturing along straight vertical planes. It is very angular in appearance, often with chimneys and crack systems remaining the same size for 100 feet (30 m) or more. Some Wingate rock—the Bride west of the Colorado River and the Coke Ovens in Colorado National Monument, for instance—is soft enough to be confused with Navajo Sandstone. When erosion has removed its Kayenta Sandstone caprock and its color has changed from russet to lighter-colored rounded domes, the rock is extremely soft, making it nearly impossible to place belay or rappel anchors.

Below Wingate Sandstone are the slope-forming Chinle Sandstone and the red/maroon Moenkopi Sandstone, both of mudflat deposition. Moenkopi is the most recognizable stratum of rock on the Colorado Plateau. It resembles a chocolate layer cake and often appears with thin horizontal bands of light green (organic deposition). At the time of deposition, the Moenkopi Formation was a 200-mile (322 km), flat, expansive flood plain which stretched from present-day western Colorado to western Utah. Few climbs exist on Moenkopi, although it is the caprock of the Fisher Towers, Onion Creek, Mystery Towers, and River Tower.

The Cutler Formation rests below the Moenkopi, often a deep bright red in color and resembling Wingate in density. Because it tends to fracture horizontally and bears a soft stucco of decomposing mud, it is loose and relatively dangerous to climb. It is the dominant rock of the Fisher Towers, Onion Creek, Mystery Towers, and River Tower.

Maps

The *Moab East* map published by Latitude 40-Degrees, Inc., of Boulder, Colorado, is the most useful for locating climbs and other features in the Moab area and east to the La Sal Mountains and the Cisco Desert to their north. It includes many names given by climbers to landforms, and an updated revision is published every year or two with future editions expected to designate additional landforms and climbing locations. It is compiled from 7.5-minute U.S. Geological Survey maps, which were field checked between 1984 and 1990 using aerial photographs. This excellent map gives a "For Your Information" section on its reverse side. Included are map-reading basics, land use information, camping etiquette, a list of archeological and historic sites, environmental considerations, personal considerations, canyon country photography, weather statistics for Moab, a brief explanation of desert ecology, elevation profiles, and a list of nearby agencies and organizations. The map is printed on 100 percent tearproof and water-resistant plastic material, but is subject to damage by petroleum products like camp fuel and sunscreen.

For Colorado National Monument, the map in the park's brochure is adequate; one may also use the 7.5-minute USGS Colorado National Monument Quadrangle. For the location of landforms not identified on the map, refer to the locator map on page 252.

Ethics

Always climb a route in the same style (or better) as the first ascent party. If the route is above your level of expertise, find a route you can climb safely and enjoyably without desecrating it and bastardizing yourself by bringing the climb down to your level. There are countless routes to choose from in the desert. Do not add bolts or fixed anchors, chisel or glue holds, or in any way alter an existing route. In simple terms, do not play God. Keep a low profile so others (climbers or not) visiting the desert are not intruded upon. Keep pets under control and boom boxes (if necessary) at low decibels. The sweet music you listen to may be noise to another. Smell the clean air and listen to the exquisite sounds of nature, all such a wonderful part of the desert experience. Have fun, and return from the desert climbing experience with the increased love, awareness, and good karma this land has to offer.

Bill Duncan relates a story of rock alteration at the head of Rough Canyon near Colorado National Monument: "On the way to climb Tabeguache Tower, there was an atrocity at the head of Rough Canyon. Someone had drilled and chiseled dozens of handholds on an overhanging wall. Bolts 5 feet apart proliferated everywhere. There was a large rock fire pit, and of course chalk everywhere. This was on BLM land, but it seemed apparent that the manufacturing of climbing holds on public land was overstepping the boundary between land use and land abuse. We reported the area to Troy, the BLM ranger, and returned one day to take photos of the place. There, we found Ed the sport climber. After a long conversation, we failed to fully convince him that what he was doing was wrong. He had a Hilti and a hammer and chisel. He said he just wanted a place to train and didn't think anyone would mind his drilling large holes in the rock. Fortunately, he got ticketed and fined, and the BLM made him remove all the bolts. I hope this is not happening elsewhere."

Please visit softly and with love.

ABOUT THIS BOOK

Each chapter in this book has the same format: The general location of the climbs are in shaded boxes; they are followed by a description of the area's location. Formation names and sub-areas are set between horizontal lines. Routes are listed from left to right on formations unless otherwise noted. Route names are followed by grade, free climbing difficulty, aid rating, number of pitches, length of route or height of the landform (measured from its longest side), and a star rating. First ascent particulars are followed by location of and access to the climb. Paraphernalia is followed by descent information.

River Road

Anasazi Buttress

Anasazi Buttress is the Navajo Sandstone wall between Short and Negro Bill Canyons.

ACQUIRED TASTE II, 5.12a/b, A1, 2 pitches, 250 feet (76 m)

First Ascent: Jeff Lowe, Teri Ebel, 3 June 1994 (on their honeymoon).

Location and Access: *Acquired Taste* is 2 cracks left of *Navajo Route*. The climb begins with 30 feet (9 m) of aid, climbed by an unknown party years ago.

Pitch 1: Begin with 4 bolts and 3 nut placements to get off the ledge at the base of the wall. Continue 5.11+ fingertips to thin hands, passing 2 fixed pitons and an anchor on the left wall. The crack widens to 4", then 6" (10–15 cm) up to a belay from 2 bolts on the left wall.

Pitch 2: Climb offwidth at 5.10+ protected by 7 bolts and drilled angles. The crux is a roof passed on its left (5.12a/b). Continue up, passing 1 bolt to a rappel station visible from below when viewed from upriver.

Paraphernalia: Friends (1) set; Big Bros (1) set; wired stoppers; quickdraws.

Descent: Rappel the route.

Rating System

Each climb is given a grade of I through VI.

I	One to two hours of climbing
II	Less than half a day
III	Half-day climb
IV	Full-day climb
V	Two-day climb
VI	Multiday ascent

Climbing difficulty is broken down into 6 classes, with Class 5 (free climbing) broken down further into 5.0 through 5.13+, and Class 6 (aid climbing) broken down into A1 through A5.

1	Trail
2	Cross-country hiking
3	Scrambling

4	Exposed scrambling, usually with rope for protection
5	Free climbing
6	Aid climbing

Ratings of free climbs range from 5.0 to 5.13+. Some additional letter ratings denote the following:

R	runout
S	hurt on fall
X	killed on fall

Ratings of aid climbs range from A0 to A5:

A0	Aid points fixed
A1	Easy, secure placements
A2	More awkward placement which will hold less weight than A1
A3	Still more difficult placement and less secure; will hold only short fall
A4	Difficult placement, not secure enough for a fall; will hold body weight only
A5	Multiple A4 placements; a fall could result in injury or death

C1, C2, etc, are ratings for *clean*, hammerless aid.

Aid Ratings by Jim Beyer

Jim Beyer's aid rating system is provided to help clarify the grades he has given to his difficult climbs on Castleton Tower, River Tower, the Fisher Towers, and at Colorado National Monument.

A0: Short sections or single points of easy aid. This ranges from a rappel, a fall, or "hangdog free climbing" to short bolt ladders.

A1: Easy aid with an occasional A2 or A3 placement but no runouts.

A2: Usually an easy pitch of aid that has a few A3 or A4 placements.

A2+: Generally an easy pitch of aid with few A3 or A4 placements.

A3: Moderately hard aid. Expect to place Leeper stacks, bashies, and hooks. Potential falls could be up to 30 feet.

A3+: Sustained A3 with possibly longer falls.

A4a: Difficult aid with at least four A4 placements in a row. This is the "old A5" standard from the 1970s. Example: *The Jagged Edge,* 4 marginal placements in a row in an otherwise A2–A3.

A4b-A4c: Harder than A4a but not "psycho aid."

A4+: Extreme aid climbing starts at this rating. 8 to 12 placement rips are possible. Potential falls are up to 50 feet. Example: Several pitches on *Deadmans Party* come to mind. The first is sustained A4–you're looking at a 40- to 50-foot fall on overhanging rock. On a higher A4+ pitch, you are standing on marginal bashies looking at a 40-foot fall. Climbs rated A4+ or harder are "psycho aid." Climbers not willing to take big falls–potentially fatal falls–should not venture into this realm.

A5a: Sustained marginal placements. Your are looking at a 60-foot fall. Example: *Worlds End* A5a, off a good bolted belay you do a peg, a hook, and 12 to 13 bashies. You are looking at a potential fall of 60 feet, if you rip. Note that a 60-foot air fall (A5a) has less potential for fatal consequences than a nasty A4+ 40-foot ledge fall.

A5b: Potential falls to 100 feet.

A5c: Potential falls of more than 100 feet. Example: *Dead Mans Party* A5c, at the top of a very long pitch you are standing on marginal bashies looking at a 100-foot to 200-foot fall: A 100-foot fall if the 3 equalized A2 pegs hold; a 200-foot fall if they rip and you rip the middle of the pitch too.

A6a: I would propose this grade for super-sick routes that include at least two pitches of extreme cutting-edge placements, a certain death fall, and no bolts. Example: *Intifada* originally met this criteria, but no longer, due to retro-bolting. Future routes will deserve A6 ratings.

The original aid rating scale proposed in the 1960s by the dominant Yosemite Valley hardmen held that 4 A4 placements in a row was as hard as it got and deserved the top rating, A5. Their belief that A5 was as hard as aid climbing could get was just as foolish as their belief that 5.10 was the tops in free climbing.

Currently, there is some sentiment in the valley that calls for the downgrading of all previously established aid routes, because harder climbs are being done, and people want to keep the grading system between 1 and 5. It's very presumptuous to assume that guidebook authors the world over are going to downgrade all the aid routes in their books just because the newest, hardest route has been done. (Aid routes *should* be down-rated when increased traffic makes them easier.) Current standards at the top of the aid game are now 2 or 3 grades harder than the first A5s, hence the need for an expanded grading system.

We should actually be into the A7s by now. Instead, I go to the valley and top psycho aid-men tell me, "There is no A5. If you get killed on your next, sickest, hardest route, maybe we will call it A5."

Oh well–it's all just numbers. It's really about adventure and that, er, adrenaline addiction.

Star Ratings

Star Ratings are based on a scale of 1 to 5. With few exceptions, they are the general consensus of those who have climbed the routes. The absence of a star rating on a climb is an indication that this information was not furnished.

Paraphernalia

A standard desert climbing rack for free climbs includes two sets of Friends, one set of TCUs , one set of stoppers, and Quickdraws with 25-inch slings for multiple pitch climbs.

There is no standard desert climbing rack for the Fisher and Mystery Towers. Steve "Crusher" Bartlett says, "Bring a lot of everything."

The following chart is designed to assist the climber in assembling and borrowing gear necessary for desert climbing. It gives a general idea of size comparisons between brands. Measurements are from the manufacturer or distributor, but are in no way guaranteed to be accurate. Provided courtesy of Moab Climbing Shop, 550 North Main, Moab, Utah, 84532, (435) 259-2725.

Paraphernalia Size Comparison Chart

Colorado Custom Hardware Aliens
Measurements are manufacturer's fully closed to fully open. Cams are not strong fully open.

.33	3/8	1/2	3/4	1	1 1/2	2	2 1/2
.33–.38	.38–.65	.53–.87	.6–1.06	.76–1.34	1.03–1.63	1.2–1.95	1.4–2.35
black	blue	green	yellow	red	orange	violet	silver

Wired Bliss TCU and FCU
Measurements are manufacturer's list of "range."

.4	.5	.75	1.0	1.5	2.0	2.5	3.0
.4–.6	.5–.8	.6–.9	.8–1.3	.9–1.4	1.2–1.9	1.4–2.2	1.8–2.8
blue	yellow	red	purple	silver	black	green	pink

Wild Country Friends and Flexible Friends
Measurements are manufacturer's list of "range."

.0	1/2	1	1 1/2	2	2 1/2	3	3 1/2	4
.52–.76	.60–.96	.76–1.16	.92–1.40	1.16–1.76	1.32–2.20	1.72–2.64	2.08–3.24	2.56–4.00
	orange	yellow	silver	pink	lt. blue	blue	purple	black

Metolius TCU and FCU
Measurements are manufacturer's list of "range."

00	0	1	2	3	4	5	6	7	8	9	10
.35–.40	.40–.60	.50–.75	.60–.90	.75–1.10	1.90–1.35	1.10–1.70	1.28–1.9	1.65–2.25	2.0–2.75	2.2–3.3	2.8–4.2
gray	purple	blue	yellow	red	black	green					

Hugh Banner (HB) Quadcams and Micromates
Manufacturer's measurement of "crack size."

00	0	.5	1	1.5	2	2.5	3	3.8	5
.42–.66	.52–.76	.60–.92	.76–1.16	.80–1.45	1.12–1.76	1.40–2.20	1.80–2.76	2.36–3.72	3.40–5.08
red	orange	yellow	lt. blue						

Black Diamond Camalot and Camalot Jr.
Manufacturer's measurements of "size range." Old style Camalots are slightly larger in sizes 1 through 4.

.5	.75	1	2	3	3.5	4	4.5	5
.8–1.3	1.0–1.6	1.2–2.0	1.5–2.5	2.0–3.4	2.56–4.0	2.9–4.8	3.74–6.0	4.2–7.0
purple	green	red	gold	blue	gray	purple	red	green

Sidewinder Protection Big Bros.
Manufacturer's measurements of "expansion range."

1	2	3	4
3.2–4.4	4.0–5.8	5.2–8.0	7.3–12.0
blue	green	blue	green

Lowe Balls
Actual minimum and maximum size "functional size is less."

1	2	3
3mm–6mm	4.5mm–9mm	6mm–12mm
yellow	red	blue

Yates Big Dudes
Manufacturer's stated "camming range."

1	2
3.74–6.0	4.5–7.0
black	blue

MAP LEGEND

STATE HIGHWAY	(128)	BUILDING	■
U.S. HIGHWAY	(191)	RIVER/CREEK	
PAVED ROAD		INTERMITTENT WATERWAY	
GRAVEL ROAD		SLICKROCK	
SINGLETRACK/TRAIL	....	CLIFF	
NUMBERED SITE	(21)		*cliff face*
TRAILHEAD	(T)	CATTLE GUARD	
PARKING	(P)	COMPASS	N
CAMPING	▲		

photo: David Nessia

Climber on *Possessed*, Ice Cream Parlor

KANE CREEK

There is a war of elements and a struggle for existence going on here that for ferocity is unparalleled elsewhere in nature.

Tones of color, shades of light, drifts of air. . . . These are the most sensuous qualities in nature and in art.

The weird solitude, the great silence, the grim desolation, are the very things with which every desert wanderer eventually falls in love.

And wherever you go, by land or by sea, you shall not forget that which you saw not but rather felt–the desolation and the silence of the desert.

–John C. Van Dyke, *The Desert*, 1903

The Kane Creek corridor was used by bands of Anasazi Indians for hunting and foraging sojourns 900 to 1,300 years ago. They left granaries and numerous petroglyph panels, but few permanent dwellings. Early white settlers of the Moab region developed the corridor into a cattle trail. In the 1950s, uranium miners built the present road to access numerous mines established along the Chinle cliffs of Kane Creek Valley and beyond. Today, Kane Creek Boulevard gives access to the Needles District of Canyonlands National Park by a multiday, long, and lonely four-wheel-drive track descending into the remote and desolate land south of Moab and east of the Colorado River. The first 12.5 miles (20 km) to Hurrah Pass have become popular with climbers, mountain bikers, and four-wheel drivers. It is this land between Moab and Hurrah Pass, and the climbing routes established there, that make up this chapter.

Kane Creek Boulevard, Potash Road (across the river), and River Road (Scenic Byway 128), a 50-mile (80km) stretch, are the only roads on the vast Colorado Plateau which parallel the river as it passes through four states and part of Mexico. Elsewhere on the plateau, the Colorado is deeply entrenched in canyons.

Location

The Kane Creek climbing area is south and west of Moab. It borders Kane Creek Boulevard, then Kane Springs Canyon, and finally Kane Creek Valley. It first parallels the east side of the Colorado River (Wall Street borders the west side) for 4 paved miles (6.4 km) before becoming dirt at a cattleguard and turning east to follow Kane Springs Canyon in a south-trending direction. The canyon then opens into Kane Creek Valley, where at its southwest edge the dirt track climbs steeply to Hurrah Pass. Since mile markers are not in place, landforms and vehicle odometer readings from the Moab McDonald's fast-food restaurant are used to designate distances.

To reach Kane Creek from Moab, turn west from Main Street (U.S. Highway 191) on Kane Creek Boulevard at McDonald's. The boulevard winds through a residential area, then at the Colorado River it turns south (left) and enters the Portal through which the river flows into the canyons from Moab Valley, approximately 1.8 miles (2.8 km).

Kane Creek

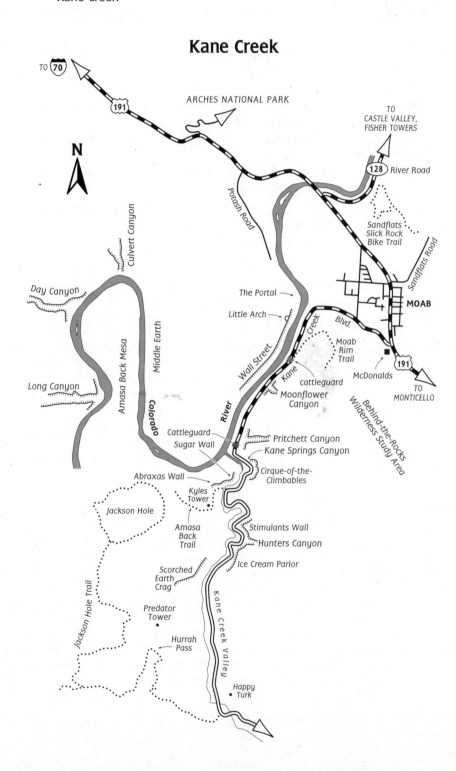

Geology

At the Portal, the walls on both sides of the Colorado rise dramatically as a result of the great Moab Valley Salt Anticline. The stratum beside the roadway is cross-bedded, stream-deposited Kayenta, which disappears below road level to reveal the aeolian Navajo Formation. As Kane Creek Boulevard turns east and enters Kane Springs Canyon, the Kane Creek Anticline is visible, and the layers of rock reverse themselves. The Navajo is uplifted, exposing first the Kayenta, then Wingate, and eventually Chinle Sandstone. At Kane Springs Canyon you pass through five distinct formations for an elevation gain of less than 100 feet (30 m). Just west on Amasa Back Mesa, as a result of the Kane Creek Anticline, the Kayenta (deposited on the level by fresh water) spans a height differential of 1,000 feet (305 m) within 2 miles (3.2 km).

Points of Interest

Worth visiting while enroute to the Kane Creek climbing areas is the 875-acre Scott M. Matheson Wetlands Preserve, purchased in 1991 and managed by The Nature Conservancy. This desert slough is the only one of its kind on the banks of the Colorado River as it passes through Utah, the second driest state in the United States. More than 180 species of birds have been identified at the preserve, which also furnishes habitat for beavers; endangered peregrine falcons, bald eagles, and other raptors; waterfowl, passerines (songbirds), and shorebirds; as well as frogs, mule deer, and river otters. The entrance to the wetlands is on the right (north), 1.4 miles (2.2 km) down Kane Creek Boulevard from its junction with U.S. Highway 191 at McDonald's. At the parking area, there is an information kiosk and passage to a scenic boardwalk leading to viewing blinds.

Little Window is in view high on the rimrock west of the Colorado from the cattleguard 2.5 miles (4 km) down Kane Creek Boulevard from McDonald's. The name Little Window is a misnomer, since it is a pothole-type arch (not a window) and is not little. It has a span of 40 feet and is 20 feet high, 25 feet thick, and 15 feet wide. There is also a sign marking the beginning of the Colorado Riverway Recreation Area. An information kiosk stands on the left just beyond the cattleguard listing the regulations that apply to the area. Signs state that camps should be in designated sites only, and outside the Riverway Recreation Area portable toilets are required.

As one descends downriver on Kane Creek Boulevard, several large humanmade caves become obvious along the cliffline 3.4 miles (5.4 km) from McDonald's. They housed an egg farm in the 1960s and 1970s. Lights were turned on eight hours, off eight hours, then on eight hours for each 24-hour period, tricking the hens into laying one-third more eggs than they would normally have done. It was a doomed business, since the eggs were pale, with more albumen and less taste than competitors' eggs.

Kane Springs

Kane Springs is 2.2 miles (3.5 km) from the cattleguard at the beginning of the dirt road marking the entrance to Kane Springs Canyon. Steep switchbacks descend to the canyon floor, where fresh water flows from the Kayenta Formation on the left side of the road. This aquifer, geologists suggest, has its origin in the 12,721-foot (3,877-m) La Sal Mountains, more than 20 miles (32 km) to the east. At the spring, rich green mosses, maidenhair ferns, wild orchids (giant *helleborine epipactis gigantes*), horsetail reeds, lush wet-site grasses and sedges, goldenrods, primroses, common reeds (*phragmites australis*), squawberry bushes, cockleburs, fleabane daisies, virgin's bower (clematis), and thistles grow in lavish variations. At Spring Campground, 500 feet (152 m) downcanyon from Kane Springs, many other trees and shrubs grow in profusion, including hackberrys, cottonwoods, junipers, scrub oaks, poison ivy, greasewoods, rabbit brush, Russian thistles, and the ubiquitous tamarisk.

Heading south from the spring, Wingate Sandstone dominates as you pass through an anticline (uplift). Scattered stumps of cottonwood trees are remnants of a beaver colony which dammed Kane Creek. The BLM relocated the colony in the late 1980s.

Map

Moab East, published by Latitude 40-Degrees, Inc., of Boulder, Colorado, is the most useful map for other sections of this guide. However, the Kane Creek region—although east of the river—is detailed only on the *Moab West* map. Identified are Kane Creek Boulevard (Road), Matheson Preserve, the Portal, Moab Rim Trail, Little Window, Moonflower Canyon, Petroglyphs, Fickle Finger of Fate, Behind-the-Rocks, Cirque-of-the-Climbables, Kane Springs, Pritchett Canyon and Pritchett Natural Bridge, Kane Springs Canyon and Kane Springs, Ice Cream Parlor, Predator Tower, Hurrah Pass, Amasa Back Mesa, Jackson Hole, and Jacob's Ladder. The next revision of the *Moab West* map will include many additional climbing routes in the Kane Creek region. Therefore, I recommend the purchase of both *Moab West* and *Moab East* maps for this guide.

Camping

There are five designated camping sites along the Colorado Riverway Recreation Area. The campsites' respective size and distance from U.S. Highway 191 are as follows: Kings Bottom (seven sites, 3 miles, 4.8 km), Moonflower Canyon (eight walk-in sites, 3.1 miles, 4.9 km), Spring (four sites, 6.7 miles, 10.7 km), Hunters Canyon (four walk-in sites, five car sites, 7.8 miles, 12.5 km), and Echo (nine sites, 8.1 miles, 13 km). Each camp area (except Spring) has vault toilets, and all have metal fire rings. Camping fee is $4 per night. Capacity at each site is limited to two vehicles, two tents, and six people. There is no water at the campsites, but great pure water can be found at Kane Springs, 2.2 miles (3.5 km) from the cattleguard at the beginning of the dirt road at the head of Kane Springs Canyon.

Road Log

Unfortunately (or fortunately) no mile markers are posted in the Kane Creek area and odometer readings may vary from one vehicle to another; thus all readings in this log are subjective.

U.S. Highway 191 JUNCTION WITH KANE CREEK BOULEVARD (McDonald's)
0.8 miles (1.2 km): 5th West.
1.4 miles (2.2 km): Scott M. Matheson Wetland Preserve. Frog on a Lily Pad Tower (a.k.a. Point of Moab) is straight ahead west of the river
1.8 miles (2.8 km): The Portal.
2.5 miles (4 km): Cattleguard with Little Arch in view west of the river.
2.7 miles (4.3 km): Moab Rim Trail.
3.0 miles (4.8 km): Kings Bottom campsites, 7 sites, $4 per night.
3.1 miles (4.9 km): Moonflower Canyon campsites and petroglyphs, 8 sites, $4 per night.

3.3 miles (5.3 km): Pit and Bear.

3.4 miles (5.4 km): First Chicken Cave.

3.5 miles (5.6 km): Mastodon Petroglyph road, which also leads to a bench with a great view of the Colorado River. Petroglyphs on Navajo Sandstone wall east of the bench.

4.4 miles (7 km): Lone cottonwood tree and Fowler Wall.

4.6 miles (7.4 km): Pritchett Canyon.

4.7 miles (7.5 km): End of Kane Creek Boulevard and beginning of Kane Springs Canyon, cattleguard, and dirt road begins. Pritchett Canyon opens on the left.

KANE SPRINGS CANYON beginning of dirt road. Straight ahead of roadway is Amasa Back Mesa.

0.1 miles (0.16 km): BLM information kiosk and parking area (on right).

0.3 miles (0.5 km): Petroglyphs are visible on the wall above the road (left). Others are in view if one hikes along the base of the wall.

0.4 miles (0.7 km): First Tombstone of the Cirque-of-the-Climbables, on the left.

0.5 miles (0.3 km): Third Tombstone and beginning of Surphase Tension Buttress, on the left.

0.7 miles (1.1 km): Large parking area on right. Trailhead on left to *Burn Victim, Dark Star, Driving While Asian,* as well as numerous petroglyphs and a good approach to the climbs on Surphase Tension Buttress. Sugar Walls in view ahead and to the west.

1.0 miles (1.6 km): *Farm* (no parking on road below the climb), above a large boulder on the talus slope, on the left. Abraxas Wall is in view to the west, right of Forming Arch.

1.3 miles (2.1 km): Beginning of signed Amasa Back Trail on the right. Forming Arch in view to the west.

1.4 miles (2.2 km): Birthing Rock, on the right.

1.5 miles (2.4 km): Upside-down rock with petroglyphs, on the right.

1.7 miles (2.7 km): Top of hill and trailhead to Funnel Arch, on the left.

2.0 miles (3.2 km): Second switchback and trailhead to *Archaic Revival* and *Kind–Other Kind*, on the right.

2.2 miles (3.5 km): Kane Springs, on the left.

KANE SPRINGS: 0.0 miles, gushing from left wall.

0.1 miles (0.16 km): Spring campsites, 4 sites, $4 per night.

0.9 miles (1.2 km): Stimulants Wall (overhanging hueco wall above the road), on the left.

1.0 miles (1.6 km): Hunters Canyon, on the left.

1.1 miles (1.7 km): *Grave* and *Unleashed*, on the left.

1.2 miles (1.9 km): Echo campsites, 9 sites, $4 per night, on the right.

1.3 miles (2 km): Ice Cream Parlor, on the left.

1.6 miles (2.5 km): Beginning of Kane Creek Valley. Big boulder on right and sign that reads "Leaving Riverway Recreation Area." This location is also the approach drainage to the grassy ledge leading to Scorched Earth Crag, on the right, and approach to *Charlie's Sorry* and *Sorry Charlie*, on the left.

2.2 miles (3.5 km): Petroglyph of a bighorn sheep, anthropomorphic figure, and centipede-like creature, above the road on a large boulder, on the left. Predator Tower is in view, with the right kind of lighting, to the far right.

3.2 miles (5 km): Note the improbable location of a large uranium loading dock high on the Chinle slope, on the east (left) side of Kane Creek Valley.

3.4 miles (**5.4 km**): Happy Turk (left) and Pensive Putterman (right).
4.2 miles (**6.7 km**): Cutler Towers, on the left. Shelbyville is on the right.
4.3 miles (**6.9 km**): Kane Creek (road crosses the drainage).
6.8 miles (**11 km**): Hurrah Pass. High atop the rimrock, Anticline Overlook is in view.

KANE CREEK BOULEVARD CLIMBING ROUTES

Climbing routes at Kane Creek Boulevard are established on Navajo Sandstone cliffs paralleling the Colorado River. Moonwalker Tower, high above the boulevard, is best viewed from the first Indian writing sign down Potash Road, on the west side of the river. Access the tower from Pritchett Canyon at the south end of Kane Creek Boulevard. Routes are listed from left to right, from Kane Creek Boulevard south to Kane Springs Canyon.

Wetlands Routes, Endless Cave

Wetlands Routes climb the best-looking crack systems on the dark varnished portion of the Wingate buttress (Birdwall) opposite the Scott M. Matheson Wetlands Preserve. To reach them, drive 1.4 miles (2.2 km) west from U.S. Highway 191 on Kane Creek Boulevard to the Wetlands entrance and hike up the Chinle slope to the buttress (south of the boulevard). Birdwall is the Wingate buttress high above the boulevard. From near the top of the Moab Rim Trail, there is a deep fissure at the edge of the cliff known locally as the Endless Cave. *Pigeon Crack* climbs the outside wall of the fissure.

1   BIRDWALL—PIGEON PARTY I, 5.10, 3 pitches, 350 feet (107 m)

First Ascent: Todd Madaux, Millie Birdwell, Brent Russel, Spring 1993.

Location and Access: *Pigeon Party* climbs a right-facing dihedral up a dark varnished buttress one crack right of a tall column leaning against the Wingate wall. Double rappel slings are in view the left of the route. Look for white guano on the wall above the rappel anchors. Information on Pitches 2 and 3 is unknown.

Paraphernalia: Standard desert rack.

Descent: Two double-rope rappels from double bolts down *Bird Crack.*

2   BIRDWALL—BIRD CRACK I, 5.11+, 3 pitches, 350 feet (107 m)

First Ascent: Pitch 1: Todd Madaux, Millie Birdwell, 1993. Pitches 2 and 3: Todd Madaux solo.

Location and Access: *Bird Crack* ascends a splitter crack just right of *Pigeon Party.* Climb to double anchors on the left, located approximately 10 feet (3 m) lower than the anchors visible on *Pigeon Party.* Todd Madaux: "Fun, excellent, high quality with a spectacular view of Moab valley." Information on Pitch 3 is unknown.

Pitch 1: Climb a flake left of a large block at the foot of the buttress, then continue to the beginning of an offwidth, 5.10.

Pitch 2: Angle left and up ending with thin cracks at a double-bolt rappel station, 5.11+.

Pitch 3: Information is unknown.

Paraphernalia: Standard desert rack with extra #2.5, #3, #3.5; a selection of knifeblades.

Descent: Two double-rope rappels from double bolts.

3   PIGEON CRACK I, 5.11, A1, 2 pitches, 250 feet (76 m)

First Ascent: Todd Madaux, Millie Birdwell, 1993.

Location and Access: Begin up the steepest, desert-varnished section of the buttress at the entrance to the Portal. Further information is unknown.

Paraphernalia: Friends (2) #3 through #4; Camalot (1) #4. Thin pitons and 3/8" angles for Pitch 2.

Descent: Walk down the Moab Rim Trail.

Arnold Ziffle

Arnold Ziffle is reached via a half hour hike up the difficult Moab Rim Jeep Trail, which begins 2.7 miles (4.3 km) from the intersection of Kane Creek Boulevard and U.S. Highway 191, or 0.1 mile (0.16 km) south of the first cattleguard on Kane Creek Boulevard. From the trailhead, the semi-detached tower is in profile on the right wall. It may also be identified as directly across the Colorado River from mile marker 12 on Potash Road. With binoculars, a rappel chain can be spotted halfway up the tower.

An information kiosk marks the beginning of the trail. It reads in part: *Moab Rim Trail, a mile plus bedrock incline. The trail is both rugged and technical for any vehicle, and simply taxing for the self propelled. Moab's Red Rock Four Wheelers have accorded the Rim Trail their maximum difficulty rating of "4+". To quote veteran member Jack Bickers, such routes should be driven by "world class Yahoo Jeepers not much concerned with vehicle durability or personal safety."* . . . *The trail is 3 miles one way to connect with Hidden Valley Trail (allow 4 hours round trip) and marks the boundary of Behind-the-Rocks Wilderness Study Area. Please keep all vehicles, including bicycles, on the existing trails.* . . . *It is 1.4 miles to the Moab Valley Viewpoint.* . . . *Beware of gnats April through June.*

4   ARNOLD ZIFFLE (a.k.a. Moab Rim Tower) I, 5.9, A1, 2 pitches, 200 feet (61 m)

First Ascent: Todd Madaux solo, 12 June 1992.

Location and Access: Begin on the downhill side of the tower and climb to a bolt, then through a wide and awkward crack to the summit.

Paraphernalia: Standard desert rack with extra Friends #3.5, #4; a selection of pitons; (1) quickdraw.

Descent: Rappel the route.

Projects, Bounce Test

There are several projects (unfinished routes) up the mastodon petroglyph road, 0.4 mile (0.6 km) south of Moonflower Canyon. From the mastodon petroglyph, hike right approximately 200 feet (61 m) along the south-facing buttress. There are three bolts, 25 feet (7.6 m) left of an old juniper, and six bolts, 10 feet (3 m) right of the juniper, protecting a 5.7 Navajo Sandstone slab to double anchors.

Another project is 35 feet (10.6 m) left of the petroglyphs. The unfinished route (20 feet [6 m] high) is protected by two bolts up a heavily lichened wall.

To reach a final project, continue north on the mastodon road until it descends steeply to the rim of Moonflower Canyon. Park, then hike approximately ten minutes to the buttress on the right and traverse left (north) to dark varnished rock at a point where the BLM rail fence, below in Moonflower Canyon, is visible. There are rappel slings 70 feet up (21 m) between double rock columns 2 feet and 4 feet (0.6 m, 1.2 m) wide, respectively. The column on the left arches out from the buttress to form an arch. The route is clearly in view from the rail fence, below, as one looks east to the Navajo Buttress.

5   BOUNCE TEST III, 5.9, A0, 6 pitches, 900 feet (274 m)

First Ascent: Andy Roberts, Jason Schroeder, Jason Hodgeman, with Liz Devaney pitch 1, 4 April 1998. Upper pitches: Andy Roberts, Jason Hodgeman, 22 April 1998.

Location and Access: *Bounce Test* ascends the first fin right of the mastodon petroglyph.

Pitch 1: Begin at the base of the fin and climb past 3 bolts, then 3 drilled pitons to a flat belay stance. A #2 Camalot may be helpful between the last piton and the belay, 5.8, 100 feet (30 m).

Pitch 2: Scramble 350 feet (107 m) over 2 low angled slabs, then continue until the wall steepens.

Pitch 3: Ascend the crack on the right for 25 feet (8 m), then angle left following the fin straight up and belay in a groove, 5.6, 200 feet (61 m).

Pitch 4: Continue up the fin (5.5) belaying when the rope runs out at 200 feet (61 m).

Pitch 5: Climb a groove for 30 feet (9 m) to anchors on the left.

Pitch 6: Continue up the groove until it ends, then move right and up passing 4 drilled pitons, 5.9, A0. Follow scary rock to the summit 90 feet (27 m).

Paraphernalia: Camalots (1) #0.75, #1, #2; Metolius #2, #3; nuts (1) set; quickdraws (7).

Descent: Three double-rope rappels down the gully left of the route.

Anasazi Chimney, Moonflower 40, Moonflower 39, Wallflower

These four routes are in Moonflower Canyon, 0.5 mile (0.8 km) down Kane Creek Boulevard from the cattleguard at the beginning of the signed Colorado Riverway Recreation Area. At the right entrance to the canyon, an information kiosk reads: *Moonflower dates from the Archaic to Formative period. There is a barrier canyon style figure (a large triangular shape with head dress), deer, bighorn sheep and a number of abstract elements.* **The routes are illegal and should not be climbed due to the nearby ancient rock art panel.** Please be a responsible visitor and respect the BLM's efforts to protect this priceless national treasure. The routes are listed only for historic documentation, with paraphernalia and descent information omitted.

At Moonflower Canyon there are eight walk-in camping sites with pit toilets. Charge is $4 per night.

6   ANASAZI CHIMNEY I, 5.6, 1 pitch, 60 feet (18 m)

First Ascent: Anasazi Indians, circa 800 years B.P. (before present).

Location and Access: *Anasazi Chimney* climbs a deep cleft, which is to the left of the rock art panel at the right entrance to Moonflower Canyon. In the chimney are aid logs (some original) used to reach a 5.6 crux at the top left of the climb. There is a line of ascent pecked into the rock from bottom to top by the first ascent party. The area is cordoned off by a rail fence put up by the BLM to protect the vulnerable rock art.

NOTE: The route is illegal to climb and is included here only for historic documentation.

7   MOONFLOWER 40 I, 5.12, 1 pitch, 50 feet (15 m)

First Ascent: Unknown.

Location and Access: *Moonflower 40* climbs a thin crack between *Anasazi Chimney* and *Moonflower 39*.

8   MOONFLOWER 39 I, 5.9+, 1 pitch, 50 feet (15 m)

First Ascent: Tony Valdes, Bego Gerhart, November 1985.

Location and Access: *Moonflower 39* climbs the wall right of *Moonflower 40*, beginning above the number 39 etched deeply in the rock. A handcrack leads to an offwidth near the top of the route.

NOTE: The climb is within the BLM split rail fence and is illegal to climb. The route is included here only for historic documentation.

9   WALLFLOWER I, A2, 1 pitch, 40 feet (12 m)

First Ascent: Bego Gerhart, Eric Bjørnstad, November 1985.

Location and Access: *Wallflower* climbs a left-trending thin aid crack to a single rappel bolt right of the split rail fence protecting the rock art panel.

NOTE: The climb is not recommended due to the nearness of the Indian writings and degradation to the rock resulting from piton placements. The route is included here for historic documentation only.

Pit and Bear

Pit and Bear is approximately 50 feet (15 m) right of the first "Chicken Cave," 3.3 miles (5.3 km) from the junction of Kane Creek Boulevard and U.S. Highway 191, or 0.2 mile (0.3 km) downriver from Moonflower Canyon.

10   PIT AND BEAR I, 5.10+, 1 pitch, 50 feet (15 m) ★★

First Ascent: Jimmy Dunn, Betsi McKittrick, 5 October 1991.

Location and Access: Climb a smooth left-facing dihedral up a straight crack with an offwidth in the middle. Rappel slings are visible from below. Jimmy Dunn: "Pit and Bear climbs a left-facing dihedral resembling the classic Heart of the Desert route in Arches National Park."

Paraphernalia: Friends (2) sets including a #5, #6.

Descent: Rappel the route from 2 fixed pitons.

Fowler Wall

Fowler Wall is left (north) of Pritchett Canyon, at the first cottonwood tree on the cliff side of the boulevard.

11   CHICKEN LITTLE I, 5.10, 1 pitch, 40 feet (12 m) ★★★

First Ascent: Charlie Fowler, Franci Stagi, March 1991.

Location and Access: *Chicken Little* climbs a large right-facing corner 3 cracks right of a lone cottonwood tree. Begin up a hand- and fingercrack and continue through a small roof (the crux) to the bench above. There are no fixed anchors on the route.

Paraphernalia: Friends (3) #1, #1.5, #2.

Descent: Walk off to the left.

12   RAINDANCE I, 5.9+, 1 pitch, 40 feet (12 m)

First Ascent: Charlie Fowler, Franci Stagi, March 1991.

Location and Access: *Raindance* is 3 cracks right of *Chicken Little*. Climbs mostly fingers up a right-angling, thin crack with a bush visible at the top.

Paraphernalia: Friends (2) #1, #1.5; large to medium nuts (2).

Descent: Walk off to the left.

13   FOWLER MYSTERY ROUTE #I I, 5.10, 1 pitch, 70 feet (21 m) ★★★

First Ascent: Charlie Fowler, Franci Stagi, March 1991.

Location and Access: *Fowler Mystery Route #I* is one crack right of *Raindance*. Begin above a shelf with face climbing, then stemming ending in offwidth stemming up a right-facing dihedral which changes to left-facing higher up. The first crux is getting to a stance, second crux getting above the stance.

Paraphernalia: A selection of thin nuts.

Descent: Walk off to the left.

14   FOWLER MYSTERY ROUTE #II I, 5.11, 1 pitch, 40 feet (12 m)

First Ascent: Charlie Fowler, Franci Stagi, March 1991.

Location and Access: *Fowler Mystery Route #II* is 2 cracks right of *Fowler Mystery Route #I*. Stem, then climb thin fingers up a large left-facing dihedral.

Paraphernalia: Standard desert rack.

Descent: Walk off to the left.

Fickle Finger of Fate

When viewed from Potash Road at the first Indian Writing sign, Fickle Finger of Fate is very thin and reminiscent of the famous photo of Gaston Rébuffat atop La Flama in the French Alps. To reach, drive to Pritchett Canyon (on the left where Kane Creek Boulevard turns to dirt and Kane Creek Canyon begins). Hike upcanyon 0.2 mile (0.3 km) to the first draw on the left (east). Scramble up the drainage, past some easy class 5, then to the mesa top, 1.5 miles (2.4 km). Traverse left (north) over obvious ground to the base of the spire. **BEWARE:** There are healthy patches of poison ivy on the approach hike.

An alternate approach is to drive 0.5 mile (0.8 km) past Moonflower Canyon to a dirt road accessing the gravel bench above. Hike south 0.25 mile (0.40 km) to the power lines. Continue along the lines to the second canyon. Scramble up (east), staying on the right (south) side of the drainage. Near the top, 4th-class scrambling leads to the base of the spire.

NOTE: While hiking up the draw from Pritchett Canyon, the delicate No Pool Arch is in view not far from the mesa top as one looks back (up and left) to the southwest. At the top of the mesa, a few yards east, is the impressive Pool Arch which has a span of 63 feet (19 m), a height of 85 feet (26 m), a thickness of 35 feet (10.6 m), and a width of 12 feet (3.6 m). Please do not pollute the pool by swimming in it. It is a source of life-sustaining water for numerous desert creatures.

15   FICKLE FINGER OF FATE—MOONWALKER II, 5.9, A2, 2 pitches, 165 feet (50 m)

First Ascent: Kyle Copeland, Marc Hirt, Alison Sheets, 10 October 1989. Eric Bjørnstad, Ron Wiggle to within 20 feet (6 m) of the summit, late 1960s.

photo: Eric Bjørnstad

Fickle Finger of Fate, Kane Creek

Location and Access: *Moonwalker* climbs the north face of the spire.

Pitch 1: Begin 5.7, then continue 5.9 hands up a crack system in the center of the face to a belay shelf.

Pitch 2: Climb a bolt ladder, then make a short 5.7 move to the tiny exposed summit.

Paraphernalia: A selection of Friends; machine nuts 1/4" and 3/8"; (15) 3/8" hangers may be required; quickdraws.

Descent: One double-rope rappel down the north side of the spire.

Pritchett Canyon

Pritchett Canyon begins to the east (left) of Kane Creek Boulevard, at the south end of the pavement. It is blocked by a fence and a privately managed campground. A lawsuit is pending to reopen (through a grandfather clause) the long-used four-wheel-drive trail crossing the private property at the canyon's entrance. To avoid going through the commercial property, access the canyon on foot by 4th-class scrambling up the cliff, to the right of the fenced area. From the shelf above, walk through a cleft in the wall and descend to the floor of the canyon beyond the private property.

Pritchett Canyon also leads to Pritchett Arch–4.5 miles (7.2 km)–which is a large pothole (water tank) collapsed into a cave below it. Subsequent erosion has formed a symmetrical, well-rounded arch in the Navajo Sandstone. With a span of 105 feet, a height of 71 feet, a thickness of 15 feet, and a width of 42 feet, it is a worthy side venture.

Pritchett Canyon is a frequent approach to the complicated Behind-the-Rocks region, a high, remote mesa between Moab Valley and the Colorado River, which is presently a designated Wilderness Study Area. It is a tilted land of striking Navajo Sandstone fins, panels of rock art, arches, and water-carved bridges–truly a hiker's paradise. One of the best views of this landscape is from the Maverick or Reptilian buttresses, high up Long Canyon (see Wall Street to San Rafael guide, described on page 3).

Approach Last Arrow Spire on foot up Pritchett Canyon from Kane Creek Boulevard, or from above with four-wheel drive. To reach the spire from the upper route, drive approximately 13 miles (21 km) south from Moab on U.S. Highway 191. Turn west (right) at the first dirt road after climbing out of the Moab Valley, up a grade known as Blue Hills. The four-wheel-drive trail to Pritchett Canyon is reached by following the most used track west after turning off U.S. 191. This region is publicly owned land with great views, isolation, and excellent camping. BLM regulations apply, prohibiting off-road vehicle travel. See "Environmental Considerations of Desert Rock Climbing," by Jeff Widen, page 3.

photo: Eric Bjørnstad

Last Arrow Spire

16   LAST ARROW SPIRE II, 5.8, A4, 3 pitches, 225 feet (69 m)

First Ascent: Dave Dawson, Kyle Copeland, 18 May 1989.

Location and Access: Last Arrow Spire is near the top of Pritchett Canyon and is obvious to the south, positioned only a few feet from the higher Wingate rimrock behind it.

Pitch 1: Begin on the north face and climb a right-facing dihedral, traversing right onto the west face and up to the prominent bedding seam below the summit block. There are 2 fixed anchors in place, A3, 165 feet (50 m).

Pitch 2: Traverse right to the west face, then to the south face where 3 fixed anchors are in place. Leave a fixed rope for the return.

Pitch 3: Climb past 4 fixed anchors to a second bedding seam (A3–A4), then free climb to the top, 50 feet (15 m).

Paraphernalia: Friends (2) sets #1 through #3.5 and #1 through #5; TCUs; a light piton rack 1" through 5" with knifeblades, Leepers; bolt hangers; quickdraws.

Descent: Rappel the south face 60 feet (18 m), then 165 feet (50 m) to the ground.

Kane Springs Canyon

Kane Springs Canyon begins at the dirt road where the paved Kane Springs Boulevard ends and Pritchett Canyon enters from the left (east). It is a steep-walled, picturesque drainage carved over aeons through hundreds of feet of aeolian and stream-deposited sedimentary rock. Kane Creek flows only intermittently; its sources are high in the La Sal Mountains. It crosses U.S. Highway 191, 14 miles (22.5 km) south of Moab at the Hole 'n' the Rock tourist extravaganza and Kane Springs highway rest stop. Because the narrow corridor of Kane Springs Canyon has the potential for violent flashfloods, camping is restricted to posted areas. It is managed by the BLM and is subject to its rules. Please observe them.

Cirque-of-the-Climbables (a.k.a. Tombstones, Pharaoh Rock)

Cirque-of-the-Climbables is the wall looming above the road on the left, 0.5 mile (0.8 km) into Kane Springs Canyon from the cattleguard at the end of the pavement of Kane Creek Boulevard. It comprises three Navajo Sandstone "tombstones." Hunter (from Salt Lake City, surname unknown) base-jumped from the middle tombstone in November 1996, referring to it as "One of the greatest base-jumps in the Southwest." Routes are listed from left to right.

17   KANE CUTTER III, 5.10+, A3+, 4 pitches, 375 feet (114 m) ★★★

First Ascent: Keith Reynolds, Kevin Chase, September 1992.

Location and Access: *Kane Cutter* is 100 feet (30 m) left of *I Dream of Jeannie* at the left side of the first tombstone of the Cirque-of-the-Climbables. Pitches 2 and 3 are climbed with much clean aid and Pitches 3 and 4 with sections of free climbing. Rappel slings are visible from below.

Pitch 1: Begin up an expanding crack system, A3+, 115 feet (35 m).

Pitch 2: Continue free, then on aid as the crack becomes wide, A2, 90 feet (27 m).

Pitch 3: Climb mostly free, 5.9, A1, 100 feet (30 m).

Pitch 4: Continue free, then aid past 2 bolts; 4th class to the summit, 5.10+, A1, 70 feet (21 m).

Cirque-of-the-Climbables

photo: Eric Bjørnstad

Paraphernalia: Friends (2) sets; TCUs (2) sets; nuts (2) sets; 4–7" units; knifeblades and Lost Arrows (4–6); angle pitons (2–3) 1/2" and 5/8"; Fish Hook (1); quickdraws.

Descent: Rappel the route.

18   I DREAM OF JEANNIE III, 5.7, A2+, 3 pitches, 330 feet (101 m)

First Ascent: Rick Donnelly, Scott DeCapio, May 1995.

Location and Access: *I Dream of Jeannie* is 100 feet (30 m) right of *Kane Cutter*.

Pitch 1: Climb an expanding crack past 7 holes (climbed with hooks), 4 drilled angles, 2 baby angles, 5.7, A2, 140 feet (43 m).

Pitch 2: Tension traverse to the crack system on the right. Climb the crack (aid) until it is possible to continue with clean gear. Belay at triple drilled angles.

Pitch 3: Climb A2+ with beaks up rotten rock to a drilled angle.

Paraphernalia: Friends (2) sets; TCUs (3) sets; #6 stoppers; hexes; Bird Beaks (5); knifeblades (10); Lost Arrows (10): (4) each 0.5", 3/4"; (1) 1" through 3" ; all size hooks.

Descent: Rappel the route.

19   DEEP VOODOO III, 5.10, A3, 4 pitches, 315 feet (96 m) ★★★★

First Ascent: Pitches 1 and 2: Kyle Copeland, Ron Olevsky, 1992. Pitches 3 and 4: Charlie Fowler, Peter Verchick, Bob Novellino, September 1993.

Location and Access: *Deep Voodoo* is right of *I Dream of Jeannie* and climbs the south face of the first tombstone. Two pitches climb a dihedral, then up the left wall by a crack system on the face between a gully and the right corner of the rock. Kevin Chase: "Good winter route."

Pitch 1: Climb a 7-bolt ladder (drilled pitons) to a belay ledge with double anchors on the left wall, 35 feet (11 m). The bolt ladder may be bypassed by a 5.9 hand traverse right to a ledge (with anchor).

Pitch 2: Climb 5.7 up a left-facing corner to double belay anchors on the left wall, 40 feet (12 m).

Pitch 3: Continue with some aid (past a bulge) to a double-anchor belay, 160 feet (56 m).

Pitch 4: Good nailing, A2, 80 feet (24 m).

Paraphernalia: Friends (2) sets #1 through #5; TCUs (2) sets; nuts (2) sets; knifeblades and Bugaboos (10–12); Lost Arrows (8–10); pitons (2–4) 0.5", 5/8"; short shallow angles (3–4); Bird Beaks (3).

Descent: Rappel the route.

20   CORNER ROUTE III, 5.12-, 6 pitches, 400 feet (122 m) ★★★

First Ascent: Pitches 1 through 3: Ron Olevsky, Kyle Copeland, with aid, November 1994. Pitches 4 and 5: Jimmy Dunn, Kevin Chase, Betsi McKittrick, 18 May 1995.

Location and Access: *Corner Route* is at the right edge of the first tombstone, right of *Deep Voodoo*. Kevin Chase: "Good winter route."

Pitch 1: Climb up and right of the bolt ladder on *Deep Voodoo* Pitch 1, then traverse left to a belay, 5.8.

Pitch 2: Climb a wide crack, 5.7.

Pitch 3: Climb up the corner, 5.10+.

Pitch 4: Continue up the corner past rappel slings to a ledge with a drilled piton, 5.9 offwidth.

Pitch 5: Climb to a left-trending splitter crack, then back to the corner, 5.12-.

Pitch 6: Climb a chimney to the top, 5.10.

Paraphernalia: Friends (2–3) sets through #5; Camalots (1) #5; TCUs (2) sets; wires (1) set.

Descent: Rappel *Kane Cutter.*

21   HIGHER REALITY (Corner Route Top-rope Variation) 5.11+, 1 pitch, 100 feet (30 m)

First Ascent: Ralph Ferrara, Kevin Chase, 1997.

Location and Access: *Higher Reality* is a variation to Pitch 6 of *Corner Route*. Climb a splitter crack left of the original Pitch 6.

Paraphernalia: Friends (3) sets.

Descent: Rappel *Kane Cutter.*

22   PLAYING HOOKY IV, 5.12, C2, 6 pitches, 365 feet (111 m) ★★★★★

First Ascent: Jimmy Dunn, Charlie Fowler, Peter Verchick, Kevin Chase, with Betsi McKittrick on lower pitches, 19 May 1993. First clean aid Dave Medara, Mike Pennings, October 1994. Mostly free: Dean Potter.

Location and Access: *Playing Hooky* climbs the center of the middle tombstone and was the first route on the tombstones to reach the mesa top. Rappel slings are visible from below. Jimmy Dunn: "Playing Hooky is one of the best climbs I've done in the Moab area." Kevin Chase: "The route overhangs on the upper pitches and gives excellent vertigo."

photo: David Nessia

Playing Hooky

Pitch 1: Begin with a 5.10+ direct start or 5.7 chimney to the left with one exposed move. Climb to a good ledge with triple anchors, 75 feet (23 m).

Pitch 2: Continue diagonally up and right to triple anchors, 5.12, 55 feet (17 m), 1 bolt.

Pitch 3: The pitch has been top-roped free at 5.12. Climb to triple anchors below a roof, C2, 55 feet (17 m).

Pitch 4: Climb with thin clean aid up a right-facing corner to triple anchors, C1, 70 feet (21 m).

Pitch 5: Crux pitch. Climb a wide right-leaning crack to triple anchors, free, or C2, 5.11, 60 feet (18 m).

Pitch 6: Start in an open book and climb past pods, then continue over a ledge to triple anchors, C1, 50 feet (15 m).

Paraphernalia: Friends (1) set with doubles through #3; many #0.4 TCUs and wires.

Descent: A long walk off the back to the right, or rappel the route from fixed ropes left from the top of Pitch 3 to the summit.

23 STAIRWAY TO HEAVEN (a.k.a. Jimmy's Chimney) III, 5.10+, 5 pitches, 420 feet (128 m) ★★★★★

First Ascent: Jimmy Dunn, Bob Novellino to summit, with Betsi McKittrick, Peter Verchick, Brett Sutteer, Jay Smith, and Alf (surname unknown) on lower pitches, 1 September 1994.

Location and Access: *Stairway to Heaven* climbs free to the top of the rimrock, up a crack system in the center of the third tombstone. All fixed anchors are drilled-in, baby-angle pitons placed on lead from a free stance.

NOTE: Jimmy Dunn often rates his climbs below their actual grade, thus the 5.10+ grade is on the Jimmy Dunn downscale rating system.

Pitch 1: Begin 5.9+ up a right-facing crack system, or start way left up a chimney. Traverse right on a ledge and climb a 5.10 roof, then 5.9 crack, to a large ledge with 2 drilled-in pitons, 80 feet (24 m).

Pitch 2: Climb 5.10, then angle left up a stairway of loose rock (5.8). Move diagonally up a right-trending ramp, then up past 2 fixed anchors. Continue to the right of overhanging rock past a white sandstone section to a ledge, 5.10, 100 feet (30 m).

Pitch 3: Begin at the right side of the belay ledge. Climb 5.7 past double anchors on the left side of the crack system. Continue past loose rock, then make an easy traverse left and climb a handcrack up the right side of a tower to a ledge with double anchors, 50 feet (15 m).

Pitch 4: Climb up, angling right to a chimney (tricky #5 wired Rock). Continue past 5 fixed anchors up an 8–9" crack (20–23 cm) to a ledge with double anchors, 5.10, 150 feet (46 m).

Pitch 5: Climb 5.10, then easier fingercrack up a system to the left of a large chockstone at the top of a chimney, 1 anchor in place, 40 feet (12 m).

Paraphernalia: Friends (1) #0.75, (2) #1, (1) #1.5, #2, #2.5, (2) #3, (1) #3.5, (2) #4; wired Rocks (1) #5 for Pitch 4.

Descent: Lower to the top of Pitch 4. Rappel 150 feet (46 m) to the top of Pitch 3. Rappel 150 feet (46 m) to the top of Pitch 1. Rappel 80 feet (24 m) to the ground.

(23)

Stairway to Heaven

23a   STAIRWAY TO HEAVEN—AID VARIATION Rating unknown

First Ascent: Unknown.

Location and Access: *Aid Variation* climbs the first pitch of *Stairway to Heaven*, then continues left on aid up a thin crack for 2 more pitches. Piton scars and rappel slings are visible from below.

Paraphernalia: Thin pitons.

Descent: Rappel the route.

Surphase Tension Buttress

Surphase Tension Buttress is the long Navajo Sandstone wall right of the third tombstone (right of *Stairway to Heaven*). Routes are listed from left to right. Parking for these climbs is on the right, 0.7 mile (1.1 km) from the beginning of the dirt road.

Unknown climbs the first crack right of *Surphase Tension*. *Learning Experience, Pigadoon,* and *Leave Your Purse at Home* begin from a grassy bench (approached from the left) approximately 300 feet (91 m) right of the Cirque-of-the-Climbables. *No Name* and *Dark Star* are right of the grassy bench and approached from a trail up the talus below the right end of Surphase Tension Buttress.

24   SURPHASE TENSION (a.k.a. Linus's Corner) I, 5.11+, 1 pitch, 130 feet (40 m) ★★★★★

First Ascent: Linus Platt belayed by Lisa Hathaway, fall 1991.

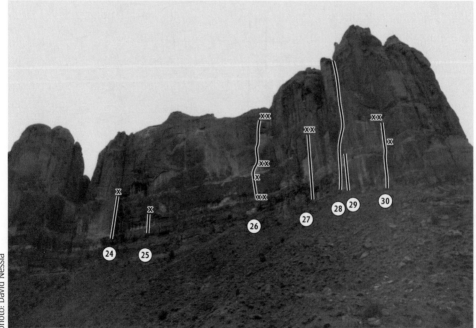

photo: David Nessia

Surphase Tension Buttress

Location and Access: *Surphase Tension* ascends the first crack right of the third tombstone (the leftmost crack system on Surphase Tension Buttress). Climb fingers-to-thin-hands-to-lieback up a corner where smooth rock on the left meets heavily lichened rock on the right. Rappel slings are visible from the road.

Paraphernalia: Friends (1) set; TCUs with many #0.75, #1, #1.5, #2.

Descent: Rappel the route.

25   UNKNOWN I, Rating unknown

First Ascent: Unknown.

Location and Access: *Unknown* is one crack right of *Surphase Tension* and climbs to rappel slings visible from the road.

Paraphernalia: Unknown.

Descent: Rappel the route.

26   LEARNING EXPERIENCE III, 5.8, A2, 3 pitches, 250 feet (76 m) ★★

First Ascent: Pitches 1 and 2: Peter Verchick, Eric Decaria, fall 1993. **Pitch 3:** Kevin Chase, Peter Verchick, fall 1994.

Location and Access: *Learning Experience* ascends the first continuous crack to the top of the buttress right of *Surphase Tension.* Begin up heavily lichened rock. Climb out 2 diagonal roofs, then a horizontal roof. Rappel slings are visible from below.

Pitch 1: Begin up a soft seam and climb past 3 fixed anchors to a double-anchor belay on the right wall, A2, 65 feet (20 m).

Pitch 2: Climb clean roofs (may go free). A #7 Big Dude or #7 Friend is useful. Climb a 6-inch (15 cm) crack, then A2 past a fixed anchor (overhang on right). Pass a second fixed anchor and belay from triple fixed anchors, left of a loose area, 5.8, A2, 120 feet (37 m).

Pitch 3: Climb off the belay ledge past a fixed nut. Climb "strange" 5.8 pods to a double-anchor belay ledge, A2, 65 feet (20 m).

Paraphernalia: Friends (1) set with (2) #1.5, #2, #2.5, (1) #7 or 6" piece; TCUs (2) sets; knifeblades and Bugaboos (7–8); Lost Arrows (5–6); angles (3–4) 0.5", 5/8"; (2) 3" through 5" angles; quickdraws (6).

Descent: Rappel the route. The first ascent party got a rope stuck on Pitch 3; a (long) walk off may be safer.

27   PIGADOON I, 5.10+, 1 pitch, 120 feet (37 m)

First Ascent: Kyle Copeland, Paul Seibert, Ryan Talbot, 29 June 1991.

Location and Access: *Pigadoon* is approximately 4 cracks right of *Learning Experience* and one crack left of a large, deep chimney. Begin up a wide crack/chimney at the far right end of the grassy ledge. Climb through light-colored rock, then over dark varnished rock to a 2-bolt anchor straddling the crack.

Paraphernalia: Friends (1) #1, #1.5, (2) #2, (3) #2.5, (4) #3, #3.5, (2) #4; Big Bros (1) #3; knee pads or long pants.

Descent: Rappel from 2 drilled pitons on either side of the crack system.

28   LEAVE YOUR PURSE AT HOME II, 5.11a, 3 pitches, 300 feet (91 m) ★★★★

First Ascent: Bob Novellino, Jimmy Dunn, Craig Luebben, November 1994.

Location and Access: *Leave Your Purse at Home* is 2 major crack systems left of *Dark*

Star. Begin up the right side of the pillar right of *Learning Experience* (the last crack system at the right end of the grassy ledge). The route climbs to the mesa top. Anchors are **NOT** visible from below, except from the left side of the pillar at the bottom of the climb.

Pitch 1: Climb bad rock passing 2 drilled anchors to a ledge 25 feet (7.6 m) up, traverse right to a left-facing crack system, then continue at 5.10a to a fixed belay anchor. Protect with a #3.5, then #3 Friend.

Pitch 2: Climb 5.10 offwidth to double anchors at the base of a chimney.

Pitch 3: Climb the chimney, move left, then climb hands-to-fingers at 5.11a to double anchors at the mesa top, 150 feet (46 m).

Paraphernalia: Friends (2) sets; TCUs (1) set; a selection of stoppers; Hexentrics (1) #7, #9; Big Bros (1) #1, #2, (2) #3, #4; quickdraws (2).

Descent: Rappel 150 feet (46 m) to the top of Pitch 2, then 150 feet (46 m) to the ground.

29   DARK STAR (a.k.a. Linus's Other Corner) I, 5.11 R, A1, 2 pitches, (pitch 1) 140 feet (43 m) ★★★★★

First Ascent: Pitch 1: Marc Hirt, Linus Platt, 2 July 1993. Pitch 2 by an unknown party.

Location and Access: *Dark Star* climbs a clean left-facing dihedral at the right side of a stout pillar that is obvious from the road. Above the top anchor on an overhanging wall (visible from below the route as well as from the road) is a large capital A inscribed by lightning.

Pitch 1: Begin on the right side of a block (left side is offwidth) and climb a chimney (hidden in a corner), 5.8 R. Move right past a bolt, 5.11 and AO, then past a second bolt, 5.11, and up a left-facing corner at 5.11 ending with A1 left to a double-bolt belay, 140 feet.

Pitch 2: The pitch climbs up the left-facing book above to rappel anchors visible from below.

Paraphernalia: Friends through #3.5 with extra #1.5, #2, #2.5; nuts; quickdraws.

Descent: Rappel the route.

Burn Victim, Driving While Asian

Burn Victim is on the left side of the canyon around the corner (south) from *Dark Star*. It is located two cracks right of three petroglyph bighorn sheep in a line and facing left. *Driving While Asian* ascends the buttress on the right (south) side of the same canyon.

30   BURN VICTIM I, 5.9, 1 pitch, 85 feet (26 m)

First Ascent: Kevin Chase, Susan Knott, November 1995.

Location and Access: *Burn Victim* begins where the trail along the petroglyph wall crests. One crack right is a glob of eroding white rock. Climb up a splitter handcrack on buff-colored rock through a small roof, then continue over broken rock to a belay ledge at dark rock. Double rappel slings are visible from below on the right dark varnished wall.

Paraphernalia: Many large hand-sized Friends.

Descent: Rappel the route.

31 DRIVING WHILE ASIAN I, 5.10+, 1 pitch, 150 feet (46 m) ★★★★★

First Ascent: Millie Birdwell, Todd Madaux, Spring 1992.

Location and Access: *Driving While Asian* ascends a handcrack up a left-facing dihedral with white bird guano at its top, visible from Kane Creek Road at the entrance to the canyon right of *Dark Star*. The route is on the opposite side (south) of the canyon from *Burn Victim*. Todd Madaux: "Thin and way pumpy, excellent Wingate, and a woman's climb for sure, Millie loves thin cracks."

Paraphernalia: Standard desert rack with many #2.5 Friends.

Descent: Rappel the route from anchors not visible from the road.

Sugar Walls, Farm

Sugar Walls is the Navajo buttress in view south of Cirque-of-the-Climbables on the west side of Kane Creek. It is a pitted, light-colored sugary-looking wall right of the dark varnished Abraxas Wall. To reach, hike the Amasa Back four-wheel-drive trail, which is signed and begins across from Forming Arch (the large arch-in-the-making) obvious on the west side of the creek. Cross Kane Creek, then contour right, and ascend a low-angle slope to the wall above. *Farm* is on the left (east) side of the road across from Forming Arch. There is a large boulder on the slope below the climb.

NOTE: There is an Anasazi granary right of Forming Arch and a life-sized shaman and owl petroglyph to the left.

photo: Eric Bjørnstad

Sugar Walls

32   SUGAR WALLS IV, 5.9, A2, 4 pitches, 285 feet (87 m)

First Ascent: Kevin Chase, Peter Verchick, fall 1993.

Location and Access: *Sugar Walls* climbs light-colored rock to rappel slings visible from below or from the road with binoculars.

Pitch 1: Climb a 5.7 chimney, then continue 5.9 ending with A1 at a sandy ledge (right of a long, vertical pod) with triple anchors (on the right wall) at the belay station, 5.9, A1, 75 feet (23 m).

Pitch 2: Continue up the pod and out a roof. Go right into another crack system and up to an area of chimneys, 5.8. Anchors are on the left wall, A1, 80 feet (24 m).

Pitch 3: Wide to start (5-inches, 12.7 cm), then the crack thins. Pass a small roof (A2) and cross to the crack system on the right in a left-facing corner and climb to triple anchors (on right wall) below a prominent ceiling, 90 feet (27 m).

Pitch 4: Climb out the right side of a short roof to a soft rock headwall and double anchors on the right wall, 40 feet (12 m). The remaining 70 feet (21 m) to the mesa top are blank.

Paraphernalia: Friends (2) sets; TCUs (1) set with double 4–7" protection; nuts (1) set; knifeblades and Bugaboos (7–8); Lost Arrows (5–6); angle pitons (4) 0.5", (3) 5/8", (1) 1.5".

Descent: Rappel the route.

33   FARM I, 5.10+, 1 pitch, 80 feet (25 m) ★★★★★

First Ascent: Kyle Copeland, Daryl Miller, fall 1990.

Location and Access: *Farm* is across from Abraxas Wall directly above and east of the Kane Springs Canyon Road. Drive south from the large parking area across from Surphase Tension Buttress. The climb is above the road at the first right curve, 0.9 mile (1.4 km) from the beginning of the dirt road. Begin up a pointy pillar and climb dark varnished rock passing an overhang on its right, then continue to a rappel chain visible from the road.

Paraphernalia: Friends (1) set with extra #2, #2.5, #3; TCUs (1) set.

Descent: Descend from a rappel chain on the right wall.

Abraxas Wall

Abraxas Wall is on the right (west) side of Kane Springs Canyon on the dark varnished prow of rock between Forming Arch and Sugar Walls, directly across the creek from *Farm*. To reach, hike the signed Amasa Back four-wheel-drive trail, cross Kane Creek, then contour right and hike up the gentle slopes right of the wall above. Routes are listed from right to left.

NOTE: As one travels uphill from Amasa Back Trail, the large boulder on the right (below road level) has petroglyphs on four sides. Pecked into the face toward the road is the famous "Birthing Scene." Farther up the road, 0.1 mile (0.16 km), is a large boulder (right side) that was bulldozed aside during road construction. It also has petroglyphs which are now upside down.

34   SUGAR KANE I, 5.10a, 1 pitch, 45 feet (14 m) ★★

First Ascent: Kevin Chase, Mark Bower, 1995.

Location and Access: *Sugar Kane* is one crack right of the south prow, right of *Abraxas Right*. Climb a handcrack up a right-facing smooth dihedral to rappel slings visible from below the route.

photo: Eric Bjørnstad

Abraxas Wall

Paraphernalia: Friends #3 through #5.

Descent: Rappel the route.

35   ABRAXAS RIGHT I, 5.11b, 1 pitch, 80 feet (24 m) ★★★★

First Ascent: Linus Platt et al, spring 1991.

Location and Access: *Abraxas Right* climbs with tight hands on the left-facing dihedral one crack left of *Sugar Kane*. The crux is the first 15 feet (4.5 m) of #2 placements. Rappel anchors are shared with *Abraxas Left*.

Paraphernalia: Friends (1) #1.5, (3) #2, (2) #2.5, #3, (2) #4, (1) #5.

Descent: Rappel the route from anchors shared with *Abraxas Left*.

36   ABRAXAS LEFT I, 5.10c/d, 1 pitch, 80 feet (24 m) ★★★

First Ascent: Linus Platt, Earl Wiggins, spring 1991.

Location and Access: Ascend a right-trending handcrack one crack left of *Abraxas Right*. Climb past an angular pod positioned above the start of the route, with perfect hands to offwidth to rappel anchors shared with *Abraxas Right*. The crux is an awkward finger start.

Paraphernalia: Friends (1) set with extra #2.5, #3, (1) #4, (1) #5.

Descent: Rappel the route.

37   PROJECT I, 1 pitch, 30 feet (9 m)

First Ascent: Kevin Chase, solo, fall 1995.

Location and Access: *Project* is an unfinished route on the face between the first and second crack systems left of *Abraxas Left*. *Project* climbs past 3 bolts up a scalloped wall. Rappel slings are visible from below the route.

Paraphernalia: Quickdraws (3).

Descent: Rappel the route.

38   XYLOKANE I, 5.11d/5.12a, 1 pitch, 70 feet (21 m) ★★★★★

First Ascent: Jay Smith, fall 1995.

Location and Access: *Xylokane* is the first crack left of *Project* and climbs, with tight fingers, a right-facing dihedral, then a roof to rappel slings visible from below.

Paraphernalia: Many small cams #0.5 through 2".

Descent: Rappel the route.

39   KRACK PIPE I, 5.10a, 2 pitches, 100 feet (30 m) ★★★

First Ascent: Pitch 1: Linus Platt, Earl Wiggins, 1991. **Pitch 2:** Bob Scarpelli, spring 1997.

Location and Access: *Krack Pipe* starts up the left side of a pillar one crack left of *Zylokane*. Begin up the right of 2 cracks, then switch to the left crack and continue fingers to offwidth, to rappel slings visible from below on the left wall.

Paraphernalia: Camalots (3) #1 through #5.

Descent: Rappel the route.

40   KRACK KOKANE I, 5.10+, 1 pitch, 50 feet (15 m) ★★★

First Ascent: Kevin Chase, Mark Bower, 1995.

Location and Access: Ascend a right-facing corner one crack left of *Krack Pipe*. Anchors are visible from below.

Paraphernalia: Friends (2) #0.5 through #2.

Descent: Rappel the route.

41   DRUGSTORE COWBOY I, 5.11a, 1 pitch, 65 feet (20 m) ★★★

First Ascent: Eric Decaria, Kevin Chase, 1995.

Location and Access: *Drugstore Cowboy* is one crack left of *Krack Kokane*. Climb a V-formation with a single bolt on the right wall at the bottom of the route, then continue up a thin crack with pods. Rappel slings are visible on the right wall. It is possible to climb 20 feet higher (6 m) through bad rock to another set of anchors.

Paraphernalia: Many small Friends and TCUs; quickdraws (1).

Descent: Rappel the route.

42   NAVAJO WARRIOR I, 5.11+, 1 pitch, 170 feet (52 m) ★★★★

First Ascent: Dave Medara, Kevin Chase, September 1995. First free ascent: Shamick, Dave Medara, September 1995.

Location and Access: *Navajo Warrior* is 75 feet (21 m) or one crack left of *Drugstore Cowboy*. The route is climbed with a 200-foot (60 m) rope. Begin behind a large boulder. Climb a shallow left-facing dihedral with the crux ascending face moves. There are 3 bolts low on the route. Rappel anchors are visible below a prominent bulge.

Paraphernalia: Friends (3) sets #0.75 through #4; quickdraws (3).

Descent: Rappel the route with 200-foot (60 m) ropes.

Slick Trick, Kyle's Tower, Scarpelli Finger Crack

Slick Trick is approximately 100 feet (30 m) up the drainage left of Forming Arch. *Kyle's Tower* is obvious from Kane Springs Road left of Forming Arch. Approach by contouring south (left) from *Slick Trick*, or hike the Amasa Back four-wheel trail which passes below the tower. *Scarpelli Finger Crack* is 100 feet (30 m) left of *Kyle's Tower.*

43   SLICK TRICK I, 5.9, 1 pitch, 70 feet (21 m) ★★

First Ascent: Kevin Chase, 1995.

Location and Access: *Slick Trick* climbs a handcrack in an open book to rappel anchors visible on the right wall from below.

Paraphernalia: Friends (1) set.

Descent: Rappel the route.

44   KYLE'S TOWER I, 5.11+, 2 pitches, 200 feet (60 m)

First Ascent: Jim Beyer, Kyle Copeland, 5.8+, A2, early 1990s. First free ascent: Clay Patton, Travis Spitzer, 1993.

Location and Access: *Kyle's Tower* climbs hard offwidth up the east face (facing Kane Springs Road). A bolt on the right wall protects the move around a loose block low on the route. Continue past a drilled piton on the right wall and a second piton where the crack angles right and up to a deep chimney.

Paraphernalia: Standard desert rack; quickdraws.

Descent: Rappel the route or the lesser angled back side of the tower.

photo: Eric Bjørnstad

45   SCARPELLI FINGER CRACK I, 5.11a, 1 pitch, 100 feet (30 m)

First Ascent: Kevin Chase, Bob Scarpelli, May 1997.

Location and Access: *Scarpelli Finger Crack* is just left of *Kyle's Tower*, faces the road, and follows an overhanging, left-facing, left-leaning corner (up light-colored rock), then up double cracks to Metolius rappel hangers visible from below.

Paraphernalia: Friends (1) #3, (6) #3.5; Camalots (3) #4 through #5.

Descent: Rappel the route.

Funnel Arch

Funnel Arch is weathered from Navajo Sandstone and has a span of 42 feet (13 m), a height of 35 feet (11 m), a thickness of 21 feet (6 m), and a width of 12 feet (3.6m). It is left (north) of the top of the hill, 0.3 mile (0.4 km) beyond the birthing scene rock. (If you start down the steep switchbacks leading to Kane Springs you have gone too far.) Scramble easy 5th class up the steep drainage left (north) of the roadway. At the top of the vertical section, continue right, following the drainage until the arch becomes visible, less than 0.5 mile (0.8 km) from the parking area. To reach the top of the arch, hike left, beyond the span, and ascend a bench where steel cable (placed by Lin Ottinger in the early 1960s) protects the scramble to the top of the mesa. Contour right to reach the arch. From the top of the cable, a large and rarely visited area of the Behind-the-Rocks region is accessible.

WARNING: Please avoid damaging the deep, rich cryptobiotic soil on the approach.

46   FUNNEL ARCH (Top-rope) I, 5.4, 1 pitch, 35 feet (11 m)

First Ascent: Lin Ottinger, belayed by Eric Bjørnstad, late 1960s.

Location and Access: Lin was belayed to the top center of the exposed arch from the plateau above, then climbed the span back to the belay.

Paraphernalia: Top-rope.

Descent: Reverse the route.

Archaic Revival, Kind–Other Kind

Archaic Revival and *Kind–Other Kind* are down the drainage from Kane Springs. Park at the lower of the two switchbacks descending to the spring, then scramble down the talus slope (right) to the creek. Hike approximately 0.75 mile (1.2 km) downstream to the second arête (formed by a right-angle bend of the Wingate wall) on the right side of the canyon. *Archaic Revival* is the first right-facing dihedral right of the prominent arête and *Kind–Other Kind* climbs the first crack (right-facing dihedral) right of *Archaic Revival*. Since Kane Creek meanders in a long right curve a short distance below Kane Springs, the easiest approach is to hike benches that form on the inside curve, or the right side of the canyon. The left side will present difficult bushwacking through tamarisk growth lining the creek. The debris found on the broad bench in the area of the routes is from thoughtless campers using the now closed walk-in campsites at the top of the wall in the region opposite Funnel Arch Trailhead.

WARNING: The canyon is subject to flash flooding during periods of storm and should be avoided if the sky appears threatening.

47   ARCHAIC REVIVAL I, 5.11-, AO, 1 pitch, 150 feet (46 m) ★★★

First Ascent: Kyle Copeland, David Widden, Linus Platt, April 1993.

Location and Access: *Archaic Revival* begins up a cottonwood log leaning against the wall. From the top of the log, a good handcrack is reached and ascended up a right-facing dihedral to rappel slings visible from below.

Paraphernalia: Small Friends and TCUs.

Descent: Rappel the route.

48   KIND—OTHER KIND I, 5.10a, 1 pitch, 140 feet (43 m) ★★★★★

First Ascent: Kyle Copeland, David Widden, Linus Platt, April 1993.

Location and Access: *Kind–Other Kind* climbs the first crack right of *Archaic Revival*. Ascend a right-facing dihedral up dark varnished Wingate to a rappel chain visible from below.

Paraphernalia: Hand-sized Friends.

Descent: Rappel the route.

Stimulants Wall (a.k.a. Heuco Wall)

Stimulants Wall is on the left (east) side of Kane Creek Canyon, 2.9 miles (4.6 km) from the cattleguard at the dirt beginning to the canyon, or 0.7 mile (1.1 km) downcanyon from Kane Springs. Stimulants Wall is also easy to locate by driving 0.2 mile (0.3 km) upcanyon from Hunters Canyon. Routes are listed from left to right.

49   VIVARIUM I, 5.11b, 1 pitch, 80 feet (24 m) ★★★

First Ascent: Jim Beyer, solo, January 1997.

Location and Access: *Vivarium* is obvious above the road with 2 bolts close to the ground and rappel slings visible from below. The crux is at the start of the climb.

Paraphernalia: Many #4 Friends; long slings; quickdraws.

Descent: Rappel the route.

50   ADRENALINE I, 5.10d/5.11a, 1 pitch, 45 feet (14 m) ★★★★★

First Ascent: Jim Beyer, solo, January 1997.

Location: *Adrenaline* is right of *Vivarium* and climbs to double bolts. Rappel slings are visible from below.

Paraphernalia: Friends #0.5 through #4; long slings; quickdraws.

Descent: Rappel the route.

51   EARL GREY I, 5.10b/c, 1 pitch, 65 feet (20 m) ★★★★

First Ascent: Jim Beyer, solo, January 1997.

Location and Access: *Earl Grey* is right of *Vivarium* and shares double bolts. Begin 5.9, then continue up and right to triple rappel anchors. The crux is high on the climb.

Paraphernalia: Many 4" camming units; long slings; quickdraws.

Descent: Rappel the route.

photo: Eric Bjørnstad

Stimulants Wall

Hunters Canyon

Hunters Canyon is 0.2 mile (0.32 km) downcanyon from Stimulants Wall. There are nine campsites with a pit toilet and fire rings, and a charge of $4 per night. Hunters Arch is on the right 0.5 mile (0.8 km) upcanyon. It is eroded in the Kayenta Formation (in rock that is 190 million years old), with a span of 63 feet, a height of 74 feet, a thickness of 9 feet, and a width of 9 feet.

Grave, Unleashed

Grave and Unleashed are on the left (east) side of the roadway, 2.3 miles (3.7 km) from the cattleguard at the dirt beginning of Kane Springs Canyon, or 0.1 mile (0.16 km) beyond (south) the drainage crossing the road at Hunters Canyon. When viewed from the road, the crack systems and rappel slings are obvious. Grave curves right, Unleashed curves left, with both climbs meeting at a shared rappel station. Park below the climbs and hike up and left to a ledge, then traverse right passing a "scary" boulder. Third class up boulders to a 2-bolt belay/rappel anchor on a ledge.

52   GRAVE I, 5.11c, 1 pitch, 180 feet (30 m) ★★★★

First Ascent: Tom Gilje, August 1994.

Location and Access: Grave climbs a right-facing dihedral past a fixed piton, up a 2-inch (5 cm) crack, then 1-inch (past a fixed piton) to double rappel anchors shared with Unleashed.

Paraphernalia: Friends #1 through #4; a selection of small nuts; quickdraws.

Descent: Rappel the route.

53   UNLEASHED I, 5.11c, 2 pitches, 180 feet (55 m) ★★★★★

First Ascent: Tom Gilje, August 1994.

Location and Access: Approach same as for Grave. Face climb past 1 bolt, then continue right to a left-facing corner which is 1.5 inches to 2 inches wide (3.8–5 cm). The route shares rappel anchors with Grave.

Paraphernalia: Many #1, #1.5 Friends.

Descent: Rappel the route.

Ice Cream Parlor

Climbs at Ice Cream Parlor are on the left (east) side of the road beginning 500 feet (152 m) past the Echo campsites and extending to where the canyon opens into Kane Creek Valley. Routes are listed from left to right.

54   SPACE GHOST I, 5.10, 3 pitches, 300 feet (91 m)

First Ascent: Tom Gilje, Jasper Groff, 1995.

Location and Access: Space Ghost is one crack system left of Juggernaut at the far left side of the Ice Cream Parlor.

Pitch 1: Climb a handcrack to a belay ledge.

Pitch 2: Continue offwidth to a double-bolt belay station, 5.10.

Pitch 3: Ascend a flared chimney to a ceiling, then veer left and up to rappel anchors.

Paraphernalia: Friends (1) set; extra large cams.

Descent: Rappel the route.

photo: Eric Bjørnstad

55   JUGGERNAUT I, 5.10, 2 pitches, 100 feet (30 m)

First Ascent: Tom Gilje, Mike Camps, Bob Novellino, 1995.

Location and Access: *Juggernaut* is one crack left of *Wolverine*. Climb a wide crack system to bolts, then move right. Climb past 4 bolts to a belay. Rappel to a ledge and belay as for *Wolverine*.

Paraphernalia: Many #4, #5 Friends; quickdraws.

Descent: One double-rope rappel down *Wolverine*.

56   WOLVERINE I, 5.11 R, 2 pitches, 80 feet (24 m)

First Ascent: Tom Gilje, 1995.

Location and Access: *Woverine* has same beginning as *Crack One*, then climbs the obvious corner and roof above. Rappel slings are visible from below the route. Tom Gilje: "A scary traverse ledge at the rappel leads you to the *Juggernaut's* wide crack; heads up!"

Paraphernalia: Friends and TCUs to #3; nuts (1) set; quickdraws.

Descent: Rappel the route.

NOTE: Cracks One, Two, and Three on Easy Slab may be top-roped from one another.

57   EASY SLAB—CRACK ONE I, 5.8, 1 pitch, 80 feet (24 m) ★★★★★

First Ascent: Tom Gilje, Julie Gilje, 1995.

Location and Access: *Crack One* is the left-most of 3 cracks close to one another on a sloping wall near the lower portion of the Ice Cream Parlor Wall.

Paraphernalia: Nuts (1) set.

Descent: Rappel the route from double anchors visible from below.

58   EASY SLAB—CRACK TWO I, 5.8+, 1 pitch, 80 feet (24 m) ★★★

First Ascent: Tom Gilje, Julie Gilje, 1995.

Location and Access: *Crack Two* is the center of 3 cracks that are close to one another on the sloping wall near the lower portion of the Ice Cream Parlor wall.

Paraphernalia: Nuts (1) set.

Descent: Rappel from *Crack One* anchors.

59   EASY SLAB—CRACK THREE I, 5.8, 1 pitch, 80 feet (24 m) ★★★

First Ascent: Tom Gilje, Julie Sheld, 1995.

Location and Access: *Crack Three* is the rightmost of 3 cracks close to one another on the sloping wall near the lower portion of the Ice Cream Parlor Wall.

Paraphernalia: Nuts (1) set.

Descent: Rappel from *Crack One* anchors.

60   RP CITY I, 5.10, 1 pitch, 100 feet (30 m)

First Ascent: Tom Gilje, Julie Sheld, 1995.

Location and Access: *RP City* climbs the crack system at the far right side of the smooth slanting wall of the Easy Slabs. Approach by traversing on a ledge right of the beginning of a left-facing corner. Face climb past a bolt, then right to a left-facing dihedral. Rappel slings are visible from below on light-colored rock.

photo: Eric Bjørnstad

Paraphernalia: RPs (10); small nuts.

Descent: Rappel the route from double bolts.

NOTE: *Good Day to Die, Pork Soda, Ice Cream Parlor Crack,* and *Pulp Friction* are approached from a ledge which begins right of the climbs.

61 GOOD DAY TO DIE I, 5.9, 1 pitch, 80 feet (24 m) ★★★

First Ascent: Tom Gilje, Julie Gilje, 1995.

Location and Access: *Good Day to Die* is the first crack 45 feet (13 m) left of *Ice Cream Parlor Crack*. Climb a dark varnished wall up a right-curving crack past 3 bolts, then double bolts side by side on a smooth wall. Rappel or traverse right a few feet to *Ice Cream Parlor Crack* anchors.

Paraphernalia: Tri-cams (1) #2; quickdraws (4).

Descent: Rappel *Ice Cream Parlor Crack*.

photo: Eric Bjørnstad

62   BEEN THERE DONE IT (Top-rope) I, 5.11, 1 pitch, 70 feet (21 m)

First Ascent: Tom Gilje, Julie Gilje, 1995.

Location and Access: *Been There Done It* climbs a right-facing dihedral to the ledge and beginning of *Good Day to Die*. Begin below and just right of *Good Day to Die*. The route may be top-roped from *Ice Cream Parlor Crack* or *Good Day to Die*.

Paraphernalia: Top-rope.

Descent: Rappel *Good Day to Die*.

63   PORK SODA I, 5.9, 1 pitch, 120 feet (36 m)

First Ascent: Tom Gilje, Bob Novellino, 1995.

Location and Access: Begin up *Good Day to Die*. Above the first fixed anchor (in right-facing corner) climb the roof above, then flakes to double rappel anchors visible from the road.

Paraphernalia: Friends (1) set; Tri-cams (1) #2; quickdraws.

Descent: Rappel the route.

64   ICE CREAM PARLOR CRACK I, 5.11a, 1 pitch, 90 feet (27 m) ★★★★★

First Ascent: Dan Mannix, Alison Sheets, 1986.

Location and Access: Climb dark varnished rock past a fixed piton on the wall right of the right-facing corner of *Good Day to Die*. Protect low on the route with a #4 Camalot before continuing up a fingercrack in a right-facing dihedral. The route may be top-roped from *Good Day to Die* or vice versa. The route was one of the first established in the Kane Creek area.

Paraphernalia: Friends (1) #0.4, (2) #0.5, (5) #0.75, (2) #1; Camalots (1) #4.

Descent: Rappel the route from one piton and double bolts.

65   PULP FRICTION I, 5.11 R, 1 pitch, 90 feet (27 m) ★★★★

First Ascent: Tom Gilje, solo, 1995

Location and Access: *Pulp Friction* climbs the left-facing dihedral one crack right of *Ice Cream Parlor Crack*. Begin up boulders, then climb the left-facing corner until it is possible to move right, passing a bolt, and onto the arête formed by the dihedral. Continue with face climbing past 2 bolts on the left wall to rappel anchors which are above the dihedral and visible from below.

Paraphernalia: Friends (1) #1, #3; quickdraws.

Descent: Rappel the route.

66   COFFIN I, 5.10, 1 pitch, 75 feet (23 m)

First Ascent: Tom Gilje, Bob Novellino.

Location and Access: *Coffin* is one crack right of *Pulp Friction*. Begin below a roof, then continue up a chimney.

Paraphernalia: Friends (1) set.

Descent: Rappel the route.

photo: Eric Bjørnstad

photo: Eric Bjørnstad

67   POSSESSED I, 5.11+ R, 1 pitch, 75 feet (23 m)

First Ascent: Eric Decaria, Brent Barthomew, 1995.

Location and Access: *Possessed* is approximately 20 feet (6 m) or one crack right of *Coffin*. Climb the face of a column (with a flat top) leaning against the buttress behind it. There are 6 bolts on the route visible from the top of the approach trail.

Paraphernalia: Quickdraws (6).

Descent: Rappel the route.

68   KNEE GRINDER I, 5.9, 1 pitch, 80 feet (24 m)

First Ascent: John Varco, Eric Decaria, 1995.

Location and Access: *Knee Grinder* climbs the right side of the pillar of *Coffin* and *Possessed*, and shares anchors.

Paraphernalia: One set of the larger size Friends; quickdraws.

Descent: Rappel *Possessed*.

69   DEATHTRAP I, 5.8, 1 pitch, 75 feet (23 m)

First Ascent: Tom Gilje, solo, 1995.

Location and Access: *Deathtrap* is approximately 100 yards (91 m) right of *Possessed*. Begin on the right side of obvious pillarlike formations near the start of *T-Rex*. Climb through the pillars and chimney to the top.

Paraphernalia: Friends (1) set; TCUs (1) set.

Descent: Rappel the route.

70   T-REX (a.k.a. Roofs from Hell) II, 5.11c, 4 pitches, 350 feet (107 m) ★★★★★

First Ascent: Tom Gilje, Bob Novellino, 1995.

Location and Access: *T-Rex* begins right of *Deathtrap*, 100 yards (91 m) right of *Possessed* and climbs to the rimrock past 20+ bolts.

NOTE: To climb only the roof at the top of *T-Rex*, continue down the road to where Kane Creek Valley opens up (directly opposite Scorched Earth Crag). Hike up weaknesses in the Wingate wall on the left (5.7), then traverse back to the route from the mesa top. Rappel from fixed anchors to the beginning of the roof pitch. Kevin Chase: "Face climb to the crack then pull the moves and enjoy the exposure."

Pitch 1: Climb a pitch protected with bolts, 5.11c, 100 feet (30 m).

Pitch 2: Climb a corner past bolts, 5.10, 100 feet (30 m).

Pitch 3: Climb a short pitch to a belay ledge, 5.11a, 50 feet (15 m).

Pitch 4: Continue up the roof, 5.11c. **BEWARE** of ropes being cut on the arête. Hike to the top of the wall above the overhang, 100 feet (30 m).

Paraphernalia: Friends (1) #1.5, (2) #2, (1) #2.5; quickdraws.

Descent: Rappel from double anchors to the base of a small roof immediately south (right) of *T-Rex* roof, then to the ground.

Space Tower, Checkmate, Gilje Route

Space Tower is a semidetached stout tower across (west) Kane Creek from Ice Cream Parlor. *Checkmate* is right of Space Tower and *Gilje Route* approximately 100 yards (91 m) right of *Checkmate*. Some route finding will be required to locate the climbs. Routes are listed from left to right.

71   SPACE TOWER—HALLOW SOULS I, 5.9, 1 pitch, 165 feet (50 m) ★★★★

First Ascent: Kevin Chase, Tom Gilje, September 1995.

Location and Access: *Hallow Souls* begins up loose rock and a chimney on the right side of the tower. Continue stemming approximately 15 feet (4.5 m) up the inside of the landform to a bolt on the wall behind the tower, then follow a handcrack which leads to the summit.

CAUTION: There are loose blocks at the base of the tower; belayer beware.

Paraphernalia: Camalots (1) set; TCUs (1) set; long runners.

Descent: Rappel the route.

72   CHECKMATE I, 5.10+, 3 pitches, 165 feet (50)

First Ascent: Jimmy Dunn, Bob Novellino, 1995.

photo: Eric Bjørnstad

Location and Access: *Checkmate* is right of Space Tower and climbs to the top of the wall.

Paraphernalia: Standard desert rack.

Descent: Rappel the route.

73   GILJE ROUTE I, 5.9, 1 pitch

First Ascent: Tom Gilje, Julie Gilje, 1995.

Location and Access: *Gilje Route* is right of *Checkmate*.

Paraphernalia: Standard desert rack.

Descent: Rappel the route.

Charlie's Sorry, Sorry Charlie

Charlie's Sorry and *Sorry Charlie* are on the left side (east) of Kane Springs Canyon high on the Wingate Sandstone buttress, 3.5 miles (5.6 km) from Kane Springs. The routes may also be identified by their position 500 feet (152 m) beyond a sign reading "End of Riverway Recreation Area." Approach left or right of the green (ferrous iron) Chinle cliff bands below the routes.

74   CHARLIE'S SORRY I, 5.10, 1 pitch, 80 feet (24 m)

First Ascent: Dan Mannix, Bret Sutteer, Linus Platt, Charlie Fowler, 1990.

Location and Access: *Charlie's Sorry* is one crack right of an obvious oblique angle in the Wingate buttress. Begin with hands and fists at 5.10. Pass a small roof (angling right), then climb larger-than-fists to a rappel piton at a small stance on the left wall and visible from the road.

Paraphernalia: Camalots #4 and larger; many large nuts.

Descent: Rappel the route.

75   SORRY CHARLIE I, 5.10b, 1 pitch, 50 feet (15 m)

First Ascent: Dan Mannix, Bret Sutteer, 1990.

Location and Access: *Sorry Charlie* is 3 cracks right of *Charlie's Sorry* and climbs a splitter crack up the center of a large rectangular block attached to the wall behind. Begin up a 3.5-inch crack (8.9 cm), then climb (5.9+) a 2-inch system (5 cm) which becomes 1-inch (2.5 cm) before continuing with tiny fingers (5.10b) up a left-facing corner to a rappel stance and slings visible from the road.

Paraphernalia: Friends (1) #1, #2.5, #3.5.

Descent: Rappel the route.

Kane Creek Valley

Kane Creek Valley is 4 miles (6.4 km) from the cattleguard at the end of the paved Kane Creek Boulevard where Kane Creek Canyon begins. It starts where the canyon opens into a scenic valley rimmed with vertical Wingate walls skirted by Chinle slopes. At the southwest border of the valley, a narrow four-wheel-drive trail serpentines through the Moenkopi's layer cake of mud and shalestone on its improbable path to Hurrah Pass, where there are sensational vistas of the Colorado River and the desolate no man's land beyond. Visible to the south from the climb to Hurrah Pass, high on the mesa top, is the chainlink fence guarding Anticline Overlook at the northern edge of the BLM-managed Canyon Rims Recreational Area. It is a worthwhile visit, accessible from U.S. Highway 191, 30 miles (48 km) south of Moab.

Scorched Earth Crag

Scorched Earth Crag is a Wingate wall on the right (west) side of upper (north) Kane Creek Valley. Access is by the drainage, 1.6 miles (2.6 km) from Kane Creek Spring, or just right of the sign reading "Leaving Colorado Parkway Recreation Area." Routes are listed from right to left.

76   CREEKER I, 5.9, 1 pitch, 60 feet (18 m)

First Ascent: Kevin Chase, Eric Decaria, 1995.

Location and Access: *Creeker* is 150 yards (137 m) right of the prow at Scorched Earth Crag.

Paraphernalia: Friends (2) #0.4 through #3.

Descent: Rappel the route.

77   DANTE I, 5.9+, 1 pitch, 70 feet (21 m) ★★★

First Ascent: Kevin Chase, Lisa Hathaway, 1995.

Location and Access: *Dante* is 10 feet (3 m) left of *Creeker* and ascends a splitter crack, which is identified by a tall tree growing near the start of the climb. Begin up a bulge and continue up a crack system to face climbing.

Paraphernalia: Friends #0.75 through #3.

Descent: Rappel the route.

78   SILENT BOB I, 5.10+, 1 pitch, 100 feet (30 m) ★★★★

First Ascent: Dave Medara, Kevin Chase, October 1995.

Location and Access: *Silent Bob* is 1,000 feet (305 m) left of the prow. Climb a shallow right-facing corner above the mining road (when viewed from Kane Creek Valley Road), or left of obvious sloping ramps. The route has a plaque with an inscribed 5.10 rating.

Paraphernalia: Friends (2) sets.

Descent: Rappel the route.

79   DARK PATH I, 5.11b, 1 pitch, 80 feet (24 m) ★★★★★

First Ascent: Dave Medara, 1995.

Location and Access: *Dark Path* is, approximately 100 feet left of the prominent prow of Scorched Earth Crag. Begin up the left side of a ledge, then move right and belay from a single bolt. Climb past 3 fixed anchors to a rappel station with slings visible from below.

Paraphernalia: Friends #0.4 through #3; quickdraws (3).

Descent: Rappel the route.

80   SCHIZO (Top-rope) I, 5.11+, 1 pitch, 100 feet (30 m) ★★

First Ascent: Dave Medara, Lynn Romano, fall 1994.

Location and Access: *Schizo* is one crack system right of *Split Personality.*

Paraphernalia: Top-rope.

Descent: Rappel the route from *Split Personality* anchors.

81   SPLIT PERSONALITY I, 5.11a, 1 pitch, 100 feet (30 m) ★★★

First Ascent: Dave Medara, Lynn Romano, 1995.

Location and Access: *Split Personality* is left of a prominent prow on the Scorched Earth Crag, at the left side of the ledge of *Dark Path*. Climb a right-facing dihedral (tight hands) that becomes left-facing, then right-facing again, before reaching double anchors on light-colored rock (difficult to see from below).

Paraphernalia: Many #1.5 Friends.

Descent: Rappel the route.

82   STILETTO (a.k.a. Hueco Route) I, 5.11+, 1 pitch, 50 feet (15 m) ★★★★

First Ascent: Kevin Chase, Lisa Hathaway, Dave Medara, October 1995.

Location and Access: *Stiletto* is 150 feet (46 m) left of *Schizo* (250 feet left of the prow). Climb a splitter crack to anchors visible from below.

Paraphernalia: Friends #0.4 through #2; Lowe Balls; many small nuts.

Descent: Rappel the route.

Predator

Predator Tower is near the southwest perimeter of Kane Creek Valley where the Organ Rock Member of the Cutler Formation forms towers and fins of purple, brick red, and maroon sandstone. Predator is visible from the road as the formation at the end of a right-trending

photo: Cameron M. Burns

Jimmy Dunn and Keith Reynolds on the first ascent of *Rain of Dust*

ridge. Approach by walking in drainages cross-country to the landform. Be careful not to hurt the dirt (cryptobiotic soil).

83   REIGN OF TERROR II, 5.11-, 2 pitches, 150 feet (46 m) ★★★★★

First Ascent: Jimmy Dunn, Kyle Copeland, Eric Johnson, 17 August 1990.

Location and Access: *Reign of Terror* begins on the west face of Predator and finishes on the south side of the tower.

Pitch 1: The crux. Crack climb to a ledge, 5.11-, 60 feet (18 m).

Pitch 2: Climb atop a loose block, then pass a fixed piton at a dirty section and traverse (5.3) right to a 5.9 handcrack which leads to the summit on the south side of the tower, 90 feet (27 m).

Paraphernalia: Friends (2) #1.5, #2, #2.5, #3, (1) #3.5, #4; 7" piece optional; long runners; quickdraws (1).

Descent: Rappel the south face from (2) 0.5" fixed angles.

84   RAIN OF DUST II, 5.11+, 3 pitches, 150 feet (46 m) ★★★★

First Ascent: Jimmy Dunn, Keith Reynolds, 31 October 1994.

Location and Access: *Rain of Dust* climbs the north side of Predator.

Pitch 1: Climb a thin crack, traversing right to a belay ledge, 5.11+.

Pitch 2: Continue up 20 feet (6 m), then traverse right and belay.

Pitch 3: Follow Pitch 2 of *Reign of Terror* to the top of the spire.

Paraphernalia: Same as *Reign of Terror*.

Descent: Rappel the south face from (2) 0.5" fixed angles.

Happy Turk, Pensive Putterman, Shelbyville, Anticline Overlook Buttress

Happy Turk is a hoodoo 3.9 miles (6.2 km) south of Kane Springs. It is visible on the left (east) side of the road 0.8 mile (1.2 km) before crossing the Kane Creek drainage in Kane Creek Valley. A high-clearance vehicle can drive directly to the tower on a faint dirt road 500 feet (152 m) south of the hoodoo, or make a 5-minute approach hike from Kane Creek Valley Road.

Pensive Putterman is a 120-foot (37 m) tower of deep red Cutler Sandstone, on the west side of the road, opposite Happy Turk. There are double bolts on the right side of the route and on the small wall behind the tower which were placed by Kevin Chase and Ronda (surname unknown) for a tyrolean traverse during a car commercial in the fall of 1995.

Shelbyville is approximately 0.5 mile (0.8 km) south of Happy Turk and Pensive Putterman on the west side of the Kane Creek Valley road. East of the road, two other small towers have anchors, but further information on their routes is unknown.

Anticline Overlook Buttress is the long Wingate Wall bordering Kane Creek Valley to its south. Anticline Overlook is in view on the rim (south) as Kane Creek Valley Road begins the climb to Hurrah Pass. The southern portion of the buttress is approached by a sandy four-wheel-drive road branching left just past where Kane Springs Valley Road crosses Kane Creek. In the general area, two other routes have been climbed by Peter Verchick and others, but further information is unknown. Also in the area, Anticline Overlook Buttress climbs to the rim top, but its precise location is unknown.

85 HAPPY TURK (a.k.a. The Devil's Golf Ball) I, 5.8, 1 pitch, 20 feet (6 m)

First Ascent: First ascent unknown. Probable second ascent Kevin Chase, solo.

Location and Access: *Happy Turk* follows a 6-bolt route on the east side of the tower. Kevin Chase: "5.8, but scary." The hoodoo's first ascent was probably climbed with aid.

Paraphernalia: Quickdraws (6).

Descent: Rappel the route, although during the second ascent it was downclimbed.

86 PENSIVE PUTTERMAN—ALL ALONG THE PUTT-TOWER I, 5.7, A1, 1 pitch, 60 feet (18 m) ★

First Ascent: Jesse Harvey, Cameron Burns, 15 November 1997.

Location and Access: *All Along the Putt-Tower* climbs the west face of the landform from the saddle behind the tower. Approach 3rd class from the right side and climb a 15-foot (4.5 m) 5.7 handcrack to a ledge. Move left 7 feet (2 m) and continue with aid (0.5" crack, 1.2 cm) to a roof, past a fixed piton, then move right and pass a second fixed piton on the way to the summit.

Paraphernalia: Friends (1) #2, #2.5; Camalots (1) #1; stoppers (1) set of small to medium; angle pitons (1) 5/8"; quickdraws (2).

Descent: One single-rope rappel down the route.

87 SHELBYVILLE—MR. PUTTERMAN GOES TO WASHINGTON II, 5.9, A1, 4 pitches, 200 feet (61 m) ★★★★★

First Ascent: Cameron Burns, Jesse Harvey, 21 February 1998.

Location and Access: The route begins on the southwest face of the tower, then meanders to the summit.

Pitch 1: Begin 10 feet (3 m) below and right of obvious rappel anchors on the southwest face and continue (5.9) up a long chimney crack system (6" then 12", 15 cm then 30 cm) which crests at 2 bolts at the top of the south ridge, 150 feet (46 m).

Pitch 2: A traversing pitch. Continue up 15 feet (4.5 m) with one move of aid, then walk right 50 feet (15 m) and scramble up a block-filled gully (30 feet, 9 m) to a belay at a notch, 120 feet (36 m).

photo: Cameron M. Burns

Pensive Putterman

Pitch 3: A bolt, then aid (A1) up several moves to easy ground, 40 feet (12 m).

Pitch 4: Scramble north to the summit (no anchor), 100 feet (30 m).

Paraphernalia: Camalots (2) sets with (1) extra #4, #5; baby angles (1); 5/8" angle (1); Lost Arrow (1); quickdraws (10).

Descent: Downclimb along the south ridge to double bolts, then rappel 110 feet (34 m).

88   ANTICLINE OVERLOOK BUTTRESS III, 5.7, A3, 5 pitches, 400 feet (122 m)

First Ascent: Ralph Nathan et al, 1996.

Location and Access: Begin up a splitter crack and climb past a death block. Continue mostly on aid to the mesa top. Further information is unknown.

Paraphernalia: Standard desert rack; a selection of pitons.

Descent: Rappel the route.

photo: Cameron M. Burns

Homer and Marge

Hurrah Pass Area

Homer and Marge are two towers 1.7 miles (2.7 km) up the Kane Creek Valley Road (toward Hurrah Pass) from where Kane Creek Road branches left a short distance beyond the crossing of Kane Creek. Marge has broken off and is leaning against Homer. To reach, climb a slot in the south side of a small amphitheater on the left side of the road. Fifty feet (15 m) up, there is a bench, and Homer and Marge are 500 feet (152 m) to the north. *Crusty the Clown* is 100 feet (30 m) west of Homer and Marge. *CB's Love Muscle* is a dramatic hoodoo approximately 0.4 mile (0.6 km) south of Hurrah Pass. *Mt. Everest* is approximately 0.5 mile (0.8 km) before the pass.

89   HOMER AND MARGE—CHILI COOK OFF I, 5.5, A1, 1 pitch, 100 feet (30 m) ★★

First Ascent: Jesse Harvey, Cameron Burns, Erik Cook, 21 November 1997.

Location and Access: *Chili Cook Off* climbs the north side of the tower. Begin with a mantle to a shelf (5.5), then climb a 6" (15 cm) crack (A1). Continue up a 5-bolt ladder to a low-angled ridge, then 4th class ending at 5.5 to the summit.

Paraphernalia: Camalots (1) #5; (1) 1/4" bolt hanger; quickdraws (6).

Descent: One-rope rappel from double bolts.

photo: Cameron M. Burns

Mount Everest

90   CRUSTY THE CLOWN—ITCHY AND SCRATCHY I, 5.10b, 1 pitch, 60 feet (18 m)

First Ascent: Cameron Burns, Jesse Harvey, Erik Cook, 5.8, A1, 21 November 1997. First free ascent: Alan "Heavy Duty" Stevenson, Kevin Chase, March 1998.

Location and Access: Climb up the southwest corner of the tower. Begin up loose rock, then 5.8 to a mantle with a fixed anchor. Continue 5.7, then 5.10 past 2 more fixed anchors to a shoulder, then past a fixed anchor to the summit.

Paraphernalia: Angle pitons (1) 5/8", 3/4", 1"; Quickdraws (5).

Descent: One single-rope rappel from triple bolts.

91   CB'S LOVE MUSCLE—PUTTERMAN SEX MACHINE, 5.5, A1, 1 pitch, 60 feet (18 m) ★★

First Ascent: Cameron Burns, Jesse Harvey, 16 November 1997.

Location and Access: *Putterman Sex Machine* climbs the north side of the tower ascending 5.5 to the summit block, then 2 bolts (A1) lead to a 3-bolt rappel station at the top of the hoodoo.

Paraphernalia: Angle pitons (1) 0.5", 3/4", 1"; quickdraws.

Descent: Rappel the route.

92   MOUNT EVEREST—KANGSHUNG FACE I, 5.8, 1 pitch, 60 feet (18 m) ★★★

First Ascent: Cameron Burns, Jesse Harvey, 16 November 1997.

Location and Access: *Kangshung Face* climbs a prominent corner crack system on the northwest side of the tower to double-bolt rappel anchors. The crux is a mantle over a roof (5.8) high on the route.

Paraphernalia: Friends (1) #4; Lost Arrow (1); baby angles (2); quickdraws (4).

Descent: Rappel the route.

Jackson Hole–Amasa Back

Jackson Hole is a dramatic rincon (abandoned meander of the Colorado River) on the south side of Amasa Back Mesa. It is visible from across the river at the Potash Mine. Moonlight Spire is hidden. To reach the tower, take a long hike from Amasa Back Mesa, or drive (four-wheel) over Hurrah Pass.

To hike to Jackson Hole, drive to the end of the pavement of Kane Creek Boulevard and park at the BLM information kiosk on the right. Drop down the bank (right) into tamarisk and willow, then bushwack through the drainage (left) to the mouth of Kane Creek. Cross the creek and follow the obvious trail which parallels the south bank of the Colorado River, eventually topping out on Amasa Back Mesa near the high-tension powerlines running to the Potash Mine. The trail follows an old gas pipe which originally ran to a uranium mine south of the Potash Mine. At the top of the mesa, look for the pipeline. Jacob's Ladder is a steep, 350-foot (107 m), switchbacking, abandoned cattle trail that descends a few yards right of the pipeline. At the bottom of the rincon, contour left to Moonlight Spire.

An alternate approach by foot is to continue down Kane Springs Canyon, 1.3 miles (2.1 km) from the end of the paved portion of Kane Creek Boulevard. Park at the beginning of the signed four-wheel-drive Amasa Back Trail, located across from the large and obvious Forming Arch (arch-in-the-making). Hike the trail until you reach the powerlines that top the mesa from the north, then descend Jacob's Ladder cattle trail. The four-wheel-drive trail is very rough and best reserved for the occasional macho jeeper who visits canyon country.

To reach Jackson Hole and Moonlight Spire by four-wheel drive, continue on the Kane Springs Valley Road to Hurrah Pass. Descend the other side of the pass (four-wheel drive only). **BEWARE**: At the time of this writing, a 2-wheel-drive vehicle was not an option from the south side of the pass, but road improvement is planned for some time in the future. Turn right (west) at the first drivable drainage to the right (near river level). Continue down the wash approximately 0.5 mile (0.8 km), then turn right and follow an old trail around limestone ledges to Jackson Hole Loop Road which follows the entrenchment of the rincon. The loop road takes you to Moonlight Spire.

A third and shorter approach to Jackson Hole is from Potash Road. Cross the Colorado River by inner tube, canoe, or raft from opposite the Potash Mine, and hike up the rincon to the spire.

Ethyl Zwink is a small tower in view across the Colorado River (on Amasa Back Mesa) from the Middle Earth region of Potash Road. It is reached from the Amasa Back Trail, beginning at the end of Kane Creek Boulevard.

93   MOONLIGHT SPIRE II, 5.11, A2, 3 pitches, 155 feet (47 m)

First Ascent: Steve Anderton, Bill Duncan, 21 November 1993.

Location and Access: *Moonlight Spire* is on the east side of the Jackson Hole rincon. The route climbs the east face of the tower.

Pitch 1: Ascend A2 to the col between the tower and the butte behind.

Pitch 2: Continue 5.11 up steps and a chimney to a ledge on the right profile of the spire. Pendulum from a drilled piton down and left to a ledge protected with small cams. Climb with aid and small hands (5.9), then fist (5.9) to a belay ledge at the beginning of Pitch 3.

Pitch 3: Climb A1 past holes and fixed anchors, then 5.7 to double summit anchors.

Paraphernalia: Standard desert rack with extra small and wide gear; a selection of knifeblades and baby angles through 5/8"; quickdraws.

Descent: One double-rope rappel down the east face reaches the ground.

94   ETHYL ZWINK I, 5.9, 1 pitch, 100 feet (30 m)

First Ascent: Todd Madaux, Millie Birdwell, 1992.

Location and Access: The small tower is climbed by a crack system on the north face. The first ascent party was impressed by a large pack rat nest with numerous cactus spines.

Paraphernalia: Standard desert rack.

Descent: Rappel the route.

The Canyon curves deeply to the left and right, sinuous as a snake, no more willing to follow a straight line than is anything else true and beautiful and good in this world.

–Edward Abbey, *Slickrock*, 1971

When your spirit cries for peace, come to a world of canyons deep in an old land; feel the exultation of high plateaus, the strength of moving waters, the simplicity of sand and grass, and the silence of growth.

–August Frugé

photo: Bjørnstad collection

Eric Bjørnstad leading *Disappearing Angel*

MOAB VALLEY

This is the most beautiful place on earth. There are many such places. Every man, every woman, carries in heart and mind the image of the ideal place, the right place, the one true home, known or unknown, actual or visionary. A houseboat in Kashmir, a view down Atlantic Avenue in Brooklyn, a gray gothic farmhouse two stories high at the end of a red dog road in the Allegheny Mountains, a cabin on the shore of a blue lake in spruce and fir country, a greasy alley near the Hoboken waterfront, or even, possibly, for those of a less demanding sensibility, the world to be seen from a comfortable apartment high in the tender, velvety smog of Manhattan, Chicago, Paris, Tokyo, Rio or Rome–there's no limit to the human capacity for the homing sentiment. Theologians, sky pilots, astronauts have even felt the appeal of home calling to them from up above, in the cold black outback of interstellar space. For myself I'll take Moab, Utah. I don't mean the town itself, of course, but the country which surrounds it–the canyonlands. The slickrock desert. The red dust and the burnt cliffs and the lonely sky–all that which lies beyond the end of the roads.

–Edward Abbey, *Desert Solitaire*, 1968

Moab Valley is a geologic anomaly. It was not carved by a glacier or river as most valleys are, but was created by faulting. There is a displacement of more than 2,600 feet (792 m) between the stratum atop the west side of the valley and the corresponding rock high on the east side. There is a viewing area with a plaque describing the Moab Fault at the top of Headquarters Hill, above the visitor center at Arches National Park, 5 miles (8 km) north of Moab. Routes in Moab Valley are on the west walls south of town above U.S. Highway 191 and are listed from right to left.

Hidden Valley, Petroglyph Wall

Hidden Valley is a hanging valley sequestered just below the west rim of Moab Valley. Hidden Valley Trail is popular with mountain bikers and hikers; it presents exceptional vistas of Moab Valley east to the Sand Flats and the La Sal Mountains, and gives access to the Behind-the-Rocks Wilderness Study Area. At its northwest end (on the right) are two long buttresses of dark varnished rock, which extend parallel to one another in a generally east-west direction. Both walls are canvases for hundreds of Anasazi petroglyphs, with the northernmost (second) wall ending at a high lookout with the ruins of an ancient circular lowstone wall. South of the buttress, a four-wheel-drive trail extends from the head of Hidden Valley northwest to the difficult Moab Rim Trail, which then descends over rough terrain to Kane Creek Boulevard.

George Hurley, in his foreword to *Canyon Country Climbs*, eloquently describes Hidden Valley: "Recently a friend led me up a winding trail through a barren, rocky gap to a hidden valley west of Moab. Steep red walls rose on either side of a flat meadow covered in blue-green grass with clusters of yellow flowers. Clouds were low, covering the tops of the canyon walls. It was a hidden place of great beauty, one version of Shangri La. This would have been reward enough, but the meadow led us to a rock wall covered with dozens of petroglyphs. The most exciting were long lines of figures, human and animal. Some of the humans had shields, some were ghostly, some had animal heads. They were intermingled with bighorn sheep and deer. Some stood alone and some seemed to dance in long processions."

To reach Hidden Valley from Center and Main Streets, drive south on U.S. Highway 191 (Main Street) 4.1 miles (6.5 km) to Angel Rock Road and turn right (west), then in 2 blocks right again onto Rimrock Road, where, a short distance farther, the road ends at a BLM register box and the posted Hidden Valley Trailhead. The trail climbs a series of steep switchbacks before entering Hidden Valley. The elevation gain is close to 1,000 feet (305 m) from Moab Valley to the upper end of Hidden Valley. It is approximately 8 miles (12.8 km) from Hidden Valley Trailhead to Kane Creek Boulevard after one of the most scenic traverses in the Moab area.

Crackapelli on Petroglyph Wall climbs a splitter crack approximately 200 yards (183 m) down the first buttress encountered from the upper end of Hidden Valley.

1   PETROGLYPH WALL—CRACKAPELLI I, 5.12a, 1 pitch, 80 feet (24 m) ★★★★★

First Ascent: Tom Gilje, solo, 1994.

Location and Access: *Crackapelli* is approximately 200 yards (183 m) beyond the upper end of Hidden Valley on the first buttress to the right. Climb a splitter crack past 2 bolts high on the route. Anchors are visible from below the climb. Begin with a step across Indian writings low on the wall.

Paraphernalia: Friends (many) #2.

Descent: Rappel the route.

Disappearing Angel, Love is a 45, Pygmy, Old Dad Spire

Disappearing Angel is a prominent tower on the western rimrock above Moab Valley, approximately 3 miles (4.8 km) south of downtown. North of town, the spire is visible south of mile marker 129 (between Potash Road and the Colorado River Bridge). It is also visible as one drives toward Moab from several miles south of town. The tower hides against higher Wingate cliffs as you approach it from either north or south, hence its name. Approach Disappearing Angel from the end of Hance Road, south of mile marker 122, south of Moab city limits. Park and hike the talus right of the tower.

Love is a 45 is approximately 100 yards (91 m) south of Disappearing Angel. *Pygmy* is high on the Wingate buttress south of the end of the pavement on Rim Rock Lane, south of *Love is a 45*. There is a small pillar at the base of the route.

Old Dad Spire is approximately 1 mile (1.6 km) south of Ken's Lake at the southern end of Moab Valley. Approach from the dirt road south of the lake. Hike east up a small canyon about 15 minutes from the road.

2   DISAPPEARING ANGEL (a.k.a. Vanishing Angel) II, 5.11+, 2 pitches, 225 feet (69 m) ★★★★

First Ascent: Eric Bjørnstad, Jim Hudock, Stan Hollister, 5.8+, A2, 30 August 1971. Second ascent: Hooman Aprin, Mike Graber, Frank Trummel, March 1975. First free ascent: Kevin Chase, Jim Symans, February 1995. Kevin Chase: "One bolt was added and three bolts were removed during a fall on the free ascent." First solo ascent: Jon Butler, fall 1995.

Location and Access: The original ascent line climbs the southwest face from the notch between the tower and the rimrock behind it, 130 feet (40 m). The tower is 225-feet high (69 m) on the valley side.

Pitch 1: Begin up a small overhang (5.11+ mantle), then continue to a fistcrack, and finally armcrack to a belay stance.

Pitch 2: Continue free or on clean aid up overhanging rock to the summit area, negotiated with aid and 5.8+ climbing, or 5.11+ face (small nuts essential, #4 Stopper).

Paraphernalia: Friends (2) sets; Camalots (2) #4; wired nuts (1) set; possibly hangers for 1/4" bolts, or many rivet hangers.

Descent: One double-rope rappel down the route.

3   DISAPPEARING ANGEL—SATAN'S REVENGE II, 5.12a, 2 pitches, 225 feet (69 m) ★★★★

First Ascent: Tom Gilje, Julie Gilje, 1994.

Location and Access: *Satan's Revenge* climbs the north face of Disappearing Angel. Double ropes are recommended to ease rope drag.

Pitch 1: Climb a vertical crack to a horizontal fracture.

Pitch 2: Follow bolts to the summit.

Paraphernalia: Friends (1) set; quickdraws.

Descent: Rappel the original route.

NOTE: A number of crack climbs have been established by Kyle Copeland, Tom Gilje, Bob Novellino, and Craig Luebben in a hidden valley behind Disappearing Angel. To reach them, hike up the talus from Disappearing Angel, then hike south down a 2-mile-long (3.2 km) hidden valley. Bob Novellino: "The hike up the talus is notoriously brutal, but the Indian Creek–quality cracks are worth the effort."

4   LOVE IS A 45 I, 5.11a, 1 pitch, 140 feet (43 m)

First Ascent: Craig Luebben, Bob Novellino, fall 1995.

Location and Access: *Love is a 45* climbs an obvious splitter crack on the northeast face of a tower. To reach it, traverse south from Disappearing Angel.

Paraphernalia: Friends (2) sets, nuts.

Descent: Walk west of the route, then 4th class from the back of the formation.

5   PYGMY I, 5.10+, 1 pitch, 150 feet (46 m) ★★★

First Ascent: Kyle Copeland, Diane (surname unknown), unknown date.

Location and Access: *Pygmy* is one major drainage south of *Disappearing Angel*. The route climbs dark varnished rock up an Indian Creek–style handcrack on a prow for 150 feet (46 m) to a drilled anchor.

Paraphernalia: Friends (many) #2, #2.5, #3.

Descent: Rappel the route.

6   OLD DAD SPIRE II, 5.10c, AO, 2 pitches, 190 feet (58 m)

First Ascent: Linus Platt, John Rzcezcki, Brad Bond, April 1998. Second ascent: Steve Seats et al, the following day.

Location and Access: The route ascends a prominent offwidth/chimney facing west.

Pitch 1: Climb an obvious crack/chimney on the west face, 5.10c, 150 feet (46 m).

Pitch 2: Aid past bolts and scramble to the summit, AO, 40 feet (12 m).

Paraphernalia: Cams up to 8"; nuts (1) set; quickdraws.

Descent: Rappel the route.

DESERT ROCK III
Moab Valley

A billion, a million, a thousand–these numbers seem so great to us who count our years in decades. Feeling the age of the earth and its rock layers comes hard. Perhaps the easiest way to become familiar with Plateau rocks is simply to make friends with each one as it comes your way. Most have distinctive personalities, and the most distinctive give you anchor points in the stack which you can recognize everywhere.

–Frank Waters, *The Colorado*

SAND FLATS

The landscape everywhere, away from the river, is of rock–cliffs of rock, plateaus of rock, terraces of rock, crags of rock–ten thousand strangely carved forms. Rocks everywhere. . . . When speaking of these rocks, we must not conceive of piles of boulders, or heaps of fragments, but a whole land of naked rock, with giant forms carved on it: cathedral-shaped buttes, towering hundreds or thousands of feet; cliffs that cannot be scaled, and cañon walls that shrink the river into insignificance, with vast, hollow domes, and tall pinnacles, and shafts set on the verge overhead, and all highly colored buff, gray, red, brown, and chocolate; never lichened, never moss-covered, but bare, and often polished.

–John Wesley Powell, 1875

The Sand Flats Recreation Area was designated by the Bureau of Land Management in 1994 to protect the scenic and recreational values of a unique area of Navajo Sandstone domes and fins. It is located just east of Moab, sandwiched between Negro Bill Canyon (Wilderness Study Area) to the northeast and Mill Creek Canyon (Wilderness Study Area) to the southwest. It is accessed by Sand Flats Road.

Starting from the Moab Information Center (at Center and Main Streets), drive 4 blocks east to 400 East and turn south (right). Continue 4 blocks to Mill Creek Drive, then bear left at the stop sign onto Sand Flats Road (where signs lead to the famous Slickrock Bike Trail). At the Recreation Area kiosk, 1.7 miles (2.7 km) from Mill Creek Drive, a nominal user fee is collected to maintain campsites and vault toilets, revegetate areas damaged by past misuse, furnish education programs, maintain trails, and provide other facilities to the region. In recent years the area has experienced a dramatic increase in use, with more than 100,000 mountain bikers visiting per year. The fee may be bypassed if one is driving the Sand Flats Road to areas outside the recreation area or en route to its junction with the La Sal Mountain Loop Road (an elevation gain of approximately 3,000 feet). The upper end of the road requires high clearance and may require four-wheel drive. Information on road conditions is available at Moab BLM offices or the entrance kiosk at the recreation area.

Several miles of Sand Flats Road is shared with the Porcupine Rim mountain bike trail. Please be courteous when meeting others by allowing enough space and maintaining slow speeds to prevent dust clouds. Porcupine Rim mountain bike trail is one of Moab's most popular and most difficult. Its high point is approximately 7,000 feet (2134 m), more than 3,000 feet (914 m) higher than Moab. The trail is extremely technical and exposed in many places. A BLM brochure cautions: "This trail is physically demanding and technically difficult. It is not recommended for children, novice riders, out-of-shape individuals, or anyone with a physically limiting medical condition. Grand County has the highest incidence of search and rescues in Utah!"

photo: Glen Dunmire

Stew Sayah rappelling off Elvis's Hammer after the first ascent

Geology

The Sand Flats area is dominated by the ancient dune-sand stratum of aeolian Navajo Sandstone. Scenic domes, fins, and rolling hills of slickrock have made the region popular among mountain bikers and hikers alike. Near the Rhino Horn, the Navajo is approximately 2,000 feet (610 m) higher than it is at the entrance to the recreation area, an illustration of how the stratum has been drastically tilted by the upthrust of the La Sal Mountains. Mill Creek has carved its dramatic canyon through the area from the La Sal Mountains west to Moab Valley.

Flora and Fauna

The Sand Flats region lies within the dwarf pinyon–juniper life zone of the high desert and presents a wide variety of shrubs and wildlife. Included is the rich variety found throughout the high deserts of the Colorado Plateau. Although rare, bears have been known to descend from the nearby La Sal Mountains to forage for edibles. Unfortunately much of the Sand Flats land has been decimated by a century of range cattle grazing, a myopic practice becoming increasingly unpopular among those who abhor the government-subsidized mutilation of lands that should be regarded as wilderness sanctuaries in our rapidly expanding mechanistic world.

Moab Sanitary Landfill

The former Moab Sanitary Landfill is 1.6 miles (2.5 km) from the beginning of Sand Flats Road at the stop sign at its juncture with Mill Creek Drive. The waste site with a lofty name took second place a few years ago in a nationwide contest to name the most scenic dump site. A site in Alaska took first place.

Map

The *Moab East* map by Latitude 40-Degrees, Inc., designates Sand Flats Road, Slickrock Bike Trail, Negro Bill Canyon, Mill Creek Canyon, Rhino Horn, and La Sal Mountain Loop Road.

Rhino Horn, Elvis's Hammer

The Rhino Horn is a tower in view on the right approximately 11 miles (17.7 km) from the junction of Sand Flats Road and Mill Creek Drive. To access the tower, descend Sand Flats Road from the scenic La Sal Mountain Loop Road. Elvis's Hammer is a prominent hoodoo beyond (and visible from) the Rhino Horn. Glenn Dunmire: "You can see air through the tower crack system which both routes (north and south) climb up. You get to sink jams into 'air,' which is outrageous as air blasts through the crack system into your face."

1   RHINO HORN II, 5.9, 2 pitches, 300 feet (91 m)

> **First Ascent:** Eric Bjørnstad, Tony Valdes, with Bego Gerhart leading Pitch 1, 3 August 1985. Second ascent: Ray Huntzinger, Miles Newby, 1990s.
>
> **Location and Access:** To approach, traverse across benches from the road rather than dropping into the valley. The route begins at the lowest point on the west side of the tower and ascends to a prominent bench at the base of the upper spire. The second lead climbs obvious cracks on the northwest side of the landform.

Paraphernalia: Friends (1) set.

Descent: Rappel the route.

BEWARE: There are several areas of soft, loose rock on the climb.

2   **ELVIS'S HAMMER—HORMONES IN WAITING I, 5.10, 1 pitch, 100 feet (30 m)**

First Ascent: Glenn Dunmire, Stew Sayah, April 1988. First free ascent by Stew Sayah, solo, May 1988.

Location and Access: *Hormones in Waiting* ascends the north side of the hoodoo.

Paraphernalia: Friends (1) #4; TCUs (2) sets.

Descent: The first ascent party suggests using 20 feet (6 m) of sling for the rappel off the east side.

3   **ELVIS'S HAMMER—BLACK ELVIS I, 5.10, A1, 1 pitch, 100 feet (30 m)**

First Ascent: Glenn Dunmire, solo, April 1991.

Location and Access: *Black Elvis* climbs the hoodoo from the south side.

Paraphernalia: Friends (1) #4; TCUs (2) sets.

Descent: Same as for *Hormones in Waiting*

Little Big Man

Little Big Man is a diminutive tower up Mill Creek's righthand branch, approximately 0.5 mile (0.8 km) from the trailhead at the end of Power House Lane. Drive right, past the turn to the Sand Flats; the next branch left is Power House Lane. Drive to its end and hike up the right-hand drainage of the creek. After approximately 20 minutes, watch for Little Big Man Tower on the right uphill slope.

An alternative approach is to drive to the end of Power House Lane and hike the four-wheel-drive road on the right. After approximately 15 minutes, the road splits. Continue left. Hike to a high point where the La Sal Mountains come into view. After a few minutes, the road levels. Bear left toward a large sandstone wall. Do not hike to where the wall turns into a fin. The tower is approximately 100 feet (30 m) down the slope that descends to Mill Creek.

4   **LITTLE BIG MAN I, 5.8, 1 pitch, 40 feet (12 m)**

First Ascent: Jimmy Dunn, Betsi McKittrick, Al (German climber, surname unknown), 14 October 1991.

Location and Access: *Little Big Man* climbs the line of least resistance.

Paraphernalia: Friends (1) #4; Camalots (1) #2; webbing for slings through holes and around horns. No pitons were used on the ascent.

Descent: Rappel the route from slings around the summit.

When I think of the desert my first reaction is to become sentimental. Probably the best days of my life so far have been spent exploring the canyon walls, climbing those amazing cracks, and sitting around the campfire at night with Steve (Hong) and other friends. The amazing part about the place is that, snowstorms and stuck vehicles notwithstanding, these wonderful weekend trips have been repeated over and over—and there are still "5 stars" to be done.

–Karin Budding, in *Canyon Country Climbs*, by Katy Cassidy and Earl Wiggins, 1989

RIVER ROAD

Perhaps this planet does somewhere else contain a thing like the Colorado River—but that is no matter; we at any rate in our continent possess one of nature's very vastest works. After the River and its tributaries have done with all sight of the upper world, have left behind the bordering plains and streamed through the various gashes which their floods have sliced in the mountains that once stopped their way, then the culminating wonder begins. The River has been flowing through the loneliest part which remains to us of that large space once denominated "The Great American Desert" by the vague maps in our old geographies.

—Owen Wister

Talus slopes of red, brown, green, gray, yellow, and white rise steeply from the meandering Colorado River. Sometimes forming huge ridges rising thousands of feet, these gargantuan talus slopes fan out below the deep red, vertical cliffs of solid Wingate Sandstone. The cliffs are topped by juniper covered mesas. Apart from these mesas are countless free-standing buttes and pinnacles.

—Katy Cassidy and Earl Wiggins, Canyon Country Climbs, 1989

River Road is the local name for Utah Highway 128, a designated Scenic Byway. This splendid road follows the Colorado River and meanders 32 miles (51 km) in a northeast vector to the barren Mancos Shale deserts of southeastern Utah. The sinuous corridor is gateway to numerous spectacular side canyons, Castle Valley (Castleton Tower), Fisher Towers, and Mystery Towers. For its first 11 miles (17.6 km), from the bridge over the Colorado River north of Moab east to its confluence with Salt Creek, it parallels the southern border of Arches National Park.

History

At the turn of the century, a rough wagon trail followed the course of the present River Road from Moab Valley to Grand Junction, Colorado. And it was still only intermittently paved more than six decades later when Layton Kor and Huntley Ingalls established the first climb in the area, ascending Castleton Tower in the autumn of 1961. In recent years the byway has experienced much "upgrading," including monotonous arrow signs warning of upcoming curves. In December 1994, four young high school students were traveling to Castle Valley on River Road when their vehicle skidded on a patch of black ice and plunged into the frigid river from the curve between mile markers 8 and 9. Seat belts may have prevented them from exiting the vehicle and they drowned. As a result of local grief and outrage, the once wonderful drive through the river corridor is slowly being tempered to protect us from ourselves and accommodate the growing number of RV and windshield tourists flocking to canyon country each year. The curve on which the fledgling drivers died has now been straightened, lined with a guard rail, and posted with warnings. Speed limits have been slowed to a creep.

River Road

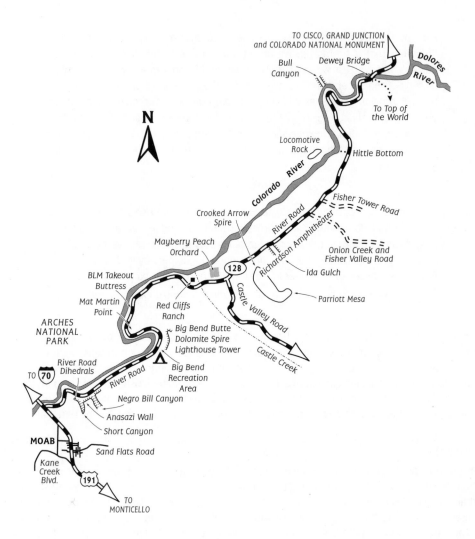

Camping and River Recreation

Only a few years ago, the Colorado River corridor was a place of unrestrained camping, travel, and recreational use. With damage to cryptobiotic crust from off-road vehicles, trees cut for firewood, the proliferation of toilet paper among groves of tamarisk and scrub oak, and other degradation to the once pristine riverway, it became increasingly clear that management of the public lands was imminent. The task fell to the Department of the Interior's Bureau of Land Management (BLM). Camping is now restricted to areas posted with a tent symbol on a brown (Karsonite) post. Off-road vehicle travel is restricted to established trails, and only driftwood from the river shore may be collected for fires. Further etiquette dictates that people use only existing campsites, do not trample untouched ground, and hike only on existing trails, in drainages, or on slickrock.

There are a number of developed campsites along River Road with restrooms, fire rings, and tables. All have an information kiosk and pipe safe for collection of a small fee. None of the sites have water, and most are posted with "no trash pickup" signs.

Potholes should not be disturbed, whether dry or filled with water. Many creatures depend on this rare water for survival. Dry potholes may contain a variety of life including fairy shrimp, snails, bug larvae, and bivalves. All are in delicate balance with life and death and are essential to the ecology of the desert.

Map

The *Moab East* map published by Latitude 40-Degrees, Inc., is the most useful for this chapter. Among designations along River Road are Matrimony Springs, Sorcerer, Sorcerer's Apprentice, all the side canyons along the river corridor, Big Bend Butte, Lighthouse Tower, Dolomite Spire, and the named beaches along the Colorado River. Farther east, the map identifies Dry Mesa, Mayberry Orchard, Parriott Mesa, and the Convent.

Road Log

This road log begins at the junction of River Road and U.S. Highway 191. Using the mile marker signs as reference points, this log gives a mile by mile window into the climbing routes, scenic features, and geologic changes as one drives the scenic byway of River Road. Together with Potash Road and Kane Creek Boulevard, River Road follows the only stretch–50 miles (80 km) long–on the vast Colorado Plateau where one can drive beside the river at river level. Elsewhere on the plateau, the Colorado is deeply entrenched in canyons.

0 to 1

Upriver Portal: Junction of River Road and US 191. Similar to the downriver Portal (at Potash Road and Kane Creek Boulevard), the rock strata at this point are dramatically tilted upward as a result of the great Moab Valley salt anticline.

Lions Park: A day use area with tables and restrooms is on the left at 0.1 mile (0.16 km). Also, there are several information plaques highlighting the history of the park, the early travel on the Colorado River, the first bridge, and a sign: "The Colorado River has extremely dangerous currents and undertows. Swimming or wading is dangerous." Another sign: "In season over 6,000 white water enthusiasts run cataract canyon downriver from here." Lions Park is the best place to scout the *El Secondo* and *Canyonlands by Night* routes on the Wingate wall on the north side of the river.

Matrimony Springs: On the right 0.2 mile (0.3 km) upriver are the perennial fresh waters of Matrimony Springs. Indian legend proclaims that those drinking from the spring will become forever wedded to the canyons and will return. The spring is the only potable water along the Colorado River corridor.

Dinosaur Age Tracks: On the slab right of Matrimony Springs are Triassic age (208–245 million years ago) tracks.

Anasazi Signatures: On the bench 500 feet (152 m) right (west) of Matrimony Springs under the overhang above a white plastic water pipe are panels of Anasazi handprints. To reach, hike the slope beside the water pipe (there is no trail). Other pictographs are on the walls above and on the cliff right of the handprints.

There are several bouldering problems up the Chinle Sandstone wall right of Matrimony Springs. The first is the overhanging crack right of the water pipe climbed by Jimmy Dunn (5.10) in the early 1970s. The second crack right of the spring involves a 5.10+ mantle and was first climbed by Mike Mayer in July 1987. The next crack right was climbed in 1986 at 5.9 by Kyle Copeland.

Updraft Arch: Upriver 0.8 mile (1.2 km), Updraft Arch is visible high on the cliff to the right (south) of the roadway. With the right lighting, the arch is also visible from the bridge over the Colorado River as one faces Moab. It was named for the air updraft experienced at its location just east of Panorama Viewpoint at the northwest end of the Slickrock Bike Trail. Updraft is an alcove-type arch with an opening of 3 feet (0.9 m) by 8 feet (2.4 m), although it appears larger when viewed from River Road.

1 to 2

Sorcerer, Sorcerer's Apprentice: Beyond Updraft Arch at mile marker 1 are two pillars leaning against the rimrock wall. The Sorcerer is the pillar to the right, the Sorcerer's Apprentice to the left.

River Corridor Information Kiosk: On the left at a large parking area.

Eye Socket Arch-in-the-Making: A prominent blind arch (in the forming stage). Light cannot be seen through its opening, although during and after heavy rains water gushing through the embryonic arch forms a dramatic waterfall.

Goose Island Campground: On the left at 1.4 miles (2.2 km) is Goose Island Campground with 17 sites with tables, restrooms, and fire rings. The charge is $6 per night. During the warmer season there is a camp host. The bottomland was named Goose Island after a sandbar that once attracted numerous Canada geese. The sandbar has since silted in and become part of the shoreline in an overall narrowing of the river due to tamarisk encroachment.

Anasazi Ruins: Navajo Sandstone (top layer at the portal) dips to river level. High under the top of the cliff, in an alcove on the right side of the roadway, is an Anasazi ruin (visible only after a short hike up the drainage). Across River Road from Goose Island Campground, on the cliff left of the drainage, is another ruin.

Rock Art Panel: At 1.9 miles (3 km), across the river on the left side of an obvious bench, is a panel of Anasazi rock art (visible with binoculars) in the dark desert varnish (manganese oxide).

2 to 3

Fun Ramp: Layton Kor/Kyle Copeland route ascends the obvious right-to-left running diagonal fracture system, which is visible across the river (part of Arches National Park) just before mile marker 2. It is also identifiable by its location straight ahead of the roadway as one drives upriver from Goose Island Campground.

Placer Gold Mine: Right of the rock art panel at 2.4 miles (3.8 km) and hidden from view by tamarisk growth are gravel benches (once at river level) that in Moab's earlier history were the site of a failed placer gold mining operation.

River Road Dihedrals: River Road Dihedrals are at 2.8 miles on the cliff facing River Road and immediately right of Short Canyon. A popular, quick-access climbing area.

Short Canyon (a.k.a. Ice Box Canyon, Sheep Canyon): The shallow canyon is obvious beyond the River Road Dihedrals. It is the first canyon upriver from the beginning of River Road. Vehicle access is blocked by large boulders. In winter the drainage is a preserve of short icefalls. In summer it is lush with deep canyon foliage (including much poison ivy). High on the left (east) wall at the canyon's entrance is a small, unnamed arch with three openings. This type of formation is possibly due to a lesser amount of calcium carbonate (the naturally occuring bonding compound in Navajo Sandstone) or (more likely) air pockets that formed during deposition of the sandstone stratum.

3 to 4

Anasazi Buttress: Located above mile marker 3, this phenomenal monolith is weathered from aeolian Navajo Sandstone, a beautiful 400-foot (122 m) overhanging desert-varnished cliff. *Artist's Tears* climbs it directly, with other routes established right and left of the impressively smooth, sheer wall.

Anasazi Granaries: High on the cliffs across the river from Anasazi Buttress, several granaries are visible.

Negro Bill Canyon: This deep canyon is located 3.1 miles (4.9 km) up River Road, just beyond Anasazi Buttress. It was named "Nigger Bill" years ago, its namesake being William Granstaff, a cowboy who settled in the area in 1877 with a companion known only as "Frenchie." They took over the old Mormon Fort in Moab and grew corn, squash, melons, and other food. Nigger Bill later raised some 40 head of longhorn cattle, grazing them in the canyon named after him. He eventually moved to La Sal Junction (south of Moab) where he faded into antiquity. The canyon has been designated an Outstanding Natural Area and is part of the Negro Bill Canyon Wilderness Study Area. It is home to a large variety of bird and animal life. There is a parking area and a BLM kiosk giving camping restrictions and other canyon information. A trail winds through a narrow riparian zone in the canyon bottom. At the BLM kiosk or office in Moab, a brochure is available detailing the animal and plant features of the zone. The canyon extends many miles into the foothills of the La Sal Mountains and Porcupine Rim (at the western border of Castle Valley) and is popular with hikers. Since it is a wilderness study area, mountain bikes are prohibited. The first few miles are composed of stream-deposited Kayenta Sandstone below round-topped Navajo cliffs. **NOTE:** Water in Negro Bill Canyon is contaminated by livestock grazing in the La Sal Mountains and, as with most water in the desert, should be treated for giardiasis before drinking.

Morning Glory Natural Bridge: This span of rock is the sixth longest in the United States (just a yard short of the fifth longest span). It is 2.5 miles (4 km) up Negro Bill Canyon. Find it by hiking 0.4 mile (0.6 km) up the second canyon on the right (about one hour's hike from River Road). The alcove-type arch, eroded from Jurassic-age Navajo Sandstone (170 million years old), was named by a visiting photographer for the area's resemblance to Morning Glory Pool in Yellowstone National Park. The bridge spans 243 feet (74 m), is 75 feet high (22.8 m), and 12 feet wide (3.6 m)–a worthwhile sojourn.

Salt Anticlines: At Negro Bill Canyon the rock strata begins to rise (most noticeably across the river). This is a result of the connected salt anticlines of Salt Valley in Arches National Park to the west and Castle and Fisher Valleys to the east. Half a mile (0.8 km) upriver from Negro Bill Canyon, Wingate Sandstone rises above river level, resting on the Chinle Formation. Atop the Wingate is the cross-bedded Kayenta caprock, and there is an occasional remnant of Navajo above the stream-deposited Kayenta. Wingate, Kayenta, and Navajo are known collectively as the Glen Canyon Group due to their extended exposure in the now inundated canyon below Lake Powell.

Indian Ruins: Opposite Negro Bill Canyon, high in the cliffs across the river, are granaries for food storage. It is believed they were built by the Pueblo Indians who inhabited the area approximately 1,000 B.P. (before present time).

Jackass Canyon to Porcupine Rim Trail: This popular mountain bike trail begins 0.3 mile (0.4 km) upriver from Negro Bill Canyon and follows an old cattle trail which parallels the river for approximately 1 mile (1.6 km) before reaching the mesa top near Big Bend, in the area northwest of Porcupine Rim. Expansive vistas north across Arches National Park make the trail a worthwhile hiking or biking excursion.

Negro Bill Recreation Site: Across from the above-mentioned trail is an information kiosk and campground. A $5 per night fee will reserve you one of the 17 campsites. Stuff your money in the pipe safe.

4 to 5

Barney Rumble Tower: The diminutive tower is obvious across the river from mile marker 4.
Milano Tower: Milano Tower is across the river at 4.8 miles.

5 to 6

Table Rock: Table Rock is a large boulder in the water near the far bank of the river 0.4 mile (0.6 km) upriver from mile marker 5. It is used by rafters to gauge the depth of the water. It generally has logs and branches caught on it from high water levels and is completely submerged during very wet springs.

Diane's Tower: Near mile marker 6 on the right (south) side of River Road. Diane's Tower is a rock column attached to the buttress behind it. Diane's identity is unknown.

6 to 7

Po-Dunk Mesa Tower: A pointy free-standing spire on the left side of the canyon.
Lower Drinks Campground, Upper Drinks Campground: There are 17 sites with pit toilets and fire rings and a $5 per night charge.

7 to 8

Moenkopi: At approximately mile marker 7, the Moenkopi Formation is visible in a few places. It is mostly obscured by colluvium (rock debris fallen from the cliffs above). Three hundred million years ago this stratum was a 200-mile long (322 km) flat and level floodplain stretching from present-day western Colorado to western Utah.

Hal Canyon, Oak Grove, and Big Bend (a.k.a. Moose Park) campgrounds: These three locations (between mile markers 7 and 8) are improved BLM campsites with a $6 per night camping fee. Hal Canyon has 11 sites, Oak Grove 7 sites, and Big Bend 22 sites. All have vault restrooms, tables, trash pickup, and fire rings—but no drinking water. Big Bend Campground (separated from the road by a rail fence) offers a large beach at the river's edge, and usually has a resident camp host during the tourist season of April through October. Also at Big Bend is a solar operated 911 telephone, installed after the 1994 auto deaths mentioned at the beginning of this chapter. The picnic area was constructed in the 1950s by volunteers from the local Moose Lodge.

Buffalo Chip Boulder: Buffalo Chip is a popular bouldering problem beside the road at the west (downriver) edge of Big Bend Campground. Harvey T. Carter first climbed it in June 1967, by seven separate routes.

Lighthouse Tower, Dolomite Spire, Big Bend Butte: A popular climbing area across from Big Bend Recreation Area and Campground on the east (right) side of River Road. A healthy hike up the rubble covering the Moenkopi and Chinle slopes brings one to wild climbing and spectacular views from the Wingate walls above. There are also several routes on the east side of the landforms not visible from River Road.

Big Bend Bouldering Area: Beyond Big Bend Campground, on the right side of the road, is the most popular bouldering in the Moab area. Kevin Chase lists close to 70 problems in his select guide to Moab climbing. High on the Wingate walls above is a Jay Smith route and several short Mark Whiton climbs.

8 to 9

Syncline: As the Colorado River meanders around Big Bend, the strata dips into the ground. The Moenkopi descends from view and the Chinle and Wingate with its Kayenta caprock dip low.

Mat Martin Point: This point is the southwest-trending, Wingate-walled peninsula around which the river meanders at Big Bend. Mat Martin and his brother John were surveyors who established ranches and settled in the Castle Valley area in the 1880s. They were also the first prospectors to venture into the Miner's Basin goldfields of the La Sal Mountains.

Upper Big Bend Campground: Eight sites with pit toilets and fire rings and a $5 per night charge.

Placer Gold Mine: On the right side of the road between mile markers 8 and 9 is a dark varnished boulder inscribed "Sahale," which was the name and location of a placer gold mining operation in the early part of the twentieth century. Another boulder is inscribed with "Big Bend Placer 1894." Just beyond, an old trail leads to a one-time cattle route to the top of the mesa. **NOTE:** All along the Chinle cliff/slope, the blue gray colors are either a result of volcanic ash or ferrous iron deposited under water. They are not oxidized in the same way as the iron that lends neighboring layers their rust color.

10 to 11

"Daily" BLM Takeout: At 10.3 miles (16.5 km), the BLM takeout has a large parking area, restrooms, and a concrete boat ramp used by a couple dozen commercial river companies running the popular "daily" rafting trip–generally originating at Hittle Bottom Campground at mile 22.5. Downriver from the boat ramp is the BLM Takeout Buttress with six routes established on the lower Chinle cliff layer.

11 to 12

Salt Wash: Across the river near mile marker 11 is the confluence of Salt Wash and the Colorado. Salt Wash borders Arches National Park on its east side; the Colorado River borders the park to its south. Salt Wash drains from Salt Valley in the park. (There is an excellent view of Salt Valley in Arches, at the overlook between Delicate Arch and Fiery Furnace.) Across the river, the land east (right) of Salt Wash is Dry Mesa. On the Wingate cliffs high on the right side of the road are several Jay Smith routes.

12 to 13

Vuja De: This incredible-feeling-that-you've-never-been-there-before route is between mile markers 12 and 13 on the right side of the road, high on the Wingate Wall as viewed from beyond the BLM Takeout Buttress.

Sandy Beach: Up River Road 11.8 miles (19 km) is Sandy Beach, with a large parking area and restrooms. There is an undeveloped boat ramp which is sometimes used by the river runners but is now closed to overnight camping.

13 to 14

Parriott Mesa, Convent Mesa, Fisher Towers, Porcupine Rim, Lower Castle Valley: In view ahead and to the east and south (right).

14 to 15

Red Cliffs Ranch (formerly White Ranch): This picturesque ranch is beside River Road at mile marker 14 (at the lower end of Castle Valley). It has long since been owned by ranchers other than the Whites and presently bears the name Red Cliffs Ranch. Until a few years ago, the ranch was home to movie sets: a large Western log fort, a Mexican village, and an Indian village. It was also the setting for numerous Western movies, including *Rio Grande*, *Ten Who Dared*, *Rio Conchos*, and *Cheyenne Autumn*. A movie site brochure from the Moab Information Center (Center and Main Streets in Moab) lists the many movies filmed at White Ranch and in the River Road vicinity.

Castle Creek: At 14.4 miles River Road crosses Castle Creek as the water drains from lower Castle Valley and crosses Red Cliffs Ranch before its confluence with the Colorado.

Moenkopi Cliffs: Beyond Red Cliffs, Ranch River Road undulates beside dramatic Moenkopi cliffs on the right and the Colorado River on the left. In this region the stratum reaches a thickness of nearly 900 feet (274 m).

15 to 16

Mayberry Orchard: Owned by The Nature Conservancy, the Mayberry peach orchard was set aside in 1994 to prevent further commercial development along the Colorado Riverway. It is marked by a locked gate with the name on it and an obvious peach orchard left (north) of River Road before the right (south) turn to Castle Valley and La Sal Mountain Loop Road.

Castle Valley, La Sal Mountain Loop Road: At 15.2 miles (24 km) La Sal Mountain Loop Road/ Castle Valley Road branches to the right. The large mesa left of the turnoff is Parriott Mesa and beyond is Convent Mesa. Farther east, the rugged spires of the Fisher Towers stand out against Top of the World Mesa.

Crooked Arrow Spire: On the left is a county road department gravel station. Right of the road on the left corner of Parriott Mesa; Crooked Arrow Spire is visible.

Ida Gulch: Noted as Rocky Rapid Day Use Area on the *Moab East* map. To reach, turn left (toward the river) just past a small white bridge. A sign reads "Ida Gulch Day Use." There are restrooms and several designated undeveloped campsites down a dirt road. The Sister Superior group is visible to the south.

17 to 18

Sorrel River Ranch: Identified as the Titus Ranch on USGS maps and *Moab East* map, but like the White Ranch at mile marker 14, owners change and names change.

18 to 19

Petroglyphs: The large boulder 0.5 mile to the south has petroglyphs on it.

Professor Valley Ranch: Home of CFI (Canyonlands Field Institute) camps. CFI is a nonprofit educational company based in Moab that gives highly recommended canyon country field trips.

20 to 21
Onion Creek: On the right, Onion Creek turnoff is identified by a sign reading "Taylor Livestock–Fisher Valley Ranch." The rugged road fords Onion Creek 31 times en route to Fisher Valley, passing beneath Mongoose, Sari, and Hindu Towers and the trailhead to the Mystery Towers.

21 to 22
Fisher Towers: The turn to Fisher Towers is 21.1 miles (33.9 km) up River Road on the right (south). A 2.5-mile (4 km) dirt road winds to a BLM-managed campground, where there is the trailhead for the 2.2-mile (3.5 km) hike through the Fishers to the Titan. Among the movies filmed near the trailhead are *The Comancheros, Wagon Master, Against a Crooked Sky, Rio Conchos,* and *Choke Canyon.* The left turn off River Road (across from Fisher Towers) takes you to a locked gate and private property (the site of Eddy Rock identified in the original *Desert Rock,* but now on private property). Take a left branch at the gate to reach good camping sites on BLM land.

Locomotive Rock: On the left side of River Road, past the Fisher Towers turn, is Locomotive Rock, a landform well known to locals. On the river side of Locomotive Rock is Eddy Rock, climbed solo by Harvey T. Carter, April 1979. The route (in the original *Desert Rock*) is not included in this volume because it is now private property with access blocked by a locked gate.

Hittle Bottom: Hittle Bottom, an early homestead, is 22.5 miles (36 km) up River Road. Now the Hittle Bottom boat ramp, the area put-in point for the Colorado River "Daily," a 13-mile stretch of river with six rapids and riffles. There are 12 campsites with restrooms, fire rings, and an $8 per night charge. A sign reads "In the early 1900s the Tom Kitsen family lived here. Tom carried the mail with his team of horses from the Cisco Post Office to the Castleton P.O. (Castleton was a thriving town beyond Castle Valley on Loop Road). He used this place as a halfway stop to change his teams. All that remains of his homestead is the rock walled dug-out. The grave site south of the dugout is his mother's. Evidently she went to the river to get water, fell in, caught pneumonia, and died. The site is named for a later resident."

23 to 24
River Tower: The approach to River Tower is by a dirt road branching right off River Road from the left turn to Hittle Bottom.

26 to 27
Kings Toll Road Buttress: On the left side of the road, a rock is incribed "Kings Toll Road," dating from the turn of the century when a toll was charged for using the stretch of dirt road to the Dewey Bridge. Across the river is Kings Toll Road Buttress and an unknown splitter crack route.

Bull Canyon: The narrow canyon opening across the river is Bull Canyon, leading into the historic Yellow Cat Uranium mining district of the 1950s and 1960s.

Fisher Towers: When driving downriver (toward Moab) the often-photographed vista of the Fisher Towers with the snowcapped La Sal Mountains comes into view.

27 to 28
Indian Chief Tower: High above the road on the right is a tower, resembling an Indian with a feather in his headband, that is semi-detached from the wall behind it.

29 to 30
Movie Site: Across from the mile marker is an old wooden ladder ascending the Wingate buttress. It is the site of a Western movie set from the 1950s.

Mule Shoe Rincon: On the right is a county gravel pile and the beginning of an abandoned meander of the Colorado River. It is identified as Mule Shoe on the *Moab East* map. *Rincon* is a geologic term derived from the Spanish word for "corner."

Dewey Recreation Site: The recreation site is on the left before the Dewey Suspension Bridge, 29.9 miles (48 km) up River Road. It has a boat launch, restrooms, fire rings, and tables. A sign reads: "Colorado River Recreation Area. Camp only at sites posted with a tent symbol, and carry a portable toilet system. Campers not carrying toilet equipment must camp at sites with constructed facilities. Leave vegetation and wood intact. Bring a stove or commercially obtained firewood. Keep vehicles off vegetation and soil crust. Use a firepan or designated ring. Carry out coals and ashes. Keep vehicles on established routes. Let the desert impact you–not the reverse." Another sign reads "Common take-out point for Dolores River whitewater trips originating from Gateway, Colorado. Also put-in point for calm water float to the Hittle Bottom boat ramp, as well as beyond."

Kokopelli Trail: The 128-mile (206 km) Kokopelli Mountain Bike Trail stretches over easy-to-difficult desert sandstone terrain from the Loma Boat Launch near Grand Junction, Colorado, to Moab, Utah, crossing River Road east (upriver) of the Dewey Bridge (across from mile marker 30). Most of the trail is on remote, unpatrolled BLM land and requires users to be cautious, personally responsible, and self-sufficient. The trail is marked by brown fiberglass posts placed approximately every 0.5 mile (0.8 km) and at intersections. It has an elevation variation of about 5,400 feet (1646 m), from 3,000 feet (914 m) to 8,400 feet (2,560 m). The eastern end of the trail is at the Loma Boat Launch, 15 miles (24 km) west of Grand Junction. The western end is at the Sand Flats road down the Slick Rock Bike Trail, 2 miles (3.2 km) east of Moab.

The trail was named after Kokopelli, a magical being recognized by many Native American groups of the Colorado Plateau. In petroglyphs Kokopelli is portrayed in a humpback position, playing a flute. He is associated with the Flute Clan of the Hopi Indians. One myth says that with the magic of his flute playing, Kokopelli brought warmth, hope, and prosperity to people and places of desperate need, and that he was able to drive back winter with his music. He wandered from village to village with a bag of songs on his back and, as a symbol of fertility, was welcome during spring planting.

The figure of Kokopelli appears in many forms across the Colorado Plateau, from paintings on pottery to numerous petroglyph carvings on desert-varnished walls. He also appears painted on Hohokam and Mimbres pottery as the Hopi Kachina Kokopelli.

Dewey Suspension Bridge: At the south end of the Dewey Suspension Bridge (29.9 miles, 48 km up River Road) a sign reads: "Dewey Bridge, constructed 1916 at a cost of $15,000, is on the National Register of Historic Places. In its prime it was designed to support the weight of 6 horses, 3 wagons, and 9,000 pounds of freight. Dewey Bridge is Utah's longest suspension bridge, and at the time of its construction was the second longest suspension bridge west of the Mississippi." It is also the state's longest clear span bridge, measuring 500 feet (152 m).

31 to 32

Proudfoot Bend Ranch: The ranch is upriver from the Dewey Bridge between mile markers 30 and 32. West (downriver) from mile marker 31 (100 feet, 30 m), is an abandoned house-in-the-rock (not in view from the road), an excellent shelter should your visit include the vicissitudes of inclement desert weather. Please obtain permission to use the shelter from the Proudfoot Bend Ranch. To reach, hike approximately 100 feet (30 m) north through a wire fence toward an alcove with a seep at its back. At the alcove, follow an old path left up a bench to the abandoned shelter.

Dolores River, Rock Art: Upriver from Proudfoot Bend Ranch, between mile markers 31 and 32, is the confluence of the Colorado and Dolores Rivers. Just beyond, on the left side of the road, is a rock canvas of Anasazi petroglyphs.

River Road leaves the Colorado at this point.

RIVER ROAD CLIMBING ROUTES

The Coup (a.k.a. Coo), El Secondo, Canyonlands by Night, Fun Ramp, Barney Rumble, Milano Tower

The Coup, El Secondo, Canyonlands by Night, Fun Ramp, Barney Rumble, and Milano Tower are on the north side of the river and technically within the boundary of Arches National Park. They are included in this volume because you approach them from River Road. Routes are listed from left to right (downriver to upriver). This section is followed by routes on the right side of River Road beginning with Sorcerer.

The Coup is on the upper Kayenta bench, north (opposite) of the river bridge, at the junction of U.S. Highway 191 and River Road. El Secondo and Canyonlands by Night are on the Wingate corner below The Coup. Fun Ramp climbs the obvious right-to-left diagonal ramp in view across the river (north) between mile markers 1 and 2. Barney Rumble is across the river from mile marker 4. Milano Tower is obvious across the Colorado River 0.2 mile (0.3 km) downriver from mile marker 5. To reach, cross the river by canoe or raft, and hike to the base of the tower.

1   THE COUP (a.k.a. The Coo) I, 5.10-, 1 pitch, 140 feet (43 m) ★★★★

First Ascent: Mike Baker, Leslie Henderson, Wilson Goodrich, 30 November 1997.

Location and Access: The Coup climbs the middle (best looking) of 3 left-facing Navajo Sandstone corner systems with a large cave at its top. The crux is where the corner pinches off and the ascent changes from liebacking and stemming to bolt-protected face climbing. To reach, from the concrete boat ramp south of the bridge and on the north side of the river, hike upriver to the first drainage where it is possible to ascend slabs up and right to the bench at the top of the Kayenta Formation. Contour left to the western end of the landform. The climb is identified by a large cave above 3 left-facing dihedrals.

Paraphernalia: Camalots (1) #1, #2, #3, #4; TCUs (1) set; quickdraws (3).

Descent: One double-rope rappel from double drilled angle pitons.

2   EL SECONDO I, 5.9, 1 pitch, 150 feet (46 m)

First Ascent: Marabel Loverage, Kyle Copeland, April 1992.

Location and Access: Park at a designated site on the north (right) side of U.S. Highway 191, a few hundred yards north of the bridge across the Colorado River. Approach from the trail to the Moab Panel (Courthouse Wash) pictographs, where an information kiosk describes the Indian writings. From the rock art, traverse right toward the river, 3rd class. Make a 5.2 step over a gap (bad place to fall), and continue to the corner of the wall where the left buttress faces US 191 and the right wall faces the Colorado River. Climb a right-facing dihedral, 5.8 fingers, then 5.9 hands to double rappel anchors on the right, light-colored wall at a ledge visible from below the route.

Paraphernalia: Light standard desert rack 1" through 3".

Descent: Rappel the route.

photo: Mike Baker

3   EL SECONDO DIRECT START (Top-rope) I, 5.11, 100 feet (30 m)

First Ascent: Kyle Copeland, Marabel Loverage, April 1992.

Location and Access: The direct start begins directly below the upper pitch. To reach, turn right after crossing the river bridge and park. The direct start is obvious up a fingercrack below visible anchors at the top of the route.

Paraphernalia: Top-rope.

Descent: Rappel the route.

4   CANYONLANDS BY NIGHT I, 5.10, 3 pitches, 200 feet (62 m)

First Ascent: Ron Wiggle, Chad Wiggle, Joe Nowak, August 1988.

Location and Access: *Canyonlands by Night* climbs the third crack right of *El Secondo* on the prow of the Wingate buttress north of the river.

Pitch 1: Begin left of the ascent line and climb up broken rock and around bulges right to a belay ledge, 5.7, 100 feet (30 m). Rappel slings are visible from across the river with binoculars.

Pitch 2: Climb a slot to the base of an offwidth and belay in a deep pod, 5.3, 75 feet (23 m).

Pitch 3: Continue up and right, then up an offwidth (Big Bro) and finally a chimney to an overhang and broken rock at the top of the chimney. There are no anchors on the pitch, 5.10.

Paraphernalia: Standard desert rack with large units; Big Bros.

Descent: The first ascent party reversed the chimney to the top of Pitch 2 where a rappel was made with slings around a chockstone, then rappelled Pitch 1 from anchors visible from below.

5   FUN RAMP III, 5.9 A2, 6 pitches, 350 feet (107 m)

First Ascent: Layton Kor, Kyle Copeland, October 1988.

Location and Access: When looking downriver from mile marker 2, *Fun Ramp* is the obvious right-to-left diagonal fracture, accessed by face climbing across the initial flake. The route was climbed with only 2 points of aid.

Paraphernalia: Friends (1) set.

Descent: Walk east along the rim to a low-angle slab with a bolt. Rappel 90 feet (27 m) to the ground.

6   BARNEY RUMBLE—RAVEN'S DELIGHT II, 5.9+, 2 pitches, 140 feet (43 m)

First Ascent: Bego Gerhart, Jeff Widen, Tony Valdes, Don Burke (support), 28 November 1986.

Location and Access: Barney Rumble Tower is across the river (north) from mile marker 4. After crossing the river, approach from a roped pitch up ramps left of the

photo: Eric Bjørnstad

Fun Ramp

photo: Jeff Widen

Barney Rumble Tower

tower. The route follows weaknesses on the east side of the landform.

Pitch 1: Begin up a corner system, then traverse left to a belay at loose blocks, 5.9.

Pitch 2: Climb a crack up a right-facing system, 5.9+, to rappel anchors. The crux is a 5.9+ hands move below the summit.

Paraphernalia: Friends (2) sets; TCUs.

Descent: Rappel anchors are hidden on a lower tier on the north side of the tower. Make 1 double-rope rappel to the north.

7   MILANO TOWER—POP TART II, 5.7, A2, 3 pitches, 250 feet (76 m)

First Ascent: Al Torrisi, Barry Roberts, Jim Bodenhamer, 3 November 1995.

Location and Access: Milano Tower is across the river (north) of mile marker 5. Rappel slings are visible low on the wall left of the tower. The route was dedicated to Rob Slater, killed in an avalanche after summiting K2. He loved mint Milano cookies and Pop Tarts.

Pitch 1: Begin 5.7 below the notch on the left side of the tower, 100 feet (30 m).

Pitch 2: Climb a chimney to a ledge, then 5.7 face to the notch and a small tree, 80 feet (24 m).

Pitch 3: Continue A2 to triple summit anchors, 70 feet (21 m).

Paraphernalia: Standard desert rack with (4) #1.5 Friends; a selection of pitons; canoe or raft to cross the river.

Descent: Rappel the route.

Sorcerer, Sorcerer's Apprentice

These two pillars are semi-detached from the rimrock wall above mile marker 1. Sorcerer is the pillar to the right and Sorcerer's Apprentice to the left.

8   SORCERER II, 5.11-, 3 pitches, 280 feet (85 m)

First Ascent: Chris Wood, Jimmy Dunn, 1977. First free ascent: Jimmy Dunn, Leonard Coyne, 1978.

Location and Access: Sorcerer ascends the left side of the pillar.

Pitch 1: Small units and 3 fixed bolts protect the pitch. Begin 5.10 offwidth, then climb a 5.9+ chimney to where it is possible to walk through (behind) the tower to the right side.

Pitch 2: Continue up a 5.9+ chimney.

Pitch 3: The crux. Climb a 5.11- offwidth up the left side of the landform to the summit.

Paraphernalia: Standard desert rack.

Descent: Rappel the route or rappel Pitch 3 to a ledge, then walk off to the left.

9   SORCERER'S CROSSING II, 5.11+, 3 pitches, 280 feet (85 m)

First Ascent: Jeff Achey and Craig Luebben, with 2 points of aid, April 1994. First free ascent: Craig Luebben, Jeff Achey, Kennan Harvey, November 1994.

Location and Access: Sorcerer's Crossing climbs the left side of Sorcerer, then traverses behind the pillar to join the original route. There are bolt anchors on the inside of the crossover.

Pitches 1, 2: The left side of the tower, making the crossover at the top of Pitch 2, 5.2, 5.9.

Pitch 3: Climb 5.10, passing 2 fixed anchors at the start, then ascend a 5.11+ squeeze to summit anchors. (Same as Sorcerer.)

Paraphernalia: Good selection of wide crack gear; light rack of wires through 3"; many 4–6" units for Pitch 1; several 6–8" pieces for Pitch 3; quickdraws.

Descent: Same as *Sorcerer's Apprentice Right*.

10   SORCERER'S APPRENTICE RIGHT II, 5.10+, 3 pitches, 280 feet (85 m) ★★★★

First Ascent: Chip Chace, Jeff Achey, April 1981.

Location and Access: *Sorcerer's Apprentice Right* ascends the right side of the tower.

Pitch 1: Climb fingers to lieback, 5.10+ ending 5.8 to a belay. An optional start is a crack left of the right edge of the tower, 60 feet (18 m).

Pitch 2: Begin up a wide crack, 5.10+. Continue through all sizes to fingers in a corner. Belay in a little alcove where it is possible to traverse through to the top of Pitch 2 of *Sorcerer's Apprentice Left*, 5.10+, 140 feet (43 m).

Pitch 3: Continue with thin stemming up an overhanging dihedral (5.10+ crux) to the tower's soft summit, 80 feet (24 m). Doug Hall: "Awesome!"

Paraphernalia: Friends (2) sets; wired stoppers for Pitch 3.

Descent: Rappel the left side 80 feet (24 m), then 3rd class from a broad ledge back to River Road or make two rappels (beginning from the ledge) directly down the tower, 200 feet (61 m) to the ground.

11   SORCERER'S APPRENTICE LEFT II, 5.11c, 2 pitches, 280 feet (85 m)

First Ascent: Pitch 1: Jimmy Dunn, Bryan Becker, Ed Webster, 1976. Pitch 2: Begun with Jimmy Dunn and Martha Morris, 1980. Summitted by Jimmy Dunn, Australian climber Maureen Gallagher, 21 July 1986.

Location and Access: *Sorcerer's Apprentice Left* ascends the left side of the pillar. The first pitch may be bypassed by a 3rd-class approach from the left side of a large ledge.

Pitch 1: Begin 5.10 and climb to a stance. Continue 5.10+, stemming to a belay where the descent ledge meets the tower and it is possible to traverse (behind) to the top of Pitch 2 of *Sorcerer's Apprentice Right*, 150 feet (46 m).

Pitch 2: Climb 5.11c to the top of the pillar, 80 feet (24 m).

Paraphernalia: Friends (2) sets with extra #0.5 through #1.5; wires, RPs.

Descent: One rappel down the left side of the tower allows a walk off from a broad ledge.

Split Pillar

Split Pillar is a tower, semi-detached from the rimrock wall behind it, approximately 180 feet (55 m) right of *Bloody Knees*.

12   SPLIT PILLAR (a.k.a. Green Crack) III, 5.10, A3, 4 pitches, 400 feet (122 m)

First Ascent: Steve Cheyney, John Hall, 5.9, A3, 1972. Second ascent: Jimmy Dunn, Doug Snively, 5.10, A3, early 1970s.

Location and Access: *Split Pillar* climbs between the tower and the rimrock wall behind, beginning above a 40 mph sign between mile markers 2 and 3. It is 2 crack systems right of *Bloody Knees.*

Pitch 1: Begin up the crack system below and right of the leaning pillar and climb to a good ledge at the base of tower, 5.7.

Pitch 2: Move left to the base of the tower, then climb past 2 fixed anchors, and up 5.10 offwidth, past a fixed anchor and continue up 5.9 hands to a belay station with a single anchor midway up the pillar.

Pitch 3: Climb 5.10 fist past a fixed anchor, then A3 to 5.10 to a belay behind the top of the pillar.

Pitch 4: Continue up the obvious crack above the pillar to the rim top.

Paraphernalia: Standard desert rack; quickdraws (4).

Descent: From the top of the rimrock, contour 0.25 mile (0.4 km) left, then right along the right side of Short Canyon, then rappel from bolts to the canyon floor. After thundershowers there is a waterfall close to the rappel line.

13 RICK'S ROTTEN RAMP VARIATION 5.7, 1 pitch, 80 feet (24 m)

First Ascent: Rick Norman, Mike Mayer, Brett Maurer, Christine Beekman, 26 July 1987.

Location and Access: This variation is to Pitch 1 of *Split Pillar* and begins behind a scrub oak tree 30 feet (9 m) or 2 cracks right of the start to *Split Pillar.* Work left on a sloping, ramplike formation that leads to a grassy ledge at the base of the upper tower.

14 LAST SUPPER III, 5.10+, 4 pitches, 400 feet (122 m)

First Ascent: Chip Chace, Jeff Achey, April 1981.

Location and Access: On the first ascent, bolts from an unknown party were found leading to the second belay. *Last Supper* shares Pitch 1 with *Split Pillar* (5.7), then climbs a 5.10+ groove with poor protection before angling left (5.9+) to continue up the prominent crack system on the face of the pillar 1 crack left of *Split Pillar.* The summit pitch follows Pitch 4 of *Split Pillar.* Pitch 2: Begin as for *Split Pillar* Pitch 2, then move left where possible and climb an obvious splitter crack for 2 pitches before finishing up the rimrock to the summit.

NOTE: Pitons are not necessary; please repeat the climb in the good style of the first ascent.

Paraphernalia: Friends (1) set, including an extra #4; Camalots (2) #4.

Descent: Rappel *Split Pillar.*

River Road Dihedrals, Molar

River Road Dihedrals are on the buttress immediately right of Short Canyon (a.k.a. Ice Box, Sheep Canyon) 0.2 mile (0.3 km) before mile marker 3. Due to their short approach, proximity to Moab, and afternoon shade, the River Road Dihedrals have become some of the most frequently visited one-pitch climbs east of the Colorado River, with *Bloody Knees* being the most popular. Routes are listed from right to left . Molar is the 20-foot-high (6 m) boulder at the right entrance to Short Canyon.

15   RIVER ROAD DIHEDRALS—BLOODY KNEES (a.k.a. River Road Dihedral West, Peapod Crack) I, 5.9+, 1 pitch, 130 feet (40 m)

First Ascent: Jimmy Dunn, 1970. Second ascent: Larry Bruce, Brian Kew, Rick Jack, 1972.

Location and Access: *Bloody Knees* is 5 crack systems right of Short Canyon and 2 cracks right of *Oxygen Debt*. Begin up heavily lichened rock and climb 5.8 up a left-facing dihedral, then 5.7 to a pod. Continue 5.8 past 2 bolts on the left wall, then 5.9+ to the grassy ledge above.

Paraphernalia: Friends (2) sets #2 through #7; some larger wired stoppers protect the moves off the ground.

Descent: Make 2 rappels down the route (1 gets the rope stuck) or walk right and rappel from a small piñon tree.

16   RIVER ROAD DIHEDRALS—OXYGEN DEBT I, 5.11+, 1 pitch, 70 feet (21 m)

First Ascent: Paul Gagner, Rich Perch, 30 September 1986. First free ascent: Craig Luebben, solo, 9 April 1989.

Location and Access: *Oxygen Debt* climbs dark varnished rock up the left or outside crack of a double-crack system on a large right-facing dihedral left of *Bloody Knees*. Begin 5.11- hands and continue hands at 5.10, then 5.10+ fist. Pass a squeeze chimney and continue 5.11+ fist (or 5.12 offwidth if hands are small). Move right under a roof. The top of the route ascends easy offwidth to double-rappel anchors left of the crack system.

Paraphernalia: Friends (1) set #1.5 through #4 with (2) #4; Big Bros (2) #1, #2, (1) #3.

Descent: One single-rope rappel from fixed anchors.

17   RIVER ROAD DIHEDRALS—RIVER ROAD DIHEDRAL EAST I, 5.9, 1 pitch, 125 feet (38 m)

First Ascent: Jimmy Dunn, Doug Snively, 1972.

Location and Access: *River Road Dihedral East* ascends the next crack system left of *Oxygen Debt* and begins 5.8 thin, then 5.9 with fist near the top. Rappel anchors are visible from below the route.

Paraphernalia: Friends (2) each #0.5 through #3, (1) #3.5, #4.

Descent: One double-rope rappel down the route from fixed anchors.

18   RIVER ROAD DIHEDRALS—LITTLE CRACK I, 5.9, 2 pitches, 125 feet (38 m)

First Ascent: Unknown.

Location and Access: *Little Crack* is 1 crack left of *River Road Dihedral East*. Begin 5.9 up heavily lichened rock, climbing a splitter crack to a belay stance with bolts, then continue up an obvious crack to the bench above and a triple-bolt anchor.

Paraphernalia: Standard desert rack.

Descent: One double-rope rappel from fixed anchors.

19   MOLAR

First Ascent: Unknown.

Molar is a 20-foot-high (6 m) pillar at the right entrance to Short Canyon, left of the River Road Dihedrals. There are several difficult and alluring boulder problems on this diminutive tower sitting just above River Road.

Anasazi Buttress

Anasazi Buttress is the Navajo Sandstone wall between Short and Negro Bill Canyons. Anasazi Wall is the smooth, overhanging, water-streaked wall above mile marker 3 in the center of Anasazi Buttress. "Frog" climbs are at the left (upriver) end of the buttress. Climbing routes are listed from right to left.

20   FOAM FLAKE I, 5.10a, 1 pitch, 100 (30 m) ★★★

First Ascent: Cindy Furman, Warren Egbert, May 1993.

Location and Access: *Foam Flake* is 0.2 mile (0.3 km) before (downriver) mile marker 3, across from a pullout on the river side of the road. Begin up a left-facing corner and pass a roof on its left side (5.10a), then continue past 2 bolts. Work left to pass a second overhang (5.10a, protected with #1, #2 TCUs). Pass a bolt and protect with a #1 Friend. Continue to double-rappel anchors visible from below.

Paraphernalia: Friends (1) #1; TCUs (1) #1, #2; Quickdraws (3).

Descent: One double-rope rappel down the route.

21   ARTIST'S TEARS IV, 5.8, A4, 3 pitches, 400 feet (122 m)

First Ascent: Molly Higgins, Larry Bruce, 26–28 May 1976. Pitches 1 and 2: Eric Bjørnstad, Jimmy Dunn, early 1970s. Second ascent: Rick Jack, John Mattson, late '70s early '80s. First solo ascent (third overall, two days): Jason Keith, 14 April 1988.

Location and Access: *Artist's Tears* ascends an obvious splitter crack system right of center on Anasazi Wall. Molly Higgins: "A beautiful thin line winding up the painted and overhanging smooth sandstone face on the Colorado River. . . . The first pitch

photo: Eric Bjørnstad

Negro Bill Canyon   Short Canyon

Anasazi Buttress

involved face moves to a bolt, hook moves to another bolt, dowels and bolts to a roof, then 80 feet of A4 to the belay. A4 is so intense you don't even whimper or whine, just get very quiet." Cassidy-Wiggins: "At the time of its establishment, this route represented the cutting edge of desert nailing."

Pitch 1: Begin 5.5, then climb a bolt ladder, A1, then A4 (angles and RPs) to double belay anchors on the right wall.

Pitch 2: Continue with aid, A3, (pitons and RPs to a #3 Friend) to double-belay anchors on the right wall.

Pitch 3: Climb A2+ past many fixed bolts and drilled angles, then make a 5.8 move onto the summit.

Paraphernalia: Early ascents used numerous thin pitons.

Descent: Rappel into Negro Bill Canyon from a 2-bolt anchor which may be difficult to locate, or leave fixed ropes on the top 2 pitches of the overhanging Anasazi Wall.

22   SEAM CRACK III, A4, 2 pitches

First Ascent: Pitch 1: Ken Trout et al, late 1980s. Pitch 2: Unknown.

Location and Access: *Seam Crack* is 1 crack system left of *Artist's Tears*. There is a bolt above the Pitch 2 rappel station. It is unknown if the route continues to the top of the rimrock.

23   NAVAJO ROUTE II, 5.11-, 1 pitch, 300 feet (91 m)

First Ascent: Unknown. First free ascent: Ray Jardine, Don Peterson, 1971.

Location and Access: *Navajo Route* is directly above mile marker 3, 1 crack left of *Seam Crack*, and ascends the crack/chimney system at the left edge of the smooth Anasazi Wall. Unfortunately, "RJ" is inscribed at the base of the climb.

Paraphernalia: Standard desert rack.

Descent: Rappel the route.

24   UNKNOWN

Location and Access: Left of *Navajo Route* on a blank wall are several bolt holes leading a short distance to a bolt anchor. Further information is unknown.

25   ACQUIRED TASTE II, 5.12a/b, A1, 2 pitches, 250 feet (76 m)

First Ascent: Jeff Lowe, Teri Ebel, 3 June 1994 (on their honeymoon).

Location and Access: *Acquired Taste* is 2 cracks left of *Navajo Route*. The climb begins with 30 feet (9 m) of aid, climbed before Lowe and Ebel by an unknown party.

Pitch 1: Begin with 4 bolts and 3 nut placements to get off the ledge at the base of the wall. Continue 5.11+ fingertips to thin hands, passing 2 fixed pitons and an anchor on the left wall. The crack widens to 4" (10 cm), then 6" (15 cm) to a belay from 2 bolts on the left wall.

Pitch 2: Climb offwidth at 5.10+ protected by 7 bolts and drilled angles. The crux is a roof passed on its left (5.12a/b). Continue up, passing 1 bolt, to a rappel station visible from below when viewed from upriver.

Paraphernalia: Friends (1) set; Big Bros (1) set; wired stoppers; Quickdraws.

Descent: Rappel the route.

NOTE: The following three climbs are listed from right to left, but are easiest to identify from left to right beginning at Negro Bill Canyon.

26   FAST TIMES AT FROGMONT HIGH I, 5.10, 1 pitch, 75 feet (23 m)

First Ascent: Tony Grenko, Paul Seibert, Tony Passariello, 19 September 1989.

Location and Access: *Fast Times at Frogmont High* begins behind the largest juniper tree at the base of Anasazi Buttress, a point 4 major mid-wall crack/seam systems left of *Acquired Taste*. Climb a wide, left-facing corner with a drilled angle, then up a thin right-facing corner to rappel slings visible from below.

Paraphernalia: Friends #4; TCUs #2, #2.5, #3.

Descent: Rappel the route.

27   CHILDREN OF A LESSER FROG I, 5.10-, 1 pitch, 80 feet (24 m)

First Ascent: Tony Grenko, Paul Seibert, Tony Passariello, 19 September 1989.

Location and Access: *Children of a Lesser Frog* climbs between *Fast Times at Frogmont High* and *Froggy Horror Picture Show*. Begin up a right-facing corner above a large juniper tree. Start with 5.10- thin (through a pod), and finish with hands at double-rappel anchors on the right wall, visible from below.

Paraphernalia: Friends #2, #2.5, #3; many TCUs.

Descent: Rappel the route.

28   FROGGY HORROR PICTURE SHOW I, 5.11, 1 pitch, 100 feet (30 m)

First Ascent: Tony Grenko, Paul Seibert, Tony Passariello, 19 September 1989.

Location and Access: *Froggy Horror Picture Show* is at the far left side of an obvious grassy ledge, just before the wall makes an oblique bend into Negro Bill Canyon. Begin up broken rock, placing a #3.5 Friend for protection. Continue up a crack which finishes with hands at double-rappel anchors on the left wall.

Paraphernalia: Friends (3) sets #2 through #3; many #0.75 TCUs.

Descent: Rappel the route.

Negro Bill Canyon

Negro Bill Canyon is 0.1 mile (0.16 km) past mile marker 3. In the parking area at the trailhead of the canyon is a BLM information kiosk defining camping and other use regulations. Please be a responsible visitor.

WARNING: Water in Negro Bill Canyon is contaminated by cattle grazing in the La Sal Mountains high upcanyon.

29   NEGRO BILL FLAKE III, 5.11, A4, 4 pitches, 300 feet (91 m)

First Ascent: Earl Wiggins, Chris Wood, Jimmy Dunn, 1974.

Location and Access: *Negro Bill Flake* is approximately 200 feet (61 m) up the right wall of the canyon. The route climbs the right side of a detached pillar that is obvious when viewed from the River Road. Cassidy-Wiggins: "Combining A4 aid climbing with 5.11 off-widthing, this route was considered a test piece for many years. This fine route is capped off with a 'leaping mantle' from the main wall to the flake's summit. The leap across a 6-foot-wide chasm to a 5.10 mantle is, to say the least, very intimidating. Failure on either the leap or the mantle results in an awful plunge into the dark depths of the bottomless flake."

Pitch 1: There is a 90-foot-high (27 m) formation in front of the lower portion of the pillar. The route begins halfway up the formation by traversing in from the right to the beginning of an obvious chimney. Climb the chimney (5.9/5.10) then belay at the top of the formation.

Pitch 2: Climb 5.10 fingers and hands, then 15 feet (5 m) of A4 in a groove that leads to a hanging belay from fixed anchors. This location is obvious from below, where white rock meets an upper wall of red rock.

Pitch 3: Climb 5.11 offwidth to a belay just below the summit.

Pitch 4: The top is reached by stemming between the wall and the pillar, then making a "leaping mantle" from the wall to the pillar's caprock, 5.10+.

Paraphernalia: Standard desert rack.

Descent: Two double-rope rappels down the route.

30   MARCH HARE FLARE I, 5.11-, 1 pitch, 50 feet (15 m)

First Ascent: Bill Robins, Kirsten Davis, 1986.

Location and Access: *March Hare Flare* ascends both twin cracks (close to one another) 0.5 mile (0.8 km) upcanyon on the left side. When viewed from the parking area at Negro Bill Trailhead, a dark buttress is apparent on the left wall. The twin cracks are out of sight a few feet around the right corner of the buttress. The route is on a nose of rock between 2 relatively smooth rimrock walls. Rappel slings are obvious from below the climb.

Paraphernalia: Standard desert rack.

Descent: Rappel the route.

Jackass Canyon

Cross Jackass Canyon near River Road as you ascend to Porcupine Rim mountain bike trail (originally a cattle trail from the river to the mesa top).

31   JACKASS CORNER I, 5.11, 1 pitch, 150 feet (46 m)

First Ascent: Unknown.

Location and Access: *Jackass Corner* is 0.4 mile (0.6 km) upriver from Negro Bill Canyon. To reach, hike the drainage of Jackass Canyon (or the mountain bike trail beginning 500 feet [152 m] downriver). Climb a dark, varnished, right-facing dihedral to rappel slings visible from below.

Paraphernalia: Standard desert rack.

Descent: Rappel the route.

Pale Ale, Beer Buttress

Pale Ale and *Beer Buttress* are on the left side of an unnamed canyon on the Wingate buttress above mile marker 5 on the right side of River Road. Climbing routes are listed from right to left.

32   PALE ALE I, 5.11a, 1 pitch, 160 feet (49 m),★★

First Ascent: Jay Smith, Jo Smith, 25 April 1993.

Location and Access: *Pale Ale* is right of *Beer Buttress* at the right side of the buttress above mile marker 5. Climb 5.10c (1.25" to 1.5", 3 cm to 2.3 cm) to a roof which is passed on the right at 5.11a. Continue thin hands passing a second roof on its right, then 5.10+ up a groove and finally a right-facing corner to a ledge and double-rappel anchors visible from below.

Paraphernalia: Friends (1) #1.5, (2) #2, (4) #2.5, (3) #3, #3.5; many runners; Quickdraws.

Descent: Rappel the route.

33   BEER BUTTRESS—Triple X I, 5.11c, 1 pitch, 150 feet (46 m) ★★★

First Ascent: Jay Smith, Jo Smith, 25 April 1993.

Location and Access: *Beer Buttress* is left of *Pale Ale.* Climb the left crack to a ledge, 5.11c. It starts 1.25", then 1.5" and finally 2.5". From the ledge, traverse left 20 feet (6 m), 5.9, and climb an obvious crack system (5.10) with perfect hands finishing with 5.11. At the top, move left of a loose and rotten area (5.10+) to a ledge with double-rappel anchors visible from below.

Paraphernalia: Friends (2) #1, #1.5, (4) #2, #2.5, (2) #3, (1) #3.5; runners; Quickdraws.

Descent: Rappel the route.

Gauntlet, Frankin-Tony, Diane's Tower, Po-Dunk Mesa Tower

Gauntlet is 0.1 mile (0.16 km) upriver from mile marker 6; park at Lower Drinks camp area. *Frankin-Tony* ascends the second crack, right of the prow, on the right side of the canyon, on the buttress downriver from mile marker 6. *Diane's Tower* is 100 feet (30 m) left of *Frankin-Tony*, and is a rock pillar leaning against the second Wingate buttress right of *Po-Dunk Mesa Tower*, which is 0.2 mile (0.3 km) upriver from mile marker 6. The south (right) side of the tower is 400 feet high (122 m), steep, and uninviting.

34   GAUNTLET I, 5.10+, 1 pitch, 110 feet (34 m) ★★

First Ascent: Andy Roberts, Jay Miller, 3 June 1998.

Location and Access: Ascend the right side of a formation that appears to be a detached pillar but is not. Alternate between a hand-crack and squeeze chimney. The route is plaqued.

Paraphernalia: Camalots (1) #0.75, #1, (3) #2, (2) #3, #4, (1) #5.

Descent: Rappel the route from a double-bolt anchor.

35   FRANKIN-TONY I, 5.10d, 1 pitch, 70 feet (21 m)

First Ascent: Tony Valdes, Steve Frank, May 1987.

Location and Access: Begin 5.9 and climb to 5.10, pass a roof, then climb 5.10c offwidth and pass a second roof. Continue up 5.10d (thin) to a chimney with double-rappel anchors on the right wall (visible from River Road).

Paraphernalia: Friends (2) #0.5, (3) #2, #2.5, (2) #4.

Descent: Rappel the route.

36   DIANE'S TOWER I, 5.9+, 3 pitches, 400 feet (122 m)

First Ascent: Mark Whiton, free solo, 26 September 1988.

Location and Access: *Diane's Tower* is climbed from the left side of the landform. The first ascent party left a small cairn halfway up the tower and a second cairn on the summit.

Paraphernalia: Standard desert rack.

Descent: Rappel the route.

photo: Andy Roberts

37 PO-DUNK MESA TOWER (a.k.a. Pyramid Tower) II, 5.9+, 3 pitches, 400 feet (122 m)

First Ascent: Kyle Copeland, solo, early 1990s. Second ascent: Dave Gloudemans, solo, 19 December 1995.

Location and Access: The climb involves (2) 40 foot (12 m) sections of technical climbing, 5.9+, and an approximately 1-hour approach from River Road.

Pitch 1: Third class, diagonally right to left, ending 5.6 up to a ledge.

Pitch 2: Make a 3rd-class traverse right to a ledge below cracks leading to the summit.

Pitch 3: Climb 5.9+ loose rock to the top.

Paraphernalia: Friends (1) #1.5, (2) #3.5; Camalots (1) #4, (1) #5; Rocks (1) #3.

Descent: Reverse the route.

Buffalo Chip Boulder

Buffalo Chip is a large boulder left of River Road just outside the rail fence at the left (downriver) end of Big Bend Campground (upriver from mile marker 7).

38   BUFFALO CHIP I, easy 5th, 1 pitch, 12 feet (4 m)

First Ascent: Harvey T. Carter, solo, June 1967.

Location and Access: Carter climbed the boulder by 7 different routes.

Paraphernalia: None required.

Descent: Downclimb.

O'Grady, Notch

O'Grady is across (east) from Big Bend Recreation Area and Campground, right of Lighthouse Tower, and climbs the west (river) side of the landform. Notch is between Dolomite Spire and Lighthouse Tower. Approach the landforms from a cairn-marked trail beginning across from Buffalo Chip at the downriver side of Big Bend Recreational Area.

39   O'GRADY I, 5.12+, 2 pitches, 180 feet (55 m) ★★★★★

First Ascent: Kitty Calhoun, Jay Smith, 1997.

Location and Access: Begin up an obvious left-facing crack system right of the overhanging left profile of the Wingate Wall.

Pitch 1: Follow a right-trending crack/corner to a belay ledge with 2 fixed anchors, 5.8, and protect with a #1.5, then #3 Friend, 70 feet (21 m).

Pitch 2: Step left and climb the overhanging 5.11b crack above (protect with wires). Continue at 5.12+ (protect with a #2 Friend). Near the top, move left (#0.75) and up to double anchors, 110 feet (34 m) .

Paraphernalia: Friends (1) #0.4, #0.5, (2 to 3) #0.75, (3) #1, #1.5, (8) #2, (1) #3; medium to large wires; 200-foot (60 m) ropes .

Descent: Rappel the route.

40   NOTCH I, 5.8, A2, 1 pitch

First Ascent: Craig Francois, Amanda Tarr, 22 March 1994.

Location and Access: The route climbs from the river side (west) to the notch between Dolomite Spire and Lighthouse Tower.

Paraphernalia: Friends, Quickdraws.

Descent: Rappel the route.

Lighthouse Tower

Lighthouse Tower is the freestanding pinnacle with the ball-shaped summit block left of *O'Grady* and right of Dolomite Spire. The summit ball is approximately 3 feet by 7 feet (0.9 m x 2 m) and has no fixed summit anchors. A 5.9 S mantle must be down-led without protection after gaining the summit.

Cassidy-Wiggins speaking of the first ascent of Iron Maiden: "His (Jeff Achey) boldness and imagination resulted in a lead consisting of creative stemming for 30 feet up a blank, desert-varnished corner to an overhanging headwall. Achey hung on with one arm and beat a piton into a horizontal seam before proceeding to hand traverse across the smooth steep wall for 25 feet, finally reaching a thin fingercrack in a vertical corner. The corner led to another hand traverse, after which Achey finally decided to establish a belay. The pitch is serious, demanding, and one of the most beautiful in the desert." Routes are listed from right to left beginning on the river side of the tower. Approach as you would for *O'Grady*.

41   IRON MAIDEN III, 5.12a R, S, 4 pitches, 315 feet (95 m) ★★★★★

First Ascent: Ed Webster, Jeff Achey, 2 October 1985. Second ascent: Swiss climbers Yves Martin, Christian Muffat-Jeandet, Romain Vogler, December 1985.

Location and Access: *Iron Maiden* ascends the narrow, right-facing dihedral system right of *Poseidon Adventure* on the river side of the tower. Pitches 1 and 2 may be combined.

Pitch 1: Climb a short chimney to a broken ledge, then up a right-facing corner, 5.8, past a fixed piton, 5.10d, then stem to a possible belay on the left side of the arête. Climb 5.12a past a bolt. Make a horizontal hand traverse right past a fixed piton to a small ledge and a belay. Protect with #1, #1.5 Friends.

Pitch 2: Climb up, make a 5.10 hand traverse left, then ascend a right-facing corner, 5.8, and finally pass an overhang with a flake on its left side and continue to a small belay ledge.

Pitch 3: Climb 5.10+ hand/fist up a large overhanging, right-facing dihedral to a good ledge. From this vantage, you can make an unprotected 5.6 traverse left to *Poseidon Adventure*.

photo: Mike Baker

Lighthouse Tower (right) and Dolomite Spire

Pitch 4: Continue past 3 pitons, then up and right to join *Lonely Vigil*, 5.12a. Make an unprotected 5.9 S mantle to the top.

Paraphernalia: Friends (2 to 3) #1, (3) #1.5, (2) #2, #2.5, (2 to 3) #3, (2) #3.5, #4; wired stoppers (10), including very small sizes; Hexs #3, #4 (Pitch 3); (2) #3 Crack 'n' Ups optional for crux near bolt; quickdraws.

Descent: Rappel *Northeast Route.*

42   POSEIDON ADVENTURE III, 5.10 S R, 4 pitches, 315 feet (95 m)

First Ascent: Ed Webster, Jeff Achey, October 1984.

Location and Access: *Poseidon Adventure* follows a chimney system directly beneath the notch between the ball-shaped summit and the lower, subsidiary landform to the left of the summit as viewed from River Road.

Pitch 1: Begin up *Iron Maiden*, then traverse left to the next crack system, 5.8. Climb 5.8 to a ledge below a deep-cut chimney.

Pitch 2: Continue 5.10 up an awkward 4" to 8" (6–12 cm) overhanging, flared squeeze chimney (the crux) to hands ending at a good ledge, 150 feet (46 m) from the ground. Protect with (2) #4 and (1) #5 Camalot.

Pitch 3: Ascend a 5.8 wide crack passing a large ledge on its right, then continue 5.7 up a short chimney leading to the summit notch.

Pitch 4: Make an unprotected traverse left, out onto the northeast face, 5.6, 70 feet (21 m). Continue up, past double-anchors, to the top with an unprotected 5.9 S mantle.

photo: Glen Dunmire

Climbers on the summit of Lighthouse Tower from Dolomite Spire

Paraphernalia: Standard desert rack, including Camalots (2) #4, (1) #5 for the crux on Pitch 2; some camming units up to 7" useful.

Descent: Rappel *Northeast Route.*

43   NORTHEAST ROUTE III, 5.9+ S, 5 pitches, 315 feet (96 m)

First Ascent: Harvey T. Carter, Gary Ziegler, Tom Merrill, 28 May 1970.

Location and Access: *Northeast Route* starts on the northeast corner (opposite side from the river) right of *Jamaroni.*

Pitch 1: Climb to the notch between Dolomite Spire and Lighthouse Tower, 5.7.

Pitch 2: Continue 5.8 offwidth, then 5.9+ off width to a fixed anchor.

Pitch 3: Move right and ascend a 5.8 squeeze, then traverse left.

Pitch 4: Climb 5.7 past the left side of a loose block to bolts below the summit pitch.

Pitch 5: The first ascent party threw a rope over the ball-shaped summit and prusiked up. Subsequent ascents have climbed the pitch directly with an unprotected 5.9 S mantle.

Paraphernalia: Friends (1) set including #5, #6; Tri-cams (1) #5; small to large angle pitons.

Descent: Rappel the route.

44   JAMARONI II, 5.10 S, 3 pitches, 315 feet (95 m)

First Ascent: David and Don Pollari, 5.9, A2, 26 October 1988. Second ascent and first free ascent: Andy Oppler, Dave Pollari, fall 1992.

Location and Access: *Jamaroni* is between *Lonely Vigil* and *Northeast Route.*

Pitch 1: Diagonal slightly to the right as the crack follows breaks through bulges and overhangs, then widens into a chimney and finally opens on a spacious belay alcove, 5.10. The first ascent team used a few moves of A2.

Pitch 2: Follow an obvious shallow corner onto the eastern face from whence a traverse to the right leads to double bolts below the summit block, 5.6, 80 feet (24 m).

Pitch 3: Follow the summit pitch of the *Northeast Route,* 5.9 S mantle.

Paraphernalia: Standard desert rack; Friends (1) #1 for the alcove belay at the top of Pitch 1; Tri-cams (1) #1; small wires. Second ascent party used Friends (2) sets; TCUs; medium wires.

Descent: Rappel *Northeast Route.*

45   LONELY VIGIL III, 5.10 S, 4 pitches, 315 feet (96 m) ★★★

First Ascent: Ed Webster, Jeff Achey, October 1985.

Location and Access: *Lonely Vigil* ascends the central crack system on the northeast (opposite river) face of the tower, left of *Northeast* route. A 50-foot (15 m) 5.6 pitch ascends to the notch.

Pitch 1: Climb hands to big hands past loose rock to a belay, 5.9.

Pitch 2: Continue over a bulge to a ledge, then traverse left 25 feet (8 m), 5.10.

Pitch 3: Climb up and slightly right to a belay for the summit pitch, 5.7, 50 feet (15 m).

Pitch 4: Summit pitch is an unprotected 5.9 S mantle.

Paraphernalia: Standard desert rack through a #4 Friend.

Descent: Rappel *Northeast Route.*

46   ARE YOU EXPERIENCED I, 5.10c, 1 pitch, 165 feet (50 m)

First Ascent: Jim Howe, Tommie Howe, spring 1995.

Location and Access: The 1-pitch route ascends a crack system just left of *Lonely Vigil*.

Paraphernalia: Standard desert rack.

Descent: Rappel *Northeast Route*.

Dolomite Spire

Dolomite Spire is between Big Bend Butte and Lighthouse Tower. The following three routes climb Dolomite Spire. A tyrolean traverse was made from Dolomite Spire to Lighthouse Tower by Tom Gilje and Rene Glovis in the mid-1990s. Same approach as *O'Grady*. Routes are listed from right to left.

47   DOLOMITE SPIRE—KOR ROUTE III, 5.8, C2, 5 pitches, 350 feet (107 m)

First Ascent: Layton Kor, Joy Kor, Kordell Kor, 11 April 1969. Second ascent: Doug Robinson, Chuck Pratt, 12 April 1969. First solo ascent: Mark Whiton, May 1988, in 4 pitches.

Location and Access: The first and second ascents were made from the river side of the spire. The tower is now generally climbed in 5 pitches from the northeast (back side). The first ascent party of this variation is unknown. The first clean aid ascent is unknown.

Pitch 1: Begin with 5.8 hands, then climb left through a chimney and past a bolt to a 2-bolt belay ledge.

Pitch 2: Angle up and right (C2) past a bolt, then above a small overhang (bolt) past a fixed piton, then a bolt to a hanging belay with double bolts.

Pitch 3: Follow piton scars up a thin right-facing crack system. Continue up a bolt ladder and a thin crack (C1) to a belay ledge. At the bedding seam at the top of the pitch, there are pitons in place that lead off-route up a crack to the left, 160 feet (49 m).

Pitch 4: Continue right around the corner and up loose C2 to a "dicey" belay ledge.

Pitch 5: Climb C1 (Friends and TCUs) past a loose block, then past bolts to a right-trending ramp protected by 2 bolts. Continue right and up around a corner to the summit, 135 feet (41 m).

Paraphernalia: Friends (2) each through #3, (1) #3.5; TCUs; Lowe Balls; wires or keyhole hangers for bolts; quickdraws.

Descent: Two double-rope rappels. Rappel east to the notch between Dolomite Spire and Big Bend Butte, then to the ground on the northeast side of the tower.

48   DOLOMITE SPIRE—WHITON VARIATION III, 5.8, A2

First Ascent: Mark Whiton, solo, May 1988.

Location and Access: The variation climbs left at the beginning of Pitch 2 (rather than traversing right around the corner), then, on tension, right on a ledge to the final summit ramp.

Paraphernalia: Same as *Kor Route*.

Descent: Rappel the *Kor Route*.

photo: Andy Donson

Kath Pyke on *Dolofright*

49   DOLOMITE SPIRE—DOLOFRIGHT III, 5.11d R, 4 pitches, 350 feet (107 m)

First Ascent: Tom Gilje, Julie Gilje, September 1993. Second ascent: Dan Osman.

Location and Access: *Dolofright* climbs the right profile of the tower as viewed from River Road. Begin on the right side of the east face, left of *Kor Route*.

Pitch 1: Climb a crack past 2 fixed pitons and a bolt. Continue past a flake, then a runout to a 2.5" (6.3 cm) crack, past bolts ending on a small ledge, 120 feet (37 m).

Pitch 2: Continue past 3 bolts to a second ledge with double bolts. The crux is above the ledge, 5.11d.

Pitch 3: Continue past 4 bolts up a runout face to a belay ledge with 4 bolts, 5.10 R.

Pitch 4: Reach the summit by traversing around the right side of the tower.

Paraphernalia: Tri-cams; RPs; wires; quickdraws.

Descent: Rappel the *Kor Route*.

Big Bend Butte

Big Bend Butte is across from Big Bend Campground, halfway between mile markers 7 and 8, left of Dolomite Spire and Lighthouse Tower. Use the approach described under the listing for *O'Grady*, page 98. Routes on Big Bend Butte begin on the river side and are listed from right to left: *Infrared, Dolomite Wall, Clearlight, Vivaldi Pinnacle,* and *Fried Flounder*. Routes on the back (east) side are reached with an easy hike up the drainage left of the butte and are listed from right to left: *Grim Reaper, Psycho Toad, Refuge*.

50   INFRARED IV, 5.12a, 4 pitches, 450 feet (137 m) ★★★★★

First Ascent: Jay Smith, Conrad Anker, May 1995.

Location and Access: *Infrared* is 1 crack system right of *Dolomite Wall*.

Pitch 1: Climb soft rock over the bedding seam between the Chinle and Wingate layers, beginning with thin stemming, then wide hands to double anchors on a belay ledge.

Pitch 2: Continue past a loose block (and fixed anchor) up a right-facing corner to double anchors on a belay ledge, 5.10+.

Pitch 3: Climb wide hands (3.5", 5 cm) at 5.11 past a fixed anchor, then hands to double belay anchors.

Pitch 4: The "Endurance" pitch. Climb past several fixed anchors through the Kayenta caprock, 5.12a. Continue 5.11 to a notch, then the summit.

Paraphernalia: Friends (2) #1, #1.5, (3) #2, #2.5, #3, (4) #3.5, (3) #4; TCUs (1) #0.3, (2) #0.4, #0.5, (3) #0.75; Sliders (1) #2; wires (1) set; many long quickdraws and runners for the last pitch; 50 meter ropes .

Descent: Fix the end of the trail line to the top of Pitch 3 for the rappel from the summit.

51   DOLOMITE WALL IV, 5.10, A3, 7 pitches, 450 feet (137 m)

First Ascent: Andrew Tuthill, Mark Whiton, 25–27 March 1989.

Location and Access: *Dolomite Wall* begins up the first fracture system left of *Infrared*.

walk

chimney   5.8+

5.11

5.12A

4" to 5"

5.11   5"

hands

hands

3 1/2"

ow 6" to 8"   5.11 wide
hands

step across
chasm
5.8   5.11-

5.11+
fingers   5.10

5.10 face   5.10+

thin
hands/fingers   wide
hands

hands   5.9

5.11
fingers   thin stem

5.11

51   50   Dolomite Spire

52

Big Bend Butte

Big Bend Butte

Pitch 1: Climb through the soft rock bedding seam, then right of a threatening block and on to a belay ledge, 5.9, 100 feet (30 m).

Pitch 2: Continue up the crack to a good ledge, 5.10, A3, 100 feet (30 m).

Pitch 3: Traverse left on the belay ledge, stepping across a chasm to a 3-bolt belay/rappel station, 5.8.

Pitch 4: Climb a 3–4" crack (7.6–10 cm), then a 6–8" offwidth (9–12 cm) past 3 pitons (Big Bro offsize) and up to a "peapod" belay station with double bolts, 100 feet (30 m).

Pitch 5: Climb past a fixed piton up a 4–5" crack (10–12.7 cm) to a double-bolt belay in a chimney, 50 feet (15 m).

Pitch 6: Continue up a squeeze chimney shared with Pitch 4 of *Clearlight*, 5.10, 50 feet (15 m).

Pitch 7: Scramble to the summit, 50 feet (15 m).

Paraphernalia: Standard desert rack; large Friends; Big Bros; a small selection of pitons.

Descent: Four rappels. Rappel to the top of Pitch 5 from ledges just right of and 50 feet (15 m) below the summit. Rappel from double anchors to the top of Pitch 3. Rappel from triple anchors to a fixed piton and a bolt left of the top of Pitch 1. Rappel to the ground.

52   CLEARLIGHT IV, 5.11+ R, 4 pitches, 450 feet (137 m) ★★★★

First Ascent: Jay Smith, Kitty Calhoun, February 1997.

Location and Access: *Clearlight* begins 1 crack system left of *Dolomite Wall.*

Pitch 1: Climb 5.11 fingers, then hands to thin hands and fingers to a belay ledge with double anchors.

Pitch 2: Pass a fixed anchor, then traverse left face climbing past a second fixed anchor. Back clean and continue up 5.11+ fingers past a pod and on to a hanging belay at double anchors.

Pitch 3: Climb hands, then a 5" (12.7 cm) crack at 5.11 to triple belay anchors at a stance.

Pitch 4: Continue up a chimney with no protection, 5.8+ to the top.

Paraphernalia: Friends (5) #1, (3) #2, (4) #3, #3.5, (2) #4, (1) #6; TCUs (1) #0.3, #0.4, (2) #0.5, (4) #0.75; Quickdraws and runners; 50 meter ropes.

Descent: Fix the end of the trail line to the top of Pitch 3 for the rappel from the summit.

53   VIVALDI PINNACLE II, 5.9 R, AO, 4 pitches, 270 feet (82 m)

First Ascent: German climbers Frank Nebbe, Renate Stockburger, 15 August 1987. Second ascent: Jake Tratiak, Pat Willard, 14 June 1989.

Location and Access: *Vivaldi Pinnacle* is 200 feet (61 m) left of the notch between Dolomite Spire and the right edge of the west face of Big Bend Butte.

Pitch 1: Body jam a flare 20 feet (6 m) right of the actual right side of the pinnacle. Continue up the handcrack above (5.9), then follow cracks to a niche on the right, 5.9, 60 feet (18 m).

Pitch 2: Follow the handcrack for 20 feet (6 m), then tension traverse left to an obvious chimney. Stem past 3 chockstones to a belay in the main chimney, 5.8, AO, 60 feet (18 m).

Pitch 3: Climb the chimney toward a big chockstone (60 feet [18 m], no protection). Belay about 20 feet (6 m) farther at chockstones, 5.6.

Pitch 4: Hand-jam a crack in a corner for 30 feet (9 m), then step left and chimney to the top of the pinnacle, 5.7, 70 feet (21 m).

Paraphernalia: Standard desert rack.

Descent: Downclimb Pitch 4 on the right side of the pinnacle. Traverse to the left side on chockstones, then make 2 rappels to the ground from slings around chockstones.

54   FRIED FLOUNDER I, 5.10b, 1 pitch, 80 feet (24 m) ★★★★

First Ascent: Tony Valdes, Terre Lashier, May 1987.

Location and Access: *Fried Flounder* is approximately 350 feet (107 m) right of the left edge of Big Bend Butte, 100 feet (30 m) right of an obvious leaning flake. Climb thin fingers then hands for 65 feet (20 m) to a roof at a bedding seam. Continue hands to rappel anchors 15 feet (4.5 m) higher and visible from below the route.

Paraphernalia: Friends (3) #1.5, (5) #2.5, (3) #3, (1) #3.5, #4; wired stoppers (2) #0.5, #4.

Descent: Rappel the route from 2 fixed pitons.

55   GRIM REAPER III, 5.10a, 4 pitches, 400 feet (122 m)

First Ascent: Benny Bach, Cameron Burns, 24 March 1987.

Location and Access: *Grim Reaper* is right of *Refuge*, approximately 500 feet (152 m) right of the second gully right of Dolomite Spire.

Pitch 1: Begin at the right side of the gully with 5.10a stemming, then climb a fingertip crack formed by a large left-facing dihedral.

Pitch 2: Continue 5.5 to a ledge, then make a short right traverse before climbing 5.6 and traversing back to the original crack system.

Pitch 3: Climb first 5.8+, then angle right and continue 5.7 to pass the right side of a roof (5.8) and loose blocks on the left.

Pitch 4: From a belay ledge climb 5.7 to a chockstone. Pass the chockstone at 5.5 on the left or 5.7 on the right. Continue 5.6 and traverse left at the next chockstone, then make a 5.9 mantle and continue up easier ground to the top.

Paraphernalia: Friends (1) set, including half-sizes; Tri-cams #1 through #2.5.

Descent: Double-rope rappels down the route.

56   PSYCHO TOAD III, 5.10a, A1, 5 pitches, 400 feet (122 m)

First Ascent: Tony Grenko, Tony Passariello, September 1989.

Location and Access: *Psycho Toad* is 70 feet (21 m) left of *Grim Reaper*. The final 40 feet (12 m) follow *Grim Reaper* to the summit.

Pitch 1: Begin up a 5.9 crack system, then past a section of A1, finishing 5.9 at a belay ledge, 80 feet (24 m).

Pitch 2: Climb 5.9, then A1 past a loose ledge, passing a 5.6 chimney before reaching a belay ledge.

Pitch 3: Continue 5.9 hands, then 5.10a offwidth to a belay ledge.

Pitch 4: Climb a 5.9 roof, then on to a 5.2 right traverse to *Grim Reaper*.

Pitch 5: Follow *Grim Reaper* to the top, 40 feet (12 m).

Paraphernalia: Standard desert rack.

Descent: Rappel *Grim Reaper*.

57   REFUGE III, 5.8, A3, 9 pitches, 400 feet (122 m).

First Ascent: Harvey T. Carter, Tom Merrill, 29 May 1970.

Location and Access: *Refuge* (the first ascent of Big Bend Butte) ascends the first gully right of Dolomite Spire, beneath a prominent notch in the skyline, left of *Psycho Toad*. From the notch the route finishes up the west side of the landform. Several pitons were fixed by the first ascent party.

Paraphernalia: Friends (2) sets; a selection of pitons.

Descent: Rappel the route.

Podium Spire

Podium Spire is behind Big Bend Butte (east) and out of view from River Road. Approach from the drainage at the left side of the butte.

58   PODIUM SPIRE II, 5.9+, 2 pitches, 210 feet (64 m)

First Ascent: Tom Merrill, Wayne Poulsen, 9 October 1970. First free ascent: Tom Merrill, Bob Sullivan, 1972.

Location and Access: Climb from the west to a bench, then to the summit from the east.

Pitch 1: Begin on the west side of the tower and climb a chimney (loose 5.9+ offwidth) to a bench at the base of the spire, 150 feet (46 m).

Pitch 2: Walk left and up to the back side of the tower and an obvious crack, then climb a hand-sized crack to the top, 5.9, 60 feet (18 m).

Paraphernalia: Friends (3) sets through #5.

Descent: Rappel the back side (east) to the bench, then to the ground from a tree on the south side of the tower.

Big Bend Bouldering

This excellent bouldering area is on the right side of the road around the first curve past Big Bend Campground. It is the most popular of the many bouldering regions near Moab. Kevin Chase's *500 Select Moab Classics* identifies 63 bouldering problems on 15 boulders at the site.

Avalon, Towers A, B, C, D

Avalon is high above the Big Bend Bouldering area. Towers A, B, C, and D are small towers leaning against the south Wingate Wall of the peninsula of Mat Martin Point, between mile markers 7 and 8, upriver from Big Bend Campground. Routes are listed from right to left. The towers are located by hiking the Wingate Wall upriver from *Avalon*.

59   AVALON I, 5.10d, 1 pitch, 75 feet (23 m) ★★

First Ascent: Jay Smith, Jo Smith, March 1994.

Location and Access: *Avalon* is on the Wingate buttress above the bouldering area on the right side of River Road between mile markers 7 and 8. The route climbs the outside edge of light-colored rock right of a left-facing dihedral. Begin up a right-angling 1.25" (3 cm) crack at 5.10d. Continue up a thin crack, then ascend 5.10 hands to a belay/rappel stance with slings visible from the bouldering area.

Paraphernalia: Friends (2) #0.5, (3) #0.75, (1) #1, #2, (2) #1.5, (1) #2, (2) #3, (1) #3.5.

Descent: Rappel the route.

60   TOWER A I, 5.7, 1 pitch

First Ascent: Mark Whiton, solo, 24 September 1988.

Location and Access: Begin on the right side up a wide chimney, then climb a slab to the top where there is a small cairn and rappel anchor.

Paraphernalia: Unknown.

Descent: Rappel the route.

61   TOWER B I, 5.8, 1 pitch

First Ascent: Mark Whiton, solo, 25 September 1988.

Location and Access: Ascend the right side of the landform with a 5.8 squeeze leading to a spacious flat summit where there is a small cairn and rappel anchor. The boulder right of *Tower B* was climbed from its left side.

Paraphernalia: Unknown.

Descent: Rappel the route.

62   TOWER C I, 5.7, 1 pitch

First Ascent: Mark Whiton, solo, 25 September 1988.

Location and Access: Climb the right side of the landform. The tiny summit has a small cairn and a rappel anchor.

Paraphernalia: Unknown.

Descent: Rappel the route.

63   TOWER D Unfinished

First Ascent: Mark Whiton, solo to just below top, 25 September 1988.

Location and Access: Mark Whiton: "Didn't reach the top of this one–full body chimney just below top, so couldn't pull across. There might be ways to climb the left corner, but didn't investigate too thoroughly."

Paraphernalia: Unknown.

Descent: Downclimb the route.

Putterman's Buttress (BLM Takeout Buttress)

The following five routes are unusual in that they ascend a cliff band in the Chinle Formation, a stratum of sandstone where few routes are established. *Mt. Julian Fisher* is 500 feet (152 m) downriver from mile marker 10, and climbs a russet-colored tower barely detached from the Chinle wall behind. *Sex Therapy* ascends the obvious hueco (pock-marked) wall left of *Mt. Julian Fisher*. *Porno Night at Eric's* climbs a hueco wall left of *Sex Therapy*, to the right of a small pillar. Left of the small pillar is *Richard the 3rd*. *Playboy Channel* climbs a low-angle, right-facing (left-trending) dihedral left of *Richard the 3rd*. *Shaded Relief* is above the BLM takeout ramp, 10.2 miles up River Road.

64   MT. JULIAN FISHER—FAT BASTARD I, 5.7, 1 pitch, 70 feet (21 m) ★★★

First Ascent: Cameron Burns, Charlie French, 28 September 1997.

Location and Access: *Fat Bastard* climbs the left side of a tower 500 feet (152 m) below mile marker 10. Begin on the left side of the landform up a crack between the tower and the wall behind. Climb 5.6 to a ledge with a bolt, then 5.5 past a bolt to a second stance. Move left and continue up the north face at 5.7, past 2 bolts to the top of the tower.

Paraphernalia: Quickdraws (4).

Descent: Rappel the route from slings around the top of the tower.

65   SEX THERAPY (Top-rope) I, 5.11a, 1 pitch, 70 feet (21 m)

First Ascent: Cameron Burns, Charlie French, 28 September 1997.

Location and Access: *Sex Therapy* climbs the hueco wall right of a dark left-facing corner, left of *Fat Bastard*.

Paraphernalia: Top-rope.

Descent: Rappel from double bolts on the bench at the top of the route.

66   PORNO NIGHT AT ERIC'S I, 5.8, 1 pitch, 70 feet (21 m) ★★★

First Ascent: Cameron Burns, Charlie French, 28 September 1997.

Location and Access: *Porno Night* climbs the first hueco wall left of *Sex Therapy*. There are 4 sets of tied-off slings visible from the road. Climb to the bench shared with *Sex Therapy*.

Paraphernalia: Slings for tying off the huecos.

Descent: Rappel *Sex Therapy* or *Richard the 3rd*.

67   RICHARD THE 3RD I, 5.7, 1 pitch, 70 feet (21 m) ★★★★

First Ascent: Cameron Burns, Charlie French, 28 September 1997.

Location and Access: *Richard the 3rd* climbs the left side of a detached flake left of *Porno Night*. Climb a 5.7 crack that varies in size.

Paraphernalia: Friends (1) set.

Descent: Rappel the route from double bolts on the bench shared with *Porno Night at Eric's* and *Sex Therapy*.

68   PLAYBOY CHANNEL I, 5.5 R, 1 pitch, 90 feet (27 m) ★★★★

First Ascent: Cameron Burns, Charlie French, 28 September 1997.

Location and Access: *Playboy Channel* climbs a low-angle slab left of *Richard the 3rd*.

Paraphernalia: Camalots (1) #2.

Descent: Rappel the route from double bolts.

69   SHADED RELIEF I, 5.11b, 2 pitches, 155 feet (47 m) ★

First Ascent: Bret Ruckman, Stuart Ruckman, 20 May 1991.

Location and Access: *Shaded Relief* is 1 crack system left of the largest overhang on the face. Climb "dicey" rock to a belay ledge, then a left-facing crack (TCUs) over a roof (#2.5 Friend), and up to a double-anchor rappel with slings visible from below on the left wall, 5.11b.

Paraphernalia: Many Friends through #4; a selection of TCUs.

Descent: Rappel the route.

Pleasure-Pain Wall

Pleasure-Pain Wall is on the right side of the road, on the Wingate buttress at the top of the hill, just before mile marker 11. *Whips and Chains* and *S & M* are directly above the first pullout (riverside) downriver from the crest of the hill, just west of a 20 mph sign with a serpentine arrow.

For *Take the Pain, Bring You Pleasure, Girly Man,* and *Norbeast,* park on the left where a dirt road descends to an undeveloped campsite by the river or at a wide spot at the top of the hill, then cross the River Road and scramble up the Chinle slope to the climbs. Routes are listed from right to left.

70   WHIPS AND CHAINS I, 5.11, 1 pitch, 120 feet (37 m) ★★★

First Ascent: Jay Smith, Jo Smith, April 1993.

Location and Access: Right of *S & M* and *Bring You Pleasure*. Rappel bolts are visible below an overhang. Climb a thin right-facing corner. Stem 5.11 past 2 overhangs and a fixed anchor, then 5.10 up a left-trending system past a second fixed anchor, and 5.10+ to light-colored rock. Double rappel anchors are visible from the road.

Paraphernalia: Friends (1) #0.75, #1, #1.5, #2, #3; wires; (3) #0.4 camming units ; quickdraws (2).

Descent: Rappel the rope.

71   S & M I, 5.10+, 1 pitch, 95 feet (29 m)★

First Ascent: Jay Smith, Jo Smith, April 1993.

Location and Access: *S & M* climbs a crack to a large grassy ledge 100 feet (30 m) left of *Whips and Chains*. The rappel anchor is not visible from below. Stem a thin right-facing crack system in the center of the wall, 5.10+. Protect with TCUs and wires. Continue, as the crack becomes 1.25" hand-and-fingers, to the grassy ledge and double rappel anchors.

Paraphernalia: Friends (3) each through #3; TCUs; wires.

Descent: Rappel the route.

72   TAKE THE PAIN I, 5.10a, 2 pitches, 315 feet (96 m) ★★

First Ascent: Jay Smith, Paul Teare, April 1993.

Location and Access: *Take the Pain* is on the buttress left of *Whips and Chains*.

Pitch 1: Begin up a right-facing corner protected with a #4 Friend, 5.10a. Continue hands to a double-anchor belay ledge at the top of a small tower with bolts visible from below, 150 feet (46 m).

Pitch 2: Continue up the right-facing system at 5.10+, thin stemming to fingers and finally thin face to double-rappel anchors visible from below, 165 feet (50 m).

Paraphernalia: Friends; wires (3) #0.4, #0.5, #0.75, (3) #1, #1.5, #2, #2.5, (2) #3, (1) #4.

Descent: Rappel the route.

73   BRING YOU PLEASURE I, 5.10+, 1 pitch, 150 feet (46 m) ★★★★

First Ascent: Jay Smith, Jo Smith, April 1993.

Location and Access: *Bring You Pleasure* is far left of *Take the Pain* on the nose of the wall. The route climbs left of an obvious crack to mid-height on the buttress. Rappel anchors are visible from the road. Gain a prominent ledge from the left and ascend a right-facing corner (5.10+ fingers then hands), finishing left past blocks, then hands to a double-anchor rappel station left of the crack system.

Paraphernalia: Friends (1) #0, #0.5, (3) #0.75, #1, (4) #1.5, (2–3) #2, (3) #2.5, (2) #3.

Descent: Rappel the route.

74   GIRLY MAN I, 5.10a, 1 pitch, 150 feet (46 m) ★

First Ascent: Jay Smith, Jo Smith, May 1991.

Location and Access: *Girly Man* climbs a handcrack/lieback with an anchor visible just left of a roof crack. A vertical crack continues up through a chimney. Approach from the small white bridge on River Road near mile marker 11.

Paraphernalia: Friends (2) sets through #3; quickdraws (1).

Descent: Rappel the route.

75   NORBEAST I, 5.10d, 1 pitch, 120 feet (37 m) ★★★

First Ascent: Jay Smith, Jo Smith, May 1991.

Location and Access: *Norbeast* is 60 feet (15 m) left of *Girly Man.* Follow a crack/corner to a ceiling, then traverse left to fixed anchors. Second pitch has fallen off!

Paraphernalia: Several each finger to hand-sized pieces.

Descent: Rappel the route.

Nuke 'em Rafi, Vuja De, Mystery Route

The three routes are in view on the Wingate buttress above mile marker 12.5, and are listed from right to left. *Nuke 'em Rafi* climbs the right corner of the buttress with *Vuja De* left directly above the 12.5-mile point (20 km). *Mystery Route* is 200 yards (183 m) left of *Vuja De.*

76   NUKE 'EM RAFI I, 5.11a, A1, 1 pitch, 75 feet (23 m)

First Ascent: Jay Miller, Andy Roberts, 2 June 1998.

Location and Access: Climb a rotten squeeze chimney for 15 feet (4.5 m) passing a chockstone. Continue to a roof which is passed on the left with 1 point of aid (probably free at hard 5.11). Climb a 3- to 4-inch crack (7.5–10 cm) 35 feet (10.5 m) to a small stance and a double-bolt anchor. The crack system continues another 80 feet (24 m) but becomes wide and overhanging.

Paraphernalia: Standard desert rack; Camalots #3, #5; long sling for chockstone (1).

Descent: Rappel the route.

photo: Andy Roberts

77   VUJA DE I, 5.10+, 2 pitches, 110 feet (34 m)

First Ascent: Bret Ruckman, Tim Coats, 25 March 1989.

Location and Access: *Vuja De* (the incredible feeling that you've never been there before) is 12.5 miles (20 km) up River Road. Climb a left (north-facing) corner. Rappel slings are visible from below. Bret Ruckman: "Fun corner, north-facing. Wild getting off with 1 rope."

Pitch 1: Begin 5.8 over a broken area to a belay ledge. Protect with a selection of nuts.

Pitch 2: Climb a left-facing corner up good rock, first 5.10+, then 5.9 to a belay from a fixed Hex atop a "bucket." Protect the pitch with (in ascending order) Friends #3, #3.5, #4.

Paraphernalia: Friends #3, #3.5, #4; nuts for Pitch 1.

Descent: Rappel the route.

78   MYSTERY ROUTE I, 5.10, 1 pitch

First Ascent: Unknown.

Location and Access: *Mystery Route* climbs a right-facing crack (#2 Friend) past a fixed anchor to rappel slings visible from below the route. There is graffiti etched in the wall by the first-ascent climbers of the unknown route.

Paraphernalia: Friends (1) #2; quickdraws (1).

Descent: Rappel the route.

Red Cliffs Ranch (a.k.a. White Ranch)

Red Cliffs Ranch, the site of numerous Western movies, is obvious across from mile marker 14.

79   WAY NICE WIFE I, 5.10a, 1 pitch, 90 feet (27 m)

First Ascent: Unknown.

Location and Access: *Way Nice Wife* is approximately 200 yards (183 m) left of where the Wingate buttress above the Red Cliffs Ranch comes closest to River Road. Climb a right-facing dihedral with light-colored rock on the right and dark rock on the left. Further information is unknown.

Paraphernalia: Standard desert rack.

Descent: Rappel the route.

River Tower

River Tower is a distinctive fin of Cutler Sandstone capped with Moenkopi, on the right (east) side of River Road, approximately 1 mile (1.6 km) north of the Fisher Towers. It is obvious at the eastern perimeter of Richardson Amphitheater, a nondescript belly of land bordering the river from the Convent to Hittle Bottom, east to Adobe and Fisher Mesas, and north to Pole Rim Mesa. To reach, drive to mile marker 22 and turn right (across from the turn into Hittle Bottom); then follow the faint track 0.6 mile (0.9 km) up a wash, park by a large juniper tree, and hike cross-country to the tower. Routes are listed from right to left.

80   RASTA WALL IV, 5.7, A4, 5 pitches, 480 feet (146 m) ★★★

First Ascent: Jim Beyer, solo, 18–20 December 1985.

Location and Access: *Rasta Wall* climbs the opposite side of the tower (side facing the Fisher Towers) from *Savage Master* and the *North Face*.

River Tower, south and west faces

Pitch 1: Aid thin cracks to a pendulum swing (right) to a loose flake. Aid out right under a roof, then up a pebbly crack to a belay in an alcove, 140 feet (43 m).

Pitch 2: Aid over a roof (TCUs) to a short A2 flake, 60 feet (18 m).

Pitch 3: Aid a long crack to a "mud glob," then continue past a bolt to a belay on the left, 100 feet (30 m).

Pitch 4: Aid a wide crack out a rotten roof (#4 Friend, #4 Camalot, big hexes) to a belay at a stance, 100 feet (30 m).

Pitch 5: Climb a 5.7 chimney on the caprock to the summit ridge, then 4th class right (80 feet, 24 m) to the summit.

Paraphernalia: The first ascent used many pitons, 13 bolts, a full rack that included (10) knifeblades, (15) Lost Arrows, many angles, and Bongs through 4".

Descent: Downclimb to the 4th belay, then rappel 155 feet (47 m) to the 2nd belay. Finally rappel 140 feet (43 m) to the ground.

81 THE FLOW III, 5.8, A2+, 4 pitches, 450 feet (137 m) ★★★★

First Ascent: Mike Baker, Cameron Burns, April 1997.

Location and Access: The Flow climbs the western prow (tallest side) of River Tower.

Pitch 1: Begin on a ledge on the northwest corner of the tower (the left-hand edge of the western prow) and climb up and right (several bolts) on mixed free and aid to a 2-bolt belay on a large, prominent ledge on the southwestern corner of the prow (A2+).

Pitch 2: Climb a perfect 2- to 3-inch crack for 30 feet (9 m), then up and left on a bolt ladder to a 2-bolt belay at a stance.

Pitch 3: Move left round the northwest corner on several bolts, then continue up a

Ralph E. Burns on *Rasta Wall*

wide crack on mixed free and aid. The pitch ends at a 2-bolt belay ledge below the caprock.

Pitch 4: Aid up and left through a small roof, then climb right up 2 bulges, traverse right 15 feet (4.5 m) on a large ledge, and scramble to the summit. Cameron Burns: "This route will definitely go clean, perhaps on the second ascent."

Paraphernalia: Friends through #4; a selection of small pitons; 1/4-inch hangers (12), 2 ropes.

Descent: Four double-rope rappels down the route.

82   NORTH FACE (A.K.A. WYRICK-MERRILL, NW CORNER) III, 5.8, C1, 4 pitches, 540 feet (165 m) ★★★

First Ascent: Originally 5.8, A2 by Ken Wyrick and Tom Merrill, 8–9 November 1973. First solo: Jon Butler, fall 1995. Mike Baker, solo, 14 November 1996. First clean ascent party is unknown.

Location and Access: *North Face* climbs near the center of the north face of the landform.

Pitch 1: Climb a bolt ladder, then 20 feet (6 m) of C1 to a belay station, 130 feet (40 m).

Pitch 2: Climb mostly free up a chimney (C1, 5.4) to an anchor, 90 feet (27 m).

Pitch 3: Scramble to the false summit ridge, 4th class, 60 feet (18 m).

Pitch 4: From the summit block, rappel 20 feet (6 m) into the notch (no fixed anchors) and reascend to the true summit, 5.8. The first ascent party looped a rope around the summit block and made a 15-foot (5 m) Tyrolean traverse.

Paraphernalia: The first ascent party used a large selection of knifeblades and angle pitons. For the clean ascent bring Camalots (1) set; Tri-cams (1) #0.5, #1, #1.5; Stoppers (1) set; a few 3/8-inch nuts, and hangers with many 1/4-inch nuts and hangers.

Descent: Rappel Pitch 4 to the notch and ascend rappel ropes left to initially gain the notch, then downclimb to the top of Pitch 2 and rappel the route.

83   NORTH FACE VARIATION 5.7, C2

First Ascent: Unknown. Second ascent: Kris Pietryga, 15 November 1997.

Location and Access: Variation to Pitch 2. Climb 15 feet (4.5 m) of Pitch 2, then angle left on an obvious loose chimney (mostly free) to a large ledge with natural protection. Continue 15 feet (4.5 m) right and traverse 20 feet (6 m) to the original anchors.

Paraphernalia: Same as *Wyrick-Merrill*.

84   SAVAGE MASTER III, 5.8 S, A5-, 4 pitches, 225 feet (69 m)

First Ascent: Jim Beyer, solo, 8.5 hours, climbed originally at A5-, 30 September 1986. Retro-bolting by repeat climbers has lowered the rating.

Location and Access: *Savage Master* is on the uphill (shorter) north face of River Tower. To reach, approach *Rasta Wall*, then go over the saddle between the tower and the rimrock behind and continue down the other side to the start of the route. Begin the climb left of *North Face*. The route was rated A5- because there is a possible 40 foot (12 m) ground fall on Pitch 1.

Paraphernalia: Many pitons were used on the first ascent, including (5) RURPs; (15) knifeblades; (10) Lost Arrows; several angles; 4" Bongs; several 1.5" to 2.5" nuts.

Descent: Reverse Pitch 4 (the prusik out of the notch), then rappel *North Face*.

photo: Cameron M. Burns

River Tower

Richardson Amphitheater

Climbs in the Richardson Amphitheater area are on a northwest-southeast–running ridge of the northernmost sector of Richardson Amphitheater, a cirque of rim rock visible on the right from River Road across from the Hittle Bottom boat launch and campground managed by the BLM (restrooms available) between mile markers 23 and 24. At the turn into Hittle Bottom, there is a pioneer gravesite with an iron cross and rail fence. Various dirt tracks branch east (right) from River Road toward the climbs, but the most direct begins just before the cemetery and is passable for 1 mile (1.6 km) with a 2-wheel-drive vehicle. The climbs are a short hike beyond and are most easily reached by dropping over the bank to the left at the end of the dirt road, then hiking up a dry wash. There is a spring at the head of the drainage, right of the towers, but it runs intermittently and may only be reliable in early spring. The northwest-southeast–running ridge on which the climbs are located is easily reached by hiking from the wash in line with the col between *Hidden Tower*, *Scorpion*, and *Dark Spire* (the farthest right of the group). *Hidden Tower* is the butte adjacent to the left. *Scorpion* is the landform farthest left (north) on the ridge. Routes are listed from right to left.

85   DARK SPIRE II, 5.7, A4, 2 pitches, 150 feet (46 m)

First Ascent: Jim Beyer, solo, 22 December 1985. Second ascent: Brad Bond, Stu Ritchie, Rob Slater, October 1993.

Location and Access: The tower was climbed from the notch on its left side.

Pitch 1: Climb the rotten band on the north face on a stack of loose blocks. Traverse right on A1 under a 3-foot roof (0.9 m), then free climb up a right-facing dihedral to the col below the spire. Continue 10 feet (3 m) up the north corner to a small ledge. Step right to the center of the northwest face and face climb to a higher ledge. Walk to the west face to a good belay ledge, 5.7, A1, 100 feet (30 m).

Pitch 2: Step back to the north face. Stacks and bashies lead past 1 bolt to an A1 crack near the top of the rock, A4, 50 feet (15 m).

Paraphernalia: The first ascent used a regular nut rack; knifeblades and Lost Arrows (8); (2) each angle pitons through 2"; Leepers (6); a wide selection of copperheads and bashies. **Note:** Please repeat the climb in Jim Beyer's good style or climb something within your ability. Do not degrade the route (or any desert climb) with additional anchors.

Descent: Rappel from a 1.5" angle near the top of the rock.

86   HIDDEN TOWER I, 5.7, 2 pitches, 150 feet (46 m)

First Ascent: Harvey T. Carter, solo, late 1960s.

Location and Access: *Hidden Tower* ascends the south edge of the landform beginning a few feet left of the *Dark Spire* notch.

Paraphernalia: Friends (1) set; nuts (1) set. An assortment of pitons were used on the first ascent.

Descent: Rappel the route.

87   STINGER—WEST FACE II, 2 pitches, 200 feet (61 m)

First Ascent: Unknown.

Location and Access: The *West Face* route climbs the obvious crack system on the river side of the tower.

Pitch 1: Begin up thin cracks which become wide at a bulge. Pass 2 bolts and continue up a chimney to a double-bolt belay, 165 feet (50 m).

Pitch 2: Scramble up poor rock to the summit, 35 feet (11 m).

Paraphernalia: Thin units up through 5"; quickdraws.

Descent: Rappel the route.

88   STINGER—EAST FACE II, 5.9, A2, 2 pitches, 200 feet (61 m)

First Ascent: Brad Bond, Alden Strong, April 1998.

Location and Access: *East Face* was the second ascent of Stinger.

Pitch 1: Aid through rotten rock for 25 feet (7.6 m), then follow a wide crack to the bench above, 165 feet (50 m).

Pitch 2: Scramble to the summit following Pitch 2 of the *West Face* route.

Paraphernalia: Two sets of Friends and TCUs through 5"; Stoppers (1) set; a few long thin Lost Arrows for the start of the climb.

Descent: Rappel the *West Face* route.

89   SCORPION II, 5.9 R, 2 pitches, 165 feet (50 m)

First Ascent: Harvey T. Carter, Eric Bjørnstad, 23 April 1987. Second ascent Brad Bond, Stu Ritchie, Rob Slater, October 1993.

Location and Access: *Scorpion* begins on the west face, 20 feet (6 m) left of the crack and chimney system which leads to the prominent notch in the skyline left of a tower.

Pitch 1: Traverse up and right over a layer of mud along a ramp which passes beneath an 8-foot (2 m) guillotine-like flake leaning out from the wall. Gain the obvious crack and chimney system above. Climb to the large chockstone at the notch, pass under it to the east side of the rock, then continue up cracks to the top of the chockstone.

Pitch 2: Climb from the chockstone directly to the summit platform. The highest point of the rock is obvious—it's a 3rd-class hike to the northernmost tip of the landform.

Paraphernalia: Friends (2) sets; nuts (1) set.

Descent: Downclimb the chimney to the top of the chockstone at the notch, then rappel 150 feet (46 m) to the ground.

Kings Toll Road Buttress

Unknown Splitter is on the Wingate buttress across the river from the rock inscribed "Toll Road," between mile markers 26 and 27.

90   UNKNOWN SPLITTER II, Rating unknown

First Ascent: Unknown.

Location and Access: The route climbs an obvious splitter crack at the left end of the Wingate buttress on the north side of the river.

Paraphernalia: Standard desert rack.

Descent: Rappel the route from anchors visible with binoculars from River Road.

Indian Chief

Indian Chief is a Wingate tower above mile marker 28. It is named for its obvious profile as you drive upriver on River Road.

91   INDIAN CHIEF—TALKING BULL I, 5.7, 2 pitches, 100 feet (30 m) ★

First Ascent: FBI (Fat Bastards International) Climbing Team, 1 March 1998.

Location and Access: *Talking Bull* is accessed by hiking the drainage left (north) of the tower, then back right (west) along a bench 100 feet (30 m) below the mesa top. Approximately 150 feet (46 m) left of the base of the tower is a gully (5.7) that leads to the mesa top. There are 2 bolts (for the descent) at the top of the gully. Walk along the mesa top to a 15-foot gap separating the mesa from Indian Chief. Downclimb into the notch, then to the summit of the spire.

Paraphernalia: Friends (1) set; TCUs (1) #0.

Descent: Reverse the route, then rappel the gully.

Dewey Bridge Area

Fear and Loathing Towers are obvious to the north of Dewey Bridge. To reach, take the dirt road (signed Kokopelli Mountainbike Trail) at the upriver end of the Dewey Bridge 0.2 mile (0.3 km) to a fork. Drive 0.1 mile (0.16 km), then turn right and pass through a red cattle gate (leave it as you find it, open or closed). Continue southwest to the east face of the towers. Hike around the southern end of the ridge on which the towers stand to reach the west face of the landform and the start of the routes.

Spite Wider is left of a lone, large cottonwood tree on the left side of the road just beyond mile marker 30. *Feasant Plucker* is 30 feet (9 m) right of *Spite Wider* and also left of the lone cottonwood tree. *Albino Groove* is 0.3 mile (0.4 km) west of Proud Foot Bend Ranch.

92   FEAR—MORE BEER I, 3rd class, A2-, 2 pitches, 80 feet (24 m) ★★★

First Ascent: Cameron Burns, Charlie French, 30 September 1997.

Location and Access: *Fear* is the left tower when viewed from the Dewey Bridge. *More Beer* climbs the west face of the tower.

Pitch 1: From below *Loathing*, scramble up and right (south) along a bench (class 3) that leads to the base of the top portion of *Fear*. Belay below an obvious crack on the northwest side of *Fear's* summit. An alternate approach is by a 4th class chimney directly below the landform.

Pitch 2: Cameron Burns: "Classic A2- nailing leads up the 50-foot crack. The rock is excellent." Begin C1, then continue with A2- climbing to a 3-bolt summit anchor.

Paraphernalia: Camalots #0.5, #1, #3; medium stoppers; angle pitons (2) 0.5, 5/8"; Lost Arrows (2).

Descent: Make a 1-rope rappel down the west face.

93   LOATHING—LESS CLOTHING I, 5.7, C1 (1 move of aid), 2 pitches, 80 feet (24 m) ★★

First Ascent: Charlie French, Cameron Burns, 30 September 1997.

Location and Access:

Pitch 1: From below the tower, scramble right (south) along a bench (class 3) that

Fear (left) and Loathing

leads to the base of the top portion of *Fear*. Move left (north) along an obvious ledge that leads to the base of the summit pinnacle of *Loathing* and belay.

Pitch 2: Traverse left 30 feet (9 m) to an obvious crack that varies in width. Climb 5.7 to a stance below the summit. Mount the summit with an etrier (the only aid move on the route).

Paraphernalia: Camalots (1) set; etrier (1).

Descent: Make a 1-rope rappel down the west face from double-bolt anchors.

94   SPITE WIDER I, 5.8, 1 pitch, 60 feet (18 m)

First Ascent: Cameron Burns, Charlie French, 29 September 1997.

Location and Access: *Spite Wider* climbs an obvious right-leaning corner at the left end of a light-colored Navajo Sandstone slab. Rappel anchors are visible from below the route.

Paraphernalia: Friends (1) set; stoppers (1) set.

Descent: Rappel the route.

95.   FEASANT PLUCKER (Top-rope) I, 5.11a, 1 pitch, 60 feet (18 m) ★★★★★

First Ascent: Cameron Burns, Charlie French, 29 September 1997.

Location and Access: *Feasant Plucker* climbs a smooth white slab right of *Spite Wider*.

Paraphernalia: Top-rope.

Descent: Rappel the route from anchors shared with *Spite Wider*.

photo: Cameron M. Burns

Charlie French on Loathing Tower

photo: Cameron M. Burns

96 ALBINO GROOVE I, 5.9, 1 pitch, 60 feet (18 m) ★★★★★

First Ascent: Charlie French, Cameron Burns, 29 September 1997.

Location and Access: *Albino Groove* is 500 feet (152 m) right of *Feasant Plucker* on the left side of the road across from a lone, large juniper tree. It may also be identified by its position at the point where white Navajo Sandstone first comes within 5 feet (1.5 m) of the roadway. Begin up a seam at 5.9, then continue 5.7 to 2 drilled angles (rappel anchors.)

Paraphernalia: Small Friends (1) set; stoppers (1) set.

Descent: Rappel from anchors barely visible from below the route.

You want a place where you can be serene, that will let you contemplate and connect two consecutive thoughts, or that if need be can stir you up as you were made to be stirred up, until you blend with the wind and water and earth you almost forgot you came from. There must be room enough for time— where the sun can calibrate the day, not the wristwatch, for days or weeks of unordered time, time enough to forget the feel of the pavement and to get the feel of the earth, and of what is natural and right.

–David Brower, *The Place No One Knew*

XX

5.7

5.9

96

photo: Ed Cooper

Left to right: **The Priest, The Nuns, The Rectory (large butte) and Castleton Tower**

CASTLE VALLEY

A weird, lovely, fantastic object out of nature . . . has the curious ability to remind us–like rock and sunlight and wind and wilderness–that OUT THERE is a different world, older and greater and deeper by far than ours, a world which surrounds and sustains the little world of men as sea and sky surround and sustain a ship. The shock of the real. For a little while we are again able to see, as the child sees, a world of marvels. For a few moments we discover that nothing can be taken for granted, for if this ring of stone is marvelous then all which shaped it is marvelous, and our journey here on earth, able to see and touch and hear in the midst of tangible and mysterious things-in-themselves, is the most strange and daring of all adventures.

–Edward Abbey, *Desert Solitaire*, 1968

Castle Valley lies in a northwest-to-southeast direction, approximately 7 air miles (11.3 km) northeast of and parallel to Moab Valley. It is 4,400 feet (1341 m) above sea level at its lower northwest end near the Colorado River, and 5,600 feet (1707 m) at its higher southeast end where it abuts the 12,721-foot (3877 m) La Sal Mountains. The noncommercial valley (a salt valley like Moab Valley) has been subdivided with a grid of roads (paved and unpaved) and is home to more than 200 residents. Most of the climbing interest in the area has centered around Castleton Tower (a.k.a. Castle Rock), which presides over the valley and is more frequently climbed than any other tower on the Colorado Plateau. The south face *Kor-Ingalls* route is one of Steck and Roper's *Fifty Classic Climbs of North America.*

In the distant past, all the formations visible from Castle Valley–Parriott Mesa, Convent, Sister Superior, Priest and Nuns, Rectory, Castleton Tower– were part of a vast mesa separating Castle Valley from Professor Valley and Adobe Mesa to the east. The Sister Superior group will likely be the first of the units to crumble to a talus slope. Perhaps by then the Convent and Rectory will have weathered into a group of dramatic free-standing pinnacles.

Map

The *Moab East* map published by Latitude 40-Degrees, Inc., is the most useful for this chapter. In the Castle Valley area it names Dry Mesa, Mayberry Orchard, Parriott Mesa, Convent, Priest and Nuns, Rectory, and Castle Rock. In the Fisher Towers region it names Hindu, Mystery Towers, Titan, Echo, Cottontail, King Fisher, and Lizard Rock.

Parriott Mesa

Parriott Mesa is at the entry to Castle Valley. It is on the left (east) after you turn right from River Road just beyond mile marker 15. A sign reads "Castle Valley, La Sal Mountain Loop Road." The road parallels Parriott Mesa as it winds up Porcupine Canyon and over Pace Hill, then descends right into Castle Valley town. There are several climbing routes on the Wingate Wall parallel to the road, and three routes along the south end of the mesa where it borders Castle Valley. No

photo: Eric Bjørnstad

Parriott Mesa and Crooked Arrow Spire (left)

routes exist along the east walls except for Crooked Arrow Spire at the northeast tip of the mesa (approached from River Road). At the southeast point of the mesa there is an easy, yet challenging 5th-class route (protected by a steel cable at one spot) that is popular with enterprising local hikers. Climbing routes are listed from left to right along the west, south, then east walls of the mesa.

1   ALICE IN SAND I, 5.8+, 1 pitch, 100 feet (30 m)

First Ascent: Tony Grenko, Tony Passariello, 1989.

Location and Access: *Alice in Sand* is below a large roof, 400 yards (366 m) right of the left edge of the mesa's west-facing buttress. Climb an offwidth chimney 100 feet (30 m) left of *Frogger Sanction Marble*.

Paraphernalia: Protection for an offwidth chimney.

Descent: Rappel the route from double anchors.

2   FROGGER SANCTION MARBLE I, 5.10a, 1 pitch, 100 feet (30 m)

First Ascent: Tony Passariello, Tony Grenko, 1989.

Location and Access: *Frogger Sanction Marble* is 100 feet (30 m) right of *Alice in Sand*. Begin with fingers up a right-facing crack system, past a roof, and end at a pillar with 5.10a hands.

Paraphernalia: Friends (1) set.

Descent: Rappel the route from slings around a pillar.

3   **LEAP FROGGIN' FOOL MARBLE I, 5.10c, 1 pitch, 100 feet (30 m)**

First Ascent: Tony Passariello, Tony Grenko, 1989.

Location and Access: *Leap Froggin' Fool Marble* is approximately 200 yards (183 m) right of *Frogger Sanction Marble*. Climb a left-facing crack system to a 2-foot (0.6 m) ledge, then continue up a wide right-facing crack to a fixed hexentric below a roof.

Paraphernalia: TCUs #0; tiny nuts.

Descent: Rappel the route from a fixed hexentric.

4   **SOUTHWEST ROUTE III, 5.8, 6 pitches, 450 feet (137 m)**

First Ascent: Harvey T. Carter, free solo, 28 April 1966.

Location and Access: *Southwest Route* follows weaknesses on the southwest end of the mesa. Approach from the top of Pace Hill where a dirt road branches left to the base of the mesa. This is an excellent area to camp when mosquitos, no-see-ems, and other flying biters are about the riverlands.

Paraphernalia: None used on original ascent.

Descent: Same as for *Ascended Yoga Masters.*

5   **ASCENDED YOGA MASTERS III, 5.10 R, AO, 5 pitches, 435 feet (133 m) ★★★★**

First Ascent: Earl Wiggins, Katy Cassidy, George Hurley, 25 March 1988.

Location and Access: Same approach as *Southwest Route,* see above. *Ascended Yoga Masters* climbs the southwest end of the mesa, up the most obvious crack system, starting small and becoming 4 feet (1.2 m) wide and very deep by the third lead. To locate the start of the climb, look for a TV antenna which runs from Castle Valley to an anchor at the base of the mesa. From the antenna, walk left on a ledge to the start of the route.

Pitch 1: Lieback a few feet to an offwidth, then climb a tight chimney. The belay stance is on chockstones where the chimney widens. The belay anchor is a drilled 5-inch piton and a large tied-off chockstone, 5.10, 130 feet (40 m).

Pitch 2: Continue up an easier chimney, climbing to a ledge and a large chockstone. Protect with Friends and TCUs, 5.8, 100 feet (30 m).

Pitch 3: Chimney (very wide) or stem deep into a "bottomless gash" to reach a Friend crack approximately 50 feet (15 m) out from the belay stance, then continue to 2 drilled-in Warthogs, 5.9 (with no protection for the first 50 feet, 15 m), 155 feet (47 m). George Hurley: "It is on the third lead that you need your ascended yoga training."

Pitch 4: Free climb easily up and right from the 2 Warthogs to a large ledge which spirals back over the top of the crack/chimney/gash previously climbed. Anchor to a large block on a ledge, 5.5, 20 feet (6 m).

Pitch 5: From the left edge of the ledge step up onto a block, then aid up 3 bolts (AO). Face climb up and left to the top, 5.7, AO, 30 feet (9 m).

Paraphernalia: Friends (1) set; TCUs (1) set; a few wired nuts; 6" or 7" tube chocks (2) or Big Bros.

Descent: Walk east to the high point of the southern end of the mesa, then go north to find the upper end of *Cable Route.* Some route finding will be required. Lower, on the descent trail down the Chinle slope, go east around the southern end of the mesa, then south to the road.

photo: Cassidy/Wiggins

George Hurley on first lead of *Ascended Yoga Masters*

6   FAT CRACK NAMED DESIRE III, 5.11-, 4 pitches, 430 feet (131 m) ★★

First Ascent: Keith Reynolds, Bob Novellino, December 1993.

Location and Access: *Fat Crack Named Desire* climbs a splitter crack on the blank wall right of *Ascended Yoga Master.*

Pitch 1: Begin with fists up a right-facing corner to double handcracks and a belay stance, 120 feet (37 m).

Pitch 2: Climb past a block, up a left-facing corner (#4 Friends), then offwidth to a belay in a pod (no fixed anchors), 5.10+, 100 feet (30 m).

Pitch 3: Climb offwidth past a bulge, then 5.10 hands to a belay from drilled pitons, 5.11-, 120 feet (37 m).

Pitch 4: Climb sloping rock with offwidth to the top, 5.7, 90 feet (27 m).

Paraphernalia: Friends (2) #1.5, (1) #3, (5) #4; Camalots (2) #4, (1) #7; Big Bros (1) #2, #3; Hexentrics (1) #11.

Descent: Downclimb sloping rock to the top of Pitch 4, then make 3 rappels down the route.

7   KING KRIMSON II, 5.11-, 2 pitches, 260 feet (79 m)

First Ascent: Jay Smith, Jo Smith, April 1994.

Location and Access: *King Krimson* climbs the right-facing corner at the far right side of the south face of Parriott Mesa (far right of *Fat Crack Named Desire*). *King Krimson* ends about three-fourths of the way up the Wingate wall, not reaching the mesa top.

Pitch 1: Begin 5.10-, then 5.10 to a belay ledge. Scramble 4th class up and left to a second belay ledge.

Pitch 2: Climb a right-facing corner with liebacking, 5.11-, to double rappel anchors.

Paraphernalia: Friends (2) #0.75, #0.4, #0.5, (3) #1, (4) #1.5, (5) #2, (2) #2.5, #3; stoppers (1) #7.

Descent: Rappel the route.

8   CABLE ROUTE II, 5th class, approximately 400 feet (122 m)

First Ascent: Unknown.

Location and Access: *Cable Route* has a fixed cable protecting a steep section of the ascent. It has long been popular with adventurous local hikers. It is on the east side of the southernmost tip of Parriott Mesa, facing north, directly opposite the *Southwest Route.* Much route finding is required to ascend this old line to the top of the mesa.

Paraphernalia: You may want a rope and protection for a belay.

Descent: Downclimb the route.

9   CROOKED ARROW SPIRE—LONGBOW CHIMNEY III, 5.8+, A1, 2 pitches, 300 feet (91 m) ★★

First Ascent: Harvey T. Carter, Ken Wyrick, 27 September 1974. Second ascent: Mark Rolofson, Mack Johnson, 3 March 1978.

Location and Access: *Crooked Arrow* is an aesthetic spire which continues to attract climbers even though the summit is reached by a 21-bolt ladder. It is in view from River Road, at the northeast tip of Parriott Mesa, across from the county gravel pile, 0.5 mile (0.8 km) upriver from the junction of Castle Valley Road and River Road.

Pitch 1: Begin on the left side of the spire up a chimney to the col between the tower and the mesa behind it.

Pitch 2: Climb a thin crack, then a bolt ladder to the summit.
Paraphernalia: Friends (2) sets (Pitch 1 only); Stoppers (4) medium; wires (2) for Pitch 2.
Descent: Rappel to the north, then down the chimney of Pitch 1.

Castleton Tower (a.k.a. Castle Rock)

From the entrance to Castle Valley, this 400-foot (122 m) stout tower is obvious southeast of Parriott Mesa where it is perched atop a 1,000-foot (305 m) talus pedestal of Chinle Sandstone. The summit of the spire is 6,656 feet (2015 m) above sea level. Castleton Tower is named for an early settlement in upper Castle Valley. It is known by locals and identified on maps as Castle Rock. To reach, drive 0.7 mile (1.1 km) beyond the right turn into the town of Castle Valley. Park/camp at the draw closest to the south face of the tower (0.5 mile [0.8 km] past a cattleguard). The BLM and American Mountain Foundation have constructed a 2.4-mile (3.8 km) trail (approximately 1 hour) to the base of the north face. Please use it to protect endangered plant communities (*Mantzelia shultziorum* and *Cycladenia humilis* var. *ionesii*) and delicate cryptobiotic crust on the Chinle approach slope. It is estimated that in the past there were 5.5 miles (8.8 km) of social trails which severely diminished the aesthetic and ecological value of the area. The BLM trail is reached from the gully leading toward Castleton from the parking/camping area. Climbing routes are listed from right to left, beginning on the south face.

White crystallization on the faces and in the fractures of Castleton Tower are aragonite and calcite minerals formed by geyser activity long before the tower was sculpted by millions of years of erosional forces. Castleton, Rectory, Nuns, Priest, and Convent probably owe their existence to this mineral, which hardened their surfaces and, in turn, slowed their erosion.

CAUTION: More than most towers in the desert, Castleton is a natural lightning rod. Harvey T. Carter was knocked unconscious by a strike at the base of the tower after making the second ascent in 1962. In 1995, a climber was killed in the North Chimney by lightning, and later in the year another climber was struck on the Kor-Ingalls route and air-rescued to a Grand Junction hospital. **NEVER** attempt a desert tower climb during inclement weather. We don't have earthquakes, widespread floods (occasional local flash floods), or tornados on the high deserts of the Colorado Plateau, but each year in the Moab area lives are lost to lightning, as well as drowning in the Colorado River.

Chronology of Ascents: Route; Date; Party

1. *Kor-Ingalls*; 14–15 September 1961; Layton Kor, Huntley Ingalls
2. *Kor-Ingalls*, first free ascent; 23 May 1962; Harvey T. Carter, Cleve McCarty
3. *Kor-Ingalls*; October 1963; Chuck Pratt, Steve Roper
4. *Kor-Ingalls*; 1968; Royal Robbins, Liz Robbins, Pat Ament
5. *North Chimney*; 2 April 1970; Daniel Burgette, Allen Erickson
6. *Kor-Ingalls*; September 1970; Jimmy Dunn, Stewart Green
7. *North Chimney*; September 1970; Jimmy Dunn, Dan Porter
8. *West Face*; 20–21 November 1971; Jimmy Dunn, Billy Westbay, Stewart Green
9. *North Face*; spring 1972; Jimmy Dunn, Doug Snively,
* *Kor-Ingalls*, first solo ascent; 1977; Mark Hesse
* *West Face*, first free ascent; June 1978; Ed Webster, Mark Rolofson
* *North Face*, first free ascent; April 1994; Jay Smith, Mark Hesse

photo: Cameron M. Burns

Climbers on Pitch 3 of the Kor-Ingalls route

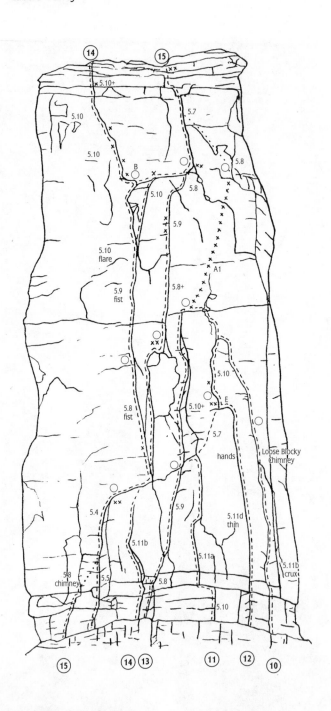

Castleton Tower, South Face

South Face

10 ARROWHEAD—LITTLE WHITE LIEBACK III, 5.11b, A1, 2 pitches, 400 feet (122 m)

First Ascent: Jeff Achey, Chip Chace, 1981.

Location and Access: *Arrowhead* is a large flake system on the extreme right side of the south face. The route ascends the right side of the Arrowhead formation (5.11b) up a right-facing corner to merge with Pitch 2 of *Stardust Cowboy*, A1.

Paraphernalia: Standard desert rack.

Descent: Three rappels down *North Face* from chains.

11 STARDUST COWBOY III, 5.11, A1, 4 pitches, 400 feet (122 m)

First Ascent: Ed Webster, Chester Dreiman, November 1982.

Location and Access: *Stardust Cowboy* climbs the left side of the Arrowhead. Begin 2 crack systems right of the *Kor-Ingalls*, or 1 crack right of the left side of *Arrowhead*.

Pitch 1: Climb past a roof and up 5.11 past a second roof where the crack continues 5.9 hands to the ledge of *Kor-Ingalls'* first belay.

Pitch 2: From the extreme right edge of the belay ledge, climb a 5.7 arête (bolt) to a fragile 5.10- lieback flake, past loose blocks to a belay ledge (2-bolt anchor) on top of *Arrowhead*.

Pitch 3: An A1 bolt ladder ascends a white wall portion of the tower, at a belay ledge even with the Pitch 4 (and last) belay on *Kor-Ingalls*.

Pitch 4: Ascend up and right of a detached pillar, then behind it and back left toward *Kor-Ingalls* and the summit.

Paraphernalia: Friends (3) sets through #3; many carabiners for the bolt ladder.

Descent: Three rappels down *North Face* from chains.

12 STARDUST COWBOY—HOLLOW POINT VARIATION I, 5.11+, 1 pitch, 160 feet (48 m) ★★★

First Ascent: Jay Smith, Bob Novellino, May 1994.

Location and Access: *Hollow Point* is a variation to Pitch 1 of *Stardust Cowboy*. Begin right of *Stardust Cowboy* and left of *Little White Lieback*.

Paraphernalia: TCUs (4) #0.4, (2) #0.5, (3) #0.75, (2) #1, #1.5, #2; wires (3) 2.5, 3, (1) 3.5.

Descent: Rappel the pitch.

13 ARROWHEAD LEFT III, 5.10+, A1, 4 pitches, 400 feet (122 m)

First Ascent: Ed Webster, Chester Dreiman, October 1982.

Location and Access: *Arrowhead Left* climbs the left side of the Arrowhead.

Pitch 1: Begin 1 crack right of the *Kor-Ingalls* and ascend to a large belay ledge by a 5.8 roof, then 5.9 offwidth.

Pitch 2: Traverse (5.8) to a vertical crack system and climb with fingers up thin flakes (5.10+) past wedged blocks to the top of a flake and a bolt anchor, approximately 110 feet (34 m) up the tower. Continue to the top of the Arrowhead where the route meets *Stardust Cowboy*.

Pitch 3 and 4: Follow *Stardust Cowboy* to the summit, A1.

Paraphernalia: Standard desert rack; Quickdraws.

Descent: Three rappels down *North Face* from chains.

14   BURNING INSIDE III, 5.11b, 4 pitches, 400 feet (122 m) ★★★

First Ascent: Jay Smith, Paul Teare, Bob Novellino, May 1994.

Location and Access: *Burning Inside* begins right of *Kor-Ingalls* and left of *Arrowhead Left.* Pitches 2 and 3 follow *Black Sun.* Pitch 4 angles left to the top, passing some fixed gear, 5.10d.

Paraphernalia: Friends (3) #1, (2) #1.5, #2; TCUs (3) 0.4, (2) #0.5, (3) #0.75, (1) #2.5, #3; wires (1) set.

Descent: Three rappels down *North Face* from chains.

15   KOR-INGALLS III, 5.9, 4 pitches, 400 feet (122 m) ★★★★★

First Ascent: Layton Kor, Huntley Ingalls, 14–15 September 1961. First free ascent: Harvey T. Carter, Cleve McCarty, 23 May 1962. Second free ascent: Chuck Pratt, Steve Roper, October 1963. First solo ascent: Mark Hesse, 1977. First free solo: Mark Whiton, 1988. Second free solo: Charlie Fowler, 1988.

Location and Access: This most popular route on the tower begins on the left side of the south face and follows obvious dihedrals and crack systems angling first right then vertically to the summit. There are good belay ledges at the top of each pitch with double- and triple-bolt anchors. Huntley Ingalls: "It was late afternoon when we arrived at Castleton Valley. Above us, the 400-foot prism of Castleton Tower, topping a thousand-foot-high ridge, dominated the valley. Dark, red, old, weathered, it looked eerie in the last rays of sunlight. Next morning the desert was still and bright in the clear air. Sparsely inhabited at the time, we had the valley to ourselves. Late in the morning, trudging up the steep, loose slope, our excitement grew. This was not only an unclimbed tower, but a new area; nothing quite like the mystique of being the first to reach an untouched summit."

Pitch 1: Begin up a 5.6 crack to a ledge 20 feet (6 m) above ground, then up a squeeze chimney climbed at 5.5. Ascend a second chimney to a belay ledge, 5.4, 140 feet (43 m).

Pitch 2: Climb the right crack past a block to a belay ledge, 5.8, 100 feet (30 m).

Pitch 3: Continue (wide) up a left-facing corner at 5.8+, then 5.9 (crux). Climb past a bolt, and make face moves to a belay ledge left of a chimney, 5.9, 100 feet (30 m).

Pitch 4: Start up the chimney, then climb up, angling left (5.7, 5.8) to a ledge, then to the summit at 5.8, 80 feet (24 m).

Paraphernalia: Friends (1) set; Camalots (1) set; Big Bros #3, #4 optional.

Descent: Three rappels down *North Face* from chains, or rappel the route, taking great care with loose rocks and other parties.

16   BLACK SUN III, 5.10b, 4 pitches, 400 feet (122 m)

First Ascent: Ed Webster, Mark Hopkins, Leonard Coyne, November 1977.

Location and Access: *Black Sun* begins up *Kor-Ingalls* before branching left on the second pitch.

Pitch 1: Climb Pitch 1 of *Kor-Ingalls,* 140 feet (43 m).

Pitch 2: Continue up a squeeze chimney (5.8) above the left end of the large belay ledge at the top of Pitch 1. Belay at a stance.

Pitch 3: Climb 5.10 fist and offwidth past a small roof and up to a stance. Continue up a 5.10 offwidth. Tunnel behind a difficult chockstone, or, as did the first ascent party,

photo: Layton Kor

First ascent of Castleton Tower, 1961

over the left side of the chockstone at 5.10, and belay on a large ledge to the left of the notch reached by *Kor-Ingalls*, 60 feet (18 m).

Pitch 4: Climb to the summit up the crack system just left of *Kor-Ingalls*, 5.8.

Paraphernalia: Friends (2) sets, including #4.5, #5; Camalots (1) #5; Big Bros (1) #6.

Descent: Three rappels down *North Face* from chains.

West Face

17　RAPTOR MOSHE I, A1, 1 pitch, 50 feet (15 m)

First Ascent: Jason Keith, Dan Osman, early 1990.

Location and Access: *Raptor Moshe* is immediately left of *Kor-Ingalls* and climbs a bolt ladder to rappel anchors.

Paraphernalia: Quickdraws.

Descent: Rappel the route.

18　WEST FACE III, 5.11-, 4 pitches, 400 feet (154 m) ★★★★

First Ascent: Jimmy Dunn, Billy Westbay, Stewart Green, 20–21 November 1971. First free ascent: Ed Webster, Mark Rolofson, June 1978. Cassidy-Wiggins speaking of the first ascent: "The climb took everything the threesome could muster." Stewart Green: "Jimmy aided out over the overhang tying several large loose blocks together before beating pins all around them." Cassidy-Wiggins: "Above that the crack became too

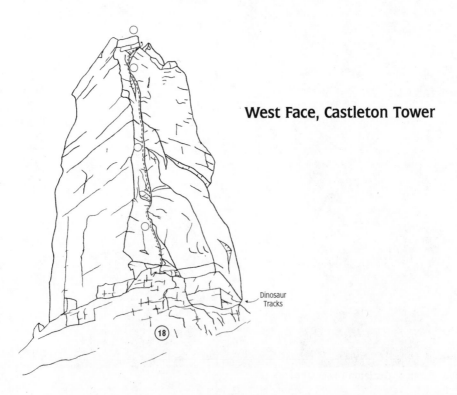

West Face, Castleton Tower

Dinosaur
Tracks

wide to nail and Billy took over the lead. He fought for several hours to inch his way up the steep pitch. . . . For protection, Westbay was stacking Bongs endwise and gently tapping them into the crack. Green: "None of us really believed they would hold a fall." Cassidy-Wiggins: "Slowly the three made progress, and by the afternoon on the second day they were safely on top, having completed one of the hardest desert climbs of the era."

Location and Access: *West Face* follows the only prominent crack system on the long west face of the tower. The cruxes are past "torpedo blocks" and wide cracks on Pitch 3.

NOTE: There are numerous dinosaur prints under the large overhang to the right of the route.

Pitch 1: Begin on the left side of the west face. Climb broken rock, then a 5.9 offwidth to 5.10 and onto a belay ledge, 100 feet (30 m).

Pitch 2: Continue up a 5.9, 3–4" (4.6–6 cm) crack system, 5.9, 60 feet.

Pitch 3: Climb a 5.9 chimney, then 5.11- past the "torpedo blocks" (4–5"). Eventually, a short traverse right gains a more moderate but exposed hand crack which gains an alcove belay. 5.11-, 160 feet.

Pitch 4: Continue up a 5.10 offwidth, then 5.9 and finally 5.6 to the summit, 5.10, 80 feet (23 m).

Paraphernalia: Camalots (2) sets through #4; a few TCUs; medium to large nuts.

Descent: Three rappels down *North Face* from chains.

North Face

---

19   SUN, MOON, AND STARS IV, 5.11d, A3+, 5 pitches, 400 feet (122 m) ★★★★

First Ascent: Jim Beyer, Pat McInerny, 25 October 1993

Location and Access: *Sun, Moon, and Stars* is between *North Face* and the *West Face* arete. Only 4 bolts were placed and pitches 1, 2, and 4 are all free. Begin up the rightmost of the three cracks on the lower wall of the north face.

Pitch 1: Climb 5.11a/b left of the arete or 5.11c up the fingertip crack to the right. Pass a bolt placed by an earlier party and belay at the top of the structure.

Pitch 2: Climb 5.10d past a fixed anchor, angling right to a double anchor belay.

Pitch 3: Ascend first with hooking, then up A3, and finally move right to climb with Bird Beaks and A3+ to a belay.

Pitch 4: Climb 5.10a/b, then move right and climb hands to a belay.

Pitch 5: Climb 5.10d offwidth past a fixed anchor to a roof. Move right and ascend A2 to 5.6 and on to the summit.

Paraphernalia: Gear to 6"; pitons (10), mostly thin; hooks and Bird Beaks.

Descent: Three rappels down *North Face* from chains.

20   ANOTHER WORLD VARIATION I, 5.11c ★★★★

First Ascent: Paul Turecki, Nancy Pfeiffer, 1988.

Location and Access: This was the first free ascent of the excellent first pitch of *Sun,*

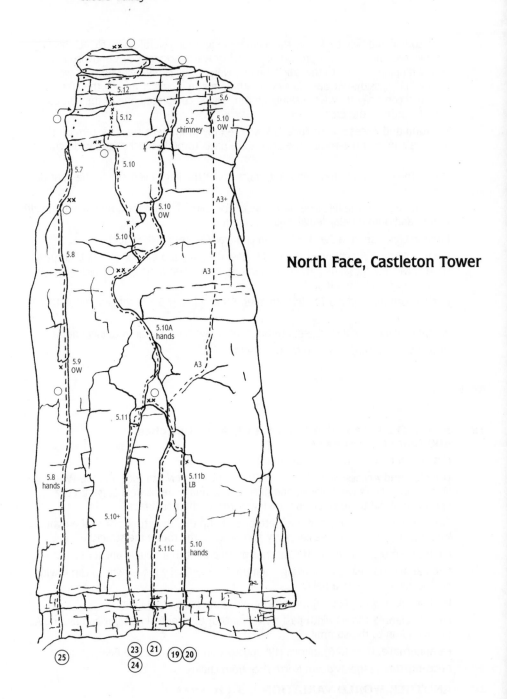

North Face, Castleton Tower

Moon, and Stars. This was originally climbed in two short pitches up to the bolt anchors atop pitch 1 of *North Face*.

Paraphernalia: Friends (3) #3, #3.5, #4; Tri-cams (1) #1, (2) #1.5, (3) #2 through #3.5.

Descent: Rappel the pitch.

21   SACRED GROUND IV, 5.12b, 4 pitches, 400 feet (122m) ★★★★

First Ascent: Jay Smith, 1994.

Location and Access: *Sacred Ground* begins up the thin crack left of *Sun, Moon, and Stars* and right of the hand crack of *North Face* route. Pitches 3 and 4 angle left from *North Face* near the top of pitch 2.

Pitch 1: Climb 5.11c to a double anchor belay stance shared with the top of pitch 1 of *North Face*.

Pitch 2: Follow pitch 2 of *North Face* but belay at two bolts where *North Face* makes a right diagonal climb ending at the top of its pitch 2, 5.10a. The pitch climbs right of dinosaur footprints.

Pitch 3: Branch left and climb past two fixed anchors and up a 5.10 lieback to a double anchor belay.

Pitch 4: Climb 5.12b (crux) past 8 bolts and on to the summit.

Paraphernalia: TCUs (2) #0.4, #0.5, (3) #0.75, (2) #1, (3) #1.5, (2) #2, #2.5, #3; small to medium wires, quickdraws.

Descent: Three rappels down *North Face* from chains.

22   NORTH FACE—ORIGINAL LINE, MIXED AID/FREE

First Ascent: Jimmy Dunn, Doug Snively, 1973.

Location and Access: The original line up the face started up the first pitch of what is now *Sun, Moon, and Stars*, thereafter joining the current standard free route at the end of pitch 1.

Paraphernalia: Original ascent rack included pins.

Descent: Three rappels down the route from chains.

23   NORTH FACE IV, 5.11b, 3 pitches, 400 feet (122 m) ★★★★

First Ascent: Ed Webster, Buck Norden, May 1979. This was the first free ascent of the north side of the tower, incorporating an all-new first pitch.

Location and Access: *North Face* follows the obvious interconnecting cracks winding up the north face of Castleton.

Pitch 1: Climb an off-hand sized crack in a dark-varnished, right-facing dihedral which becomes good hands at a small roof. Above, the crack thins to a fingertip lieback (crux). Easier climbing up ledges leads to a good belay at double bolts.

Pitch 2: Continue up a splitter hand-crack past a pod to a belay on ledges just before a steep fist/offwidth crack behind a left-facing flake, 5.10. There are dinosaur footprints to the left of and below the belay.

Pitch 3: Climb the wide crack, then move right to another 5.10 fistcrack. Finish up the chimney above, 5.10, then 5.9 offwidth, and finally 5.7 to the summit.

Paraphernalia: Friends (2) #1.5, #2; (3) #2.5, #3, (5) #3.5; Camalots (1) #4; TCUs (1) #0.75, #1; medium-large nuts (6).

Descent: Three rappels down the route from chains.

Cameron Burns on the first pitch of the *North Chimney*, Castleton Tower

24   NORTH FACE—LELLA-ROTERT VARIATION I, 5.11a, 1 pitch ★★★★★

First Ascent: Bruce Lella, Bob Rotert, 1980.

Location and Access: This variation is to the top 15 feet (4.5 m) of pitch 1 and allows the route to be done at a slightly easier free standard. Undercling right at the small roof, then lieback to easier climbing, 5.11a. This has become the standard way of doing *North Face* and the 5 stars are given for the whole route done this way.

25   NORTH CHIMNEY III, 5.9-, 4 pitches, 400 feet (122 m) ★★★★★

First Ascent: Daniel Burgette, Allen Erickson, 5 hours, 2 April 1970. Second ascent: Jimmy Dunn, Dan Porter, September 1970.

Location and Access: *North Chimney* is obvious at the left side of the north face of the tower, 40 feet (12 m) left of *North Face* route. It is thought by many to be a little less difficult than the *Kor-Ingalls* south face route of the same rating.

Pitch 1: The pitch ascends vertical-to-overhanging rock which is climbed with jams and liebacks. The first ascent party used a shoulder stand. There is a small ledge 50 feet (15 m) above the ground. The crux is a bulge 130 feet (40 m) up the pitch. Belay from double bolts 10 feet (3 m) above the bulge, 5.9-, 140 feet (43 m).

Pitch 2: Climb a smooth-walled dihedral with bulges on the left wall. In the corner, a constricting crack narrows from 1 foot to 2 inches. Climb with jams and little protection except in the corner cracks. Above, the climbing eases as it ascends a moderate chimney with a few difficult chockstones. The pitch ends 135 feet (41 m) up, at a flake at the back of the chimney. At this belay, light shines through the crack from the south side of the tower, 5.8, 135 feet (41 m).

Pitch 3: Continue right into an adjacent chimney when possible and on to the notch between the main and secondary towers, 5.8.

Pitch 4: Lead out of the notch and traverse left to *Kor-Ingalls*, then continue 30 feet (9 m) to the summit, 5.8, 50 feet (15 m).

Paraphernalia: Friends (1) #1, (2) #2.5, (1) #3, #3.5, (1) #4; Tri-cams #1 through #3; medium stoppers; large nuts; long runners, helmet for second on Pitches 3 and 4.

Descent: Three rappels down *North Face* from chains.

Rectory

Rectory is the small mesa north of Castleton Tower and adjacent to the Priest and Nuns. Approach up the BLM and American Mountain Foundation trail used to reach Castleton Tower. Climbing routes are listed from right to left.

26   FAREWELL TO THE DESERT II, 5.8, A2, 4 pitches, 400 feet (122 m)

First Ascent: West German climbers Frank Nebbe, Renate Stockburger, 25 August 1987.

Location and Access: *Farewell to the Desert* climbs the east side of the Rectory and is 200 yards (183 m) south of the north edge of the mesa. An 85-foot (26 m) partially detached flake marks the start of the climb.

Pitch 1: Begin at the left side of the flake and climb a short chimney 15 feet (5 m), then move over a short roof and climb the 20-foot (6 m) crack above with aid. Where the crack ends, move left 8 feet (2 m), then climb up over jammed blocks into the

photo: Chris Beque

The Rectory

chimney behind the flake and the wall. Tunnel right (north) to the other side of the flake and chimney to a ledge, 5.7, A1, 110 feet (34 m).

Pitch 2: With aid, ascend the knifeblade seam right of a 5" crack (12.7 cm). Continue into a chimney. Where the chimney ends at an overhang, a few aid points lead up and right to a broad ledge, 5.7, A2, 80 feet (24 m).

Pitch 3: This mixed pitch leads up the right crack above the ledge. Where it widens, make an awkward tension traverse into the left crack. The crack widens into a chimney, at the end of which you climb up and left to blocks and ledges. There is considerable rope drag on the pitch, 5.8, A2, 110 feet (34 m).

Pitch 4: Move left about 20 feet (6 m) before climbing up through cracks and corners to the top, 5.8, 100 feet (30 m).

Paraphernalia: Standard desert rack; knifeblades (3).

Descent: Rappel *Empirical Route,* which is reached at the extreme north end (west side) of the landform.

27   COYOTE CALLING III, 5.11+, 4 pitches, 410 feet (125 m) ★★★

First Ascent: Scott Lazar, Kent Wheeler, March 1995.

Location and Access: *Coyote Calling* is at the far left (south) end of the east face, right of *Fine Jade.*

Pitch 1: Begin up a fingercrack, then traverse left to slightly overhanging rock and a right-facing dihedral. Continue up a thinning crack system, climb a roof (the crux) and establish a hanging belay, 5.11, 100 feet (30 m).

Pitch 2: Traverse left 10 feet (3 m) and climb to a belay, 5.11, 100 feet (30 m).

Pitch 3: Follow a fingercrack around an arête and up with tight hands and a fingercrack to a hanging belay station, 5.11+, 100 feet (30 m).

Pitch 4: Traverse left on thin face holds, then climb a handcrack and on to the summit, 5.11+, 110 feet (34 m).

Paraphernalia: Friends (2) sets; TCUs (3) sets; wires (2) sets; quickdraws.

Descent: Rappel *Fine Jade,* which is reached at the extreme south end (west side) of the landform.

28   FINE JADE III, 5.11-, 4 pitches, 375 feet (114 m) ★★★★★

First Ascent: Originally 6 pitches by Chip Chace, Pat Ellinwood, 1984.

Location and Access: *Fine Jade* ascends the crack system on the narrow south prow of Rectory, facing Castleton Tower. The original ascent used no bolts, although bolts have now been added to belay stations. The route is climbed in 3 pitches if done with the direct finish, or 4 pitches if done with the original finish.

Pitch 1: Climb the right side of a pedestal, 5.2. From the pedestal climb with offwidth fist past a 5.10+ hands overhang, then to a belay ledge. Continue with 5.10 thin hands, then climb with 5.10- fingers to a belay ledge with a block on its right side. There are 2 metolius hangers below the crux finger bulge.

Pitch 2: Climb 5.10+, then make 2 moves of 5.11 fingers past a bulge. Continue 5.9 hands past a second small roof, 5.9+, to a belay stance.

Pitch 3: Begin with a 5.10a lieback/hands move and continue 5.9 past a rotten section to a triangular roof. Climb 5.10- to a large ledge with a large block on its right side. Continue up a bolted face at 5.11- to the top, a variation to the original route, or follow Pitch 4 to the summit.

photo: Steve "Crusher" Bartlett

Gary Ryan and Julia Warwick on *Fine Jade*

Pitch 4: Traverse 5.7 left and belay around the corner. Continue up the corner at 5.8, then traverse left below a roof, past a block, then climb to the summit, 5.9.

Paraphernalia: Friends (2) #1, #1.5, (3) #2, #2.5; Camalots (1) #4; TCUs (1) #1, (2) #2; medium nuts (6).

Descent: Make 3 full-rope rappels down the route.

29   WEST SIDE STORY III, 5.11, 4 pitches, 375 feet (114 m)

First Ascent: Fred Vandenberg, Noah Bigwood, 1992.

Location and Access: *West Side Story* is a crack system left of *Fine Jade*.

Pitch 1: Begin 5.7 to a ledge, then climb a 5.10 fist-to-hands, right-facing corner to a belay below a roof, 100 feet (30 m).

Pitch 2: Ascend the roof, 5.10, with fingers and footholds, then continue up a splitter crack to a belay, passing a flake protected by a bolt on its right side, 100 feet (30 m). Fred Vandenberg: "Flake feels loose, but won't budge."

Pitch 3: Climb 5.11 thin, then right to a belay anchor in a window opening to the other side of the rock, 80 feet (24 m).

Pitch 4: Make 5.9 face moves past the anchor, then climb a 5.7 face to connect with the final 20 feet (6 m) of *Fine Jade*.

Paraphernalia: Friends (2–3) #0.5 through #1.5, (2) #2.5, (3) #3, #3.5, (3–4) #4; stoppers (1) set.

Descent: Rappel *Fine Jade*.

30   BROKEN ARROW III, 5.10, 4 pitches, 375 feet (114 m)

First Ascent: Dan Grandusky, Henry Lester, Easter Sunday 1980.

Location and Access: *Broken Arrow* ascends a large, right-curving dihedral right of *Crack Wars*, left of *Fine Jade*.

Pitch 1: Climb 5.5 to a belay ledge.

Pitch 2: Continue 5.6 to a belay ledge.

Pitch 3: Climb 5.10 offwidth to a belay.

Pitch 4: Traverse right, then climb 5.9 to a second right jog before reaching the summit.

Paraphernalia: Standard desert rack.

Descent: Rappel *Empirical Route* or *Fine Jade*.

31   CRACK WARS III, 5.11, 4 pitches, 375 feet (114 m) ★

First Ascent: Glenn Randall, Charlie Fowler, October 1982.

Location and Access: *Crack Wars* is right of *Emperical Route*.

Pitch 1: Begin atop a block, climbing thin hands. After 15 feet (5 m) of 5.10+ the crack widens to perfect hands and fist. Traverse left to belay.

Pitch 2: Climb 5.10 offwidth to a belay.

Pitch 3: Continue 5.9 hands to a fist roof slot (5.11), then to a rotten belay, protect with #3.5 Friend and #3 Camalot.

Pitch 4: Climb 5.9 fingers in a corner, then a 5.9+ squeeze.

Paraphernalia: Standard desert rack with extra #3.5 Friends and #3 Camalots; Big Bro 8–10" for Pitch 2.

Descent: Two long, double-rope rappels down the route, or rappel *Empirical Route* or *Fine Jade.*

32 OFF TO SEE THE ALLAH I, 5.11b, 1 pitch, 200 feet (61 m) ★★★

First Ascent: Jay Smith, Kitty Calhoun, April 1997.

Location and Access: *Off to See the Allah* climbs the center of the west face right of a prominent calcite wall. Ascend a left-facing corner with fingers to a left-trending hand traverse. Above, climb a hand-sized splitter crack to anchors. A second set of anchors was placed near the hand traverse so climbers can split the pitch.

Paraphernalia: Many finger- to hand-sized pieces.

Descent: Rappel the route.

33 EMPIRICAL ROUTE III, 5.9 R, 2 pitches, 375 feet (114 m) ★★

First Ascent: Harvey T. Carter, Cleve McCarty, with Annie Carter on Pitch 1, 22 May 1962.

Location and Access: *Empirical Route* ascends the crack system separating the southern edge of the Nuns from the northern edge of the Rectory.

Pitch 1: Begin up a 5.8 chimney and climb to the beginning of a handcrack, 5.9.

Pitch 2: Climb a handcrack to a chimney leading to the summit, 5.8 R.

Paraphernalia: Standard desert rack; 200-foot (60 m) ropes .

Descent: Rappel the route.

34 EAST FACE I, 5.11, 1 pitch, 150 feet (46 m) ★

First Ascent: Jay Smith, Mark Hesse, May 1995.

Location and Access: Approximately 500 feet (152 m) left of the Nuns. Climb a right-facing dihedral to double fixed anchors. The route does not reach the mesa top.

Paraphernalia: Finger- to hand-sized units.

Descent: Rappel the route.

Nuns

Nuns are the two (connected) shorter towers attached to the north end of the Rectory. Approach up the BLM trail as for Castleton Tower, then traverse left past the Rectory to the Nuns.

35 WHERE HAVE THE WILD THINGS GONE? III, 5.11, 3 pitches, 325 feet (98 m) ★★★

First Ascent: Swiss climbers Romain Vogler, Christian Schwarz, 6 August 1985. Second ascent: Charlie Fowler, Jimmy Dunn, with Australian climber Maureen Gallagher on Pitch 1, 1986.

Location and Access: *Where Have the Wild Things Gone?* climbs the west face of the tower up the prominent crack system separating the 2 Nuns, then summits on the Rectory.

Pitch 1: Begin up the 5.9 right side of a 25-foot (8 m) pillar at the base of the crack system left of the Rectory's *Empirical Route.* Continue above the pillar, with a 5.11 lieback (Friends [3] #2), then 5.10 face to a hanging belay at bolts placed by the second ascent team.

photo: Ed Cooper

The Priest (left) and the Nuns

Pitch 2: Climb with sustained finger and face moves, 5.11, then follow a ledge that is on the back (east) side of the Nuns to the second rappel point of *Empirical Route* at a bolt with slings in a chimney.

Pitch 3: Continue to the summit of the Rectory up *Empirical Route*.

Paraphernalia: Friends (4) #1.5, #2, #2.5, #3, #4; stoppers (1) set.

Descent: Rappel *Empirical Route*.

36   BAD HABIT II , 5.11c, 3 pitches, 250 feet (76 m) ★★★★

First Ascent: John Catto, Jay Smith, Mark Hesse, 1995.

Location and Access: *Bad Habit* climbs the east face of the tower.

photo: Jimmy Dunn

Where Have the Wild Things Gone?

Pitch 1: Begin with thin stemming up a left-facing corner, 5.11c. Continue with thin hands to a belay, 5.11c.

Pitch 2: Climb 5.10 to double anchors 50 feet (15 m) below the summit.

Pitch 3: Continue 5.10- to rappel anchors on the summit, 50 feet (37 m).

Paraphernalia: Friends (1) #2; wires (1) #0.4, #2, #2.5.

Descent: Rappel the route.

37 **HOLIER THAN THOU II, 5.11c, 3 pitches, 250 feet (76 m) ★★★★★**

First Ascent: Jay Smith, Mark Hesse, 1995.

Location and Access: *Holier Than Thou* ascends the north face of the tower.

Pitch 1: Climb 5.11c past 11 bolts to double belay anchors, 120 feet (37 m).

Pitch 2: Continue 5.9+ past 3 bolts for 80 feet (24 m) to double anchors.

Pitch 3: Follow *Bad Habit*'s Pitch 3 to the summit, 50 feet (15 m).

Paraphernalia: Quickdraws.

Descent: Rappel the route.

38 **NORTH FACE RIGHT II, 5.10a, 3 pitches, 250 feet (76 m) ★★★**

First Ascent: Mark Hesse, Jay Smith, 1995.

Location and Access: *North Face Right* is just right of *Holier Than Thou*. Climb 5.10a, curving left to meet the top of *Holier Than Thou*'s Pitch 1. Continue on *Holier Than Thou* to the summit.

Paraphernalia: Friends through #2.5.

Descent: Rappel *Holier Than Thou*.

Priest

Priest is a freestanding tower north of the Nuns. The approach is the same as for Rectory.

39 **HONEYMOON CHIMNEY (a.k.a. West Face) III, 5.11, 4 pitches, 330 feet (101 m) ★★★★**

First Ascent: Harvey T. Carter, Layton Kor, with Annie Carter on Pitches 1 and 2, 16–17 September 1961. First free ascent: Chip Chace, Jeff Achey, April 1981. First solo ascent: Jeff Widen, 15 November 1986.

Location and Access: *Honeymoon Chimney* begins right of the prominent chimney on the west face. Fred Knapp: "The Priest is the wildest tower in the Castle Ridge area. Rumor has it that a famous mathematician and climber backed off the route, claiming that the geometry was too weird. This route involves offwidths, tunneling, wild stemming, face climbing, and even occasional jamming."

Pitch 1: Start at a flake at the base of the main seam of the Priest's robe on the west face and squeeze past a retro-bolt, then past an old piton on the right, into an open chimney of 5.9 offwidth. Bypass a large chockstone on its left at 5.9, then tunnel through to a belay from a large ledge not visible from the ground, 130 feet (40 m). From the belay, light is seen from the east through a window in the rock. It is possible to traverse through the window west to east.

Pitch 2: Climb a 5.6 chimney to a belay from bolts on a good ledge on the west face, 60 feet (18 m).

The Priest, Honeymoon Chimney

photo: Fred Knapp

Bret Ruckman on the Priest

Pitch 3: Crux pitch. Continue up the chimney as it widens, then face climb on a 6-bolt ladder on the arête. Traverse left at 5.7 to a shallow cave and a sloping belay stance. Belay from a bolt and fixed piton, 5.11, 80 feet (24 m).

Pitch 4: Traverse 20 feet (6 m) around the left corner and climb fingers-and-hands at 5.8 to the summit, 60 feet (18 m). The first ascent party climbed straight to the summit with aid.

Paraphernalia: Friends (1) #0.5, #1, #1.5, #2, #3, #4; large cams for Pitch 1; a selection of nuts; quickdraws (6).

Descent: Rappel with double ropes from slings around a boulder to the top of Pitch 2, then rappel west to the ground or through the chimney to the top of Pitch 1, and finally to the ground down the east face, or with a 200-foot (60 m) rope rappel to the top of Pitch 2, then to the ground.

40   KOR-BECKEY VARIATION III, 5.9, A2, 4 pitches, 330 feet (101 m)

First Ascent: Fred Beckey, Layton Kor, 18 September 1961.

Location and Access: This second ascent of the Priest was executed with a direct start variation to Pitch 1. Begin below and just left of the prominent chimney on the west face of the tower.

Paraphernalia: Friends (1 set); knifeblades.

Descent: Rappel *Honeymoon Chimney*.

41   EAST FACE III, 5.11, 4 pitches, 330 feet (101 m) ★★★★

First Ascent: Joede Schoeberlein, Mike Mayers, October 1977. Second ascent: Joede Schoeberlein, John Schoeberlein, August 1980.

Location and Access: The first 2 pitches are new and on the east face of the tower. The climb then joins *Honeymoon Chimney* on the west face for the final 2 pitches.

Pitch 1: Scramble onto a ledge directly opposite the crack system followed on *Honeymoon Chimney*. Continue with 5.10 lieback and offwidth, then climb a 5.7-to-5.9 chimney to the top of a large chockstone. Pass the chockstone on the left and belay on top. This is the same belay as at the top of Pitch 1 on *Honeymoon Chimney*; you can traverse to that route or continue the climb above, 130 feet (40 m).

Pitch 2: Continue up the chimney to a window and traverse to the top of *Honeymoon Chimney* Pitch 2, 5.6, 60 feet (18 m).

Pitch 3 and 4: Follow *Honeymoon Chimney* to the summit, 5.11.

Paraphernalia: Friends through #4; stoppers.

Descent: Rappel *Honeymoon Chimney*.

Sister Superior Group (a.k.a. The Professor and Students)

The pinnacles of the Sister Superior Group are east of Parriott Mesa and are easily viewed from River Road east (upriver) of the Castle Valley turnoff. Approach from Castleton Tower, or from between mile markers 17 and 18 on River Road. Turn onto a dirt road branching right (south) at a small, white bridge over Ida Gulch. This road is an access to range where cattle graze and is generally kept in good repair, provided you have a high-clearance vehicle. It is important for those using the access to leave gates as they are found (open or closed). Approximately 2.5 miles (4 km) up the road, park at a large cairn on the left, which marks the start of the trail to

photo: Mike Baker

Left to right: **Cubic Sister, Chimney Rock, Unknown Sister, North Sister, Sister Superior**

photo: Topher Donahue

Jeff Ofsenko below Sister Superior

the towers. Hiking time is about 1 hour from the trailhead. There are restrooms and camping north at Ida Gulch, left of the access road to the Colorado River.

The Professor and Students has long been the local name for the Sister Superior spires, the Priest and the Nuns; that's why the locals call this Professor Valley. Climbers, however, are not generally familiar with local names and so climber-given names are used in this guide.

The spires of the Sister Superior Group are (south to north): Sister Superior, North Sister, Unknown Sister, Crazy Little Sister (not in view until you're at the southwest corner of Chimney Rock), Chimney Rock, Cubic Sister, and Baby Sister.

42   SISTER SUPERIOR—SAVIOR III, 5.11c R, 3 pitches, 330 feet (101 m)

First Ascent: Harvey T. Carter, David Bentley, 17 May 1965. First free ascent: Marco Cornacchione, Steph Davis, 1994.

Location and Access: *Sister Superior* is a sharp-edged pinnacle with 3 facets. *Savior* begins at the east corner and continues to the summit.

Pitch 1: Begin opposite *Jah-Man* on the northeast side of the tower, up a 5.9 offwidth, then move to the far right and belay in an alcove.

Pitch 2: Climb a splitter crack with fingers to hands. Continue past old bolts and loose flakes, then hand traverse left to belay at the top of a steep corner.

Pitch 3: Follow Pitch 4 of *Jah-Man* to the summit.

Paraphernalia: Friends (2) sets #1 through #3, with extra #2.

Descent: Rappel the route.

43   SISTER SUPERIOR—SAVIOR VARIATION III, 5.8, A2, 3 pitches

First Ascent: Harvey T. Carter, Dave Hiser, Steve Miller, early 1960s.

Location and Access: Although *Savior Variation* was the first route established on the tower, it did not climb the blank summit headwall. It is now considered a variation of *Savior* which climbs to the top of the spire. Pitches 1 and 2 climb 2 5.8 chimneys to a large ledge, level with the notch west of the spire. Pitch 3 traverses south on the ledge and climbs a steep wall on the east face with aid.

Paraphernalia: Same as *Savior*, including a selection of pitons.

Descent: Rappel the route.

44   SISTER SUPERIOR—JAH-MAN III, 5.10d, 5 pitches, 330 feet (101 m) ★★★★★

First Ascent: Ken Trout, Kirk Miller, 1984.

Location and Access: *Jah-Man* ascends the southwest face of the tower. A great sunny winter day route.

Pitch 1: Begin with face climbing. Traverse right and continue up a wide system with a 5.9 pull over a roof, then move on to a ledge, move right on the ledge and pull a 5.9 move onto another ledge. 5.9, 40 feet (12 m).

Pitch 2: Continue up a left-facing corner, "Sister Squeeze" (5.8) to a belay ledge with double anchors, 5.8, 90 feet (27 m).

Pitch 3: Climb 5.10 thin hands to a roof, then pass a fixed anchor and face traverse left at 5.10d. Climb 5.9 hands up a left-facing, right-trending corner to a belay ledge with triple anchors, 5.10d, 90 feet (27 m).

Pitch 4: Climb 5.10b thin hands. Move to the next crack left and continue 5.10b thin hands to a belay ledge with triple anchors, 5.10b, 100 feet (30 m).

photo: Mike Baker

Jah Man

Pitch 5: Move right and climb past 4 fixed anchors, then make a 5.10a face move to the summit, 50 feet (15 m).

Paraphernalia: Friends (2) sets #1 through #3, with (5) extra #2; wires (1) set; Quickdraws.

Descent: Rappel to the top of Pitch 4, 50 feet (15 m). Rappel from Pitch 4 to the top of Pitch 2, 150 feet (46 m), then 140 feet (43 m) to the ground. A single 60 m rope also works from the top of Pitch 2 to a ledge with anchors 60 feet (18 m) above the ground.

45 SISTER SUPERIOR—JAH-MAN DIRECT START III, 5.10+, 1 pitch ★★

First Ascent: Dougald MacDonald, Mark Hammond, 29 March 1997.

Location and Access: This direct start to *Jah-Man* begins 40 feet (12 m) right of the original route. Jamming and stemming up a short overhanging corner protected with small cams leads to a fingercrack directly below "Sister Squeeze" chimney.

Paraphernalia: Friends (2) #0 through #1.5.

Descent: Rappel original route.

46 NORTH SISTER—GAG ROUTE III, 5.10, 4 pitches, 250 feet (76 m) ★★★

First Ascent Pitch 1: Ken Trout, Kirk Miller, 17 May 1995. To the summit: James Garrett, Will Gilmer, Dave Anderson, 2 October 1988.

Location and Access: North Sister is the bulbous landform north of and semi-attached to Sister Superior. *Gag Route* climbs the next prominent crack system 100 feet (30 m) left of *Jah-Man*, on the west face of the tower.

Pitch 1: Begin with a 5.8 scramble to a broken section of rock. Climb past an old fixed piton up a left-facing dihedral to a good ledge, 5.9.

Pitch 2: Ascend the wall of the tower proper. Climb 5.9 up a straight-in crack to a right-facing, left-to-right-trending dihedral ending at a good ledge.

Pitch 3: Continue up a crack system above the belay ledge with 5.8 hands, widening and decreasing in angle before reaching a ledge.

Pitch 4: Climb a short 5.10 offwidth ending on another ledge, then scramble 5.6 to the summit.

Paraphernalia: Friends (3) sets with (1) large unit.

Descent: Rappel 165 feet (50 m) to the shorter east side of the tower.

47 NORTH SISTER—WEST FACE III, 5.10+, 1 pitch, 150 feet (46 m)

First Ascent: Ken Trout, Kirk Miller, 17 May 1975.

Location and Access: Ascend the obvious weaknesses (corner system) on the west face of the spire. This may be pitch 1 of *Gag Route*.

Paraphernalia: Standard desert rack.

Descent: Rappel the route.

48 UNKNOWN SISTER II, 5.10+, A1, 1 pitch, 100 feet (30 m) ★★★

First Ascent: Harvey T. Carter, 1960s. Second ascent: Rob Slater, Jim Bodenhamer, November 1994.

Location and Access: Unknown Sister is the tower north of North Sister. A bolt on the west face leads to a thin crack which gradually widens to 5 inches (12.7 cm) near the top.

photo: Jim Bodenhamer

Unknown Sister

Paraphernalia: Friends (1) set; quickdraws (1).

Descent: Rappel south from a double-bolt anchor.

49   CRAZY LITTLE SISTER I, 5.7, 1 pitch, 50 feet (15 m) ★★★

First Ascent: Rob Slater, Becky Hall, Jim Bodenhamer, Al Torrisi, November 1994.

Location and Access: Crazy Little Sister is a detached spire off Chimney Rock and not visible until you are at the southwest corner of Chimney Rock. From the main trail, hike around Sister Superior, then on the east side of the landforms past Unknown Sister (slender spire), continue west of Chimney Rock to Crazy Little Sister. Short, fun route with excellent photo potential.

Paraphernalia: Friends (1) #3.5.

Descent: Downclimb the route, no summit anchors.

50   CHIMNEY ROCK— NORTH FACE II, 5.7, 1 pitch, 80 feet (24 m)

First Ascent: Mark Rolofson, Mack Johnson, spring 1978.

Location and Access: The route is obvious on the north face of the spire.

Paraphernalia: Friends (1) set.

Descent: Rappel the route from a drilled-in angle.

51   CUBIC SISTER (a.k.a. Cuboid Sister) II, 5.10, C1, 1 pitch, 80 feet (24 m) ★★

First Ascent: Rob Slater, Jim Bodenhamer, Barry Roberts, Al Torrisi, November 1994.

Location and Access: *Cubic Sister* passes 2 bolts on the northwest corner, then climbs to a thin crack which diagonals to the summit. Rob Slater: "The route will probably go free at 5.11+."

Paraphernalia: Friends (1) set; quickdraws (2).

Descent: Rappel the route.

photo: Jim Bodenhamer

Becky Hall on Crazy Little Sister

photo: Fred Knapp

Sharon Sadleir on Baby Sister

52 BABY SISTER I, 5.8, A0, 1 pitch, 60 feet (18 m) ★★

First Ascent: Mark Rolofson, Mack Johnson, Spring 1978.

Location and Access: *Baby Sister* is the northernmost formation on the ridge. While *Baby Sister* is probably not worth the hike by itself, it is a recommended climb along with *Jah-Man* and/or *Gag Route* on Sister Superior. Ascend the obvious line on the south side, passing 1 fixed anchor on the way to the diminutive tower's summit.

Paraphernalia: Friends (1) set.

Descent: Rappel the route from a drilled-in angle piton.

53 BABY SISTER—EAST FACE I, 5.8, 1 pitch, 60 feet (18 m)

First Ascent: Jim Bodenhamer, Al Torrisi, Spring 1990.

Location and Ascent: On the east side of the landform. Begin up an obvious hand-to-finger–sized crack system, then traverse left (south) to the southeast corner and on to summit.

Paraphernalia: Friends (1) set.

Descent: Rappel the route.

Convent

Convent is a mesa approaching the size of Parriott. It lies north of and in line with Castleton, Rectory, Nuns, Priest, and Sister Superior Group. All of the landforms are island formations, remnants of a once continuous plateau. Convent is the mesa on the right side of River Road beyond Ida Gulch. Approach from River Road.

54 SALVATION CHIMNEY III, 5.10, 4 pitches, 450 feet (137 m)

First Ascent: Harvey T. Carter, Steve Miller, 4 November 1965. First free ascent: Lou Dawson, Kendall Williams, Mike Pokress, May 1975.

Location and Access: *Salvation Chimney* is one-third of the way from the left edge of the mesa when viewed from the west. Begin at a small leaning tower and a straight-in crack which opens into a chimney higher on the wall. The route then tunnels behind a large flake and chockstone at a left-facing dihedral with a bombay chimney.

Paraphernalia: Standard desert rack.

Descent: Double-rope rappels down the route.

55 RENATE GOES TO AFRICA IV, 5.9, A1, 5 pitches, 540 feet (165 m)

First Ascent: West German climbers Frank Nebbe, Renate Stockburger, 19 August 1987.

Location and Access: *Renate Goes to Africa* is approximately 350 yards (320 m) from the north end of the west face of the Convent, at a chimney/corner that is blocked 60 feet (18 m) up by large chockstones. Right of the route, 265 feet (81 m), is a small tower with a balanced rock on top. The climb follows the chimney/corner system, then a prominent right-slanting ramp. From the end of the ramp, ascend a chimney to broken rock and the summit. Only 5 points of aid were used on the first ascent.

Pitch 1: Climb the crack in the corner to the roof, which is formed by chockstones. A few aid points lead to the left edge of a roof. Ascend the corner above the roof to a belay in a recess between 2 chockstones, 5.9, A1, 90 feet (27 m).

Pitch 2: The pitch climbs the left corner to a large ledge covered with debris, 5.7, 60 feet (18 m).

photo: Jim Bodenhamer

Rappelling off the Convent

Pitch 3: Follow a ramp with easy climbing to a belay at a small rock spike, 5.5, 120 feet (37 m).

Pitch 4: Continue up the ramp and gain entrance to the upper chimney system. Follow the chimney for 50 feet (15 m), then step right (west) to a belay on a small ledge, 5.8, A0, 140 feet (43 m).

Pitch 5: Climb short cracks above the belay to easy ramps and a short corner leading to the summit, 5.4, A1, 130 feet (40 m).

Paraphernalia: Friends (1) set; wired stoppers; Hexentrics through #8.

Descent: Make 4 rappels down the route. The first rappel is from an angle piton, 85 feet (26 m) to a block with slings. The second is 160 feet (49 m) to the rock spike at the top of Pitch 3. The third rappel is 85 feet (26 m) to a ledge with a block, then rappel the arête immediately right (south) of the large chockstones using a block in the chimney for an anchor. Keep to the left or north side of the rappel ledge.

56   VALUE OF AUDACITY IV, 5.11+, 5 pitches, 450 feet (137) ★★★★★

First Ascent: Earl Wiggins, Keith Reynolds, April 1994.

Location and Access: *Value of Audacity* climbs the northwest corner of the mesa. There are no fixed anchors in place.

Pitch 1: Begin in a corner under a right-facing roof. Climb thin fingers out and around the roof, then continue up a wide, flaring crack/alcove to a stance at the base of a fistcrack, 5.11+, 100 feet (30 m).

Pitch 2: Climb a fist/offwidth crack through pods to a belay, 5.10, 100 feet (30 m).

Pitch 3: Climb hands to a small roof/bulge on fingers to a belay ledge, 5.11+, 150 feet (46 m).

photo: Harvey T. Carter

Summit of the Convent

Pitch 4: Climb a wide crack through pods to a chimney, 5.10, 100 feet (30 m).

Pitch 5: Fourth class to the top.

Paraphernalia: Friends (2) sets; Camalots (1) #5; TCUs.

Descent: Rappel *West Face Dihedral*.

57   WEST FACE DIHEDRAL Rating unknown, 1 pitch, 90 feet (27 m)

First Ascent: Earl Wiggins, George Hurley, late 1980s.

Location and Access: *West Face Dihedral* is 300 yards (234 m) left of *Renate Goes to Africa* and 160 feet (49 m) right of the north edge of the west face. Climb to double rappel anchors and slings visible from below on the left wall.

Paraphernalia: Standard desert rack.

Descent: Rappel the route.

58   JUNIOR BUTTRESS IV, 5.10 R, A2, 4 pitches, 450 feet (137 m) ★★★★

First Ascent: Jim Bodenhamer, Rob Slater, Bruce Hunter, Tom Cotter, May 1992.

Location and Access: When viewed from the west, *Junior Buttress* climbs the right edge of the mesa and follows a clean crack system to the summit.

Pitch 1: Traverse left on a ledge and climb a left-facing corner to an open slab. Pass 1 drilled angle and belay from a large ledge, 5.10.

Pitch 2: Climb A1, 5.8 up an obvious crack to a belay ledge with double anchors.

Pitch 3: Move right and climb a perfect TCU crack to a large block. Pass the block on the right and belay from a good ledge on the prow of the buttress (Jr's Brow), 5.8, A2.

Pitch 4: Continue with bolts and easy free climbing up an arête to the summit, 5.5, A1.

Paraphernalia: Friends (3) sets through #4; TCUs; Tri-cams (1) #7; wires (3) sets; a few knifeblades, Lost Arrows and small angle pitons; quickdraws.

Descent: Downclimb to the top of Pitch 3, then make 3 rappels down the route.

For all the toll the desert takes of a man it gives compensations, deep breaths, deep sleep, and the communion with stars.

–Mary Austin, 1903

To many of us, the wilderness truly unaltered by human interference, the wilderness with its wealth of life rolling across it in great surges, ebbing and flowing with the seasons of the year, is inseparable from our innermost being.

–Ian McTaggert Cowan

FISHER TOWERS

In all of Canyonlands, no single grouping of towers is as grand and majestic as the Fishers; but by the same token, no other group of towers is as intimidating or outright dirty as these mud covered giants. Wild summits, fins, gullies, and erosion at work are all elements of the mud experience. The actual Cutler rock that is found underneath the mud is quite good, but the mud casing makes placements difficult, tie-offs scary, anchors untrustworthy, and belayers miserable.

–Fred Knapp, *Classic Desert Climbs*, 1996

Steep walls with mud curtains, fluted chimneys, and undulating bulges soar overhead. Stone diving boards protrude from grotesquely twisted summits. . . . To climb here is to submit oneself to several days of abuse, including fear, frustration, intimidation, and an all-encompassing grime. When touched, the dry mud veneer disintegrates to pebbles and grit, filling the air to the point of suffocation.

–Katy Cassidy, Earl Wiggins, *Canyon Country Climbs*, 1989

The Fisher Towers are approximately 23 miles (37 km) east of Moab. To reach them, drive River Road to mile marker 21, where a sign directs you southeast (right) along a 2-mile (3.2 km) dirt road to the Fisher Towers Recreation Site. The small campground has restrooms and fire grills, but no running water. Camping is also available along River Road where there are numerous campsites, both undeveloped and semideveloped, only a few miles from the Fisher Towers.

At the south end of the Fisher Towers parking area is a register box and trailhead to the impressive 2.2-mile (3.5 km) hiking path (marked by rock cairns) meandering past the main towers and ending at a panoramic view beyond the Titan. The trail is worth hiking, even for those who have come only to climb.

Several of Jim Beyer's difficult routes are located on the Fisher Towers. For a breakdown of his innovative aid ratings see the "Aid Ratings" section, page 15.

Geology

The Fisher Towers are composed of Cutler Sandstone capped with Moenkopi. Cutler is similar to Wingate in density and would present some of the best climbing in the desert if it fractured vertically and weren't coated with a stucco of soft mud. The stratum is made up of relatively recently disintegrated granitic rocks (sands and gravels with interbedded red mudstones and siltstones). Moenkopi is widespread throughout the Colorado Plateau. It is a soft, crumbly stone (with a few hard layers) consisting of muds and silts distributed by tidal currents across mudflats in tidal channels. The Cutler Sandstone originated in the ancient Rocky Mountains (the Uncompahgre), east of the Fisher Towers. It is distinct in appearance and easily recognizable as a brown, red, and maroon chocolate layer cake formation.

photo: Duane Raleigh

The Fisher Towers, seen from the summit of the Titan.

A Brief History of Climbing in the Fisher Towers by Mike Baker

The Fisher Towers are named for a miner who, in the 1880s, lived near them, working the area in pursuit of mineral riches. Although Fisher surely scrambled among the now-coveted towers, it was 80 years before the first climber took note of them. Huntley Ingalls, while employed by the U.S. Geological Survey, gazed at these amazing towers and decided they were way beyond his ability. By the fall of 1961, feeling more confident on sandstone after his success with Layton Kor on Castleton, Ingalls once again returned to the Fishers, this time to reconnoiter possible climbing routes.

Although the rock was coated with mud, it did appear climbable. That winter, on a trip back east, he showed a couple of slides of the Fisher Towers to acquaintances at the *National Geographic* magazine and, to his surprise, they expressed interest in sponsoring an attempt on the largest of the towers. *National Geographic* would not only pay money, but would supply one of their photographers, Barry Bishop, to document the adventure. After some persuasion, Kor agreed to make a reconnaissance with Ingalls to the Fisher Towers. By spring the unstoppable Kor had decided that the project was an excellent way to kick off the new climbing season.

Kor and Ingalls reasoned that three climbers would be safer and faster than two, and decided that George Hurley was their man. With Hurley enlisted, the climbing team was off to the desert, with sights set on the summit of the largest tower, later to be known as the Titan. The approach was long, the cracks were coated in petrified mud, the climbing was difficult and almost all of it was artificial. After two days of climbing, with Kor in the lead, the trio had only been able to gain 300 feet, and the most difficult part of the route was yet to come. Somewhat defeated, they left fixed ropes for their return, loaded their car, and drove back to Boulder, Colorado, and their Monday morning jobs. On Thursday, after much anticipation and some anxiety, they were again off to the Fishers. As Ingalls put it, "In the early '60s, speed limits were high and gasoline was cheap."

They had previously arranged to meet Bishop (the photographer) in Grand Junction. Bishop had recently returned from Europe where he had acquired a pair of mechanical ascenders that Kor and Ingalls would use on their fixed lines. This was notable, since it was the first time ascenders were used in the United States. Hurley was slightly more skeptical and went with the tried and true prusiks.

At their high point, Kor again took the lead and continued to work his way up virgin rock. After another day of climbing, the trio discovered a small yet adequate bivi ledge and decided to spend the night instead of returning to the ground. The following day Kor was off on the final pitches. The relatively blank rock required a 70-foot bolt ladder to reach the more solid caprock and finally the summit.

Layton Kor, George Hurley, and Huntley Ingalls summitted the Titan via the *Finger of Fate* on May 13, 1962. Bishop, having hired a plane for aerial photography, had flown to Moab for fuel. When he returned, the team had already summitted and was on its way down. Ingalls wrote an article in the November 1962 *National Geographic* entitled "We Climbed Utah's Skyscraper Rock." Hurley would return to do the second ascent of the Titan in 1966, and went on to pioneer many routes on the desert, including several on the Mystery Towers. Both Kor and Ingalls moved on to other areas, and neither did any substantial climbing in the Fishers again. With so many other unclimbed towers in the area, this may seem a little strange, but when in 1991 I asked Kor if he would like to join me for a climb in the Fisher Towers he replied, "Why? I've already climbed the Titan."

Fisher Towers

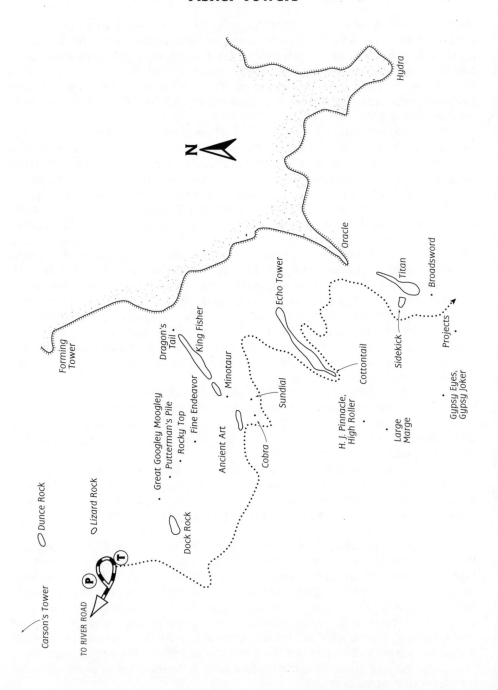

In the spring of 1962, Harvey T. Carter arrived at the Fisher Towers planning to make what he thought would be the first ascent of the largest tower. After a long hike to the base of the Titan he saw signs that the tower had recently been climbed (it turns out only one week prior). Somewhat discouraged, he chose the second largest tower, King Fisher, for his endeavor. In 1966, Carter teamed with Fred Beckey and Eric Bjørnstad to make the first ascent of Echo Tower, the third summit to be reached in the Fishers.

Cottontail, the fourth and last of the major towers, was climbed in 1967 by Carter, Art Howells, Don Ducette, Mike Dudley, Morgan Gadd, and Herbie Hendricks. For the next 10 years, Carter would continue to pioneer routes in the Fisher, Mystery, and Onion Creek areas, many of which have proved to be classics. While Carter dominated Fisher and Onion Creek climbing, Bill Forrest, George Hurley, and Don Briggs racked up many fine climbs in the Mystery Towers. By the close of the '60s, all of the major summits in the Fishers had been reached. It was late in the '70s when Jim Beyer first appeared on the scene, and by the '80s, Beyer's solo first ascents added aesthetic and bold new lines to all of the major towers and many of the smaller ones. Beyer's solo ascents continue to push the standard of sandstone climbing in difficulty, excellence, and purity, with routes like *Intifada*, the first A6 (proposed). (See the "Aid Ratings" section, page 15.)

With the '90s came a major increase in the number of desert sandstone climbers, and many rapid repeats of established lines were accomplished, as well as the addition of new ones. Rob Slater was the first to reach all the summits listed in the Fisher Towers chapter of the original *Desert Rock*. Every climb has now been repeated at least two or more times, and many have become trade routes. The once peaceful and seldom climbed Fishers are often crowded (and sometimes a bit of a scene). On any given weekend in the spring or fall, one party can usually be seen on every major tower, as well as a line waiting to climb Ancient Art. With such a dramatic increase in visitation, the Fisher and Mystery Towers, already threatened by regulation and/or closure, have become even more deserving of our protection. It is paramount that we all tread as lightly as possible on the approaches, camouflage bolt hangers and rap slings, and not reach for the drill or the hammer just because we are scared. After all, it is the softness of the rock, the uncertainty of the placements, and the problem-solving on lead which set the summits of the Fisher Towers apart. Let's do our best to preserve this truly unique and magical area for future ascentionists.

Fisher Towers Rack

The following list is, of course, arbitrary since each route has different needs: Camming units (3) sets from 0.25" through 6"; Stoppers (3) sets from RPs through 2" (these "stopper heads" can be beaten into old piton scars); Tri-cams (small sizes) are also useful for clean aiding piton scars; Bird Beaks (3) or more on harder routes; Toucans (3) sets (the leverage is far superior to knifeblades); knifeblades and Bugaboos (12) assorted, mainly long and thin; Lost Arrows (8); angles (3) each baby angles, (5) standard angles, (4) each up to 1 1/2", (1) each larger sizes; Leepers (4–6); Pika Hooks (1 set); Alumiheads, Bashies–mandatory for the harder routes.

Carson's Tower

Carson's Tower is a diminutive landform in view diagonally left and ahead of the dirt approach road to the Fisher Towers.

1   CARSON'S TOWER I, 5.7, 1 pitch

First Ascent: Mark Whiton, solo, fall 1995.

Location and Access: There are double-drilled angle pitons fixed on the route.

Paraphernalia: Quickdraws.

Descent: Rappel the route from a single drilled anchor.

Lizard Rock (a.k.a. Dragon Rock), Dock Rock, Great Googley Moogley, Putterman's Pile, Rocky Top

Lizard Rock is in the back of the camping area, east of the trailhead. Dock Rock, Great Googley Moogley, Putterman's Pile, and Rocky Top are south (left) of the trailhead.

2   LIZARD ROCK—ENTRY FEE I, 5.8+ S, 1 pitch, 60 feet (18 m) ★★

First Ascent: Harvey T. Carter, Annie S. Carter, 1 June 1962.

Location and Access: Begin up a wide crack on the southwest corner and climb to a flake. Stand on the point of the flake, then traverse right (5.8+ and unprotected). Continue up easier rock to an old ring bolt (of questionable value) and mantle onto the summit.

Paraphernalia: Large Friend for the flake; a selection of nuts; quickdraws.

Descent: Rappel off bolts on the west side of the landform.

3   LIZARD ROCK—LEAPIN' LIZARD I, 5.10-, 1 pitch, 60 feet (18 m) ★★★★

First Ascent: Ed Webster, Patrick Griffin, May 1984.

Location and Access: *Leapin' Lizard* begins left of *Entry Fee*. Climb a thin crack to a bolt, using small nuts for protection, 5.10-. Move right, then out left, before climbing overhanging jugs to the top.

Paraphernalia: Friends through #3; TCUs (1) set; stoppers (1) set; quickdraws (2).

Descent: Rappel from bolts on the west side of the landform.

4   LIZARD ROCK—ENTRY LIZARDS I, 5.10-, 1 pitch, 60 feet (18 m) ★★★★★

First Ascent: Unknown.

Location and Access: *Entry Lizards* climbs a combination of the first 2 routes. Climb the first part of *Entry Fee* to a large horn at the traverse, then straight to the top on unprotected rock to a hidden bolt.

Paraphernalia: Camalots (1) #4; slings.

Descent: Rappel from bolts on the west side of the landform.

5   DOCK ROCK—LOOK SEE I, 5.7, 2 pitches, 80 feet (24 m)

First Ascent: Harvey T. Carter, solo, 13 April 1969.

Location and Access: *Dock Rock* is the first formation approached on the left (east) from the start of the hiking trail. It is a small butte-shaped formation. To reach, hike left of the trailhead. The route ascends the most prominent crack/chimney on the west face.

Paraphernalia: Standard desert rack.

Descent: Rappel the route.

photo: Cameron M. Burns

Fisher Towers

---

6   DOCK ROCK VARIATION 5.8+

First Ascent: Harvey T. Carter, solo, 1985.

Location and Access: The variation climbs the first crack right of the original route.

7   DOCK ROCK—IMPISH I, 5.4, 2 pitches, 80 feet (24 m)

First Ascent: Layton Kor, solo, April 1970.

Location and Access: *Impish* is at the right edge of the landform when viewed from the trailhead.

Paraphernalia: Standard desert rack.

Descent: Rappel the route.

8   DOCK ROCK—SMASH I, 5.8, A4, 2 pitches, 80 feet (24 m)

First Ascent: Harvey T. Carter, Larry Lane, 21–22 April 1979.

Location and Access: *Smash* ascends the north face of the landform beginning at the far left side when viewed from the approach trail.

Paraphernalia: Standard desert rack.

Descent: Rappel the route.

9   GREAT GOOGLEY MOOGLEY I, 5.10+, 1 pitch, 100 feet (30 m) ★★★★

First Ascent: Walt Shipley, aid solo, November 1997. Second ascent and first free ascent: Keith Reynolds, Walt Shipley, November 1997.

King Fisher

Great Googley
Moogley

Rocky
Top

Putterman's
Pile

photo: Jesse Harvey

Fisher Towers

Location and Access: Great Googley Moogley is a formation with several rounded summits in view from the trailhead, left of Dock Rock and south of Lizard Rock. Begin on the northwest side of the landform and climb a wide crack (5.9) to a right-angling ramp. Continue up the ramp, then up a bulging offwidth (5.10+ crux) to a double-bolt summit anchor.

Paraphernalia: Friends #1 through #6.

Descent: Rappel the route.

10   PUTTERMAN'S PILE—BEYOND THE VALLEY OF THE PUTTERMAN I, 5.8, A1, 1 pitch, 100 feet (30 m) ★★

First Ascent: Cameron Burns, Mike Baker, Jesse Harvey, 13 December 1997.

Location and Access: Putterman's Pile is approximatey 300 feet (91 m) south of Great Googley Moogley. Climb the southeast ridge to a subsidiary summit (5.8), then lower into the notch between the subsidiary summit and the true summit. Continue (A1) past 3 bolts to the higher summit.

Paraphernalia: Angle pitons (1) 0.5", 5/8"; Lost Arrows (1); quickdraws (4); ropes (1).

Descent: Make a 1-rope rappel west from double summit bolts.

11   ROCKY TOP—TUKTOOLONG I, 5.7, A1, 1 pitch, 80 feet (24 m) ★★★

First Ascent: Jesse Harvey, Cameron Burns, Mike Baker, 14 December 1997.

Location and Access: Rocky Top is an obvious mallet-shaped spire in view directly below King Fisher from the trailhead. To reach, hike east from the trailhead directly toward King Fisher. Descend a gully and walk past Great Googley Moogley, then follow the ridge behind Putterman's Pile and 3rd-class 40 feet (12 m) to a shelf leading to the base of the Rocky Top formation. *Tuktoolong* climbs an obvious dirty crack system on the northeast side of the tower beginning up 5.7 rock protected with cams and pitons. Continue to an offwidth crack between blocks, C1 (#3 and #4 Camalots). Short but solid mud aid leads to a bolt ladder out a roof. More aid, then a bolt and a mantle lead to a ledge below the summit where a belay is made from a slung block. From the anchor, it is 6 feet (1.8 m) to the top.

Paraphernalia: Camalots (1) #2, #3, #3.5, (2) #4; angle pitons (2) 0.5", 5/8", (3) 1", 2"; tie-offs (6); rappel sling.

Descent: One single-rope rappel down the route from webbing around a block on the summit.

Dunce Rock, Forming Tower

Dunce Rock is a small formation (with a rappel sling visible from below) in a gully northeast of the trailhead. Forming Tower is a large partly formed formation of major proportions upslope from the parking area, on the north side of the main arroyo. A trail leads up 400 feet (122 m) on a steepening dirt ridge to where a 300-foot (91 m) leftward traverse across rocky scree places you at the base of the tower.

12   DUNCE ROCK—NORTH FACE I, 5.8, 1 pitch, 100 feet (30 m)

First Ascent: Harvey T. Carter, solo, April 1970.

Location and Access: The route is obvious from the north side of the landform.

Paraphernalia: Friends (1) set.

Descent: Rappel the route.

13   DUNCE ROCK—JAM A CRACK I, 5.8, 1 pitch, 100 feet (30 m)

First Ascent: Harvey T. Carter, Dave Erickson, 20 April 1971.

Location and Access: *Jam a Crack* climbs 2 short jam cracks up the west edge of Dunce Rock to a bolt from which the summit was lassoed. Sadly, someone retro-bolted the lasso move in 1997.

Paraphernalia: Friends (1) set.

Descent: The first ascent team rappelled from a single piton on the north side of the formation.

14   FORMING TOWER—RUNAWAY CRACK IV, 5.8+ R, A2+, 4 pitches, 325 feet (99 m) ★★★

First Ascent: Harvey T. Carter, Paul Disnard, with Ken Wyrick to the halfway point, 15–16 May 1975.

Location and Access: Begin up a classic diagonal crack (first soloed by Carter) on the southeast face.

Pitch 1: Climb past a fixed piton, a bolt, then a fixed piton over a roof (diagonally left) and past 2 bolts to a belay, A2+, 150 feet (46 m).

Pitch 2: Ascend a chimney past a roof and a bolt, then 5.8+ sand (funky runout) past a bolt. Continue at 5.5 to a good ledge, 105 feet (32 m).

Pitch 3: Climb a right-facing wide crack past loose blocks to a sloping belay ledge, 5.9 or C1, 60 feet (18 m).

Pitch 4: Fourth class to the summit.

Paraphernalia: Camalots (2) sets #1 through #4, (1) #0.5, #0.75; nuts (1) set; angles (3) 0.5", 3/4", 5/8", 1-1/4", 1.5", (1) 2"; sawed-offs (2) 5/8"; Lost Arrows (2); knifeblades (2); Bird Beaks (1).

Descent: Rappel the route.

15   FORMING TOWER—FULL METAL JACKOFF III, 5.7, A3, 4 pitches, 330 feet (100 m) ★★★★

First Ascent: Eric Kohl, Pete Takeda, 8 June 1996. Second ascent: James Garrett, Franziska Garrett, Angus Finney, fall 1996.

Location and Access: *Full Metal Jackoff* climbs the northwest face of the tower. The route follows the crack system which bisects the entire formation, directly opposite *Runaway Crack.*

Pitch 1: Climb A3 to double belay anchors.

Pitch 2: Climb free to a single anchor.

Pitch 3: Continue with 5.7 to a belay.

Pitch 4: Ascend 4th class to the summit.

Paraphernalia: Standard desert rack; angles (8–10) 1.5".

Descent: Rappel the route or make 3 rappels down the original route on the southeast face.

Fine Endeavor

Fine Endeavor is the only fin uphill from Lizard Rock.

16   FINE ENDEAVOR III, 5.8, A1, 3 pitches, 200 feet (61 m)

First Ascent: Harvey T. Carter, Bruce Hamilton, 30 March 1990.

Location and Access: Pitch 1 climbs 5.5, Pitch 2 is 5.8, and Pitch 3 is 5.7, A1.

Paraphernalia: Standard desert rack.

Descent: Rappel the route.

Dragon's Tail Rock

Dragon's Tail Rock is the landform behind (east of) King Fisher.

17   DRAGON'S TAIL ROCK IV, 5.8, A3, 4 pitches, 250 feet (76 m) ★★

First Ascent: Mike Baker, solo, with Leslie Henderson on Pitches 1 and 2, May 1993.

Location and Access: Begin near the northeast side of the tower. Pitches 1 and 2 can be combined (double gear list).

Pitch 1: Climb A3 into A2+ to a 1-bolt and gear belay stance, A3, 75 feet (23 m).

Pitch 2: Climb A3 past a fixed anchor, then up A2+ to a double-anchor belay ledge, A3, 75 feet (32 m).

Pitch 3: Continue past a fixed anchor at 5.8, then angle up and right past a fixed anchor and a single point of aid. Downclimb (5.6) on the back side, traverse left to triple anchors and belay, 5.8, AO, 75 feet (32 m).

Pitch 4: Step across a gap and climb past 4 fixed anchors, then 5.8 to a sling around the "Dragon's Tail". Traverse right and make a wild step across before climbing past a fixed anchor and up to the highest summit, 5.8, AO, 75 feet (32 m).

Paraphernalia: Standard desert rack; knifeblades (5); Lost Arrows (1); angles (3) 1/2".

Descent: Rappel from slings around the highest summit to the Dragon's Tail summit. Rappel to the top of Pitch 3. Rappel from bolts east to the ground.

King Fisher

King Fisher is the nearest major tower in view south of the Fisher Towers parking area. When Harvey T. Carter discovered, in mid-May 1962, that the Titan had been climbed the week before, King Fisher–the second largest tower in the Fishers–became the team's second-choice pioneer objective and the second tower in the Fishers to be climbed. Routes are listed from right to left (east, south, west, north). A register was placed on the summit in 1995, with eight ascents recorded before 5 November 1995.

Chronology of Route Ascents: Route; Date; Time; Party

1. *Colorado Ridge*; 27–31 May 1962; 5 days; Harvey T. Carter, Cleve McCarty
2. *Jagged Edge*; 28–30 October 1986; 3 days; Jim Beyer, solo siege
3. *Death of American Democracy*; 27–30 December 1986; 4 days; Jim Beyer, solo
4. *Dead Again*; spring 1993; Pete Takeda, Duane Raleigh
5. *Hazing*; May 1997; Eric Kohl, Bryan Law, Pete Takeda

King Fisher/Ancient Art Summits

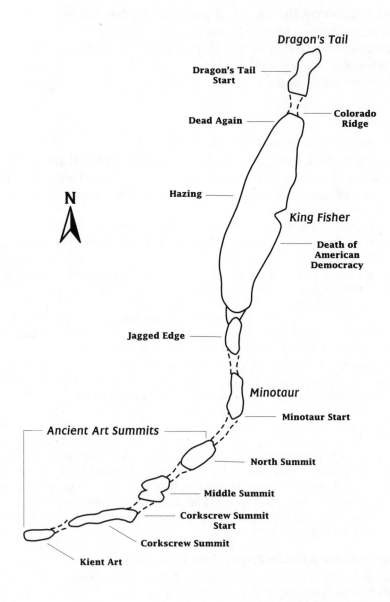

North face of King Fisher

18 COLORADO RIDGE (a.k.a. Northeast Ridge) IV, 5.8, C2, 7 pitches, 500 feet (152 m) ★★★

First Ascent: Harvey T. Carter, Cleve McCarty, 5.8, A2, 27–31 May 1962. First clean ascent unknown.

Location and Access: *Colorado Ridge* ascends the relatively narrow and steep northeast ridge, which is the left skyline profile when approaching the parking area from River Road. It is the easiest route on King Fisher. To reach, hike the Fisher Tower Trail approximately 0.5 mile (0.8 km), then turn left where the trail makes a sharp left turn and begins to descend between Ancient Art and Echo/Cottontail towers. Ahead on the left is the impressive Cobra hoodoo. To this point, the approach has been the same as for Ancient Art. Before the Cobra, scramble up a steep slope on an established climber-use trail to the uphill (east) side of the tower and the obvious bolt ladder of Pitch 1.

Pitch 1: Begin up a bolt ladder on a blank wall at the northeast edge of the tower, C1, 90 feet (27 m). Pitches 1 and 2 are often combined for (1) 140-foot (43 m) pitch.

Pitch 2: Free climb a muddy chimney which connects to the edge of the ridge. Belay from a perch on a saddle (protect with #1 through #4 Friends and 2 #2 Friends), 5.8, 50 feet (15 m).

Pitch 3: Crux pitch. Climb a narrow ridge (15 feet, 4.5 m) past a false belay to a belay in a saucer-like formation 15 feet higher (4.5 m), 5.8, C2, 120 feet (37 m). Protect with Friends #1.5 through #3.

Pitch 4: Climb a bolt ladder up an arête to a hanging belay below the caprock, 115 feet (35 m). Pitches 4 and 5 may be combined.

Pitch 5: Surmount the overhang above (caprock) and follow pitons and bolts to a large ledge, 50 feet (15 m).

Pitch 6: Climb a short wall past ledges, 5.8, to a final tight chimney which exits onto the summit, 80 feet (24 m).

Pitch 7: Boulder to the high point, 5.7, 12 feet (4 m).

Paraphernalia: Friends (1) #1, (2) #2, (1) #2.5, (2) #3, (2) #4; several TCUs; many rivet hangers or stoppers for bolts without hangers; hero-loops (12); carabiners (50); many quickdraws.

Descent: Rappel the route to the large ledge at the beginning of Pitch 6. Free rappel 150 feet (46 m) off the caprock and (with a slight swing) reach the saucer belay at the top of Pitch 3. Rappel to the top of the muddy chimney at the top of Pitch 2. Finally, rappel 150 feet (46 m) to the ground.

19 WALKER-FORREST VARIATION I, 5.10, A2, 1 pitch, 100 feet (30 m)

First Ascent: Ken Walker, Bill Forrest, 1970s

Location and Access: The variation to Pitch 1 of *Colorado Ridge* begins 50 feet (15 m) right of the original route and climbs 5.10 to an A2 traverse (left) back to the original route line. This was the second overall ascent of King Fisher.

Paraphernalia: Same as *Colorado Ridge.*

Descent: Rappel *Colorado Ridge.*

photo: Jeff Widen

Colorado Ridge of King Fisher, pitch 1

South face of King Fisher

20   DEATH OF AMERICAN DEMOCRACY V, 5.9, A4+ R, 5 pitches, 700 feet (213 m) ★★★★★

First Ascent: Jim Beyer, solo, 27–30 December 1986. Second ascent: Chris Kalous, Rob Van Aernum, Pitch 1, 6 hours, 2.5 days overall, spring 1993. Jim Beyer: "Several of the pitches are run out, thus the A4+ rating."

Location and Access: *Death of American Democracy* climbs the south face of King Fisher. Jim Beyer: "I think the best 2 aid routes in Utah are *Death of American Democracy* and *World's End* as far as quality and difficulty."

Pitch 1: Begin 35 feet (11 m) left of a cave formation on the south face of the tower. Pass fixed anchors and go right, past an A3+ expanding flake, then A4 and more bolts to A2 up a left-facing corner to a hanging belay from triple anchors.

Pitch 2: Continue left past fixed anchors, then up A4 to a right-facing corner, A1, and finally A3 mud to A2 Bongs ending at triple belay anchors at a ledge.

Pitch 3: Move right and climb past fixed anchors up a 5.9, A0 face to A3+. Descend right to a ledge and continue right and up, A2, then A4 to a triple-anchor hanging belay, 5.9.

Pitch 4: Climb A3, then A4 past fixed anchors (hollow/loose), then A2 hands, and finally A3 (steep) to A1 to a ledge with double anchors.

Pitch 5: Move right and past a chockstone on its left, 5.9, then up a slot, 5.9, to the summit.

Paraphernalia: First ascent list: RURP (10); knifeblades and Bugaboos (20); Lost Arrows (20–25); Leepers (8); baby angles (2), 3/4" (3); (2) 1"; (1) 1 1/4"; Bong-Bongs through 4"; nuts (10) 1/8" to 3"; copper and aluminum heads; bolt hangers. Updated list: Friends (1) set #0.75 through #5; TCUs (1) set; stoppers (1) set; keyhole and rivet hangers; heads (5); Bird Beaks (5); knifeblades (15); Lost Arrows (15); angle pitons (4) 0.5", (3) 5/8", 3/4", (2) 1", 1.5", (2) 2", Bong-Bongs (1) 2.5" through 4".

Descent: Rappel *Colorado Ridge*. The route was originally rappelled with ropes fixed on Pitches 2, 3, and 4.

21   JAGGED EDGE V, 5.9, A4, 8 pitches, 700 feet (213 m) ★★★★

First Ascent: Jim Beyer, solo siege, 38 bolts, 28–30 October 1986. Second ascent: Keith Reynolds, Matt Laggis, 8 hours at the crux, March 1993. Second solo ascent: Andes "The Chile Dog" Zegers, May 1995.

Location and Access: *Jagged Edge* ascends a diagonal crack system on the north face, beginning on the downhill arête of the tower. From the parking area, walk to the ridge of yellow talus, then contour to the base of the main north face. Descend a chimney/ gully and traverse right. Ascend a short lieback/traverse to the beginning of Pitch 1. The route's name is from a Jimi Hendrix song, "Dolly Dagger": "She drinks your blood from the jagged edge, you better watch out baby, here comes your master." Jim Beyer: "I free soloed the first ascent of the last pitch (5.9, 70 feet)–up and down–didn't have any fun after finally reaching the top–I was gripped-out thinking about downclimbing that crack with 700 feet [of] exposure."

Pitch 1: Nail a diagonal crack up and right. Traverse left and up to a long, wide crack (mostly 3") to a good ledge on the south side, below an obvious gargoyle. Avoid a chopper chockstone on the pitch, 5.8, A3+, 160 feet (49 m).

Pitch 2: Climb (5.7) to a large ledge. Mantle to a higher ledge and make an unprotected 5.8+ move left to a hidden bolt. Pendulum left to a short A1 crack. Stem 5.9 to a bolt ladder (A0) which ends on a good ledge, 5.9, A1, 130 feet (40 m).

King Fisher

Pitch 3: Tension traverse left to an A3 crack. Mantle onto the notch. Climb triple unprotected mantles (5.9, 5.7, 5.6) to an aid crack which leads to large but sloping ledges (5.7, A3 on south face), 5.9, A3, 135 feet (41 m).

Pitch 4: Pendulum left to 2 hidden bolts on the north side of a rib. Do another pendulum left to a crack (A3+ is followed by A4). Establish a hanging belay low on a bolt ladder, A4, 95 feet (29 m).

Pitch 5: Climb the bolt ladder (some 5.8 and A3+) to good ledges above the caprock roof, 5.8, A3+, 125 feet (38 m).

Pitch 6: Continue 4th class 70 feet (21 m). Scramble 20 feet (6 m) up a gully and down the other side, then traverse left (on the north face) on ledges to a belay just before a chimney.

Pitch 7: Climb the chimney for 80 feet (24 m) at 5.7 to a belay through the chimney on the south face.

Pitch 8: Traverse right on the south face to a bulging hand-and-fist crack that leads to the top, 5.9, 70 feet (21 m).

Paraphernalia: Nuts and cams 1" through 4"; pitons; RURPS (1); Bird Beaks (3); knifeblades (12); Lost Arrows (15); Leepers (8); angle pitons (3) each through 4"; Bashies; belay bolts have hangers, all others have nuts and washers but are hangerless; slings for rappel anchors (10); quickdraws; bolts, total used on first ascent (38). All bolts have nuts and washers and are Red Head "Wedge" type anchors. Jim Beyer: "Do not tighten the bolts any more as this will pull the bolt out beyond its sleeve and reduce its outward pull strength to zero."

Descent: On the first ascent, Beyer downclimbed the top 3 pitches, then rappelled the route. Pitches 2 and 3 must be fixed to descend this way. Since the summit boulder is only 30 feet (9 m) from the first rappel anchor of the *Colorado Ridge* it may be easier to descend that route.

22   HAZING V, 5.8, A3+, 6 pitches, 700 feet (213 m)

First Ascent: Eric Kohl, Bryan Law, Pete Takeda, May 1997.

Location and Access: *Hazing* begins up slabs right of *Dead Again*. The route was begun by Duane Raleigh in 1991. Eric Kohl: "*Hazing* should become a trade route."

Pitch 1: Climb past broken rock, passing 2 fixed anchors, then continue A3 to a double anchor belay.

Pitch 2: Continue up A3, passing fixed anchors to a double-bolt belay.

Pitch 3: Follow the obvious crack system with A3+, passing a fixed anchor. Belay from double anchors.

Pitch 4: Continue A3+ to a belay.

Pitch 5: Ascend A3, then 5.8 past a bowl. Continue 5.8, then A1, passing death blocks on the right before reaching a double-anchor belay.

Pitch 6: Follow a chimney and finally a 5.8 crack system to the summit.

Paraphernalia: Standard desert rack; thin pitons, many Beaks and mudbeaks (a Bryan Law invention of blunt aluminum hooks pounded into drilled holes bathook style). The first ascent team also used ground-down Black Diamond Spectres and Pika Arkees.

Descent: Rappel *Colorado Ridge*.

photo: Takeda collection

Bryan Law on *Hazing*

23   DEAD AGAIN V, 5.10 R, A4, 6 pitches, 700 feet (213 m)

First Ascent: Pete Takeda, Duane Raleigh, spring 1993.

Location and Access: Approach as for *Jagged Edge*. *Dead Again* follows an obvious crack system just right of the left skyline. All belays are hanging.

Pitch 1: Scramble in from the left to access a short bolt ladder which is interspersed with difficult Beaking. Free climb (mostly unprotected) up an obvious slot and belay.

Pitch 2: Climb 30 feet (9 m) above the belay, then lower to below the belay and swing right to access a trough/crack which is climbed with difficult ice axe hooking and tied-off dirt bollards.

Pitch 3: Continue up an obvious crack.

Pitch 4: Follow a wide crack to the caprock, move right, then ascend to a pendulum off a drilled angle piton. Exit left with difficult and unprotected free climbing to reach a belay station on *Colorado Ridge*.

Pitches 5 and 6: Follow *Colorado Ridge* to the summit.

Paraphernalia: SLCDs through 5"; TCUs (2) sets; Bird Beaks (4); ice axe for hooking; many pitons through 4".

Descent: Rappel *Colorado Ridge*.

Ancient Art

Ancient Art is the four-summit tower beside the trail between King Fisher and the Echo/Cottontail complex, and is the most frequently reached summit in the Fishers. Approach as for *Colorado Ridge* on King Fisher. Fred Knapp: "The true summit is the corkscrew-shaped feature resembling a child's drip sand castle that appears to defy gravity."

Chronology of Ascents: Route; Date; Party

1. North Summit, *Hippie Route*; 6–11 June 1967; Herbie Hendricks, Dennis Willis
2. Corkscrew Summit, *Stolen Chimney*; 29 April 1969; Bill Roos, Paul Sibley
3. Corkscrew Summit, *Continuation Variation*; April 1971; Harvey T. Carter, Dave Erickson, Ken Wyrick
4. Middle Summit, *Purebread*; 14–15 September 1972; Harvey T. Carter, Will Marshall
5. Middle Summit, *Baker Variation*; 1991; Mike Baker, solo
6. Corkscrew to Middle, *Summit Variation*; 18 August 1991; Jimmy Dunn, Chad Wiggle
7. Kient Art, *Adjacent Art*; 6 April 1996; Pete Takeda, Eric Kohl

24   NORTH SUMMIT—HIPPIE ROUTE IV, 5.10+, 6 pitches, 500 feet (152 m) ★★★★★

First Ascent: Herbie Hendricks, Dennis Willis, 6–11 June 1967. First free ascent: Harvey T. Carter, Tim Jennings, November 1967.

Location and Access: The north tower is climbed from the southeast side.

Paraphernalia: Standard desert rack.

Descent: Four rappels down the route.

photo: Duane Raleigh

Ancient Art

25   MIDDLE SUMMIT—PUREBREAD IV, 5.10, A2, 8 pitches, 500 feet (152 m) ★★

First Ascent: Harvey T. Carter, Will Marshall, with Mike Flynn working on the first 6 pitches, 14–15 September 1972.

Location and Access: *Purebread* climbs to the highest summit of the tower by its west face. The climb is predominantly free, with only 4 aid bolts.

Paraphernalia: Standard desert rack.

Descent: Rappel the route.

26   BAKER VARIATION III, 5.10, A0, 4 pitches, 500 feet (152 m)

First Ascent: Mike Baker, solo, 1991.

Location and Access: *Baker Variation* climbs the Middle Summit with only 3 points of aid. Climb the first 3 pitches of the Corkscrew Summit, then tension traverse at the top of Pitch 2 and join *Purebread*. The relationship between this route and route 28 is unknown.

Paraphernalia: Standard desert rack.

Descent: Rappel from slings around a nubbin to the tension traverse, then free climb to the top of Pitch 2 on the Corkscrew summit. Make 2 double-rope rappels to the ground.

27   CORKSCREW SUMMIT—STOLEN CHIMNEY III, 5.11a, 5 pitches, 500 feet (152 m) ★★★★★

First Ascent: Bill Roos, Paul Sibley, 29 April 1969. Second ascent: David Kozak, Steve Spaar, fall 1983. First free ascent: Keith Reynolds, Burton Moomaw, May 1991. Second free ascent: Jimmy Dunn, Kyle Copeland.

Location and Access: *Stolen Chimney* may be climbed 5.9 and AO or at the more difficult rating of 5.11a. Begin up the southeast ridge of the tower, 30 feet (9 m) beneath an obvious chimney, or approximately 200 feet (61 m) above the Fisher Towers Trail. The route climbs to the Corkscrew (southwest) Summit.

Pitch 1: From the southeast side of the tower near the Cobra hoodoo, scramble from the trail to the shoulder at the base of the tower, below a prominent chimney leading to the corkscrew summit, 5.7, 50 feet (15 m).

Pitch 2: Make an easy stem (5.7), then climb 4 bolts of 5.10d (or AO) to a belay ledge with triple anchors, 30 feet (9 m).

Pitch 3: Continue up a chimney system (5.8) passing 2 bolts to a commodious belay ledge to the right of a chockstone at the top of the chimney, 140 feet (43 m).

Pitch 4: Move left of the chockstone and climb 5.10 (or AO) past 3 anchors to the "Sidewalk" and belay from triple anchors, 50 feet (15 m). **NOTE:** From the Sidewalk, one may traverse and climb to the other summits of Ancient Art.

Pitch 5: Traverse left on the Sidewalk and climb past double-anchors to the "Diving Board" with a 5.8 mantle. On the back side of the Corkscrew, stem at 5.9+ past fixed anchors and make a right traverse, then a 5.9 mantle to the top.

Paraphernalia: Technical Friends (1) each; Camalot (1) #3; stoppers #4 through #7; carabiners (12); runners (6); short Quickdraws (6).

Descent: Lower the leader to the Diving Board and reverse the Sidewalk. Do a short rappel to the top of Pitch 3, then 2 double-rope rappels to the ground.

photo: Mike Baker

Corkscrew Summit, Ancient Art

28 CORKSCREW TO MIDDLE SUMMIT VARIATION III, 5.10-, 1 pitch, 80 feet (24 m)

First Ascent: Jimmy Dunn, Chad Wiggle, 18 August 1991.

Location and Access: Begin from the top of Pitch 2 of the standard Corkscrew Summit route. Climb through a hole to the north side of the formation, then downclimb a chimney for a few feet and traverse left at a weakness (5.10) to an old belay (not used). Continue up a short offwidth (5.10-), then stem past 2 ancient bolts to the top of the middle formation.

Paraphernalia: Camalots (1) #4; small nuts; quickdraws.

Descent: Wrap the rope around a summit spike and rappel to the ledge at the corkscrew summit's second belay.

29 CORKSCREW SUMMIT— CONTINUATION VARIATION III, 5.10, 2 (new) pitches

First Ascent: Harvey T. Carter, Dave Erickson, Ken Wyrick, April 1971.

Location and Access: This direct-start variation climbs 2 new pitches beginning directly off the trail on the southwest side of the tower. Ascend the lower wall to the start of the original Corkscrew route by short steep bands, overhanging bulges, and jam cracks.

Paraphernalia: Standard desert rack.

Descent: Four rappels down *Stolen Chimney*.

30 KIENT ART—ADJACENT ART III, 5.8, A3, 3 pitches, 500 feet (152 m) ★★

First Ascent: Pete Takeda, Eric Kohl, 6 April 1996.

Location and Access: *Adjacent Art* scales the previously unclimbed minor summit due west and attached to the Corkscrew Summit.

Paraphernalia: Standard desert rack.

Descent: There are no anchors on top. Downclimb to the belay and rappel the route.

Minotaur

Minotaur is the landform east of Ancient Art. Minotaur is the half-man, half-bull Greek mythological monster.

photo: Jimmy Dunn

Betsi McKittrick and Chad Wiggle on the Corkscrew summit

31   MINOTAUR IV, 5.9+, C2, 7 pitches, 500 feet (152 m) ★★

First Ascent: Duane Raleigh, Lisa Raleigh, 5 1/2 hours 1995.

Location and Access: Begin at the left edge of the landform, just right of the col east of Ancient Art. Only 2 bolts were placed on the first ascent.

Pitch 1: Climb dirt 5.9+, A0 to a belay.

Pitch 2: Continue up a 5.9 offwidth to a belay at the top of a formation with no anchors.

Pitch 3: Lower to the notch right of the Pitch 2 belay.

Pitch 4: Climb past a bolt, then a 5.9 chimney to a bolt belay.

Pitch 5: Move left (C2), then up 30 feet, back right, and up onto the ridge.

Pitch 6: Continue up, traversing right, 5.8, and belay below the summit glob.

Pitch 7: Ascend to the summit.

Paraphernalia: Friends (2) sets #0.5 through #4; bolt hangers (1) 3/8". No pitons required.

Descent: Make a 165-foot (50 m) rappel down the route to a hanging station, then continue to the ground.

Cobra, Sundial

Cobra is a hoodoo above the trail as it serpentines between Ancient Art and the Echo/Cottontail landforms. Sundial is 150 feet (46 m) east of Cobra.

32   COBRA (a.k.a. ET Tower) I, 5.11 R, 1 pitch, 40 feet (12 m) ★★★★★

First Ascent: Jimmy Dunn, Chad Wiggle, Betsi McKittrick, 23 August 1991.

Location and Access: Cobra is climbed from the north (uphill) side of the hoodoo facing Ancient Art. Begin 5.5 and climb to a fixed piton below the caprock. The crux is above the piton. At the lip of the caprock, make a couple of moves left to a point of less overhang, then clip into a drilled angle piton on the summit. Leg-over onto the top. Chad Wiggle: "5.11R, harder for shorter people."

Paraphernalia: Friends (1) #4; quickdraws, webbing.

Descent: Lower (with the aid of a ground party) off the southeast edge or rappel from a single bolt.

33   SUNDIAL I, 5.9, 1 pitch, 20 feet (6 m) ★★

First Ascent: Eric Kohl, Bryan Law, June 1997.

Location and Access: Eric Kohli: "The 20-foot high obliquely slanting Pizza Hut–box disk of death. A saucer-like landform precisely placed by a higher life form than our own."

Paraphernalia: A selection of pitons.

Descent: Rappel from a single anchor on the summit.

H.J. Pinnacle, High Roller, Large Marge

H.J. Pinnacle is a prominent, distinct spire on a fin west of the main trail as it meanders between King Fisher and Cottontail Towers. The identity of H.J is unknown. High Roller is the hoodoo right of H.J. Pinnacle. Large Marge is a small tower in the drainage west of Cottontail Tower.

photo: Sharon Sadleir

Fred Knapp atop the Cobra

34   H.J. PINNACLE I, 5.7, A3, 1 pitch, 90 feet (27 m)

First Ascent: Jim Beyer, Buck Tilley, October 1985.

Location and Access: *H. J. Pinnacle* is climbed by its north face to a ledge halfway up the landform, then traverse left to an overhanging knifeblade crack. From the second bolt make a placement to the right and free climb past a bolt to the top. Five bolts were placed by the first ascent team (2 rappel bolts).

Paraphernalia: A selection of knifeblades; quickdraws (5).

Descent: One rappel from double bolts.

35   HIGH ROLLER I, 5.8, A1, 1 pitch, 50 feet (15 m) ★★

First Ascent: Eric Kohl, Bryan Law, June 1997.

Location and Access: Climb a 5.8 crack system to an A1 anchor near the summit, then make a 5.8 mantle to the top.

Paraphernalia: Quickdraw (1).

Descent: Rappel from a single anchor.

36   LARGE MARGE—MY CLEANEST DIRTY SHIRT I, 5.5, C1, 1 pitch, 100 feet (30 m) ★★★

First Ascent: Cameron Burns, Jon Butler, 27 April 1997.

Location and Access: Follow the Titan Trail to its westernmost point as it circumnavigates King Fisher and Ancient Art. Descend to the northwest into the shallow draw west of the trail. The draw curves west, then southwest, and points towards Castleton Tower. After about 0.5 mile (0.8 km), the draw meets a major drainage coming from the left (east). Turn right (west) at the junction of the two and hike west for approximately 300 yards (91 m). Large Marge is on the left side of the draw. Begin on the east side of the rock, climbing a 10-foot (3 m) chimney between Large Marge and the pinnacle left of it (5.5), then scramble to the notch proper. Angle right over 4th-class ground to a band of loose rock, then climb the band by a small rotten gully on the right (5.4). Three bolts (C1) lead to a double-bolt rappel on the summit. Cameron Burns: "You can do them drunk."

Paraphernalia: Angles (1) 0.5", 5/8", 3/4"; (5) 3/8" bolt hangers or tie-off slings.

Descent: Single-rope rappel down the route.

Echo Tower

Echo Tower lies east of and adjacent to Cottontail Tower. Routes on the north side are reached by a scramble from the Fisher Towers Trail beginning near Cobra and the approach to the *Colorado Ridge* on King Fisher. *Tapeworm* and *Run Amok* (south and southeast side routes) are approached from the Fisher Towers Trail as it descends along the south side of the tower. (See the Fisher Towers map on page 170.) Climbing routes are listed from left to right.

Chronology of Ascents Route; Date; Time; Party

1. *North Chimney*; 14–19 October 1966; 5 days; Fred Beckey, Eric Bjørnstad, Harvey T. Carter
2. *Run Amok*; March 1979; 4 days; Jim Beyer, solo
3. *Phantom Sprint*; 25–26 February 1986; 18.5 hours up; Jim Beyer, solo
4. *Tapeworm*; 5 February 1994; Brian Warshaw, Brad Jarrett
5. *Phantom Sprint* speed ascent; 1994; 5 hours 15 min.; Duane Raleigh, Lisa Raleigh

photo: Jon Butler

Cameron Burns on the first ascent of Large Marge

Echo Tower/Cottontail Tower

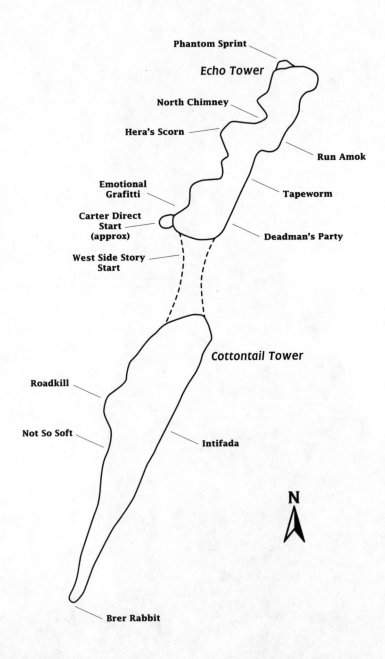

Phantom Sprint

Echo Tower

North Chimney

Hera's Scorn

Run Amok

Emotional
Grafitti

Tapeworm

Carter Direct
Start
(approx)

Deadman's Party

West Side Story
Start

Cottontail Tower

Roadkill

Not So Soft

Intifada

N

Brer Rabbit

6. *Emotional Graffiti*; May 1994; Mike Baker, Leslie Henderson, with Zach Merritt lower pitches
7. *Deadman's Party*; 1989; Jim Beyer, solo
8. *Hera's Scorn*; March 1995; Keith Reynolds, solo, with Courtney Scales on first and second pitches

* *Phantom Sprint* hammerless ascent; 2–3 September 1996; Dougald MacDonald
* *Phantom Sprint* first free ascent; spring 1997; Stevie Haston, Laurence Gouault

37 PHANTOM SPRINT IV, 5.12 or 5.8, C2+, 6 pitches, 450 feet (137 m) ★★★★★

First Ascent: Jim Beyer, solo, 19.5 hours up, 1 bolt, 5.9, A3, 25–26 February 1986. Second ascent: Steve "Crusher" Bartlett, Bill Roberts, 5 May 1988. Phantom Sprint is the first major tower in the Fishers to be climbed free.

Location and Access: Approach from the climber-use trail which ascends from the Cobra hoodoo to the *Colorado Ridge* (east ridge) of King Fisher. From the trail, traverse right on a bench to the start of the route. Alternate approach: Hike the trail to the back (south) side of the tower, then scramble easy 5th class to the route. The climb begins 60 feet (18 m) left of *North Chimney* and ascends the tower's northeast arête. Jim Beyer: "A great route with minimal hard climbing. Generally of relatively clean and easygoing climbing. Duane Raleigh: "It is your standard Fisher Towers mange, with mandatory dirt clawing, slot wallowing, and general funkiness–a must for all manic-depressives and others with similar mental disorders." Doug Hall: "Originally climbed in seven pitches, the route is easily done in four pitches by combining the original Pitches 1, 2 and 6, 7." Michael Benge: "Like all Fisher routes, the free version is scary, with pitches of poorly protected 5.11+, 5.11, 5.12-, and 5.12, and offers everything from finger cracks to offwidth."

Pitch 1: Begin up a short 5.4 chimney to a belay ledge, 45 feet (14 m).

Pitch 2: Continue up a crack (up to 4-inches wide, 6 cm) climbing a right-facing corner to a belay, 5.8, C2+, 140 feet (43 m). (5.11+.)

Pitch 3: Angle up and right to a hanging belay, C2+, 120 feet (36 m). A Fishhook is useful. (5.11.)

Pitch 4: Continue up, then under a roof, then climb with tension right to a hanging belay from a fixed anchor, 85 feet (26 m). (5.12b.)

Pitch 5: Climb a groove (the crux) which leads right (with tension) to a wide crack belay at 2 bolts at the beginning of an 8 bolt ladder, 5.9 offwidth. C2+ (5.11.)

Pitch 6: Continue up the bolt ladder to the top. The free version traverses far right from halfway up the bolt ladder to a scary mantle. (5.11+.)

Paraphernalia: Friends (1) #4, #5; Camalots (2) #5; Tri-cams (1) set; TCUs (1) set; SLCDs (2) sets to 5"; medium to large Hexcentrics; Fishhooks (1); quickdraws.

Descent: Rappel to the belay at Pitch 3, then to the belay at the top of Pitch 2, then to the ground.

38 NORTH CHIMNEY IV, 5.9, A2+, 6 pitches, 550 feet (158 m)

First Ascent: Fred Beckey, Eric Bjørnstad, Harvey T. Carter, 2 bivouacs, 14–19 October 1966. First solo ascent: Scott Riley 4 days, January 1996.

Left to right: **Titan, Echo Tower, Cottontail Tower**

photo: Mike Baker

Location and Access: *North Chimney* ascends the obvious large chimney system at the middle of the north face. The climb was the third ascent made in the Fisher Towers and involved five days of climbing with two cold bivouacs after a heavy snowfall in the nearby La Sal Mountains. Fred Beckey, writing in the American Alpine Journal: "Much of the route lay up a very vertical couloir with its inside walls sculptured into a continual succession of caves and overhangs."

Pitches 1–3: Climb a bolt ladder with occasional piton placements.

Pitch 4: Continue up the chimney system negotiating an expanding flake. Protect with #4 and #5 Camalots.

Pitch 5: Chimney 40 feet (12 m) to a ledge, then make a 3-bolt traverse to the left to join *Phantom Sprint* .

Pitch 6: Climb 40 feet (12 m) to the top on bolts, then traverse right to the highest point.

Paraphernalia: The first ascent used 55 pitons and placed 71 bolts. Standard desert rack; Camalots (1) #4, #5 for pitch 4; medium and baby angles; selection of Lost Arrows; quickdraws.

Descent: Rappel *Phantom Sprint.*.

39   CARTER VARIATION I, 5.8, 1 pitch, 150 feet (46 m)

First Ascent: Harvey T. Carter, solo, mid-1970s.

Location and Access: The first pitch variation climbs direct from the Fisher Towers Trail to the beginning of the *North Chimney*, eliminating the circuitous traverse to the start of the *North Chimney*.

Paraphernalia: Unknown.

Descent: Rappel the pitch or walk off the original *North Chimney* approach.

40   HERA'S SCORN VI, 5.9, A3+, 5 pitches, 570 feet (174 m) ★★★★

First Ascent: Keith Reynolds, solo, March 1995. Pitches 1 and 2 with Courtney Scales.

Location and Access: Climbs the middle pillar of Echo Tower when viewed from the trailhead, just right of *North Chimney*.

Pitch 1: Free climb, then aid up 2 bolts to a double-bolt belay, 5.8, A1, 70 feet (21 m).

Pitch 2: The *Spiral Chimney Pitch*. Climb a 7-bolt ladder up and right to the base of an obvious chimney, then free climb to a ledge and belay, 5.9, A1, 140 feet (43 m).

Pitch 3: Continue with a few aid moves up and right to a slung horn. Aid through a bulge, then make free moves to a bolt. Continue on aid past 2 more bolts to a flaring dihedral which changes into a thin crack and leads to a 3-bolt anchor (with a fourth bolt out right), 5.9, A3+, 150 feet (46 m).

Pitch 4: Continue up a thin crack through bulges leading up and right with some free climbing to a roof. Make aid moves off a bolt to a crack in the roof. Above the roof, free climb large cracks to a belay alcove with 2 bolts, 5.9, A3, 130 feet (40 m).

Pitch 5: Climb right to a corner, then up, passing several bollards, to cracks leading to the third summit from the left. Belay at 2 bolts below the summit, then scramble to the top, 5.9, 80 feet (24 m).

Paraphernalia: Friends (2) sets; Camalots (1) set #1 through #5; Bird Beaks to Bongs, Warthogs (2); medium and large hooks.

Descent: Rappel the route.

41   EMOTIONAL GRAFFITI V, 5.9, A4, 7 pitches, 665 feet (203 m) ★★★

First Ascent: Mike Baker, Leslie Henderson with Zach Merritt on lower pitches, May 1994.

Location and Access: Approach as for *North Chimney*, then traverse on a ledge (5.8) to the right (west) and a 2-bolt anchor. Climb to a ledge with double anchors. Mike Baker: "Great bivy ledge." The route ascends a pillar then moves onto a south-face arête. Finish on the southwest face up an obvious crack system.

NOTE: Zinc-coated nail drive bolts on the route (if any remain) should not be trusted.

Pitch 1: From double bolts at the start of the route, climb a crack system left of a chimney. Make a tension traverse right to the chimney and climb 5.8, A2 to double anchors at the top of the chimney. Continue over a small roof and past a fixed anchor, then 5.8, A2 to a belay ledge with triple anchors, 165 feet (50 m).

Pitch 2: Traverse right on the "Traverse of Tears" (5.9), then up, passing 4 fixed anchors (AO) to a double-anchor belay ledge, 60 feet (18 m).

Pitch 3: Continue up, passing 4 fixed anchors, 5.9, A3+/A4, to a ledge with double anchors, then pass a roof and climb past a fixed anchor to a belay ledge with double anchors, 5.8, A3+/A4, 100 feet (30 m).

Pitch 4: Climb a bolt ladder (A3) and move left, 5.8, then climb, passing a ledge and roof on the left side, 5.9. Continue up a 5.9 face past fixed anchors and 1 A3+ move to double anchors at a belay stance below a roof.

Pitch 5: Pass the roof on its right side and climb past 2 fixed anchors, A2+, then pass another roof and follow a crack system to a triple-anchor belay.

Pitch 6: Traverse right making 1 A3+ move. Climb a left-facing corner, A2, past 2 fixed anchors ending with 5.9 and a belay ledge with double anchors.

Pitch 7: Climb 5.8, A2 to the summit, 40 feet (12 m).

Paraphernalia: Camalots (1) #0.5, #0.75, #1, (2) #2, #3, #4; TCUs (1) each; Tri-cams (1) #0.5, #1, #1.5; Bird Beaks (3); RURP (1); knifeblades (2); shallow angles (1), (3) 0.5" angles (3), (1) 5/8", 3/4", 1"; bolt hangers (10); quickdraws.

Descent: Make 7 double-rope rappels down the gully left of the climb. Rappel 1 is 40 feet (12 m) to the top of Pitch 6. Rappel 2 is 165 feet (50 m). Rappel 3 is 145 feet (44 m). Rappel 4 is to the top of Pitch 1, 150 feet (46 m). Rappel 5 is to the double anchors on the ledge at the start of the route,165 feet (50 m). Rappels 6 and 7 are directly to the trail below the tower.

42   DEADMAN'S PARTY VI, 5.10 S X, A5, 8 pitches, 625 feet (191 m) ★★★★★

First Ascent: Jim Beyer, solo, 1989. Second ascent: Tim Wagner, Lance Bateman, April 1997.

Location and Access: *Deadman's Party* is left of *Tapeworm*, climbs the south face to the notch between Echo and Cottontail, and involves 200 feet (61 m) of A5. Jim Beyer: "This is the best route in the Fisher Towers." No bolts were placed on the first ascent.

Pitch 1: Begin up 5.6, A1 mud to a belay at the base of a chimney.

Pitch 2: Climb left of a chimney (climbed by Tom Cosgriff at an earlier date), A4, to a belay and anchor at an expanding flake.

Pitch 3: Continue A4 to an anchor beside loose blocks. There is a potential 40-foot (12 m) ledge fall on this pitch.

Pitch 4: Pass an overhang on its left side and continue A4 to a belay.

Pitch 5: Climb A1, then A4+ and finally A5 to a belay. There is a possible "big fall" on near-vertical rock at the A5 area of the pitch.

Pitch 6: Climb A3+ expanding rock to a belay just below the summit.

Pitch 7: Continue up a 5.10 face, moving to the west face of the tower.

Pitch 8: Traverse over summit rock to the highest point.

Paraphernalia: Basic desert (A5) rack; many Chouinard Bashies; many blades, RURPs and hooks.

Descent: Rappel *Phantom Sprint.*

43   TAPEWORM VI, 5.8, A3, 6 pitches, 625 feet (191 m) ★★★

First Ascent: Brian Warshaw, Brad Jarrett, 5 February 1994.

Location and Access: *Tapeworm* is left of *Run Amok* and right of *Deadman's Party*, on the south face of the tower. Rappel slings are visible from the trail. The first 3 pitches were climbed by Tom Cosgriff in the '80s. Kevin Chase: "Bolts were added to Pitch 1 after the first ascent, bad ethics, bad karma."

Pitch 1: Begin A1, then traverse left over 5.6 loose rock and belay at a fixed anchor.

Pitch 2: Continue up the obvious crack system above and climb past a fixed anchor to a belay from triple anchors, A2+ then A3.

Pitch 3: Climb a right-facing corner to a triple-anchor belay, A2+.

Pitch 4: Climb past a "mud curtain" and up a chimney past several fixed anchors to a double-bolt belay station, A3.

Pitch 5: Continue up the chimney past several fixed anchors to a hole (occasional free moves) and belay at double anchors, first 5.8, then A0, 5.8, and finally A3.

Pitch 6: Pass fixed anchors on the way to the summit and double anchors, A2.

Paraphernalia: Bird Beaks through Bongs; quickdraws.

Descent: Rappel *Phantom Sprint* or the opposite side of the tower down "The Bowels of the Tapeworm."

44   RUN AMOK V, 5.9, A3+, 9 pitches, 625 feet (191 m) ★★★

First Ascent: Jim Beyer, 4-day solo with 1 bivouac, March 1979.

Location and Access: *Run Amok* climbs the southeast face of Echo Tower. Pitches 2, 3, and 4 are overhanging 5 to 30 feet (2 m to 9 m).

Pitch 1: Begin A2, then angle up and right up steps chopped in a dirt-covered slab to belay below a roof.

Pitch 2: Traverse left, 5.6, then continue A3+ passing 1/4" holes, and on to a hanging belay.

Pitch 3: Climb a right-facing corner, then up A3+ to a good belay ledge with bolts.

Pitch 4: Thin nailing to a bolt ladder leads left to a small pendulum into an A1 crack system and a hanging belay.

Pitch 5: Ascend steep A1 into A3 to a hanging belay at a small stance.

photo: Ed Cooper

Cottontail Tower (left), Echo Tower

Pitch 6: Angle up and right with A3 and rivets to a belay at a small stance with double anchors. Jim Beyer: "Sitting bivy for 1."

Pitch 7: Climb A3 with Bongs or Friends (up and right, right-facing corner). Climb a 5.9 chimney to a double-anchor and belay in a pod. Steve "Crusher" Bartlett: "Expect heinous rope drag!"

Pitch 8: Continue up a right-facing corner (5", 12.7 cm) climbing 5.9 offwidth (with some A2), then A3 to a belay at the bottom of a bolt ladder.

Pitch 9: Follow the *North Chimney* bolts to the summit. Protect with #2.5, #3 Friends.

Paraphernalia: Many Friends through #3; knifeblades (10); Bugaboos (10); Lost Arrows (12); baby angles (10); regular angles (10); 2" angles (3); nuts through 6"; bolts and hangers 3/8" and 1/4".

Descent: The first ascent party reversed the route with ropes fixed on Pitches 2, 3, and 4 which overhang 5–30 feet (1.5–9 m). *Phantom Sprint* is the recommended descent line.

Cottontail Tower

Cottontail Tower is recognized by its summit rock, the cottontail. It rises immediately above the Fisher Towers Trail west of and adjacent to Echo Tower, between King Fisher and the Titan. Climbing routes are listed left to right.

Chronology of Early Ascents: Route; Date; Time; Party

1. *West Side Story*; 6–11 June 1967; 6 days, 3 bivouacs; Harvey T. Carter, Art Howells, Don Doucette, Mike Dudley, Morgan Gadd, Herbie Hendricks
2. *Brer Rabbit*; 4–9, 15–16 April 1978; 11 days; Ed Webster, solo
3. *Brer Rabbit*; 19–20 April 1980; 2 bivouacs; Les Ellison, Mark Smith
4. *West Side Story*; November 1983; 4 days; Harvey Miller, Art Wiggins
5. *Road Kill*; 13 November 1987; Earl Wiggins, Art Wiggins, Katy Cassidy
6. *Intifada*; December 1988; Jim Beyer, solo
7. *West Side Story*; October 1989; Steve "Crusher" Bartlett, Bill Roberts
8. *Brer Rabbit*; May 1992; Chip Wilson, Steve "Crusher" Bartlett
* *West Side Story* speed ascent; 1994; 8 hours, 15 min.; Duane Raleigh, Lisa Raleigh

45   WEST SIDE STORY VI, 5.9, C3, 10 pitches, 850 feet (257 m) ★★★★

First Ascent: Harvey T. Carter, Art Howells, Don Doucette, Mike Dudley, Morgan Gadd, Herbie Hendricks, over two consecutive weekends, 3 bivouacs, 6–11, June 1967. Second ascent (fourth overall of the tower), Harvey Miller, Art Wiggins, 4 days, November 1983. Speed ascent: Duane and Lisa Raleigh, on-sight, 8 hours, 15 minutes, 1994. First clean ascent: Dave Goldstein and Mark Hammond.

Location and Access: *West Side Story* starts on the northeast side in an obvious crack system below the left end of the saddle which connects Cottontail with Echo Tower. This climb was the fourth overall ascent made in the Fisher Tower and the third first ascent in the Fishers by Carter.

Pitch 1: Begin up a right-facing corner. Climb hands and clean aid on (2) 1/4" studs over a bulge then on to an alcove. Continue offwidth to a large ledge with a tree approximately 125 feet (38 m) above the ground, 5.8+.

Pitch 2: From the left end of the ledge, climb mixed aid and free past 2 studs over bulges (some bolts for aid) to the start of an obvious chimney. Ascend the chimney to its end and a good belay ledge to the right, 5.7, C2+, 80 feet (24 m).

Pitch 3: From the belay ledge, move left a short distance into a muddy dihedral/ groove; climb this, step left (watch for old bolts) and belay on a small ledge, 5.8, C2, 80 feet (24 m).

Pitch 4: Stem over the ledge, then aid climb up the rotten crack above, or cleaner crack to the left. Gain a bolt ladder, then move right to a scary mantle to the saddle, 5.8, C3, 100 feet (30 m).

Pitch 5: Walk right along the saddle to the start of the summit ridge past 1 bolt, then belay, C2/3, 50 feet (15 m).

Pitch 6: Move right 15 feet (4.5 m) from the pillar onto the northwest face and gain a crack system, 5.9, C2, 90 feet (27 m).

Pitch 7: Traverse right (scary) to blind placements (rope drag). Ascend on devious aid to the start of a bolt ladder, 5.8, C3, 100 feet (30 m).

Pitch 8: Climb a wide crack to a belay below a chimney, 5.9, 60 feet (18 m).

Pitch 9: Follow a 5.7 chimney to a false summit, 5.7, 50 feet (15 m).

Pitch 10: Climb the east side of the Cottontail formation, C1, to the summit, 40 feet (12 m).

Paraphernalia: Friends (2) sets; Cams through 7"; Tri-cams (1) set; sliders; stoppers (1) set; Lowe Balls (1) set; large hooks (2).

Descent: Rappel the route or rappel to the belay at the northwest shoulder below the summit block, then straight down *Road Kill* instead of traversing to the *West Side Story*.

46 ROAD KILL V, 5.9, A4, 7 pitches, 750 feet (229 m) ★

First Ascent: Art Wiggins, Earl Wiggins, Katy Cassidy, 13 November 1987.

Location and Access: *Road Kill* ascends the north face and is the third route established on Cottontail Tower. The climb begins 200 feet (61 m) right of *West Side Story* at the right side of an obvious buttress with a thin-looking discontinuous crack system going straight to the summit.

Pitch 1: Climb up ledges moving right to left to a double-anchor belay.

Pitch 2: Continue up and trend left making a hard A4 placement, then pass 2 fixed anchors and climb to a belay ledge with triple anchors.

Pitch 3: Climb past 2 fixed anchors and up A4 rotten rock to double anchors below an A4 roof. Above the roof climb A3+ up bulges with thin cracks to a triple-anchor belay.

Pitch 4: Continue up and traverse left to cracks, then back right on a ledge to a bulge with bolts. Belay at triple anchors below a roof.

Pitch 5: Climb double cracks passing double anchors, then past bolts and rivets to a double-anchor belay left of bulges.

Pitch 6: Ascend thin and discontinuous cracks to a double-anchor belay ledge at the bedding seam below the caprock, A4.

Pitch 7: Continue left of a wide area to double-rappel anchors at the summit.

Paraphernalia: Friends (1) set; stoppers (1) set; a selection of knifeblades; Lost Arrows; angle pitons from baby through Bongs; small to mid-range angles (3) each, large 2" and up (3); a few RURPS useful; quickdraws.

Descent: Rappel the west face.

47 NOT SO SOFT VI, 5.8, A3+, 5 pitches, 605 feet (184 m)

First Ascent: Shawn MacRae, Chris Van Lerven, 2-5 April 1998.

Location and Access: *Not So Soft* climbs the northwest face of Cottontail beginning 300 feet (91 m) right of *West Side Story*.

Pitch 1: Pass 2 fixed anchors, then continue with Bird Beaks to a 3rd anchor below a roof. Continue over the roof and up steep rock and belay just over a second roof, A3+, 140 feet (43 m).

Pitch 2: Climb up then angle right and up passing a roof and belay at a stance from triple anchors, A3, 80 feet (24 m).

Pitch 3: Traverse right (5.6) then climb a groove to triple anchors, 5.6, A3, 70 feet (21 m).

Pitch 4: Continue with Bird Beaks and knifeblades and belay at a block, A3, 150 feet (46 m).

Pitch 5: Climb mixed free and aid up steep rock. Pass a flake on its left and continue past fixed anchors and holes joining *Brer Rabbit* at a belay ledge, 5.8, A3, 165 feet (50 m).

Paraphernalia: Camalots (2) sets with (1) #4, #5; double Aliens or TCUs; knifeblades (10); Toucans and Spectres useful; Lost Arrows (10); angles (2) 1/2", 5/8", 3/4", (1) 1", 1 1/2"; Bong Bongs through 2 1/2" for *Brer Rabbit*; Z pitons and sawed off angles useful; Bird Beaks (18); hooks (2–3) grappling; Ibis (1–2); rivets and bolt hangers (most belays do not have hangers).

Descent: Rappel the west face down *Road Kill*.

48   BRER RABBIT VI, 5.11b R, A3+, 10 pitches, 850 feet (257 m) ★★★★

First Ascent: Ed Webster, solo, April 1978. Second ascent: Les Ellison, Mark Smith, 1980. Second solo ascent: Chris Kalous, 1994.

Location and Access: *Brer Rabbit* ascends the aesthetic wind-blasted southwest ridge of the huge sandstone tower.

Pitch 1: Begin with mixed climbing up a sustained vertical crack system just left of the ridge above the trail and climb to a ledge on the left, 5.10+, A2, 140 feet (43 m).

Pitch 2: Follow a crack past an unprotected wide section to and around a small roof. Belay on a stance on the ridge to the right, 5.10, A2, 125 feet (38 m).

Pitch 3: Step right and aid a short hidden crack to a bolt ladder and free moves to a large belay ledge (excellent bivy in the cave on the left), 5.6, A2, 60 feet (18 m).

Pitch 4: Traverse straight left across the west face on a sloping ledge "the sidewalk" to a bolt belay, 5.8, 90 feet (27 m).

Pitch 5: Aid a difficult and sustained crack system up a steep wall (a few bolts) to an obvious notch and bolt anchors, A3+, 140 feet (43 m).

Pitch 6: Climb an overhanging offwidth through a bulge (5.9), then a handcrack on the left (5.8) to a horizontal ridge, 60 feet (18 m).

Pitch 7: Walk north along the ridge to a "leap across" gap. Leave slings on a bolt. Belay on a narrow fin, 85 feet (26 m).

Pitch 8: Ascend aid bolts and an A2 crack up the ridge. Walk, then aid 2 more bolts to a platform, 5.11b R, A2, 160 feet (49 m).

Pitch 9: Traverse right and aid up the back of a large fluting to a stance with bolts, 5.9+, A2+, 130 feet (40 m), or continue 30 feet (9 m) to the ridge to a giant thread belay.

Pitch 10: Aid to the final ridge, then walk north and up the summit block (cottontail) by a good 3" hand/Friend crack to the left of the *West Side Story* finish, A3, 70 feet (21 m). The pitch will probably go free at 5.10+.

Paraphernalia: Full rack, including pitons, and thin through 6" pieces; quickdraws.

Descent: Rappel the route (tricky), or the west face down *Road Kill*.

49   INTIFADA VI, 5.10 S X A6, 12 pitches, 850 feet (257 m) ★★

First Ascent: Jim Beyer, solo, December 1988. Second solo ascent: Tim Wagner, March 1997.

Location and Access: *Intifada* is right of *Brer Rabbit*, immediately above the Fisher Towers Trail on the south face of the tower. No bolts were place and no holes drilled deeper than 1/4" on the first ascent which was made with 38 hook moves (some

Chip Wilson on Pitch 9 of *Brer Rabbit*

drilled). Jim Beyer: "A6 is 2 grades harder than some A4s. A6 is 2 or more pitches with potential death falls and no bolts."

Pitch 1: Begin up an A4, then A3 rotten seam. Continue with hooks up A4 rock to a hanging belay at an A3 anchor with a sling visible from the trail below. The pitch ascends a conglomerate layer of rock (pebbles and aragonite) at the base of the tower.

Pitch 2: Climb A4 to a hanging belay at the top of the conglomerate rock, a point 165 feet (50 m) above the trail.

Pitch 3: Climb a left-facing corner at 5.8, A3 to a hanging belay at an A3 anchor in an expanding pillar.

Pitch 4: Hook traverse left A4+ ending with A1, and set up a hanging belay. The pitch has the potential for a death fall.

Pitch 5: Climb up A4, then A1 past an overhang, then up A5. Pendulum right off a micro hook at the top of the A5 climbing and establish a hanging belay. Jim Beyer suggests: "Big Fall Possible," A6.

Pitch 6: Continue with A1 into A4 to a hanging belay.

Pitch 7: Angle up and right (A4), then make hook moves left to a large (bivouac) ledge and belay.

Pitch 8–11: Follow *Brer Rabbit* up easy 5.9, A3 past many bolts to the summit pitch.

Pitch 12: Climb a sandy arête past a bulge and on to the top from a point left of the *Brer Rabbit's* summit pitch, 5.10 hands.

Paraphernalia: Cams; hooks, Bird Beaks, Bashies, many pitons.

Descent: Rappel the west face.

Gypsy Eyes, Gypsy Joker

The Gypsys are two pinnacles located west of the Fisher Towers Trail as it meanders between Cottontail and the Titan. The two hoodoos stand together, with Gypsy Eyes southeast (left) of Gypsy Joker.

50 GYPSY EYES I, 5.10, A3, 1 pitch

First Ascent: Jim Beyer, Mike Munger, fall 1983.

Location and Access: The spire is climbed by nailing the north face to the summit crack which is surmounted by free climbing an overhanging hand-and-fist crack, then an offwidth at the top. There is 1 fixed bolt on the route.

Paraphernalia: Standard desert rack; a selection of pitons.

Descent: Rappel the route.

51 GYPSY JOKER I, 5.8, A0, 1 pitch

First Ascent: Jim Beyer, Mike Munger, fall 1983.

Location and Access: Jim Beyer: "The route is destined to become a classic because it reaches a summit in the Fisher Towers on a rack of nuts, on moderate, well-protected rock." No bolts were placed on the first ascent. Begin with a shoulder stand (A0) on the southeast corner of the tower. A tricky mantle is followed by a short handcrack and chimney.

Paraphernalia: A selection of nuts.

Descent: Jim Beyer: "Rappel off the top on (2) A3 pegs."

Titan

Titan was the first tower in the Fishers to be climbed. It is at the end of the 2-mile (3.2 km) Fisher Towers Trail and is obvious from the parking area and River Road as the tallest monolith in the area. The approach requires negotiating a 10-foot (3 m) steel ladder between the Cottontail/Echo complex and Titan itself. To bypass the ladder (if you are accompanied by a canine) descend into the gully before reaching the ladder, then follow the drainage past the ladder until it is possible to regain the trail. Routes are listed left to right beginning with the *Finger of Fate*.

The historic first ascent of the Titan in May 1962 was filmed from the air for the National Geographic Society by Barry Bishop, who was one of the first Americans to summit Everest (1963). In November 1962, an article written by Huntley Ingalls and titled "We Climbed Utah's Skyscraper Rock" appeared in the *National Geographic* magazine.

After Steck and Roper's *Fifty Classic Climbs of North America* was published in 1979, the tower, included in the 50, became much sought after by those wishing to check off their list as many of the "classics" as possible. The Titan is a hauntingly awesome tower which, despite numerous ascents, has a very high ratio of failures. In a *Summit Magazine* article, Bill Forrest comments, "Somewhere between standing at the base of these grotesquely shaped, wind and water carved monoliths, and standing on their summits, is a priceless encounter with true grit."

Steck-Roper: "The Titan is much more than loose rock, sand in the eyes, shifting pitons, drizzles, and dangerous rappels, however. Anyone who walks in its vicinity will be awed by its multitude of bizarre rock forms, startling colors, and fascinating vegetation. Those who climb the Titan may find the landscape and climbing so different from that found in other areas that the experience becomes distinctly unearthly. Equally dramatic is the contrast between the glaring midday sun and the soft light from a full moon, which renders the region hauntingly beautiful. The convoluted rock casts a network of eerie shadows at such a time, and the howl of the coyote seems eminently appropriate."

Steve Roper on the 5th ascent of Finger of Fate: "The bivy ledge was like all of them: comfortable and huge at sundown, hard and tiny and repulsive at dawn . . . the rappels were endless, difficult, and scary."

Kevin Daniels: "The Titan is kind of rock, kind of mud, kind of scary, kind of climbable."

Will Oxx base-jumped off the Titan in 1995.

David Pagel: "Robed in flowing red curtains of sandstone, and topped with a solid helmet of brown caprock, the 900-foot formation presents a magnificent edifice–perhaps the tallest and certainly the proudest freestanding desert spire on Earth."

Chronology of Early Ascents: Route; Date; Time; Party

1. *Finger of Fate*; 13 May 1962; 4 days; Layton Kor, Huntley Ingalls, George Hurley
2. *Finger of Fate*; 5 March 1966; 4 days; George Hurley, TM Herbert, Tom Condon
3. *Finger of Fate*; 14 April 1969; 2 days; Paul Sibley, Bill Roos
4. *Finger of Fate Direct*; 14 April 1969; 2 days; Harvey T. Carter, Tim Jennings
5. *Finger of Fate*; 22 October 1969; 1.5 days; Royal Robbins, Chuck Pratt, Steve Roper
6. *Finger of Fate*; 14 March 1971; 1.5 days; Jimmy Dunn, Ron Cox, Larry Hamilton
7. *Sundevil Chimney*; 28 April 1971; 8 days; Harvey T. Carter, Robert Sullivan, Tom Merrill, Ken Wyrick
8. *Finger of Fate*; 13 June 1971; 11 hours; Bill Forrest, Ray Jardine

photo: Steve "Crusher" Bartlett

North side of the Titan

Titan

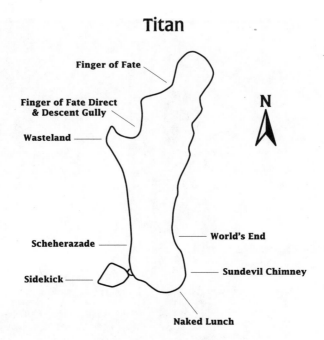

Finger of Fate

Finger of Fate Direct
& Descent Gully

Wasteland

N

Scheherazade

Sidekick

World's End

Sundevil Chimney

Naked Lunch

9. *Scheherazade*; 6 September 1973; Lou Dawson, Harvey T. Carter
* First solo; May 1980; 9 hours; Jim Beyer
* *Finger of Fate* speed ascent; February 1994; 3 hours, 22 minutes; Duane Raleigh, Lisa Raleigh
* *Finger of Fate* first clean ascent; 1996; Stevie Haston, Laurence Gouault; 5.12, C3

52   FINGER OF FATE IV, 5.8, A2+ (or 5.12, C3), 9 pitches, 900 feet (274 m) ★★★★

First Ascent: Layton Kor, George Hurley, Huntley Ingalls, 53 bolts, 1 bivouac, over 2 consecutive weekends, 5–6 and 12–13 May 1962. First clean ascent: Stevie Haston, Laurence Gauoult, 5.12, C3, 1996.

Location and Access: The *Finger of Fate* ascends the uphill northeast side of the Titan and is reached by a complete circumscription of the giant tower. Begin by hiking the trail to the western escarpment of the Titan before contouring east into a small valley. Follow this to its head, then traverse left along ledges to the base of the tower. The route begins in a shallow bowl on the northeast side of the monolith. No pitons are needed above Pitch 4. The route goes 80 percent free at about 5.11b. Jim Beyer: "The Finger of Fate route is to the Fisher Towers what the Chouinard/Herbert on Sentinel is to Yosemite."

Pitch 1: Begin up a slot, then climb C2, 5.7, pass an old triple-anchor belay. Angle up and left to a triple anchor hanging belay, 150 feet (46 m).

Pitch 2: Climb to a second triple-anchor hanging belay, 5.8, A2+, 80 feet (24 m).

Pitch 3: Ascend A2 past piton scars to a triple-anchor belay ledge, A2, 70 feet (21 m).

Pitch 4: Move down and right past double-anchors, 5.6, then climb a roof (A0) and on to a belay stance at the base of the Finger of Fate, 5.6, A0, 70 feet (21 m).

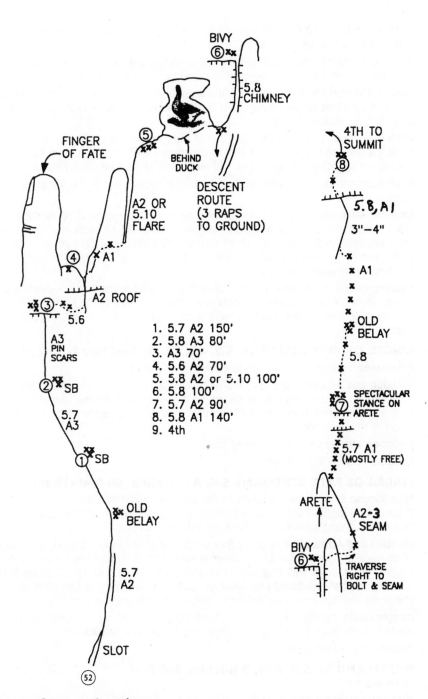

BIVY
⑥xx

5.8
CHIMNEY

BEHIND
DUCK

FINGER
OF FATE

⑤
xxx

A2 OR
5.10
FLARE

DESCENT
ROUTE
(3 RAPS
TO GROUND)

4TH TO
SUMMIT
x
⑧

5.8, A1

3"-4"

-x

x A1

x
x
x

xx OLD
x BELAY

5.8

④
xx

x A1

xxx-x-xx
③
5.6

A2 ROOF

SPECTACULAR
xx STANCE ON
⑦ ARETE
TTT
x
x

A3
PIN
SCARS

②xx SB

5.7
A3

①x SB

x 5.7 A1
x (MOSTLY FREE)
x

ARETE

A2-3
SEAM

xx OLD
BELAY

BIVY
⑥xx

TRAVERSE
RIGHT TO
BOLT & SEAM

5.7
A2

1. 5.7 A2 150'
2. 5.8 A3 80'
3. A3 70'
4. 5.6 A2 70'
5. 5.8 A2 or 5.10 100'
6. 5.8 100'
7. 5.7 A2 90'
8. 5.8 A1 140'
9. 4th

SLOT

52

Finger of Fate, The Titan
by George Bell

Pitch 5: Climb up and right through a roof (the crux) past 2 fixed anchors at A2 or 5.10 flare to a triple-anchor belay, 5.8, A2, or 5.10, 100 feet (30 m).

Pitch 6: The "Duckwalk." Climb behind the "Duck," past double-anchors, then up a 5.8 chimney to a double-anchor belay (bivouac) ledge, 5.8, 100 feet (30 m).

Pitch 7: Traverse left (5.7) to a bolt and a seam and climb A2 past an arête, past a roof, and up a bolt ladder (mostly free) to a spectacular 4-anchor belay stance on an arête, 5.7, A2, 90 feet (27 m).

Pitch 8: Continue past 2 anchors and an old triple-anchor belay, then up a bolt ladder. Move left and climb a 3–4" crack (7.6-10 cm), pass a roof, then a fixed anchor to a double-anchor belay, 5.8, A2+ tricky, 140 feet (43 m). A #5 Camalot is helpful.

Pitch 9: Pass many rivets, bolts and old bolts (A2+) before continuing 4th class to the summit.

Paraphernalia: The following is a gear list for a non-clean ascent; climbing the route clean involves tricky free climbing on shaky gear: (C3 and 5.12) Technical Friends (1) set; Camalots (1) #0.5, #0.75, #4, (2) #1 through #3; TCUs (1) set through #2.5; stoppers (4–8); Leepers (2); angles (2), 0.5", (1) 5/8", (2) 3/4", 1", (1) 1 1/4 , (3) 1.5", (2) 2"; carabiners (70); quickdraws (20).

Descent: Double-rope rappels to the top of Pitch 7, then to the notch south of the "Duck." From the notch make 3 rappels down the north side to the base of the route. Pull the knot down 30 feet (9 m) to avoid severe rope drag on the first rappel from the Duck.

53 FINGER OF FATE DIRECT IV, 5.8, A3, 13 pitches, 900 feet (274 m)

First Ascent: Harvey T. Carter, Tim Jennings, 13–14 April 1969.

Location and Access: *Finger of Fate Direct* climbs a 170-foot (52 m) direct start beginning 50 yards (46 m) right of the *Finger of Fate* route (from the southeast). The original route, which begins from the northeast, is met at a saddle at the base of the *Finger of Fate Gendarme.*

Paraphernalia: Same as for *Finger of Fate.*

Descent: Rappel *Finger of Fate.*

54 FINGER OF FATE GENDARME 5.4, A1, 1 pitch, 60 feet (18 m)

First Ascent: Brad England, 5 hours 25 minutes solo, with Phil White support, 2 October 1997. Second ascent: Brad England, 3 October 1997, to retrieve gear abandoned during a violent thunderstorm the previous day.

Location and Access: The *Finger of Fate Gendarme* is 370 feet (113 m) up the Titan. Climb the northwest corner of the tower beginning at the top of the *Finger of Fate* route's Pitch 4. Begin with exposed A1 climbing, then 5.4 to a stance. Continue left of a muddy overhang, climbing past fixed 3.5" bolts. Clipping the first bolt after the stance creates bad rope drag. Follow A1 bolts to double anchors on the summit.

Paraphernalia: Camalots (1) #0.5, #2, #3, #4; TCUs (1) #2, #3, #4; stoppers small to medium; baby angle (1); a long 1.4" angle; rivit hangers (2); quickdraws.

Descent: Rappel the route.

55 WASTELAND VI, 5.9, A3+, 9 pitches, 900 feet (274 m) ★★

First Ascent: Duane Raleigh, Walt Shipley, 20-25 October 1997.

photo: Layton Kor

First ascent of the Titan

photo: Brad England

Finger of Fate Gendarme. The route goes up the right cracks.

photo: Steve "Crusher" Bartlett

The Titan

Location and Access: Begin off the highest ledge on the northwest face.

Paraphernalia: Friends (2) #0.5 through #3.5; Camalots (1) #4; knifeblades (5); Lost Arrows (4); angles 0.5" through 3/4" (2), 1" through 1.5" (1); 3" and 4" Bong-Bongs (1); Leeper Zs (3); large hook; ice hammer; (9) 3/8" hangers.

Descent: Rappel the route or *Sundevil Chimney*, or the *Finger of Fate* to the top of Pitch 5, then make 3 rappels down the gully right of the route.

56 SCHEHERAZADE VI, 5.9, A4, 11 pitches, 900 feet (274 m) ★

First Ascent: Lou Dawson, Harvey T. Carter, with Kendall Williams, Michael Kennedy working on the first 6 pitches, approximately 55 bolts, 15–20 September 1973. Second ascent: Art Wiggins, John Myers, March 1986.

Location and Access: *Scheherazade* begins after climbing a mud chimney to the saddle between Sidekick (a small formation next to the west face) and the west face proper. From the saddle, climb several pitches through overhangs and large ledges to a 75-foot (23 m) bolt ladder in an obvious blank corner. From a hanging belay at the top of the ladder, climb several pitches directly up, then begin working a bit to the right using a tension traverse. The next-to-last pitch follows a vertical mud-encrusted crack directly to the caprock. One mixed pitch through the caprock leads to the summit.

Paraphernalia: On the first ascent, 55 bolts, 125 pitons, and 12 nuts were placed.

Descent: Double-rope rappels lead down the route, using 2-bolt belay stations for anchors, or rappel *Sundevil Chimney* or the *Finger of Fate* to the top of Pitch 5, then make 3 rappels down the gully right of the route.

57 SIDEKICK—CAMPFLOWER III, 5.10, A3, 5 pitches, 235 feet (70 m)

First Ascent: Harvey T. Carter, Ken Wyrick, 23 April 1971.

Location and Access: Sidekick is a formation beside the trail, connected to the bottom of the Titan's southwest face. Climb an awkward flaring overhanging crack on the left, then friction traverse right to a second belay. Climb a crack and wall with aid and other strenuous means to upper belay ledges. Continue up a short ,difficult wall and on to the exposed (west) summit horn.

Paraphernalia: Standard desert rack, including larger Friends and Tri-cams.

Descent: Two double-rope rappels down the route.

58 NAKED LUNCH VI, 5.10 R, A4, 8 pitches, 900 feet (274 m)

First Ascent: Pete Takeda, Duane Raleigh, 6.5 days, approximately 45 bolts, 1,100 feet of climbing, summer 1994. David Pagel: "The first ascent introduced a new bag of tricks to the Fisher Towers: ice tools and lariats."

Location and Access: *Naked Lunch* climbs the dihedral system between *Sundevil Chimney* and *Scheherazade* on the south prow of the Titan and is the longest route on the tower.

Pitch 1: Climb the first 70 feet (21 m) of *Sundevil*, and belay at double bolts.

Pitch 2: Lower to the left 40 feet (12 m) to a knifeblade crack. Hook to the left 25 feet (7.6 m) to a knifeblade crack in a roof. Follow it to a wide crack system which is taken to the top of a small, dirt pinnacle. Traverse left 30 feet (9 m) to a double-bolt belay. **NOTE:** The pitch, due to rope drag, is a mandatory solo.

Pitch 3: Gain the thin crack overhead with delicate ice axe hooking, a couple pitons, and 2 bolts. Follow a thin crack to a roof. Move right, then up to a hanging belay from a bolt.

Pitch 4: Ascend a short bolt ladder to a thin crack down and under a roof. Aid climb under the roof, then exit the right side to access a nutting section which leads to a bolt ladder.

Pitch 5: Free climb right 30 feet (9 m), unprotected, then continue to double bolts and back left to a 5.10 slot. Above the slot, do an ice axe grappling hook toss on a sharp horn out to the left. Mantle onto the horn and step left to belay (good ledges).

Pitch 6: Aid climb out the roof, then climb an obvious crack to the left with nuts. Thin nailing leads to an exposed stance to the left.

Pitch 7: Nail an overhanging sandy crack to a wide crack system. Move right at the end of the crack to a good belay/bivy ledge.

Pitch 8: Thin nailing up an obvious dihedral leads to the top.

Paraphernalia: Friends (3) sets of all sizes from #0.5 through #5; Bird Beaks (5); knifeblades (20); all angles through 2" (5); long-thin knifeblades (5); assorted Leeper Zs (10); small and medium wires; ring-angle claw; ice axe for hooking; small to medium aluminum heads; bolt hangers for 3/8" and 0.5" bolt studs.

Descent: Rappel *Sundevil Chimney* or the *Finger of Fate* to the top of Pitch 5, then make 3 rappels down the gully right of the route.

59 SUNDEVIL CHIMNEY VI, 5.9, A3+, 7 pitches, 850 feet (259 m) ★★★★★

First Ascent: Harvey T. Carter, Tom Merrill, Bob "Sully" Sullivan, Ken Wyrick, approximately 55 bolts, 20–28 April 1971. Second ascent: Italians Giorgio Bertone, Lorenzino Cosson, American Craig Martinson, October 1976. The Italian ascent was filmed by Carlo Mauri for Italian and German television. Jim Beyer: "I think the two most popular routes in the Fisher Towers in the next 10 years will be the *Sundevil Chimney* and the *Jagged Edge*."

Location and Access: *Sundevil Chimney* climbs the south face of the tower and begins 110 feet (36 m) above the trail. It is reached by contouring around from the hiking trail to the direct south face of the tower or directly up the wall from the trail.

Finger of
Fate Gendarme

Oracle

Cottontail

59

61

photo: Ed Cooper

Titan and Oracle

Pitch 1: Begin up a left-facing system (A2) past a fixed anchor, a roof, another fixed anchor, then A3 past several more fixed anchors to a triple-anchor hanging belay, A3, 155 feet (47 m).

Pitch 2: Climb A1 up a 2–3" crack (5-7.6 cm), then A2 to a 4 anchor hanging belay, A2, 125 feet (38 m).

Pitch 3: Climb A2+ into 5.8, then up a bolt ladder to A2+ and a hanging 4 anchor belay, 5.8, A2+, 130 feet (40 m). Pitches 3 and 4 are inside a muddy chimney.

Pitch 4: Continue A2 past a fixed anchor, then A2+ past another anchor. Stem in mud, 5.7, with poor protection, past a fixed anchor to a sloping stance and a 4-anchor belay, 5.7, A2+, 130 feet (40 m).

Pitch 5: Climb A1 up a right-facing corner passing a roof on its right (4 anchors), then up A2 (5") rock past a fixed anchor. Continue up a sandy ramp to a ledge. Belay from a rope lassoed around a horn, A2, 120 feet (37 m).

Pitch 6: Continue A2, move left to a fixed anchor, 5.9, then to the bedding seam (below the summit) and a fixed anchor. Climb to a ledge to belay from triple anchors, 5.7, A2, 130 feet (40 m).

Pitch 7: Ascend a right-facing chimney to the summit and triple anchors, 5.6, 60 feet (18 m).

Paraphernalia: Friends (2) sets through #3.5, (1) #4; TCUs (1) set; Tri-cam (1) #5; medium selection of mostly large stoppers; angle pitons (6) 0.5", (4) 5/8", 3/4", (1) 3", (2) 1-1/4", (3) 1.5"; Bongs (2) 2.5"; long Leepers (4); small selection of Lost Arrows; medium long knifeblades (2); Big Dudes (2) are useful on Pitch 5; quickdraws. Matt Moore: "A pair of golf cleats." Note: Clean aid as of March, 1999.

Descent: Rappel the route or the *Finger of Fate* to the top of Pitch 5, then make 3 rappels down the gully right of the route.

60   WORLD'S END VI, 5.9 X A5, 8 pitches, 900 feet (274 m) ★★★★★

First Ascent: Jim Beyer, solo, over 4 days in late February and the first of March 1987. Second ascent: Chris Kalous, solo, 30 October 1994, with a variation to the finish (further information is unknown).

Location and Access: Beyer gives the climb an A5 rating because of a 70-foot (21 m) fall potential on Pitch 3. The route begins 40 feet (12 m) right of *Sundevil Chimney* on the southwest face of the Titan. Five pitches are climbed before the route joins *Sundevil Chimney*. On the first ascent 39 bolts were placed. Jim Beyer: "I think the best two aid routes in Utah are *Death of American Democracy* and *World's End* as far as quality and difficulty." David Pagel: "The topo for this climb is covered with so many asterisks you'd swear it's the most recommended route in the world–until you realize the stars mark bad bolts. The gear list from the first ascent indicates that Beyer placed 20 RURPs in this fudge; it's no wonder he had to do the thing alone."

Pitch 1: Begin up a left-facing edge and climb A2+ to a hanging belay.

Pitch 2: Continue A1, then A4 to double anchors at a hanging belay with triple anchors.

Pitch 3: Climb A5 past fixed anchors with a couple hook moves, then A4 crossing an arête right to left. Belay at a ledge with triple anchors, A5 X.

Pitch 4: Ascend left of an arête, 5.9, A0 up a bolt ladder. Continue A1 (TCUs, small Friends), then A3+ to A4. Make a hook move and end at a hanging belay with a fixed piton.

Pitch 5: Climb past fixed anchors A2 to A4 ending with 5.9, A0 and a bivy ledge.

Pitch 6: Move up at 5.9 to a belay ledge.

Pitch 7: Climb 5.7 dirt, then A2, and 5.7 to a belay ledge.

Pitch 8: Climb to the summit A2 and 5.9 fingers, ending with 5.8.

Paraphernalia: First ascent list: Friends (1) set #0.5 through #3; TCUs #0.4 through #3/4; RURPS (20); small knifeblades (5); large knifeblades (12); Bugaboos (8); Lost Arrows (20); Leepers (8); angles (2) 0.5", 5/8", (4–5) 3/4", (3) 1", 1.5"; copperheads (5); aluminum heads (20-25); wired nuts (10); hooks; (3–4) 3/8" hangers, and up to (8) 1/4" hangers or keyhole hangers. Updated list: Friends (1) set to #3 Camalot; TCUs (1) set; stoppers (2) sets; Leepers (2); keyhole hangers (8); aluminum heads including large Chouinards (15); all hooks; Bird Beaks (13); knifeblades mostly short (15); Lost Arrows (15); angle pitons 0.5" through 3/4" (3); 1" through 2" (1).

Descent: Rappel *Sundevil Chimney* or *Finger of Fate* to the top of Pitch 5, then 3 rappels down the gully right of the route. The first ascent rappelled the route with fixed ropes left on overhangs.

Oracle, Broadsword Rock

Oracle is a spire connected to the wall northeast of the Titan. Broadsword Rock is a fin-shaped rock toward Onion Creek, southwest of the Titan.

61   ORACLE—FANTASIA VI, 5.10 S, A2, 7 pitches, 590 feet (180 m) ★★★

First Ascent: Harvey T. Carter, Tom Merrill, Steve Kentz, with Mike Pokress working on the first 5 pitches, 9–17 October 1970. Second ascent: Tom Merrill, Tom Sullivan, Ken Wyrick.

photo: Chip Wilson

Steve "Crusher" Bartlett on *Fantasia*, pitch 6

photo: Ed Cooper

Oracle

Location and Access: Oracle is uphill from Titan. *Fantasia* climbs the south face of the landform. The first ascent team placed 44 bolts, 33 pitons, and 3 nuts in a 14-pitch ascent. A summit register was left 3 March 1997, by James Garrett and Ryan Hokenson.

Pitch 1: Climb a wide clean crack left of a mud chimney to a ledge on the chimney's right side, 5.9, A2, 120 feet (37 m).

Pitch 2: Continue up a bolt ladder with occasional free moves to a belay ledge, 5.8, A0, 70 feet (21 m).

Pitch 3: Climb the short bolt ladder to a 5.8 dirt traverse right to a crack which gains the shoulder. Continue with mixed free and aid to an A2 (clean) crack to a double-bolt belay ledge, 5.8, A2, 130 feet (40 m).

Pitch 4: Traverse the south ridge on its west side with a few aid moves, then walk to the east side and proceed with easy 5th class to a belay consisting of a slung hourglass, 5.7, A1, 60 feet (18 m).

Pitch 5: Continue traversing (on the east side) past a bolt on increasingly difficult free climbing (5.7) to a short right-leaning crack. Aid the crack (A2) to a belay. Move the belay to (2) 3/8" bolts (hidden) and rappel into the notch, 5.10, A2, 80 feet (24 m). Above the rappel point, an old bolt is visible to the left; the original party continued up the wide improbable looking chimney above.

Pitch 6: Continue with serious free climbing past an old anchor using hooks and free moves to (2) 3/8" bolts, 5.10 S, 50 feet (15 m).

Pitch 7: Free moves lead to a bolt ladder leading to the summit, A2, 80 feet (24 m).

Paraphernalia: Standard desert rack with extra Friends #1 through #7; hooks; Quickdraws.

Descent: Rappel the route (tricky) or to the notch, then down the "Gastrointestinal" chimney to the east.

62   ORACLE—BEAKING IN TONGUES VI, 5.8, A4, 7 pitches, 720 feet (219 m) ★★★★

First Ascent: Steve "Crusher" Bartlett, Dave Levine, April 1997.

Location and Access: Oracle is uphill from the Titan. *Beaking in Tongues* climbs the northwest face of the landform, following an obvious left-leaning crack system. On the first ascent, the crux involved placing 12 Bird Beaks in a row. Bartlett and Levine also placed 3/8"-by-3–4" Rawl bolts at belays. No other bolts or drilled holes for aid were used on the ascent.

For Crusher, the ascent completed his goal of climbing all the major towers in the Fishers twice: King Fisher, Echo and Cottontail Towers, Oracle, and the Titan.

Pitch 1: Begin up an incipient crack system which becomes better higher up, A3, 130 feet (37 m).

Pitch 2: Continue up a muddy crack, A2, 100 feet (21 m).

Pitch 3: Follow the muddy crack up and left, A2+, 140 feet (40 m).

Pitch 4: Mud, then thin nailing leads right then left to a crack and a belay, A3, 60 feet (18 m).

Pitch 5: Traverse right along a horizontal 30-foot (9 m) section, then up a thin crack to a bolt belay, A3+, 70 feet (21m).

Pitch 6: Traverse right under a roof to a scooped-out appearing area, then continue to a saddle, A4, 40 feet (15 m).

Pitch 7: Trend up and right to a good crack, then traverse down and right to a splitter crack leading to the summit, 5.8, A3, 180 feet (24 m). **NOTE:** The first ascentionists led this pitch on 2 ropes to avoid rope drag.

Paraphernalia: Tri-cams (6); Bird Beaks (15); a few large hooks, plus a general Fisher Towers aid rack.

Descent: Rappel to the saddle, then to anchors placed 60 feet (18 m) right of the top of Pitch 3, and finally to the ground following belay anchors.

63   BROADSWORD ROCK—SOUTHWEST FACE II, 5.5, 3 pitches, 225 feet (69 m)

First Ascent: Harvey T. Carter, solo, 8 May 1973.

Location and Access: Broadsword Rock is a fin-shaped formation, which looks like a sword, with a tower (the handle) at its south end. The location of the *Southwest Face* route is uncertain.

Paraphernalia: Friends (1) set.

Descent: Rappel the route.

64   BROADSWORD ROCK—NORTHERN BLADE II, 5.10, A0, 4 pitches, 225 feet (69 m)

First Ascent: James Garrett, Franziska Garrett, 24 April 1997.

Location and Access: *Northern Blade* is visible from the trail as you walk around the exposed (south) side of the Titan (Sundevil Chimneys). The Garretts found no anchors on the summit, so they drilled 2 bolts for their rappel.

Pitch 1: Begin up the north edge of the landform, 5.7, and climb bulges to a saddle.

Pitch 2: Make a short blocky traverse, 5.4, along the Blade of the sword.

Pitch 3: Descend, then continue the traverse to the base of the tower (the Handle), 5.4.

Pitch 4: Climb the Handle beginning 5.10, then A0 to the summit.

Paraphernalia: Friends (1) set; TCUs (1) set; nuts (1) set.

Descent: Rappel with double 60 m ropes to the northeast.

Projects

Projects is a butte-shaped fin (with a large window) in the drainage west of the Titan.

65   PROJECTS—OLDE ENGLISH 800 II, 5.7, A1 2 pitches, 120 feet (37 m) ★★★★

First Ascent: Cameron Burns, Jon Butler, 26 April 1997.

Location and Access: To reach, follow the Titan Trail to Cottontail Tower. Walk past *Brer Rabbit*, then along the south face of Cottontail, passing *Intifada*. Drop into the next drainage. Follow the drainage west for approximately 0.5 mile (0.8 km), then cross the ridge to the south. Projects will be visible to the west several hundred yards away. *Olde English 800* climbs the eastern (uphill) prow of the butte-shaped tower in 2 short pitches to avoid rope drag.

Pitch 1: Begin scrambling up left of the prow, then aid up a short 10-foot (3 m) A1 crack. Continue up a 4-bolt ladder to a large ledge. Belay using natural gear.

Pitch 2: Ascend the roofs above, then follow 15 feet (4.5 m) of 4th class to a short easily protected face (5.7) to the summit.

Paraphernalia: Friends (2) #1, #1.5, #2, (1) #2.5, #3, (2) #4; large hexes (2); angles (1) 0.5", 5.8", 3/4"; double ropes; 3/8" bolt hangers (2) or tie-off slings.

Descent: One double-rope rappel down the route.

photo: Cameron M. Burns

Jon Butler on the first ascent of *Olde English 800*

Time, geologic time, looks out at us from the rocks as from no other objects in the landscape. Geologic time! How the striking of the great clock, whose hours are millions of years, reverberates out of the abyss of the past! Mountains fall and the foundations of the earth shift as it beats out the moments of terrestrial history. Rocks have literally come down to us from a foreworld. The youth of the earth is in the soil and in the trees and verdure that spring from it; its age is in the rocks. . . . Even if we do not know our geology, there is something in the face of a cliff and in the look of a granite boulder that gives us pause. . . .

The rocks have a history; gray and weatherworn, they are veterans of many battles; they have most of them marched in the ranks of vast stone brigades during the ice age; they have been torn from the hills, recruited from the mountaintops, and marshaled on the plains and in the valleys; and now the elemental war is over, there they lie waging a gentle but incessant warfare with time and slowly, oh, so slowly, yielding to its attacks! I say they lie there, but some of them are still in motion, creeping down the slopes or out from the claybanks, nudged and urged along by the frosts and the rains and the sun.

–John Burroughs

photo: Steve "Crusher" Bartlett

Ralph E. Burns on the Mongoose

ONION CREEK TOWERS

There is no royal road for the person who would explore the canyon's hidden secrets. Enthusiasm in unlimited quantities is a most needful qualification—enthusiasm in spite of discomfort, fatigue, and toil all to gain what might be a doubtful goal.

–Ellsworth Kolb, 1914

The towers of Onion Creek are visible to the right (east) as you drive between mile markers 19 and 21 on River Road. To approach, turn between mile marker 20 and 21 at a sign reading "Fisher Valley Ranch." Mongoose, Sari, and Hindu tower above the dirt road as it winds through a narrow canyon, crosses Onion Creek 16 times, then continues through multicolored gypsum beds and up Fisher Valley on the north shoulder of the La Sal Mountains. As the sinuous canyon cuts through deep red Cutler Sandstone, note the white crusty deposits in places near the creek. These are saline minerals dissolved from very old Paradox Formation salts. Gypsum, squeezed from deep within the earth, is hydrous calcium sulfate (from the Greek *gypsos* meaning "chalk"). Of Permian and Triassic age, it is now used as a retardant in portland cement and in making plaster of Paris. Onion Creek's name derives from the malodorous springs that flow from above the salts of the gypsum upthrust. As you near the springs, Onion Creek becomes increasingly sulfurous.

photo: Lin Ottinger

Left to right: **Mongoose, Sari, Hindu**

photo: Harvey T. Carter

Mongoose from the east

Hindu is the tall, thin spire obvious from River Road. The spire is known locally as The Sentinel and is designated on some maps as another Totem Pole. Mongoose (angular tower) and Sari (butte shaped) are often referred to by locals as Mother with Baby Carriage, Mother with Perambulator, Miner and Ore Cart, or Grandma and Little Red Riding Hood. Names used in this guide were given by first-ascent parties.

1   MONGOOSE—EXCALIBUR III, 5.12b, 5 pitches, 500 feet (152 m)

First Ascent: Harvey T. Carter, Kenny Williams, Mike Pokress, 5.8, A2, 4–5 June 1971. First free ascent: French alpinists Stevie Haston and Laurence Gouault, 1995.

Location and Access: *Excalibur* follows the longest possible line on the formation, starting from the low point on the east side. The back side of the tower is only 100 feet (30 m) high. The crux is on the last pitch passing bat hook holes, 5.12b.

Paraphernalia: Friends (2) sets; a selection of Tri-cams and stoppers.

Descent: Rappel the shorter back side of the tower.

2   SARI—EAST FACE II, 5.11a, 1 pitch, 130 feet (40 m)

First Ascent: Bill Forrest, solo, 5.6, A1, late 1960s. First free ascent: Rob Slater, Stu Ritchie.

Location and Access: *East Face* climbs an obvious weakness on the east face of the tower. The free ascent negotiates a 3-foot (0.9 m) roof at the crux.

Paraphernalia: Friends (1) set; selection of wide pitons.

Descent: Rappel from double anchors.

3.   SARI—STRIKEFORCE II, 5.8, A2, 3 pitches, 130 feet (40 m)

First Ascent: Harvey T. Carter, Larry Lane, 19 April 1979.

Location and Access: *Strikeforce* begins on the east ledge and moves to the south corner, then traverses to the west (5.8 then 5.5). Continue around to an aid crack that is followed to the summit.

Paraphernalia: Standard desert rack.

Descent: Rappel the route.

4   SARI—SOUTH FACE II, A3, 1 pitch, 130 feet (40 m)

First Ascent: Jim Beyer, solo, A3, spring 1983.

Location and Access: *South Face* aids the discontinuous cracks on the south face of the tower.

Paraphernalia: Unknown.

Descent: Rappel the route.

5   HINDU—MAVERICK III, 5.13a (or 5.8, C2), 3 pitches, 280 feet (85 m) ★★

First Ascent: Harvey T. Carter, Steve Miller, 4 pitches, 5.8, A2, 16 April 1964. First free ascent: Stevie Haston, Laurence Gouault, 10 April 1996.

Location and Access: Approach up the right side of the tower. *Maverick* begins on the south face, then moves west and up past many fixed pitons. Stevie Haston: "The rock is like the softer English gritstone."

Pitch 1: Climb an obvious 5.11+ crack to a thin 5.13a crux past fixed pitons.

Pitch 2: Traverse left 15 feet (5.9+), then up to easier ground. Continue up an easy groove (5.7) to a belay at a horizontal break.

photo: Jeff Widen

Hindu

Pitch 3: Climb over a 5.10c bulge to the summit.

NOTE: Steve "Crusher" Bartlett: "Maverick was a popular aid climb and will likely remain so, but as such it is easily climbed hammerless."

Paraphernalia: Friends (2) sets; Tri-cams (1) set; nuts (2) sets; quickdraws.

Descent: One double-rope rappel with 200-foot (60 m) ropes down *Maverick* to the base of the tower, then walk off.

6   HINDU—SHIVA (a.k.a. North Face) III, 5.12a, 3 pitches, 280 feet (85 m) ★★★

First Ascent: Bill Forrest, Don Briggs, 5.8, A2, 4 pitches, 8 April 1969. First free ascent: Jay Smith, Mark Hesse, April 1994.

Location and Access: *Shiva* is the free ascent of the North Face. From the shoulder at the base of the tower, traverse to the northwest corner along a narrow ledge. Climb left, then up on fairly good rock for 2 pitches. The route joins the first ascent line (*Maverick*) at a stance on the northwest corner of the tower. The final lead follows a moderate crack to the summit, 5.10c. The crux is on the second pitch.

Pitch 1: Climb up for 20 feet, (6 m), then left 60 feet (18 m) to the north face and a good bolted belay, 5.10a.

Pitch 2: Continue past fixed anchors, 5.10, then a piton, 5.12a. Make a hand traverse right and continue up at 5.11a to a belay stance with double anchors above an old bolted belay.

Pitch 3: A long pitch to the summit which meets *Maverick* halfway up. Begin with a leftward diagonal ascent, then up, passing fixed pitons, to the top, 5.10c, 160 feet (49 m).

photo: Steve "Crusher" Bartlett

Stevie Haston and Laurence Gouault on the first free ascent of Hindu–*Maverick* route

Paraphernalia: Friends (2) sets; Tri-cams (1) set; wires (3) #0.4, #0.5, #0.75, (2) #1, #1.5, #2, (1) #3, (2) #3.5.

Descent: One double-rope rappel with 200-foot (60 m) ropes down *Maverick* to the base of the tower, then walk off.

Something will have gone out of us as a people if we ever let the remaining wilderness be destroyed; if we permit the last virgin forests to be turned into comic books and plastic cigarette cases; if we drive the few remaining members of the wild species into zoos or to extinction; if we pollute the last clear air and dirty the last clean streams and push our paved roads through the last of the silence, so that never again will Americans be free in their own country from the noise, the exhausts, the stinks of human and automotive waste. And so that never again can we have the chance to see ourselves single, separate, vertical and individual in the world, part of the environment of trees and rocks and soil, brother to the other animals, part of the natural world and competent to belong in it.

–Wallace Stegner, Letter to Wildland Research Center.
The Sound of Mountain Water, 1946

MYSTERY TOWERS

I loved the approach to the Mystery Towers. I had seen them from the top of the Titan in the spring of 1962 and again in 1966, but I could see no way to get to them even though they were only a half mile east of the Fisher Towers. Bill Forrest obtained a set of stereoscopic aerial photos. We were delighted to see that a side canyon led from Onion Creek to the towers.

The high desert is unique and exotic. To someone from Europe or Japan, or from more temperate parts of the United States, the desert of Utah is as foreign as another planet. There are unusual land forms, not only towers but arches, buttes, mesas, and—most intriguing of all—deep and narrow canyons that promise fabulous discovery.

–George Hurley

The Mystery Towers present some of the wildest sandstone climbing on the Colorado Plateau. Approach as for Onion Creek Towers (Mongoose, Sari, and Hindu). Turn south from River Road beyond mile marker 20 at a sign: "Fisher Valley Ranch." After 16 crossings of Onion Creek you come to a bridge across a deep, narrow gorge. Approximately 0.5 mile (0.8 km) farther, the Titan's south face briefly comes into view to the north, with the Finger of Fate seen low on the right side. About 0.2 mile (0.32 km) beyond the crest of the hill after the bridge, the top of Gothic Nightmare is briefly visible to the east. Approach the towers from the last possible system of gullies before rising walls prevent further access. There is a brown post with a camping symbol on the left side of the road at the approach gully.

photo: Duane Raleigh

Mystery Towers from the east. *Left to right*: Fortress, Citadel, Gothic Nightmare, Atlas

Mystery Towers

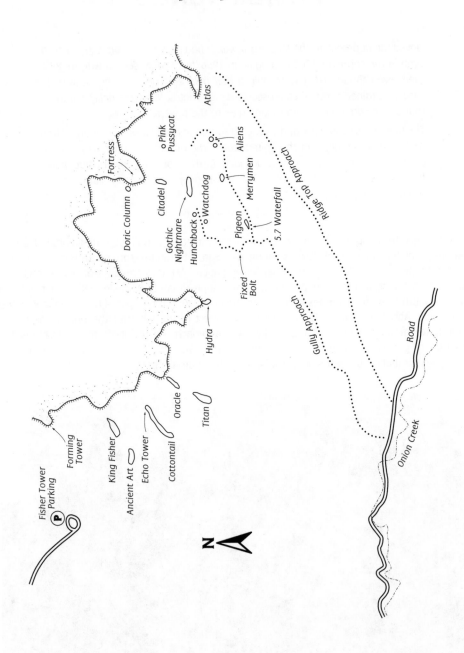

Geology

The Mystery Towers are composed of Cutler Sandstone capped by the Moenkopi Formation. Because they are even closer to the La Sal Mountains than the Fisher Towers (of the same strata) and thus receive a bit more moisture, and because there is little of the protective Moenkopi caprock remaining, they are more severely weathered and have a thicker stucco of mud on their flanks.

1   **PINK PUSSYCAT I, 5.11 R, A3, 1 pitch, 40 feet (12 m)** ★★

First Ascent: Bill Forrest, Don Briggs, 20 October 1969. Second ascent: Rob Slater, Al Torrisi, Jim Bodenhamer, November 1994. First free ascent: Alan "Heavy Duty" Stevenson, Keith Reynolds, March 1998.

Location and Access: Pink Pussycat is a hoodoo at the bottom of the wash below the Citadel. The route is obvious on the west side of the landform where it climbs past a bolt to the caprock above.

Paraphernalia: Friends (1) #1; TCUs (1) #0.75, #1.5; Lost Arrows (1); knifeblades (1); quickdraws (1).

Descent: Single-rope rappel from a summit bolt.

2   **PIGEON III, 5.10+ S, 4 pitches, 330 feet (100 m)**

First Ascent: Keith Reynolds, Alan "Heavy Duty" Stevenson, with Matt Laggis on lower pitches, April 1998.

Location and Access: The landform climbs a wall on the left past the waterfall up the right fork of the approach hike to the Mystery Towers. Climb a major groove system leading to a chimney right of the pigeon's head.

Pitch 1: Climb past a ledge (5.10+) to a 2-bolt belay.

Pitch 2: Continue to the base of a chimney, 5.9+.

Pitch 3: Climb the chimney (5.6) to a fixed piton on a shoulder, 5.6.

Pitch 4: Continue up a short pitch (5.10) to the summit and 2 bolts.

Paraphernalia: Standard desert rack.

Descent: Lasso a boulder to the north and make a tyrolean off the landform.

3   **MERRYMEN TOWER—ROBIN HOOD I, 5.9, 2 pitches, 115 feet (38 m)**

First Ascent: Matt Laggis, rope solo, 6 April 1998.

Location and Access: On the approach to the Mystery Towers, take a right fork once the top of wet slab (with a fixed rope) is gained. Merrymen Tower is the obvious 5-summited formation directly in front of the approach. To climb *Robin Hood*, grovel up the drainage west of the landform and begin up a large chimney formed by a pillar leaning against the tower. Climb 30 feet (9 m), then move right between the Merrymen and the tower to its left when viewed from the west, 5.6. From the notch, chimney up, then traverse right onto the west face. Climb right onto ledgy corners, 5.8, then 5.7 to the summit block. A 5.9 stem reaches the top. The route may be climbed in 1 pitch, but this results in considerable rope drag.

Paraphernalia: Camalots (1) set through #5.

Descent: Downclimb to an anchor on the west face and make a 115-foot (38 m) rappel to the ground.

4   MERRYMEN TOWER—FRYER TUCK I, tyrolean traverse

First Ascent: Matt Laggis, solo, 6 April 1998.

Location and Access: The first ascent of *Fryer Tuck* was made from the summit of *Robin Hood*. There are no anchors on the summit.

Paraphernalia: Rope for rope-toss.

Descent: Reverse the tyrolean.

5   ALIENS LEFT—SPACE INVADER I, 5.10, A4, 1 pitch, 60 feet (18 m)

First Ascent: Keith Reynolds, Alan "Heavy Duty" Stevenson, spring 1998.

Location and Access: The Aliens are hoodoos in a wash east of Gothic Nightmare. Aliens Left climbs 5.10 to a couple of A4 cobble moves onto the summit.

Paraphernalia: Quickdraws.

Descent: Rappel the route.

6   ALIENS RIGHT—DANGER WILL ROBINSON I, 5.11, 1 pitch, 50 feet (15 m)

First Ascent: Alan "Heavy Duty" Stevenson, spring 1998.

Location and Access: Same as Aliens Left.

Paraphernalia: The hoodoo climbs past a fixed piton and a bolt.

Descent: Rappel the route.

7   WATCHDOG I, 5.8, 1 pitch, 40 feet (12 m)

First Ascent: Alan "Heavy Duty" Stevenson, solo, April 1998.

Location and Access: Watchdog is an obvious hoodoo southwest of Gothic Nightmare and south of Hunchback. The crux involves a mantle to the summit.

Paraphernalia: None required.

Descent: Downclimb the route.

8   ATLAS—WAIT OF THE WORLD VI, 5.8, A3, 6 pitches, 600 feet (183 m) ★★★

First Ascent: Steve "Crusher" Bartlett, Chip Wilson, 20 April 1995.

Location and Access: *Webster's New Collegiate Dictionary:* "Atlas—a Titan who for his part in the Titans' revolt against the gods was obliged to support the heavens with his head and hands—one who bears a heavy burden." Atlas is the impressive buttress east of Gothic Nightmare. The climb begins in the middle of the south face, 200 feet (61 m) right of a large right-facing flake system. To approach, hike up and across the ridgetop east of the regular mystery approach gully.

Pitch 1: Begin at 2 bolts then climb up and left to a good crack. Continue up and right past a closet-sized, semi-detached block to thin nailing and a 3-bolt belay, A3, 80 feet (24 m).

Pitch 2: Continue on thin aid up and right to a bolt ladder with hooking to a ledge, A3+, 80 feet (24 m).

Pitch 3: Climb the flake system left of the ledge passing a bolt to a shallow dihedral under a large triangular roof and a 3-bolt belay, A2+, 80 feet (24 m).

Pitch 4: Make tricky moves left around the roof, then access a good 1" crack (2.5 cm), A2, 120 feet (37 m).

Atlas

Steve "Crusher" Bartlett on *Wait of the World*

Pitch 5: Move up and left into an easy dihedral, then tension left from a bolt to a shallow groove. Hooks negotiate the caprock taking you to a good belay ledge, A2+, 80 feet (24 m).

Pitch 6: Move the belay 30 feet right (9 m) to triple bolts, then scamper up a 5.8 chimney to the summit.

Paraphernalia: Friends #0.5 through #7, (3) each #1 through #4; Lost Arrows (12); knifeblades (8); Bugaboos (10); baby angles (5); standard angles (12) up to 2", up to 2–3" (5) each; many nuts, copperheads (1) each; Bird Beaks (10); Hooks/ring angle claw; Hexcentrics (9).

Descent: Rappel the route.

9   ATLAS—WONDERMONGER VI, 5.9 R, A3, 4 pitches, 450 feet (137 m)

First Ascent: Tony Wilson, Russell Hooper, November 1997.

Location and Access: *Wondermonger* climbs the sharp end of the Atlas formation up the northwest face just left of a prominent arête. The route finishes on the front end of the landform.

Pitch 1: Begin in a wide crack and climb a runout ending with A2+ aid at double belay anchors, 100 feet (30 m).

Pitch 2: Climb A2 angling left to double anchors, 100 feet (30 m).

Pitch 3: Pass a loose block and fixed anchors climbing A3 to double anchors, 160 feet (49 m).

Pitch 4: Continue up 40 feet (12 m) until it is possible to make an axe throw to the saddle above, then climb up and right passing fixed anchors to double belay/rappel anchors. 50 feet (15 m).

Paraphernalia: Friends (2) sets; Camalots (1) #4; TCUs (2) sets; Toucans (7); long Lost Arrows (6); baby angles 3/4"(6), angles 1" through 2" (2); Bird Beaks (2); Pika Peckers (1); Ice Axe (1) mandatory throw to saddle; 3/8" bolt hangers.

Descent: Rappel the route.

10   GOTHIC NIGHTMARE—NORTH FACE VI, 5.9, A4, 5 pitches, 400 feet (122 m) ★★★

First Ascent: Bill Forrest, Don Briggs, spring 1970, with George Hurley, Jonathan Hough working on the lower pitches, 1969. Second ascent: John Sherman, Mike O'Donnell, Rob Slater, Al Torrisi, 22 May 1993.

Location and Access: *Webster's New Collegiate Dictionary:* "Gothic–. . . architecture developed in northern France and spreading through western Europe from the middle of the 12th century to the early 16th century that is characterized by the converging of weights and strains at isolated points upon slender vertical piers and counterbalancing buttresses and by pointed arches and vaulting." John Sherman: "Endwise, it looks like one of the Coneheads wearing a jester's cap, dangly bells sprouting out of the top. From the side it resembles a sailfish fin." Gothic Nightmare is the first tower reached in the Mystery Towers amphitheater from the gully approach. Gothic Nightmare is climbed on its north side 40 feet (12 m) down and right of the crest of the saddle; the crux is encountered on the first pitch. The "Traverse of the Goblins" is a long western traverse (mostly on the south side of the tower) around the many stone gargoyles that are perched along the knife-edged summit ridge and leads to the highest point of the rock. John Sherman: "The rock on the Gothic makes the Titan look like granite."

Atlas

Pitch 1: Begin with aid up an incipient, rotten crack system, then climb over a roof to a sloping belay stance, A4.

Pitch 2: Move right (5.8), then up at 5.7. Continue on aid up a widening crack system to belay bolts.

Pitch 3: Chimney to a ridge (5.9), clipping into a few rivets on the way, then mantle up and traverse right to a belay.

Pitch 4: Bolts and some free climbing take you south over the "Traverse of the Goblins" to a belay on a gargoyle.

Pitch 5: Lower off the gargoyle from bolts and move right, then up, passing bolts to the summit.

Paraphernalia: Standard desert rack; a good selection of wide gear and pitons.

Descent: Rappel the route.

11   GOTHIC NIGHTMARE—NORTH FACE LEFT VARIATION

First Ascent: Keith Reynolds, Alan "Heavy Duty" Stevenson, Kevin Chase, March 1997.

Location and Access: *North Face Variation* climbs a new pitch on the original (north face) route of Gothic Nightmare. Climb the Forrest/Briggs original route for 2 pitches to the ridge, then continue (3rd pitch) with free climbing to a notch which is normally passed with aid on the left. Climb to a saddle and belay from double bolts.

Paraphernalia: Same as the original route.

Descent: Rappel the original *North Face* route.

12   GOTHIC NIGHTMARE—MEDUSA VI, 5.8, A3+, 7 pitches, 400 feet (122 m)

First Ascent: Pitches 1 and 2: Roger "Strappo" Hughes, Steve "Crusher" Bartlett. Pitches 3 and 4: Drake Taylor, Bruce Erikson, April 1996. Pitches 5 through 7: Bill Forrest, Don Briggs. Second ascent: Alan "Heavy Duty" Stevenson and Co.

Location and Access: *Medusa* is a variation to the original *North Face* route. In Greek mythology, Medusa was a Gorgon who could turn someone who beheld her face into stone. Webster describes a Gorgon as any of three snaky-haired sisters in Greek mythology whose glance turns the beholder to stone, or an ugly or repulsive woman. Begin on a rounded ridge between Gothic Nightmare and Citadel. From the top of the variation, continue with many bathooks to the original line of ascent which is the main chimney dividing the tower.

Pitch 1: Free climb a dirty crack, then free and A2 to a hanging belay from triple anchors.

Pitch 2: "Just Shut Up and Watch Me." Move right and ascend passing fixed anchors, A3, then A3+ up a right-facing corner. Belay from triple anchors at a notch on the landform's top ridge.

Pitch 3: Traverse the ridge right, slinging a window through a tower (the Seal) which is then climbed on the back side of the formation passing a fixed bolt. Move back to the north side and on to a second towerlike formation ("Ride the Horse") which is climbed before moving on to triple anchors in a notch.

Pitch 4: Continue right across the face of a tower (with bathooks and free climbing) passing fixed pitons and bolts to the notch of the original route. Belay from triple anchors.

photo: Steve "Crusher" Bartlett

Gothic Nightmare in front, Citadel in back

photo: Drake Taylor

Pitch 5: Aid a bolt ladder (A2) and continue free and with aid over 2 humps ("Rocking Horse" and "Rotten Horse") to triple anchors. Leave a fixed rope on the pitch for the descent.

Pitch 6: Pass many old bolts and rivets on the south side of the landform. Ascend a hump and belay from triple anchors. Leave a fixed rope on the pitch for the descent. Drake Taylor: "A3+ unless bolts and rivets are replaced with newer gear."

Pitch 7: Continue the traverse, climbing a bolt ladder, then on to the summit.

Paraphernalia: Friends (1) #1.5, #2, (2) #2.5, (4) #3, #3.5, (1) #4; small nuts (10); medium nuts (2); pitons (4); long knifeblades; Lost Arrows (3); angle pitons (2) 0.5", (3) 5/8", 3/4", 1", 1 1/4", 1.5", (1) 2", (2) 3"; bathooks (2); ropes (3); tie-offs.

Descent: Reverse the route if fixed ropes were left on Pitches 5 and 6, or rappel the original *North Face* route.

13   GOTHIC NIGHTMARE—SOMETHING WICKED THIS WAY COMES VI, 5.9, A2+, 5 pitches, 400 feet (122 m) ★★

First Ascent: Pitches 1 through 4: Brad Jarrett, Brian Warshaw, John Slezak, 1995. Pitch 5 to the summit by Steve "Crusher" Bartlett, Roger "Strappo" Hughes, Chip Wilson, during the 3rd ascent of the tower, March 1997.

Location and Access: *Something Wicked This Way Comes* climbs the south-southwest face of Gothic Nightmare.

Pitch 1: Climb an easy crack through an overhang to thin nailing and occasional bolts. A2+,180 feet.

Pitch 2: Follow a crack to a belay, 150 feet, A2+.

Pitches 3 and 4: Follow bolts and an occasional placement to the shoulder, A1.

photo: Kevin Chase

Southeast face of Gothic Nightmare

Pitch 5: Move the belay to the base of summit obelisk, then climb past 2 bolts and 5.9 to the summit.

Paraphernalia: Standard desert rack, pitons.

Descent: Rappel the route.

14 GOTHIC NIGHTMARE— NIGHTMARE ON ONION CREEK VI, 5.3+, A4, 7 pitches, 650 feet (192 m)

First Ascent: Alan "Heavy Duty" Stevenson, Kevin Chase, January 1997.

Location and Access: *Nightmare on Onion Creek* climbs the southeast face of the tower finishing up a bolt ladder to the second highest summit. The climb involves 500 feet (152 m) of varied aid climbing with only 5 aid bolts. Pitch 7 climbs a bolt ladder to the summit. Stevenson: "A very steep, killer route which follows a natural line of corners and grooves."

Paraphernalia: Flex Friends 1/4" through 5"; pink and red Tri-cams (1); cams (3) sets with a mandatory large unit; TCUs; Aliens; many hooks; much thin and wide gear; Leepers (12); angles 3/4" (2), 2", 3" (1); knifeblades (8); long pitons (4); short pitons (4); Bugaboos (4); Auks (3); Peckers (3); Bird Beaks (3); Toucans (6); Fish Hooks (2); grappling hooks (2); Rocks (2) sets #1 through #8.

Descent: Rappel the route.

15   HUNCHBACK I, 5.8, A1, 1 pitch, 50 feet (15 m)

First Ascent: James Garrett, John Sweeley, 17 April 1996.

Location and Access: *Hunchback* is 150 feet (46 m) left of the southwest corner of Gothic Nightmare. Ascend the east face of the tower beginning with 5.8 and finishing with A1. Pass a fixed anchor below the summit.

Paraphernalia: Friends (2–3) small; Lost Arrows (1).

Descent: Simultaneous rappel off opposite sides of the tower. There are no anchors on top.

16   CITADEL V, 5.9R, A4, 5 pitches, 450 feet (137 m) ★★★★

First Ascent: Bill Forrest, Don Briggs, October 1969. Second ascent: Rob Slater, John Sherman, 4 days, June 1992.

Location and Access: *Webster's New Collegiate Dictionary:* "Citadel–A fortress that commands a city; stronghold." Citadel is the freestanding tower beyond Gothic Nightmare. The route begins 35 feet (11 m) right of the southeast corner of the tower.

16

photo: Duane Raleigh

The Citadel

photo: Steve "Crusher" Bartlett

Chip Wilson on Double Exposure Ledge, Citadel

Pitch 1: Climb up and right to a small overhang. Aid over the overhang to a dirt ramp, then traverse left to belay bolts, 40 feet (12 m).

Pitch 2: Continue up and right into a vertical flute using pitons in dirt holes. Climb a bolt ladder with an occasional piton, to bolts at a hanging belay, 70 feet (21 m). Pitches 1 and 2 can easily be combined.

Pitch 3: Follow bolts up a poor crack, then up and left to 2 bolts at a corner. Climb up and left with bolts and a scary 5.9 mantle to a stance at the "Dragon's Head," a large standstone gargoyle, 5.9.

Pitch 4: Shinny along the "Dragon's Tail" to the southeast arête and climb shaky pitons and bolts to a mantle onto a dirt-caked, 1-foot-wide (0.3 m) horizontal stance and belay (Double Exposure Lodge).

Pitch 5: Continue up a rotten, wide crack to bolts (protect with large Friends or Bongs), then right to the solid capstone and 10 feet (3 m) of free climbing to the summit.

Paraphernalia: Friends (1) set; Camalots through #5; pitons through 3.5", knifeblades and Lost Arrows; quickdraws.

Descent: Rappel the route.

17   CITADEL—MAGICAL MYSTERY TOUR V, 5.9, A3+, 4 pitches, 400 feet (122 m) ★★★★★

First Ascent: Keith Reynolds, Alan "Heavy Duty" Stevenson, April 1997.

Location and Access: Begin on the north ridge. The first-pitch anchor is visible from below the route. Leave a fixed rope on Pitch 3 for the descent. Pitch lengths are given in rope lengths rather than vertical height.

Pitch 1: Aid and free climb out a rib to a slung horn. Make a 30-foot (9 m) rope throw, then pendulum right into a left-facing corner. Aid, then free climb to a double-bolt belay ledge, 5.9, A2, 110 feet (34 m).

Pitch 2: Step left and aid thin and wide cracks to a double-bolt belay ledge on the shoulder above, A3, 140 feet (43 m).

Pitch 3: Climb right past 2 large potatolike formations, then continue mixed free and aid on the west face passing 3 aid bolts to a double-bolt hanging belay, 5.9, A3+, 130 feet (40 m).

Pitch 4: Aid up and right past 2 bolts, then tension right into a left-leaning crack which leads to an overhanging finish to the summit, A3+, 100 feet (30 m).

Paraphernalia: Friends (2) sets; Camalots (1) set #1 through #4; TCUs; Bird Beaks (4–5); angles through 3"; Warthog and medium hook.

Descent: Rappel the route.

18   **FORTRESS—KITTY LITTER WALL V, 5.9, A3, 5 pitches, 600 feet (183 m)**

First Ascent: Keith Reynolds, Alan "Heavy Duty" Stevenson, March 1998.

Location and Access: The Fortress is north behind the Citadel. Keith Reynolds: "The Fortress holds one of the cleanest pitches, and one of the loosest, in the Mystery Towers."

Pitch 1: Climb a 5.7 crack up and left to a fixed piton.

Pitch 2: A2+ takes you up 2 bolts and a 5.8 chimney. Belay right of a large flake, 5.8, A2+.

Pitch 3: Follow the crack up and left, then back right, to a 2-bolt belay below an overhang, A3.

Pitch 4: A clean 1 1/2" crack takes you up and right, then back left to an area of loose ledges, and a double-bolt belay, A2.

Pitch 5: Free climb (5.8) through loose terrain, to a fixed piton, then right into a dihedral (5.9) to the summit, 5.9.

Paraphernalia: Many camming units 1/4" through 5"; wires (1) set; knifeblades (3); angles 1" (2); Bong Bongs 2" (2); Leepers (6).

Descent: Rappel the route, keeping to the right on the top pitch to avoid loose rock.

19   **DORIC COLUMN IV, 5.9, A2+, 5 pitches, 340 feet (104 m)**

First Ascent: Bill Forrest, George Hurley, with Rod Chuck on the lower leads, April 1969. Second ascent: Steve "Crusher" Bartlett, George "Chip" Wilson, April 1992.

Location and Access: *Webster's New Collegiate Dictionary:* "Doric–belonging to the oldest and simplest Greek architectural order." To reach, follow cairns toward Gothic Nightmare, then continue past Citadel rather than hiking directly toward the tower when it first comes into view. Doric Column is climbed by a major chimney line on the southeast (approach) side of the tower. The chimney is gained from right to left. A register was placed by the second ascent party.

Pitch 1: Start at a mound of dirt against the tower. Climb mixed free and aid 60 feet (18 m) up and left to gain a chimney to the beginning of a bolt ladder. Mantle to a double-anchor belay shelf. The old bolt near the bottom of the climb was placed by the first ascent team when the starting dirt mound was much higher, 5.9, A2+.

photo: Duane Raleigh

Doric Column

Pitch 2: Climb the bolt ladder (all bolts and rivets) to a double-bolt belay below a roof, 60 feet (18 m).

Pitch 3: Continue up bolts with 5.8 free climbing below a roof which is climbed on its right by an expanding flake with aid to a double-bolt belay (crux), 60 feet (18 m).

Pitch 4: Climb 100 feet (30 m) up a crack, then chimney (5.8) past a fixed anchor, with occasional free moves to the caprock.

Pitch 5: Easy free climbing (5.5) over better rock reaches the summit, 60 feet (18 m).

Paraphernalia: Standard desert rack; pitons (1) each through 2"; Leepers (2).

Descent: Downclimb to Pitch 5, then rappel to the top of Pitch 3. Rappel to the top of Pitch 1, then to the ground.

20   DORIC COLUMN—BIG NASTY V, 5.8 R, A4, 5 pitches, 550 feet (168 m) ★★★

First Ascent: Duane Raleigh, Walt Shipley, 21–23 November 1997.

Location and Access: Begin in the first right-facing corner, 200 feet (60 m) downhill and left of the original route. Pitch 2 moves to the west side of the tower and faces *Hydra*.

Pitch 1: Climb up (5.8 R), then left and up to a saddle at the base of a chimney (optional belay, 100 feet–30 m). Climb the chimney to its top, then step off a pedestal to a straight-up crack, A2+. Belay on a ledge with a giant horn anchor, 200 feet (60 m).

photo: Steve "Crusher" Bartlett

Pitch 2: Climb with aid 30 feet (9 m) to a saddle, then walk far left to a thin crack (A4) that gets easier up high, A2. Belay on a small stance out left, 160 feet (49 m).

Pitch 3: A few placements lead to a 5-bolt ladder, then A4, with 2 more bolts leading to a 3-bolt belay under the capstone roof, 120 feet (37 m).

Pitch 4: Climb with aid through the roof (A1), then continue mixed free and aid (5.8, A1) to a large ledge below the summit block, 70 feet (21 m).

Pitch 5: Continue 4th class to the summit.

Paraphernalia: Cams (1) 3/4", (2) 1" through 3"; Camalots (1) #4; knifeblades (8); Lost Arrows (4); angles (1) 1/2", 5/8", (2) 3/4", 1"; Leepers Zs (3); Bird Beaks (4); hangers (10) 3/8".

Descent: Downclimb the top pitch of the regular route, then rappel 150 feet (46 m) to a stance at the base of a chimney. A 165-foot (50 m) rappel then leads to the ground.

Chip Wilson on the Doric Column, pitch 3

21   PILLARS OF HERCULES—HARD SONG V, 5.9, A3+, 6 pitches, 1000+ feet (305+m)

First Ascent: Duane Raleigh, Tony Wilson, 4 days, 1995.

Location and Access: Pillars of Hercules is between *Hydra* and Doric Column. Thirty-five bolts were placed on the first ascent.

Pitch 1: Climb a bolt ladder with a 5.9 move, then sling a cobble and continue to a belay, making an ice axe hook on the way.

Pitch 2: Continue, passing fixed anchors to a belay, A2.

Pitch 3: Climb 5.9, A3 to a belay, passing a short chimney.

Pitch 4: Climb A2 to a belay.

Pitch 5: Pass loose rock, then continue A3+ passing more loose rock to a belay.

Pitch 6: Continue up a 5.8 chimney, then a right-facing corner to the top.

Paraphernalia: Friends (2) #0.5 through #5; many knifeblades; angles (2) 5/8" through 5"; Leeper Zs, 3/8" and 0.5"; bolt hangers; north wall hammer; 200-foot (60 m) ropes.

Descent: Rappel the route.

22   HYDRA IV, 5.9, A3+, 4 pitches, 300 feet (91 m)

First Ascent: Tony Wilson, Duane Raleigh, fall 1994.

Location and Access: *Webster's New Collegiate Dictionary:* "Hydra— a many-headed serpent or monster of Greek mythology slain by Hercules each head of which when cut off was replaced by 2 others. . . . A multifarious evil not to be overcome by a single effort."

Hydra climbs the prominent gargoyled fin that separates the Mystery Towers from the Fisher Towers. The route ascends the skyline edge and involves more than 500 feet (152 m) of climbing; the crux is the last pitch. Approach as for Doric Column, but branch left below Gothic Nightmare. Twenty-four bolts were placed on the first ascent.

Pitch 1: Begin 20 feet (6 m) left of the ridge by lassoing a horn. From the horn, free climb left to thin wavy cracks. Follow the cracks to their end, A3, 40 feet (12 m). Traverse right 20 feet (6 m) to a right-facing dihedral. Climb the right-facing dihedral to a ledge and 2-bolt belay.

Hydra

photo: Duane Raleigh

Pitch 2: Move left to a bolt. Difficult and loose nailing accesses an obvious crack/trough. Follow the trough to a natural belay on a ridge, A3+.

Pitch 3: Bolt/nail to an ice axe throw over a large blob. A series of mantles and steps over the blob get you to a bolt ladder, A1. Belay at a gargoyle.

Pitch 4: The crux pitch. An ice-axe throw up and to the left accesses a stance 20 feet (6 m) off the belay. Tension traverse left and free climb onto a loose ledge, 5.9, A3+. An ice axe throw up and right gains another ledge and an A1 crack leading to the summit.

Paraphernalia: SLCDs (3) sets; TCUs (3) sets; angles (4) each through 2"; assorted Leeper Zs (6); ice axe for hooking and throwing; bolt hangers to fit 3/8" and 0.5" studs.

Descent: Two 165-foot (50 m) rappels down the route.

Slowly, as I sauntered dwarfed among the overhanging pinnacles, as the great slabs which were the visible remnants of past ages laid their enormous shadows rhythmically as life and death across my face, the answer came to me. Man could contain more than himself. Among these many appearances that flew, or swam in the waters, or wavered momentarily into being, man alone possessed the unique ability.

–Loren Eiseley

photo: Pete Takeda

Joel Arellano on the south face of Independence Monument

COLORADO NATIONAL MONUMENT

The Trail of the Serpent is done. We built it so people could drive where only the birds could fly before. Folks call it the crookedest road in the world. And with fifty-four switchbacks on the way up the plateau from No Thoroughfare Canyon, I guess that's about right. Looks like Grand Canyon of the Colorado River will have to split honors with Col. Nat. Mt. from now on.

–John Otto, August 1921

Colorado National Monument is a few miles south of Interstate 70, between the towns of Fruita and Grand Junction, at the west-central edge of Colorado. The monument encompasses 20,445 acres of canyons and mesas ranging in elevation from 4,620 to 7,107 feet (1,408 to 2,166 m). It was set aside for federal protection by President William Howard Taft in 1911. This chapter includes climbs established within the monument as well as in nearby vicinities.

Rim Rock Drive

This 23-mile (37 km) loop joins the east and west entrances with roads outside the monument to form a 33-mile (53 km) round-trip Grand Loop. Along Rim Rock Drive are over a dozen viewpoints and overlooks. The visitor center is 4 miles (6.4 km) from the park's West Entrance and has a good selection of publications, maps of the monument and related areas, film, and an informative slide program which investigates the geologic, natural, and cultural history of the monument. Interpretive and campfire programs are offered, and schedules of the events are posted. Restrooms, water, and telephone are available at the visitor center.

John Otto

The farmers who settled near the present site of the monument were probably quite indifferent to the rugged canyons, cliffs, and monoliths of the area. It would not be until sometime after 1907 and the arrival of John Otto that enthusiasm for the region gained the momentum leading to the establishment of a national monument.

John Otto arrived in Fruita, Colorado, from Missouri to work as a powderman on a water flume. Earlier he was involved in gold mining in northern California and had campaigned for miners' rights. While working in Fruita, he made numerous pack trips into the wilderness at the south edge of the community and fell in love with the grandeur of the complex landscape. He camped near the northeastern mouth of Monument Canyon and singlehandedly began constructing trails to the interior of the canyons so that others might be able to enjoy the breathtaking vistas. This labor of love lasted more than ten years. In 1907 Otto encouraged the Grand Junction Chamber of Commerce to petition the U. S. Secretary of the Interior to set aside the canyon country south of Fruita as a national monument.

On May 24, 1911, President William Howard Taft signed the proclamation creating Colorado National Monument. On June 14, 1911, Otto completed the first ascent (solo) of Independence Rock, where he placed the Stars and Stripes in celebration of Flag Day. Only two pipes remain of his original pipe ladder (top of Pitches 1 and 4), but steps chiseled into the rock are still used on

Colorado National Monument

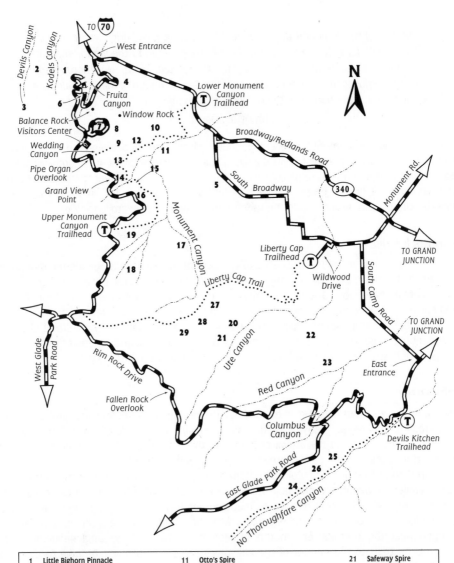

1	Little Bighorn Pinnacle	11	Otto's Spire	21	Safeway Spire
2	Phantom Spire	12	Monolith Spire	22	Gypsy Towers
3	Devil's Disciple	13	Independence Monument	23	Super Crack
4	Remnants Tower	14	Grand View Spire	24	Lost Arrow Buttress
5	Oliver Perry-Smith Buttress	15	Kissing Couple, Dirty Old Man Tower	25	Primal Instinct Tower
6	Ribbed Buttress	16	Rainbow Tower	26	Over the Edge Spire
7	Saddlehorn Bouldering Area	17	Egypt Rock, Pharaoh Point	27	Liberty Cap
8	Sentinel Spire	18	Squaw Fingers	28	Jolly Tower
9	Pipe Organ, Organ Pipe Spires	19	Coke Bottle	29	Oompah Tower
10	Lower Monument Canyon Slabs	20	WalMart Tower		

part of the ascent of *Otto's Route*. For a number of years, Otto climbed to the top of Independence Monument each Fourth of July and placed a flag to commemorate the day. The route he pioneered eight decades ago is today the most popular climb in the monument.

In Case of Accident

Attempt to notify any monument employee in the event of an accident. The visitor center is open daily (except Christmas) from 8 A.M. to 4:30 P.M., with extended evening hours during the summer months. The monument can be reached at 303-858-3617; after hours call 858-3619. Also, there are rangers living at the East Entrance station who may be reached at 242-7906. Dial 911 from any pay phone in the monument and report problems to the Mesa County sheriff's office. Pay phones are by the front door of the visitor center, by the booth at the East Entrance, and in the Saddlehorn campground.

Maps

The Trails Illustrated topo map is the most useful for Colorado National Monument, although the map on the monument brochure is also very good.

Climbing Regulations

There is no mandatory registration. There are off-limit areas near rock art sites, and in areas with active raptor nests. Please check at the visitor center for current closures. The use of any portable power tool is forbidden. Webbing of any color except brown is not permitted, as well as uncamouflaged (bright metal) anchors. The practice of chipping rock to create or enlarge hand and footholds is also forbidden. An information flier for climbers is available at the visitor center. It should be noted that Independence Monument was closed from April through August 1997 due to nesting peregrine falcons.

A Brief History of Climbing in Colorado National Monument by KC Baum

John Otto, founding father of the Colorado National Monument, moved into Monument Canyon in 1907 and remained there for the next 30 years living his dreams. Otto was a restless, tireless spirit with unlimited physical endurance. Singlehandedly, he opened this great playground to the world.

No individual had more impact on climbing in the Colorado National Monument than the man the locals called "The Hermit of Monument Canyon." He began scaling many of the smaller rock features in the monument, using pipe and rung ladders secured in the soft sandstone rock. He was intensely patriotic and raised an American flag on the small summit of Liberty Cap on July 4, 1909. He then set his sights on the most impressive rock monolith, which he named Independence Monument, and pioneered his famous "Otto's Route," carving steps in the soft rock and drilling 1-inch holes, into which he drove lead pipes to form a ladder.

In 1911, a bigger Fourth of July celebration was planned by the local Chamber of Commerce, including an Independence Day celebration in Monument Canyon. John Otto was presented with a 6 x 12-foot American flag to be unfurled on the morning of July 4 atop Independence Monument. Otto patiently climbed toward the summit, hoisting the flag and pole without incident until a pipe rung came loose just below the crux caprock, nearly ending his short climbing career. The flag he raised could be seen distinctly from town, and locals from Fruita cheered the hermit for his act of daring, then rode out to the canyon for a closer view of the banner atop the 500-foot (152 m) tower.

In 1990, to honor John Otto's patriotic endeavors, local climber Bob Fisher decided to re-enact the Fourth of July ascent pioneered by Otto 80 years prior. On July 4, Bob and KC Baum climbed in the footsteps carved by Otto and hauled with them a 3 x 6-foot American flag, with pole and ropes to secure it on the caprock of Independence Monument. A documentary photo of Bob hoisting the Stars and Stripes made national news, and the flag-raising has remained an annual event since, except in 1997 when peregrine falcons were nesting and the route was off limits.

Except for Otto's daring first ascents, monument climbs date from the spring of 1960, when the legendary team of Harvey T. Carter and Layton Kor, along with John Auld, established the first ascents of Sentinel Spire, Bell Tower, and Pharaoh Point. Numerous climbers began visiting and climbing in the monument during the '60s, including Fred Beckey, Don Doucette, Jim Dyson, Art Howells, Tom Kaufman, John Kuglin, Bill Kurimay, Rick Linkert, Steve Mack, Tom Merrill, and Gary Ziegler. During the '70s and '80s new route development in the monument continued, thanks to local activists and visiting climbers including Peter Athans, Jim Beyer, Tom Blake, Eric Boehlke, Tom Bratton, Kyle Copeland, Paul Cowan, Bill Forrest, Charlie Fowler, Steve French, Steve Johnson, Dave Kozak, Steve Kolarick, Ron Olevsky, Clay Patton, Andy Petefish, Allison Sheets, Tom Stubbs, and Ed Webster.

During the '80s and early '90s, several local climbers developed a significant number of free and aid ascents in previously unexplored areas of the monument, with first ascents established by Mike Baker, Tom Blake, Cameron Burns, Jon Butler, David Carrat, Andrea Heath, Leslie Henderson, Michael Kennedy, Luke Laeser, Guy Lord, Kurt Luhrs, Andy Petefish, Ann Robertson, and Bob Wade. KC Baum added numerous new routes with Tom Archibeque, John Culberson, Jeff Hollenbaugh, Peter Hollis, Bob Hustava, Chris Monz, Matt Simpson, Mel Thorson, and Chris Vickers. The mid-1990s saw a resurgence in aid climbing at the monument, with new route development combining both free and aided ascents. Joel Arellano, Jon Burnham, Mike Colacino, Bill Duncan, Scott Evens, Jesse Harvey, Michael Ohm, Matt Simpson, and Pete Takeda, among others, contributed to new lines.

Many secluded canyons in Colorado National Monument and adjacent areas remain unexplored and surely contain many quality climbs on Wingate Sandstone. Those with a desire for solitude, adventure, and untouched rock will appreciate this beautiful sandstone wonderland and understand why John Otto dedicated 30 years of his life to promoting its great natural resources.

Devils Canyon

Approach as for Kodels Canyon. After the turn into Kings View Estates from Broadway (Colorado Highway 340), drive 0.6 mile (0.9 km) and veer left at a Y, 500 feet (152 m) beyond the sharp left turn to Kodels Canyon. Then follow signs to Horse Thief Canyon and Devils Canyon. Park and then hike approximately 4 miles (6 km) on a sketchy trail on the east side of the canyon. Stay high (on the trail) to avoid a cliff area near the floor of the canyon. The three Devil's Disciple Towers are on the west side of the canyon. Only the two higher spires have been climbed. The

photo: Mike Baker

Phantom Spire

smaller tower is attached to the plateau behind it. Phantom Spire is across from Devil's Disciples on the east side of the canyon.

1   DEVIL'S DISCIPLE ONE II, 5.9 A2, 3 pitches, 250 feet (76 m)

First Ascent: Bill Forrest, Steve French, 1981.

Location and Access: Devil's Disciple One is the best looking and left or easternmost of the three towers near the head of the canyon.

Pitch 1: Climb to a notch from the west, then free climb up and right on friction to a belay ledge.

Pitch 2: Free climb to a thin aid crack (2 bolts are in place), then continue to the capstone and a belay in an alcove.

Pitch 3: Climb a short free pitch through an overhanging chimney to the summit.

Paraphernalia: Friends (1) set.

Descent: Two rappels down the route.

2   DEVIL'S DISCIPLE TWO II, 5.10+, A1, 3 pitches, 250 feet (76 m)

First Ascent: Bill Forrest, Steve French, 1981. Second ascent: Brad Bond, Stewart Ritchie, October 1995.

Location and Access: Devil's Disciple Two is the right or westernmost tower.

Pitch 1: Climb an obvious chimney on the west side of the tower, 5.10+, 5 inches (12.7 cm) at its top.

Pitch 2: This short pitch ascends a steep, left-facing corner (5.10+) until it is possible to step right and belay.

Pitch 3: Continue up a tight chimney which has overhanging rock near the summit.

Paraphernalia: Friends (3) sets through #5; Lost Arrows.

Descent: Rappel the route.

3   PHANTOM SPIRE (a.k.a. Kit Carson Spire) II, 5.8, A3, 1 pitch, 100 feet (30 m)

First Ascent: Mike Baker, Leslie Henderson, 7 March 1992.

Location and Access: *Phantom Spire* is obvious on the east side of Devils Canyon opposite the Disciple Towers. On the wall behind the tower, "Kit Carson 1841" is inscribed with a couple of other historic signatures and dates. Kit Carson trapped beaver in the area in the winter of 1840–1841. Ascend between the spire and the rimrock behind it. Begin 5.8, then climb A3 to a bolt ladder leading to the top.

Paraphernalia: Friends (1) set; Camalots (1) #1, #2; Tri-cams #0.5; angle pitons (2) 0.5"; knifeblades (2); short Lost Arrows (2); free carabiners and runners for the bolt ladder.

Descent: Rappel the route.

Kodels Canyon

Kodels Canyon is between Devils Canyon and Fruita Canyon at the northwest edge of Colorado National Monument. It is in view to the south as you approach the West Entrance to the monument. Approach from outside the West Entrance on Kings View Drive. Take Exit 19 at Fruita from Interstate 70 and drive south on Broadway (Colorado Highway 340) toward the monument. After crossing the bridge over the Colorado River, drive 0.3 mile (0.4 km) and turn

photo: Mike Baker

South face of Little Bighorn

photo: Leslie Henderson

Wilson Goodrich climbing, Mike Baker belaying on the first ascent of *Split Decision*

right on Kings View Drive. At the turn, a sign reads "Horse Thief Canyon State Wildlife Area." Drive through Kings View Estates. Approximately 0.5 mile (0.8 km) after the turn from Broadway take the first left turn (dirt road). Continue to the mouth of the canyon, where it is a 30-minute hike to Little Bighorn Pinnacle. Because the dirt approach road deteriorates before reaching the trailhead, a high-clearance vehicle may be required.

4   LITTLE BIGHORN PINNACLE III, 5.7, A2, 2 pitches, 120 feet (37 m) ★★★

First Ascent: Mike Baker, Leslie Henderson, Lindsey Archer, March 1993. Second ascent: Keith Bergland, Mike Baker, September 1997.

Location and Access: Climb a corner system on the north face. Little Bighorn Pinnacle was named for the desert bighorn sheep and their young seen in the area during the first ascent.

Pitch 1: Climb a right-facing corner system with a white, calcite-covered crack to a belay ledge with double anchors, A2, 80 feet (24 m).

Pitch 2: Move right and follow a 5-bolt ladder to the summit, 5.7, A1, 40 feet (12 m).

Paraphernalia: Pitch 1: Camalots (1) #0.5, (2) #1, #2, #3, #4. Pitch 2: Camalot (1) #0.75; quickdraws (5).

Descent: Rappel the route.

5   SPLIT DECISION II, 5.10a, 3 pitches, 350 feet (107 m) ★★★

First Ascent: Mike Baker, Leslie Henderson, Wilson Goodrich, October 1997.

Location and Access: *Split Decision* climbs the wall directly behind *Little Bighorn Pinnacle*. The route is obvious as the only crack that goes to the top.

Pitch 1: Lieback the edge of a solid flake until it is possible to mantle to its top. Finger jam to a small roof (5.9+) which is turned on its right side. Move right, climbing on pockets, passing 1 bolt and 2 fixed pitons, until it is possible to climb the rightmost crack to a small overhang and a gear belay in a pod.

Pitch 2: Continue up the crack system to a steep headwall of dark, desert-varnished rock. The crux. Lieback the headwall to a small ledge and a 2-bolt anchor, 5.10a.

Pitch 3: Climb the crack system passing a fixed piton until it pinches off and it is possible to face climb past 3 drilled anchors, 5.8.

Paraphernalia: Standard desert rack.

Descent: Two double-rope rappels down the route.

West Entrance

To reach the West Entrance of the monument take Fruita Exit 19 from Interstate 70 and drive south on Broadway (Colorado Highway 340) 2.6 miles (4 km) to the entrance kiosk.

6   REMNANTS TOWER (a.k.a. Defecating Monk)—SQUEEZEBOX II, 5.9, 3 pitches, 225 feet (69 m)

First Ascent: Harvey T. Carter, John Auld, Layton Kor, 2 May 1960.

Location and Access: Remnants Tower is between the entrance of Lizard Canyon and Wedding Canyon. To reach, drive just under 1 mile (1.6 km) from the West Entrance kiosk and park near Dead Man's Curve (the first hairpin switchback). Remnants Tower

photo: Harvey T. Carter

Remnants Tower

will be visible to the east, about a 15-minute hike. The route ascends an obvious crack system in the middle of the north face with a chimney visible 30 feet (9 m) up.

Pitch 1: Begin up a crack system below the chimney and climb to a belay ledge and a fixed anchor, 5.9.

Pitch 2: Climb a 5.4 squeeze chimney to a belay ledge and double anchors.

Pitch 3: Face climb, angling up and right, past a loose area to the summit with triple anchors, 5.6.

Paraphernalia: A selection of smaller-sized cams.

Descent: Rappel the route.

7   REMNANTS TOWER—SQUEEZEBOX VARIATION I, 5.7+, 1 pitch

First Ascent: David Kozak, Walt Kuentzel, 1983.

Location and Access: *Squeezebox* is a variation to Pitch 1. Begin 10 feet (3 m) left of the overhang, then diagonal back right to the chimney of the first ascent route. The variation was the second ascent of the tower.

8   REMNANTS TOWER—QUEEN AND HER JEWELS II, 5.9, 3 pitches

First Ascent: Fred Knapp, Sharon Sadlier, Jules Raymond, Richard Starnes, November 1990.

Location and Access: *Queen and Her Jewels* climbs the north side of the tower following a crack system just inside the right profile when viewed from the north (far right of the original route). Fred Knapp: "The route might be as good as any route on the tower."

Pitch 1: Climb a loose fingercrack to a better hand-and-fist crack.

Pitch 2: Step over crumbly rock into a sandy chimney. Grovel to a ledge at the top of *Squeezebox* Pitch 2. Protected with slings, there are no fixed anchors. Follow Pitch 3 of *Squeezebox* to the summit.

Paraphernalia: Rappel original route.

Descent: Rappel *Squeezebox*.

9   HARVEST MOON III, 5.11+, 3 Pitches, 240 feet (71 m) ★★★★

First Ascent: Luke Laeser, Jon Butler, 2 December 1995.

Location and Access: *Harvest Moon* climbs the prow of a buttress 200 yards (183 m) left of (before) the *Oliver Perry Smith Buttress*. Only the first three pitches were climbed to where a 4th-class traverse leads north. Two more pitches could be climbed to the rim but would probably require aid.

Pitch 1: Begin up loose but easy rock to a 5.10+ roof, then continue to a large belay ledge without anchors, 60 feet (18 m).

Pitch 2: Climb a left-facing thin dihedral (5.11) through a 5.11+, 4-foot (1.2 m) roof to a 2-bolt hanging belay 10 feet (3 m) above the roof, 100 feet (30 m).

Pitch 3: Continue up a left-facing dihedral with hands and fingers, 5.10, 80 feet (24 m).

Paraphernalia: Friends (2) #0.5 through #1, (4) #1.5 through #2, (3) #2.5 through #3, (2) #3.5 through #4; Camalots (2) #4; medium through large stoppers (1) set.

Descent: Two double-rope rappels or exit 4th class north to a gulley descending to the east.

10   OLIVER PERRY-SMITH BUTTRESS III, 5.10, 2 pitches, 350 feet (107 m)

First Ascent: Rick Linkert, Tom Kaufman, 20 August 1972. Second ascent: Kyle Copeland, Charlie Fowler, Alison Sheets, February 1987.

Location and Access: *Oliver Perry-Smith Buttress* is on the first bank of cliffs right of Rim Rock Drive, a short distance beyond the West Entrance kiosk, on the prominent recess formed by left- and right-facing dihedrals. The route ascends the left dihedral.

Pitch 1: Begin 5.9 up a corner, past a fixed anchor, then up a 5.8 offwidth to a second fixed anchor. Continue 5.10 offwidth passing 2 fixed anchors to a double-anchor belay.

Pitch 2: Climb 5.10 past a fixed anchor and on to the summit.

Paraphernalia: Standard desert rack; large Camalots.

Descent: Rappel the route or walk off to the north, then descend a gully to the east.

History: Oliver Perry-Smith Buttress was named for the American climber who, in this country and at Dresden, Germany, at the turn of the century, set standards of free climbing difficulty generations ahead of his time.

11   OLIVER PERRY-SMITH BUTTRESS—SPECIAL VERDICT I, 5.8+, 1 pitch, 100 feet (30 m)

First Ascent: Steve Johnson, Tom Blake, 1986.

Location and Access: *Special Verdict* is 50 feet (15 m) right of the first ascent route. Climb 5.8+ hands to double rappel anchors visible from below the route.

Paraphernalia: Medium to large nuts.

Descent: Rappel the route.

Fruita Canyon

Fruita Canyon is approximately 1.5 miles (2.4 km) into the park from the West Entrance kiosk, beyond Balanced Rock. Balanced Rock is signed, with a viewing pullout.

12   RIBBED BUTTRESS IV, 5.12, AO, 5 pitches, 500 feet (152 m) ★★★★

First Ascent: Ron Olevsky, solo, 5.8, A3, February 1978. Second ascent: Andy Petefish, Tom Stubbs, fall 1978. First free ascent (with exception of 10 feet- [3 m], 2 or 3 A0 moves up a bolt ladder): Andy Petefish, Tom Stubbs, June 1986.

Location and Access: *Ribbed Buttress* is approximately 100 yards (91 m) before the first tunnel on the narrow south face of the wall, above the point where the lowest part of the cliff shelf on the left comes closest to the road. The beginning of the climb is less than five minutes uphill from the roadway. A good viewing location is the pullout for Balanced Rock.

Pitch 1: Climb a handcrack to an alcove (small ledge) at the base of a large chimney, 5.7, 80 feet (24 m). From the belay it is possible to walk off to the left.

Pitch 2: Ascend the chimney to a small stance and belay from gear and a 3/8" bolt, 5.8, 100 feet (30 m). Difficult to protect. Climb a left-facing dihedral, then step left into a right-facing dihedral and continue to a hanging belay from 3 bolts, 5.10+, 80 feet (24 m).

Pitch 3: Free climb right (or traverse on bolts) to a thin crack which is climbed at 5.11 to a 5.9+ offwidth (or C1). The pitch ends on a sloping ledge with a hanging belay, 5.11, 100 feet (30 m).

Kath Pyke on Ribbed Buttress

photo: Steve "Crusher" Bartlett

Pitch 4: Continue up a 4" (10 cm) crack which widens higher up. Make an optional belay on a sloping stance 15 feet (5 m) below the "Rib Eye," 5.10, 90 feet (27 m). Climb the corner, then tension traverse left where 1 stopper placement lets you reach the base of a bolt ladder ending on a belay ledge, 5.12, A0, Protect with #4 Camalots, 80 feet (12 m). The original ascent aided straight to the bolts at A3.

Pitch 5: Climb a left-leaning corner to a series of mantles, 5.9. Move up and right with (5.6) steep jug climbing to the top, 80 feet (24 m).

Paraphernalia: Friends (2) sets; Camalots #4s; TCUs #0 through #2; 4" pieces (3); stoppers (1) set.

Descent: Walk west to Rim Rock Drive, then downhill on the road.

13   **BOOK OF PLEASURE IV, 5.9, A1+, 5 pitches, 500 feet (152 m)** ***

First Ascent: Pitches 1 through 3: Mike Baker, 7 December 1993. Pitches 4 through 5: Mike Baker, Leslie Henderson, 1 March 1994.

Location and Access: *Book of Pleasure* begins up the original *Ribbed Buttress* route. A good viewing point is the Balanced Rock pullout.

Pitches 1-2: Follow the first 2 pitches of *Ribbed Buttress*.

Pitch 3: Traverse right from the hanging belay at the top of Pitch 2 and climb loose 5.8 to the beginning of short A1+ bolt ladder ending at a 2-bolt anchor.

Pitch 4: Climb an open book (*Book of Pleasure*) with good 5.9 stemming and great hands to a 2-bolt anchor.

Pitch 5: Climb straight to a large roof, then make an A1 airy traverse out from underneath the roof until it is possible to move to a large belay shelf.

photo: Mike Baker

Fruita Canyon

Paraphernalia: Camalots (1) #0.5, #0.75, #4, (2) #1, (3) #2, (2) #3; TCUs (1) set; Big Dude (or #5 Camalot), (1) #7 for Pitch 5.

Descent: Walk west to Rim Rock Drive, then downhill.

14   **HAIRBOATIN' I, 5.10b, 1 pitch, 80 feet (24 m)**

First Ascent: Steve Kolarik, David Kozak, April 1986.

Location and Access: *Hairboatin'* is approximately 200 feet (61 m) left of *Ribbed Buttress*. Approach as for *Ribbed Buttress*, then traverse left to an offwidth crack with rappel slings visible at the 80-foot (24 m) level. View the route from the Balanced Rock pullout.

Paraphernalia: Medium to large cams.

Descent: Rappel the route.

15   **TUNNEL VISION III, 5.10+ R, A1, 4 pitches, 435 feet (133 m)**

First Ascent: Mike Colocino, Calvin Hebert, March 1990.

Location and Access: *Tunnel Vision* ascends the second crack system right of the tunnel right of *Ribbed Buttress*.

Pitch 1: Begin at a 12-foot (4 m) block, then continue 5.10 hands up a right-facing corner. Angle right, A1 (#0.5 TCUs), gaining a belay ledge at its right edge, 70 feet (21 m).

Pitch 2: Climb a face passing a fixed anchor and belay from a ledge at the base of a chimney, 5.8, 35 feet (11 m).

Pitch 3: Begin up the chimney and work into hands continuing up a left-facing dihedral. Pass a pod (the crux) and continue to a belay at a tree, 5.10+, 165 feet (50 m).

Pitch 4: Climb 5.6 with no protection past an offwidth and up broken rock to the top, 165 feet (50 m).

Paraphernalia: Standard desert rack; TCUs (2) #0.5.

Descent: Rappel the route or walk uphill at the top of the route to reach the road, then descend the road.

16   **Z-ROW GRAVITY II, 5.10, 2 pitches, 200 feet (61 m)**

First Ascent: Tom Stubbs et al, 1980s.

Location and Access: *Z-Row Gravity* is on the opposite side of the wall from *Ribbed Buttress*. Park as for that route, then hike up Rim Rock Drive to the climb. Rappel slings are visible from below.

Paraphernalia: Standard desert rack.

Descent: Rappel the route.

Saddlehorn Bouldering Area

Sixty-foot-high (18 m) cliffs offer numerous bouldering and top-rope possibilities, although the rock is composed of the relatively soft Entrada Sandstone. The region is north of the visitor center in the Saddlehorn campground and picnic area. From the West Entrance, follow Rim Rock Drive 4 miles (6.4 km) to signs giving directions to the campground.

photo: Mike Baker

Sentinel Spire

Wedding Canyon

To view the towers in Wedding Canyon, drive from the West Entrance on Rim Rock Drive to the parking area at Pipe Organ Overlook, and hike 0.5 mile (0.8 km) on Otto's Trail to the overlook for Pipe Organ. Organ Pipe Spire is the lower, outside tower adjacent to Pipe Organ Spire. Sentinel Spire is the prominent pinnacle southeast and below the Book Cliff View Point, approximately 4 miles (6.4 km) up Rim Rock Drive from the monument's West Entrance. Rainbow Tower is in Upper Wedding Canyon on the west side past Bell Tower and Pharaoh Point. It is semi-attached to the wall behind with the top 100 feet (30 m) soaring free from the wall.

The towers are reached by rappel from Pipe Organ Overlook. Don't be tempted to rappel directly to Pipe Organ Spire, because a 165-foot (50 m) rappel leaves you 35 feet (11 m) short of the ground. A better rappel point is 100 yards (91 m) west of the overlook on the north flank of the rimrock at a large, solid pinyon pine 5 feet (1.5 m) from the edge of the canyon. A 150-foot (46 m) rappel reaches 3rd-class ground from where a hike east reaches the base of Pipe Organ. An alternate (and much longer) approach is from the Lower Monument Canyon Trail. Leave the trail before reaching Independence Monument (a point where Pipe Organ and Organ Pipe spires are visible), then hike northwest to the landforms.

17   SENTINEL SPIRE (a.k.a. Watusi Spear)—FAST DRAW II, 5.10-, 2 pitches, 250 feet (76 m) ★★★★

First Ascent: Layton Kor, Harvey T. Carter, John Auld, 3 May 1960. First free ascent: Andy Petefish, John Christenson, 1978. A tyrolean traverse has been done from Sentinel Spire by a unknown party.

Location and Access: The viewing area for Sentinel Spire is off the Saddlehorn Campground loop road which is well marked from Rim Rock Drive. Park at the Book Cliff Overlook and walk south a short distance to a peninsula of rock which leads to a view of the spire. With 1 rope, rappel about 80 feet (24 m) from a piñon pine on the north side of the peninsula (left side when looking at the spire from the rim). Sentinel Spire will be due east. Leave the rope fixed for the return on ascenders. Descend a gully and short friction slabs until even with the base of the spire. Mike Baker: "This can be very scary when wet, and hard to reverse." Traverse to the northwest side of the tower and a belay ledge beneath the obvious crack line of the first pitch. Sentinel Spire may also be approached by a double-rope rappel from a tree close to the rim's edge, in line with the spire. Continue with a 1-rope rappel from 3 bolts to reach the base of the climb. Sentinel Spire can also be reached by a 1-hour hike up the Monument Canyon Trail. The tower is 120 feet (37 m) from the rimrock behind it.

Pitch 1: Step across a 2.5-foot (6 cm) gap, then climb a slightly overhanging corner (5.10-) passing old bolts. At a 2-bolt station, make a hanging belay or continue left past bolts (5.10-) to a belay in an alcove.

Pitch 2: The crux. Climb up a fingercrack until it becomes less than vertical; continue on with hands and offwidth, 5.10-, than 5.8 up a chimney system to the summit and a 2-bolt anchor. Protect the pitch from old bolts and larger-sized cams.

Paraphernalia: Friends, mostly hand-sized, with a few smaller and larger sizes.

Descent: Two double-rope rappels down the route.

18   SENTINEL SPIRE—WEBSTER-NORDEN VARIATION 5.9+, 1 pitch

First Ascent: Buck Norden, Ed Webster, April 1979.

Location and Access: The variation continues higher up the initial crack (5.9+ loose) to join the left crack; belay in a higher alcove.

19   SENTINEL SPIRE—SOUTHWEST VARIATION 5.9+, 1 pitch

First Ascent: Harvey T. Carter, John Auld, 1960.

Location and Access: The variation ascends cracks on the southwest side of the spire as a variation to the original Pitch 1 of *Fast Draw*.

20   SENTINEL SPIRE—MEDICINE MAN III, 5.12b, 4 pitches, 250 feet (76 m)

First Ascent: Andy Petefish, Tom Bratton, spring 1980. First free ascent: Alan Lester, Pete Takeda, 1993.

Location and Access: *Medicine Man* climbs the southeast face of the tower, directly opposite *Fast Draw*.

Pitch 1: Climb a 5.10- handcrack to a belay ledge.

Pitch 2: Continue up a 1.5" (3.8 cm) crack in a groove, then make a traverse left under an overhang to a bolt and continue up a 1.5" crack over 5.11 rock to a belay.

Pitch 3: Climb an overhanging 2–2.5" crack (3 cm–3.8 cm), then a 2" crack through a bulge (5.12b crux) to a belay below a roof.

Pitch 4: Traverse left beneath the roof, the crack to the right is off-route. Continue up an awkward 5.10, 3" (4.6 cm) crack to the summit.

Paraphernalia: Friends (1) #1, (4) #1.5, (5) #2, (7) #2.5, (2) #3, (2) #3.5, (2) #4, with extra #1.5 for Pitch 2 and extra #2 for Pitch 3; stoppers (1).

Descent: Two double-rope rappels down *Fast Draw*.

21   LIZARDS AND SCORPIONS ON TUESDAY WITH CLOUDS IN THE SKY III, 5.11, 4 pitches, 360 feet (110 m) ★★

First Ascent: Andy Petefish, Tom Stubbs, March 1985.

Location and Access: The route climbs the major left-facing dihedral of the canyon wall left of Sentinel Spire.

Pitch 1: Begin up a short steep left-facing dihedral (mostly fingers) to ledges, 5.11, 30 feet (9 m).

Pitch 2: Climb a corner with drilled angles, 40 feet (12 m) to a large chimney. Continue up the chimney 60 feet (18 m), then traverse left (1 or 2 bolts) to a large ledge on the left with bolts for a belay, 5.10.

Pitch 3: Continue up a 165-foot (50 m) pitch with loose rock at first, then a beautiful dihedral (hands and fists) to belay under a large roof, 5.10. Extra hand-and-fists cams.

Pitch 4: Climb up, then make a right traverse (5.7, 5.8) to the top, 50 feet (15 m).

Paraphernalia: Standard desert rack with extra hand-and-fists–cams for Pitch 3.

Descent: Rappel the route.

22   PIPE ORGAN SPIRE—SOUTHEAST III, 5.10, 3 pitches, 350 feet (107 m)

First Ascent: John Auld, Gary Ziegler, Jim Dyson, John Kuglin, 30–31 January 1961. Second ascent and direct start: Harvey T. Carter, Tim Jennings, 1963. Third ascent: Rich Perch, Mike Munger, 1978. First free ascent: Unknown party in the early 1980s.

photo: Cameron M. Burns

Pipe Organ Spire (left) and Organ Pipe Spire

Location and Access: The spire is climbed from the southeast.

Paraphernalia: Standard desert rack.

Descent: Rappel the route.

23   **ORGAN PIPE SPIRE—SIROCCO III, 5.9, A3, 5 pitches, 325 feet (99 m)**

First Ascent: Harvey T. Carter, Bill Kurimay, 13 March 1976.

Location and Access: Approach as for Pipe Organ Spire.

Paraphernalia: Selection of nuts and a few pitons.

Descent: Rappel the route.

Lower Independence Monument Trail

The first climbs you reach on the trail are established on the Lower Monument Canyon Slabs, a popular area near the mouth of the canyon, 10 minutes from the car. It is 4.9 miles (7.8 km) from Interstate 70 to the Monument Canyon Trailhead or 2 miles (3.2 km) from the West Entrance. Take Fruita Exit 19 off I-70 and drive south toward the monument. The trailhead is gained from Broadway (Colorado Highway 340) at a parking lot beside a lone two-story house approximately 2 miles (3.2 km) south of the turnoff to Rim Rock Drive and the monument's West Entrance. Follow the trail for approximately 0.5 mile (0.8 km) as it heads south, skirting the rear of the Deer Park housing development. The trail meets the Monument Canyon drainage and veers west toward Independence Monument and Upper Monument Canyon. Shortly thereafter the trail goes by a register box, then passes close to a short cliff. Fixed anchors not visible from below were placed by National Outdoor Leadership School for top-roped climbs. The anchors are reached by scrambling up obvious 3rd-class slabs on the right (east) side of the formation. The canyon in this region exposes large areas of ancient granite rock. All routes are listed from right to left (lower to upper canyon).

24 BORN TO BE WILD I, 5.10-, 1 pitch, 100 feet (30 m)

First Ascent: Unknown.

Location and Access: *Born to be Wild* is 60 feet (18 m) right of the 3rd-class slab which reaches the top-rope climbs. Face and friction climb past a drilled piton to a belay station.

Paraphernalia: Unknown.

Descent: Rappel the route.

25 BORN TO BE WILD AND HIGHER I, Rating unknown, 1 pitch, 40 feet (12 m)

First Ascent: Unknown.

Location and Access: From the top of *Born to be Wild* easy scrambling up and right brings you to the top and *Born to be Wild and Higher*. The route is protected by 3 drilled pitons.

Paraphernalia: Unknown.

Descent: Rappel the route.

26 DUDLEY-SAC I, 5.8, 1 pitch, 30 feet (9 m)

First Ascent: Mike Dudley, Dennis Willis, early 1980s.

Location and Access: *Dudley-Sac* is approximately 100 feet (30 m) west, up the trail at a slab which lies against the main wall. Third class to the top of the slab and climb the face above to the top. The route is protected by 2 bolts.

Paraphernalia: Unknown.

Descent: Rappel the route.

27 MORMON TEA I, 5.8, 1 pitch, 80 feet (24 m)

First Ascent: Dennis Willis, Brad Jenter, June 1985.

Location and Access: *Mormon Tea* is approximately 300 feet (91 m) up the trail from *Dudley-Sac*. The route climbs a handcrack (identified by a fixed piton at its beginning) to a belay ledge.

Paraphernalia: Hand-sized units.

Descent: Rappel the route.

28 CIRCLE, SQUARE, AND THE TRIANGLE II, 5.9+, 1 pitch, 155 feet (47 m) ★★

First Ascent: KC Baum, Tom Archibeque, 20 February 1988.

Location and Access: *Circle, Square, and the Triangle* is 150 feet (46 m) right of *Higher Mind Dynamics* and just right of a prominent left-facing dihedral. Begin right of an elevated left-facing dihedral 20 feet (6 m) off the ground. Follow bolts with a 5.8+ move, then continue to an alcove where it is possible to belay. Climb past bolts with a 5.9+ move and on to triple rappel bolts. Fifteen bolts were placed by the first ascent team.

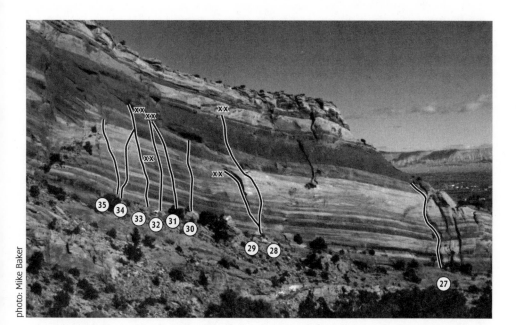

photo: Mike Baker

Paraphernalia: Small #4 TCUs or #0.5 to #1 Tri-cams to protect the belay in the alcove; Quickdraws (15).

Descent: Rappel the route from a 3-bolt anchor.

29   LUHRS ROUTE I, 5.9+, 1 pitch, 155 feet (47 m) ★

First Ascent: Kurt Luhrs et al, summer 1991.

Location and Access: *Luhrs Route* begins at *Circle, Square, and the Triangle* and clips the first 2 bolts. Move left into the left-facing dihedral and climb a crack system until the dihedral begins arching to the left, 90 feet (27 m). Make a roof move out of the dihedral and continue right on the face to join *Circle, Square, and the Triangle* to its anchors. A 2-bolt anchor was placed at the top of the dihedral in the fall of 1993 by Jon Butler and Luke Larsen.

Paraphernalia: Small to hand-sized protection.

Descent: Rappel *Circle, Square, and the Triangle*.

30   RAINBOW BRIDGE I, 5.12b/c, 1 pitch, 110 feet (34 m) ★★★

First Ascent: KC Baum, Tom Archibeque, 1 June1988.

Location and Access: *Rainbow Bridge* is approximately 100 feet (30 m) left (west) of *Circle, Square, and the Triangle*. Start right of a juniper tree and face climb past (10) 3/8" bolts with SMC hangers. Pass a small flake on its right, a small roof, then pass a second small flake on its left and continue to triple 3/8" anchors.

Paraphernalia: Quickdraws (10).

Descent: Rappel the route from a 3-bolt anchor.

31   HIGHER MIND DYNAMICS I, 5.11b/c, 1 pitch, 110 feet (34 m) ★★★

First Ascent: KC Baum, Tom Archibeque, 30 January 1988.

Location and Access: *Higher Mind Dynamics* is 30 feet (9 m) left (west) of *Rainbow Bridge*. Begin just above a large rock and climb to triple rappel anchors. Eleven bolts are in place plus belay anchors.

Paraphernalia: Nuts and hangers (14); quickdraws (11).

Descent: Rappel from a 3-bolt anchor.

32   FRIENDS CAN'T BE TRUSTED I, 5.12a/b, 1 pitch, 110 feet (34 m) ★★★★★

First Ascent: Andy Petefish, solo, spring 1988.

Location and Access: *Friends Can't Be Trusted* is 20 feet (6 m) left (west) of *Higher Mind Dynamics* and 20 feet (6 m) right of *Dihedral #I*. Fourteen bolts are in place. *Friends Can't Be Trusted* veers right after the last protection bolt to share rappel anchors under an overhang with *Higher Mind Dynamics*. Follow bolts with a 5.11+ move and a higher 5.12a/b move.

Paraphernalia: Quickdraws (14).

Descent: Rappel the route.

33   DIHEDRAL #1 I, 5.10+ A3, 2 pitches, 130 feet (40 m) ★★★★★

First Ascent: Harvey T. Carter, 1970s.

Location and Access: *Dihedral #I* climbs a prominent right-facing dihedral 20 feet (6 m) left of *Friends Can't Be Trusted*. A right-curving crack between *Dihedral #I* and *#II* ascends up and right and joins *Dihedral #I* below the rappel anchors. Right of the routes (high above) is a left-curving chimney which sounds like tin foil flapping when the wind is blowing.

Pitch 1: KC Baum: "A very popular pitch which gets the 5-star rating," 5.8.

Pitch 2: A 5.10+, A3 pitch that is rarely climbed.

Paraphernalia: Tri-cams or TCUs; small nuts; Quad-cams recommended; RPs.

Descent: Rappel from a 2-bolt anchor.

34   CARTER ROUTE I, 5.9+, 1 pitch, 100 feet (30 m)

First Ascent: Harvey T. Carter, early 1980.

Location and Access: *Carter Route* is identified by fixed pitons 3/4 of the way up the route. Climb the left of 2 right-curving cracks between *Dihedral #I* and *#II*. Ascend up and right, then join *Dihedral #I* below rappel anchors.

Paraphernalia: Nuts and cams.

Descent: Rappel the route from a 2-bolt anchor.

35   DIHEDRAL #II I, 5.9 R X, 1 pitch, 100 feet (30 m)

First Ascent: Harvey T. Carter, 1970s.

Location and Access: *Dihedral #II* is left of *Carter Route* and climbs 5.8–5.9 (much loose R X rock) left of 2 right-curving cracks in a right-facing dihedral identified by a bolt 40 feet off the ground. Continue up a corner to a ledge from which you can 3rd class to the ground to the left (west). The route may be top-roped. Rappel slings are visible from below the climb.

Paraphernalia: Top-rope.

Descent: Walk off to the left (west).

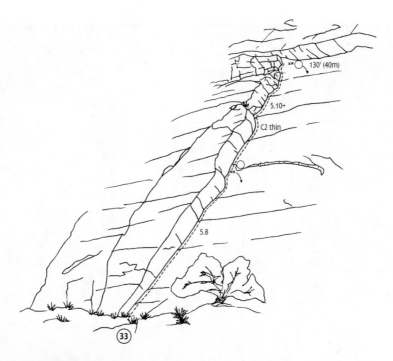

130' (40m)

5.10+

C2 thin

5.8

(33)

36   WINGATE WARRIOR I, 5.10d/5.11a, C2, 1 pitch, 170 feet (52 m) ★★★★★

First Ascent: KC Baum, Tom Archibeque, January 1989.

Location and Access: *Wingate Warrior* is approximately 100 yards (91 m) left (west) of *Dihedral #I*. Either the belayer has to climb up or a 55 m rope is needed for this 170-foot (52 m) route. Eighteen bolts are in place.

Paraphernalia: Quickdraws (18).

Descent: Rappel from a 3-bolt anchor.

37   DIHEDRAL #III II, 5.11, 2 pitches, 250 feet (76 m)

First Ascent: Unknown.

Location and Access: *Dihedral III* is 150 feet (46 m) left of *Out of the Frying Pan and into the Fire*. Begin up a short, right-facing dihedral marked by a bolt about 40 feet (12 m) off the ground. High on the climb is a light-colored, right-facing dihedral (5.11), beyond which the route ascends through a window in the upper Kayenta Formation. Rappel slings are visible from below.

Paraphernalia: Standard desert rack.

Descent: Walk off to the right.

38   ROUTE #1 Rating unknown, 1 pitch, 100 feet (30 m)

First Ascent: Unknown.

Location and Access: *Route #1* follows Pitch 1 of *The Binge*, then moves right climbing a right-angling thin crack left (west) of *Dihedral #III*. Begin at a broken face section with a large ledge approximately 100 feet (30 m) off the ground. Rappel slings are visible at the ledge.

photo: Mike Baker

Paraphernalia: Standard desert rack.

Descent: Rappel the route.

39 THE BINGE IV, 5.9 A4, 4 pitches, 400 feet (122 m) ★★★★

First Ascent: Mike Baker, solo, November 1994.

Location and Access: *The Binge* is a lone splitter crack right of *Desert Solitaire* where the Monument Canyon Trail passes between several large boulders. No bolts were placed on the first ascent, except at belays. The route is plaqued. Begin on a face with cracks 15 feet (4.5 m) right of a large, light-colored, precariously balanced flake. Begin up the first crack that goes to a loose flake, then turns into a seam.

Pitch 1: Climb A2+ up slightly overhanging rock to a ledge, then continue up a 5.8 left-facing corner to a good belay ledge, 130 feet (40 m).

Pitch 2: The crux. Begin A4 with Bird Beaks in a seam. Ascend the seam until it becomes a knifeblade crack and finally opens to 0.5 inch (13 cm). Follow the crack as it moves slightly right and it is possible to free climb to a 2-bolt belay, 5.8 A4, 130 feet (40 m).

Pitch 3: Climb a steep left-facing corner (A1) to the base of an overhang and a 2-bolt belay, A1, 70 feet (21 m).

Pitch 4: Begin A2. Climb past the overhang (5.9), then A2+ through a series of overhangs (formed by the caprock) and on to the summit, 5.9 A2+, 70 feet (24 m).

Paraphernalia: Camalots (2) #0.5, #0.75, #1, (1) #2, #3; Tri-cams (1) #0.5, #1, #1.5, #2; TCUs (1) set; Bird Beaks (4); knifeblades (4); Lost Arrows (3); angle pitons (3) 0.5"; stoppers (1) set.

Descent: Walk off east and meet the trail, or rappel from anchors at the top of *Desert Solitaire*.

40 ROUTE #2 Rating unknown, 1 pitch, 90 feet (27 m)

First Ascent: Michael Dudley et al.

Location and Access: *Route #2* is 1 crack left of *Binge*. Climb a wide left-facing dihedral with an old homemade hanger at an offwidth overhanging crux about 60 feet (18 m) up. Rappel slings are visible from below.

Paraphernalia: Several large offwidth-sized cams.

Descent: Rappel the route.

41 AID ROUTE III, A2, 4 pitches, 400 feet (122 m)

First Ascent: Unknown.

Location and Access: *Aid Route* climbs a knifeblade crack with obvious piton scars 1 crack system left of *Route #2*.

Paraphernalia: A selection of thin pitons.

Descent: Rappel the route.

42 ROUTE #3 I, 5.10a, 1 pitch, 80 feet (24 m) ★★

First Ascent: Andy Petefish, Dave Huntley.

Location and Access: *Route #3* is 1 crack left of *Aid Route*. Climb a right-facing dihedral with a small roof (the crux) approximately 45 feet (14 m) up the buttress. Begin with fingers, then large hands to a small ledge with a 2-bolt anchor.

Paraphernalia: Friends small to large with (1) big piece.

Descent: Rappel the route.

80'
(24m)

90'
(27m)

5.10 a
crux

large
hands

OW

fingers

Aid Route

42

41

40

43 PROW II, 5.7/8, 3 pitches, unfinished

First Ascent: Andy Petefish, Tom Stubbs, John Christenson, 1978.

Location and Access: *Prow* is left of *Route #3*.

Pitch 1: Climb broken blocks to a belay ledge.

Pitch 2: Move left of the ledge to a small roof with a thin knifeblade crack and slab above it. Aid up the slab to bolts below a steep headwall.

Pitch 3: Started but not finished. Aid up a crack to a bolt and rotten rock.

Paraphernalia: Standard desert rack with a selection of knifeblade pitons.

Descent: Rappel the route.

44 OUT OF THE FRYING PAN AND INTO THE FIRE I, 5.9, 1 pitch, 85 feet (26 m) ★

First Ascent: Guy Lord et al.

Location and Access: *Out of the Frying Pan and into the Fire* is approximately 100 yards (91 m) left (west) of *Wingate Warrior* at the southeastern prow of the landform, on the first buttress as you walk past the lower slab routes. Begin at a fingercrack that arches left and climbs to a good stance. Continue, face climbing, past 3 or 4 bolts to a ledge with a 2-bolt rappel anchor.

Paraphernalia: Standard desert rack.

Descent: Rappel the route.

45 SHORT ROUTE I, 5.9+, 1 pitch

First Ascent: Unknown.

Location and Access: *Short Route* is 20 feet (6 m) right of *Bigfoot*. It climbs with perfect hands 2 parallel cracks near a right-hand 5.9+ corner. The corner itself is not climbed.

Paraphernalia: Standard desert rack.

Descent: Rappel the route.

46 BIGFOOT I, 5.10c/d, 1 pitch, 60 feet (18 m) ★★

First Ascent: KC Baum, Tom Archibeque, January 1990.

Location and Access: *Bigfoot* climbs an A-frame formation on a buttress approximately 0.25 mile (0.4 km) east (right) of Monolith Spire. Ascend an overhanging hand-and-fist crack to a small right-sloping flaring squeeze, then continue with good hands to an anchor visible from below.

Paraphernalia: Small to large cams; Camalots (2) #3.

Descent: Rappel the route.

47 TOM AND ANDY I, 5.11, 1 pitch, 120 feet (37 m)

First Ascent: Tom Blake, Andy Petefish, 1992.

Location and Access: *Tom and Andy* is 150 feet (46 m) right of *Route #4*. Climb a left-facing dihedral to a ledge (mostly offwidth) using Big Bros and bolts for protection.

Paraphernalia: Big Bros; Quickdraws.

Descent: Rappel the route.

85' (26m)

5.9

fingers

(44)

48   ROUTE #4 I, 5.9+/5.10-, 1 pitch, 80 feet (24 m) ★★★

First Ascent: Unknown.

Location and Access: *Route #4* is approximately 40 feet (12 m) left (west) of *Bigfoot*. The climb may be identified by its location left of a light-colored, relatively fresh break in the rock. The route follows 2 parallel cracks, using both cracks for the ascent. Climb a double handcrack on the left face of an open book corner to a 2-bolt anchor.

Paraphernalia: Medium to hand-sized cams.

Descent: Rappel the route.

49   ROUTE #5 Rating unknown, 1 pitch, 80 feet (24 m)

First Ascent: Unknown.

Location and Access: *Route #5* is left of *Route #4* and climbs a left-facing flake into a large chimney with rappel anchors visible from the ground.

Paraphernalia: Standard desert rack.

Descent: Rappel the route.

50   ROUTE #6 Rating unknown, 1 pitch, 80 feet (24 m)

First Ascent: Unknown.

Location and Access: *Route #6* is approximately 50 feet (15 m) left (west) of *Route #5*. Rappel slings are visible from below.

Paraphernalia: Standard desert rack.

Descent: Rappel the route.

51   BIG BERTHA I, 5.10a, 1 pitch, 80 feet (24 m) ★

First Ascent: KC Baum, Matt Simpson, May 1988.

Location and Access: *Big Bertha* is approximately 100 yards (91 m) right (east) of Monolith Spire and just right of a large chimney. Begin in a right-facing dihedral and climb fingers through hands into an offwidth. Finish at a large ledge with a 2-bolt anchor.

Paraphernalia: Small- to hand-sized cams; Camalots (1–2) #3.

Descent: Rappel the route.

52   MONOLITH SPIRE—AS ABOVE, SO BELOW III, 5.10d, AO, 3 pitches, 260 feet (79 m) ★

First Ascent: KC Baum, Andrea Heath, Peter Hollis, Chris Monz, April 1989.

Location and Access: Monolith Spire is an obvious formation with 3 cracks splitting its face. It is approximately 0.25 mile (0.4 km) east of Independence Monument, in the last horseshoe-shaped bowl before reaching the monument from the east. The spire was previously called Catcher's Mitt by the first ascent party climbing *Dewar Dihedral*, but their route did not go to the top, so the formation was renamed Monolith Spire by the party finishing the climb to the summit. *As Above, So Below* follows the center crack on the landform.

Pitch 1: 5.10, AO, 110 feet (34 m).

Pitch 2: Climb 5.10 offwidth and a chimney to a large shelf/ledge on the right side of the spire, 80 feet (24 m). There is a 2-bolt rappel station off the east face.

Pitch 3: Begin from left of the shelf and ascend the 5.10d south face, then move to the east face and finish to the top, 70 feet (21 m). The pitch is protected by 6 bolts. It

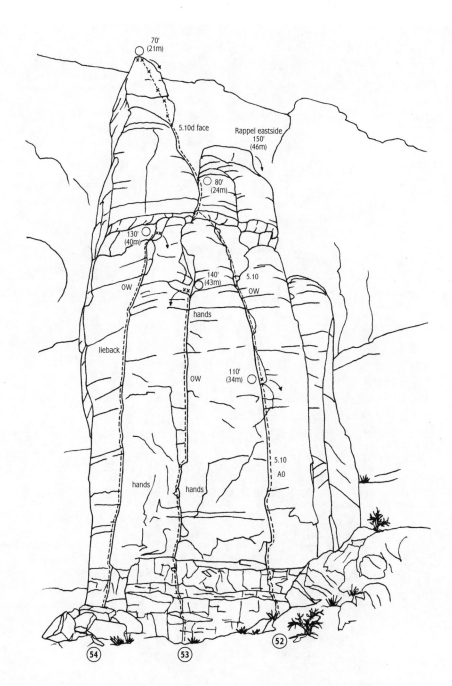

70'
(21m)

5.10d face

Rappel eastside
150'
(46m)

80'
(24m)

130'
(40m)

140'
(43m)

5.10

OW

OW

hands

lieback

OW

110'
(34m)

hands

5.10
A0

hands

hands

hands

54

53

52

photo: Photographer unknown

Monolith Spire

is possible to climb up the back (north) side of the spire by an easy 5th-class chimney and gain the large ledge at the start of Pitch 3.

Paraphernalia: Clean aid; Camalots (2–3) #4; small to large cams; stoppers.

Descent: Rappel 70 feet (21 m) to the ledge, then 1 double-rope rappel off the east face to the ground, 150 feet (46 m).

53   MONOLITH SPIRE—TAMING OF THE SHREW I, 5.12a, AO, 1 pitch, 140 feet (43 m) ★★

First Ascent: KC Baum, Tom Archibeque, December 1989.

Location and Access: *Taming of the Shrew* is 30 feet (9 m) left (west) of *As Above, So Below*. It is the overhanging westernmost crack of the 3 cracks that split the face of Monolith Spire. Begin 1 crack right of Dewar Dihedral in the Chinle Formation, then make face moves into an overhanging handcrack. Climb hands to a small stance at the base of an overhanging offwidth (5" [13 cm] parallel-sided crack). Continue up the offwidth into good hands and finish in a large alcove with a 2-bolt rappel anchor.

Paraphernalia: Small to large cams; Camalots (2–3) #3, #4.

Descent: Rappel the route.

54   MONOLITH SPIRE—DEWAR DIHEDRAL—CATCHER'S MITT I, 5.10b/c, 1 pitch, 130 feet (40 m) ★★

First Ascent: Stephen Angelini, Mack Johnson, August 1989.

Location and Access: *Catcher's Mitt*, the first route established on Monolith Spire, is approximately 25 feet (8 m) left (west) of *Taming of the Shrew* in a large left-facing dihedral on the west side of the landform. Climb good hands to a small ledge with a drilled baby angle on the right face approximately 60 feet (18 m) up the climb. Continue with a lieback up an offwidth crack to a 2-bolt rappel station.

Paraphernalia: Hand-sized protection; Friends (2) #3, (3) #3.5, #4; Camalots (2–3) #3, (1) #4; Hexentrics #10, #11.

Descent: Rappel the route. The original party rappeled from a hex and baby angle.

55   DESERT SOLITAIRE IV, 5.11a, AO (2–3 points), 6 pitches, 350 feet (107 m) ★★★★

First Ascent: KC Baum, Andrea Heath, Tom Archibeque, Peter Hollis, March 1989.

Location and Access: *Desert Solitaire* is approximately 400 yards (366 m) left (west) of Monolith Spire and 0.25 mile (0.4 km) east of Independence Monument. Approach from where the trail passes through 2 large boulders. Begin the climb at the Wingate-Chinle contact in a shallow corner. The route climbs to the top of the landform.

Pitch 1: Climb a slightly overhanging fingercrack with a good handcrack flake which arches left and leads to a sandy ledge. Climb hands into an undercling, then lieback the flake as it becomes vertical and ends on a good belay ledge, 5.11a, 100 feet (30 m).

Pitch 2: Walk east along the ledge and make an easy 5th-class mantle onto a higher ledge which leads to a 3rd-class ramp. Walk west (left) up the ramp to the base of a large block forming a right-facing dihedral with the main wall, just right of *Lightning Bolt Crack*. It is possible to 3rd and 4th class this ramp from the ground, 5.3 mantle plus a 3rd-class traverse, 30 feet (9 m).

Pitch 3: Climb the dihedral with hands to the top of the block, 5.10, 50 feet (15 m). Pitches 3 and 4 can be combined.

photo: Mack Johnson

Steve Angelini rappelling the *Dewar Dihedral*

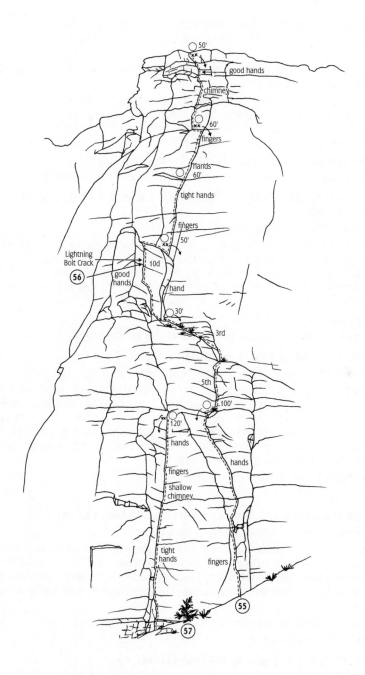

50'

good hands

chimney

60'

fingers

hands
60'

tight hands

fingers
50'

Lightning
Bolt Crack

10d

good
hands

56

hand

30'

3rd

5th

100'

120'

hands

hands

fingers

shallow
chimney

tight
hands

fingers

55

57

Pitch 4: Continue with fingers and tight hands to a blank section with 1 bolt and pass it with 2–3 points of AO. Finish in an alcove with a 2-bolt rappel anchor, 5.10 AO, 60 feet (18 m).

Pitch 5: Climb hands into a tight hand/finger crack (crux), then continue to a large ledge with rappel anchors, 5.11a, 60 feet (18 m).

Pitch 6: Climb either of 2 cracks coming off the belay ledge, into a chimney below a long, slender, protruding rectangular block. Cautiously pass the block and climb hands to a roof formed at the base of the Kayenta caprock. Continue with good hands through the roof and belay at a 2-bolt anchor, 5.9, 50 feet (15 m).

Paraphernalia: Small to hand-sized cams; Tri-cams; wires; nuts.

Descent: Rappel the route to the ramp, then downclimb to the ground.

56 DESERT SOLITAIRE—LIGHTNING BOLT CRACK 5.10d, 1 pitch, 50 feet (15 m) ★★★

First Ascent: KC Baum, Peter Hollis, September 1989.

Location and Access: *Lightning Bolt Crack* is approximately 25 feet (8 m) left (west) of a large right-facing dihedral and is a variation to Pitch 3 of *Desert Solitaire*. The route splits a large block obvious from below. Approach from the right side with a 4th-class ramp. Climb a good handcrack which forms a prominent zig-zag in the east face of the large block.

Paraphernalia: Small- to hand-sized cams.

Descent: Rappel from the block, then descend the 4th-class ramp.

57 WIZARD I, 5.10d/5.11a, 1 pitch, 120 feet (37 m) ★★★

First Ascent: KC Baum, Tom Archibeque, December 1989.

Location and Access: *Wizard* is a vertical crack with a beige stain approximately 25 feet (8 m) left (west) of *Desert Solitaire*. Begin in a 10-foot (3 m) section of Chinle Sandstone under a small roof formed by the base of the Wingate. Climb tight hands through a roof and into a shallow, flaring chimney with good face holds and a handcrack. Continue into an open book corner with a fingercrack (crux) to a small ledge. Finish with good hands to rappel chains.

Paraphernalia: Small- to hand-sized cams.

Descent: Rappel the route.

58 WINTER SOLSTICE I, 5.10b/c, 1 pitch, 120 feet (37 m) ★

First Ascent: KC Baum, Tom Archibeque, December 1989.

Location and Access: *Winter Solstice* is approximately 150 feet (46 m) left (west) of *Wizard*, and 175 feet (53 m) left of *Desert Solitaire*. Start in the Chinle Formation under a small, dark-colored roof (crux) and left-facing dihedral, then climb a small-to-large handcrack up an obscure left-facing corner to a large chimney with an alcove and rappel chains.

Paraphernalia: Small-to-large cams; Camalots (1) #4.

Descent: Rappel the route.

59 ROUTE #7 I, 5.10, 1 pitch, 60 feet (18 m) ★★

First Ascent: Andy Petefish, Marty Miller, fall 1990–1991.

Location and Access: *Route #7* is approximately 175 feet (53 m) left (west) of *Winter Solstice* and 1/8 mile (1.2 km) east of Independence Monument. When viewed from

photo: Scott Evens

Lightning Bolt Crack

photo: Fred Knapp

Bret Ruckman on *Get A Life*

the trail below *Winter Solstice*, the route ascends a dark buttress 75 feet (23 m) right of the skyline prow. Climb a right-leaning crack 60 feet (18 m) to a ledge with 2 bolts visible from below.

Paraphernalia: Standard desert rack.

Descent: Rappel the route.

60   CLUELESS TOWER—GET A LIFE III, 5.12c/d R, 5 pitches, 450 feet (137 m) ★★★★★

First Ascent: Bret Ruckman, Fred Knapp, 15 April 1993. First free ascent: Bret Ruckman, Steve Levin, 17 October 1994.

Location and Access: Clueless Tower is reached from the upper end of the 6-mile long (9.6 km) Monument Canyon Trail which descends 600 feet (183 m) into the canyon and was built by John Otto shortly after the turn of the century. The trailhead is between Artists Point (south) and Coke Ovens Overlook (west) on Rim Rock Drive near a formation called Cleopatra's Couch. After approximately 5 minutes, the Coke Oven Overlook Trail branches right. Continue into Monument Canyon (left) another 20 minutes to a detached tower that is obvious to the left. Clueless Tower is separated from the rimrock by about 8 feet (2.4 m). *Get a Life* climbs the south face of the tower. Begin left of a wide crack in a depression which leads to a left-facing dihedral. Fred Knapp: "The climb is exceptional, continuous, and exposed, making this one of the better hard routes in the desert."

Pitch 1: Climb broken rock to a left-facing corner which is ascended with stemming and crack climbing between the "mitten." Continue up a #1.5, #2 Friend crack to a belay in an alcove, 5.11a.

Pitch 2: Climb up the corner (#2 Friends) to a 2-bolt anchor at a good ledge, 5.11a.

Pitch 3: The crux; climb a 40-foot (12 m) pitch of endurance up an overhanging fingercrack in a corner to a belay on a good ledge under a pod.

Pitch 4: Climb a right-facing corner (a crack in an arête), then move right to a good belay ledge, 5.10d.

Pitch 5: Face climb past 2 bolts (5.11a) and traverse left (5.8 R) passing a drilled baby angle. Continue up a scary section (5.10 R), then to the summit.

Paraphernalia: Friends (2) #1, (4) #1.5, (5) #2, (2) #2.5, #3, (1) #3.5; Flex-Friends (1) #0.5; TCU (1) #0.4, (2) #0.75; Rocks (1) set; quickdraws (5); extra carabiners.

Descent: Begin an overhanging rappel from anchors hidden beneath the summit. Rappel 60 feet (18 m) to the top of Pitch 4, then 150 feet (46 m) to the top of Pitch 3. A final 165-foot (50 m) rappel reaches the base of the tower.

60a   NOT MUCH UPSTAIRS I, 5.11a, 1 pitch, 80 feet (24 m)

First Ascent: Bret Ruckman, Marco Cornacchione, spring 1997.

Location and Access: Climb starts 100 yards left of *Get a Life*. Climb a corner (past a fixed anchor not in view from below) with thin fingers to hands.

Paraphernalia: Friends #2 and smaller.

Descent: Rappel the route.

61   OTTO'S SPIRE—CUSTODIAN CHIMNEY III, 5.8, A3, 2 pitches, 250 feet (76 m)

First Ascent: Harvey T. Carter, Mike Pokress, 11 May 1974.

Location and Access: Otto's Spire is off the trail to Independence Monument, approximately 1 mile (l.6 km) from the trailhead. It is the landform across the drainage from the trail near Mushroom Rock. *Custodian Chimney* climbs a prominent chimney close to Mushroom Rock.

Paraphernalia: Standard desert rack.

Descent: Rappel the route.

Independence Monument

The most frequently used approach is a hike up Monument Canyon Trail to the east end of the tower. To reach *Otto's Route*, follow a climbers' trail to the north side of the monument. Approach takes approximately one hour. The quickest approach to Independence Monument is by a 150-foot (46 m) rappel from a solid pinyon tree 5 feet (1.5 m) from the cliff edge at a point on the north flank of the rimrock, approximately 100 yards (91 m) west of Pipe Organ Overlook. The direct rappel from the overlook leaves you 35 feet (11 m) short on a small stance from which a second rappel is required to reach the ground.

NOTE: On a flat-topped boulder due east of Independence Monument, where the trail changes directions from west to south, the last sentence of the Declaration of Independence, with John Hancock's signature, is inscribed by Otto's wife. Of two large adjacent boulders this boulder is nearer the monument.

photo: Layton Kor

Independence Monument

62 **OTTO'S ROUTE III, 5.9-, 5 pitches (with a scramble between pitches 2 and 3), 500 feet (152 m) ★★★★**

First Ascent: John Otto, solo, 14 June 1911. First free ascent: Unknown.

Location and Access: Otto's Route climbs the north face of the tower to Lunch Box Ledge, then the west face to the summit.

Pitch 1: Begin at a right-angling ramp near the left side of the north face. Follow a 4th-class crack system to a good ledge. Continue up the crack system (with a few chopped Otto holds) to a small ledge with 3 bolts for belay and a rappel chain, 5.4, 150 feet (46 m). Protect with wires or small Friends. A variation by an unknown party climbs a 5.9 crack 20 feet (6 m) right of the original start.

Pitch 2: Follow the crack through a chimney overhang (5.8 offwidth) to a 2-bolt stance, 50 feet (15 m). Scramble 4th class up a narrow slot behind a block (Time Tunnel) to its end on a belay ledge, 30 feet (9 m). Protect with a #3.5 Friend.

Pitch 3: Climb a steep groove utilizing a few face moves, then mantle (5.8) to Lunch Box Ledge (passing several fixed pitons) on the west shoulder of the tower, 60 feet (18 m).

Pitch 4: From Lunch Box Ledge, climb a 3rd- to 4th-class ramp until it steepens under the caprock. Make a few vertical moves, then climb the 1-foot (3 m) caprock roof (protected by 3 angle pitons) which is pulled over with strenuous hand cranks and hard footwork to a good ledge with a 3-bolt anchor (and the old flagpole pipe). This is 7 feet (2 m) from the summit, 80 feet (24 m).

Pitch 5: A 5.8 move takes you to the top, where there are no anchors.

Paraphernalia: Standard desert rack; Tri-cams #1.5, #2 in drilled holes protect the runouts.

Descent: One double-rope rappel off the north side to a point just short of Pitch 3, 140 feet (43 m). Scramble down a slot to the top of Pitch 2 and rappel 80 feet (24 m) to a large ledge. Traverse east on the ledge to the top of pitch 1 and a 3-bolt rappel anchor with chains. Make 1 double-rope rappel to the ground, 150 feet (46 m).

NOTE: Lunch Box Ledge has a 3-bolt rappel anchor, making it possible to do 4 rappels with half a rope. The last half-rope rappel puts you on a large ledge which has an easy 5.3 downclimb to the ground.

63 **SLAVERY IV, 5.10+, A3+, 5 pitches, 380 feet (116 m) ★**

First Ascent: Luke Laeser, Jon Butler, Cameron Burns, 6–7 August 1994.

Location and Access: Slavery begins on the north face left of Otto's Route. On the ascent, 18 holes were drilled. The crux is up the soft 5th pitch.

Pitch 1: Begin A2 past a small overhang and continue 5.10+ offwidth to a large ledge with a tree.

Pitch 2: Climb past 2 holes, then beaks in a slab, up A2 to a belay below an overhang.

Pitch 3: Ascend an awkward overhang, then A2 through A1 to a double-anchor belay.

Pitch 4: Climb A1, then A2 to a hanging belay.

Pitch 5: Continue up, passing 2 fixed anchors, then through a rotten section, A3+. Follow a bolt ladder angling up and right to the summit.

Paraphernalia: Friends (2) sets; many stoppers; Bird Beaks (5); baby angles (15).

Descent: Rappel Otto's Route.

photo: Mike Baker

Summit pitch of *Otto's Route*. Note the carved steps and old pipe holes.

photo: Cameron M. Burns

Independence Monument

64 INDEPENDENCE CHIMNEY (a.k.a. Scorpion Crack Variation) III, 5.8, A1, 5 pitches (4 new), 500 feet (152 m)

First Ascent: Michael Dudley, Fletcher Smith, June 1970.

Location and Access: *Independence Chimney* is a variation starting in a vertical crack at the west (left) end of the south face. Ascend to a right-slanting crack system on the southwest margin of the monument. Join *Otto's Route* at Lunch Box Ledge, and follow the original ascent line to the summit.

Paraphernalia: Standard desert rack; Tri-cam (1) large (to protect offwidth on Pitch 2).

Descent: Rappel *Otto's Route*.

65 SOUTH FACE #I III, 5.9-, A3, 4 pitches, 500 feet (152 m)

First Ascent: Andy Petefish, solo, 1990.

Location and Access: *South Face #I* is between *Independence Chimney* and *South Face Direct*. The route joins *Otto's Route* for the last pitch.

Pitch 1: Climb A3 up a corner to a horizontal break, then move right on aid to a bolt belay.

Pitch 2: Continue A3 up a thin seam past a bolt and a fixed knifeblade piton to a good thin crack (A1) ending at a double-bolt belay below a small roof.

Pitch 3: Move over the roof (A3) to a bolt and empty hole (hooking) leading to the edge of the monument and merge with the last pitch of *Otto's Route* for the belay.

Pitch 4: Follow Pitch 4 of *Otto's Route* to the summit.

Paraphernalia: Many pitons; 3/8" bolt hangers; Quickdraws.

Descent: Rappel *Otto's Route*.

South face of Independence Monument

66   SOUTH FACE DIRECT IV, 5.8, C3 (or A3), 5 pitches, 500 feet (152 m)

First Ascent: Michael Dudley, Art Howells, Don Doucette, May 1971. First clean ascent unknown.

Location and Access: *South Face Direct* begins up the center of the south face right of *Independence Chimney* at 2 boulders with blue horizontal stripes of desert varnish.

Paraphernalia: Many pitons were used on the first ascent, but Friends are highly recommended for present day ascents.

Descent: Rappel *Otto's Route*.

67   RED DESERT V, 5.10a, A4+, 4 pitches, 505 feet (154 m)

First Ascent: Jim Beyer, solo siege, 21 hours to the summit, 6–8 February 1987.

Location and Access: *Red Desert* ascends the fracture line a few yards right (east) of *South Face Direct*. The top of the route overhangs the bottom by 25 feet (8 m). Four drilled angles and 1 bolt were fixed on the first ascent. Pitches were lead on double 11 mm ropes.

Pitch 1: Begin up a left-facing corner, 5.10a, then A2. Move left with hooks and bashies, then A4+ to A3+ to double anchors at a hanging belay, 5.10a A4, 150 feet (46 m).

Pitch 2: Climb A3+ past an overhang, then A4 to a hanging belay from a single anchor, A4, 130 feet (40 m).

Pitch 3: Continue A1 to a hanging belay, A1, 85 feet (26 m).

Pitch 4: Climb A1, then move right (A3) and continue up "The Frozen Sands" (A3+), past a loose ledge and on to the summit, A3+, 140 feet (43 m).

Paraphernalia: Friends (1) set #0.5 through #3; small TCUs; Bugaboos (8); Lost Arrows (15); Leepers (12); angles (3) 0.5", 5/8", (4) 3/4", (2) 1", (1) 1 1/4", (2) 1.5"; Bong-Bongs (1) 2.5", 3"; small knifeblades (8); large knifeblades (12); RURPS (8); nuts (10) 1/4" through 1"; copperheads (10); aluminum heads (15); hooks.

Descent: Rappel *Otto's Route*.

68 SOUTH FACE #II V, 5.9, A3, 6 pitches, 500 feet (152 m)

First Ascent: Mike Darrah, Dave Dow, 30 March 1992.

Location and Access: *South Face #II* is 50 feet (15 m) right of *Red Desert*, and left of *Sundial Dihedral*. The pitches are rated 1-C2+, 2-A3, 3-A3 (with bolts added after an A4 fall), 4-A3, 5-A3, and 6-A1, which joins the *Sundial Dihedral* bolt ladder. The route has occasional free moves but is mostly aid climbing. Only 1 bolt was used for an aid move. All belays are protected with 3" bolts.

Paraphernalia: Standard desert rack; a selection of pitons; quickdraws.

Descent: Rappel *Otto's Route*.

69 SUNDIAL DIHEDRAL III, 5.11b, A1, 6 pitches, 490 feet (149 m) ★★★★

First Ascent: Ed Webster, Peter Athans, 19–20 April 1986.

Location and Access: *Sundial Dihedral* climbs the prominent corner line on the right-hand (north) side of the east face. Begin below a 60-foot (18 m) detached pillar. The left side of the pillar was first climbed by Mike Dudley and partner in the 1960s. The first ascent party used aid on Pitch 2 and 6. Ed Webster: "The route is one of the best and longest in the monument. Ascends the prominent corner line on the right-hand (north) side of the east face. The rock is superb and cleanly sculpted."

Pitch 1: Begin on either the left (5.8) or the right side (5.10-, large Friends) of a 60-foot (18 m) detached pillar and climb to a good ledge at its top, 60 feet (18 m).

Pitch 2: Follow a thin vertical crack to a ledge with a fixed piton, then continue up more thin cracks on a 95-degree headwall, 5.11b, to free moves up a better crack to a belay ledge, 5.11b, A1, 100 feet (30 m).

Pitch 3: Climb a chimney/corner system to a large belay ledge, 5.8, 60 feet (18 m).

Pitch 4: Jam and lieback a strenuous wide crack (#7 Tri-cam) out to the lip of an overhanging amphitheater, 5.11, then hand-jam to a roof passing it on the left (5.9) to a perfect stance with a 2-piton anchor, 5.11, 90 feet (27 m).

Pitch 5: Lieback a flake to a rest, then stem corners to reach a large ledge (with a piton anchor) on the northern arête to the right, 5.9+, 80 feet (24 m).

Pitch 6: Move over the gap and follow a ladder of 13 bolts up a white arête to the top, 5.7, A1, 100 feet (30 m).

Paraphernalia: Friends through #4; Tri-cams (1) #7; knifeblades through baby angles (2).

Descent: Rappel *Otto's Route*.

Upper Monument Canyon

Routes in Upper Monument Canyon include *Grand View Spire, Bell Tower, Egypt Rock, Pharaoh Point, Squaw Fingers,* and *Chimney Tower.* These landforms are accessible from Upper Monument Canyon Trail off Rim Rock Drive at the Coke Ovens Overlook Trailhead. The well-marked Coke Ovens Trail and Upper Monument Canyon Trail descend into the canyon together before separating, and provide access to all formations. *Grand View Spire* may also be reached more directly from a 165-foot (50 m) rappel down the south-facing gully, then downclimbing and walking 20 feet (6 m) east to the base of the tower. Leave a fixed rope for the return.

70   GRAND VIEW SPIRE—SOUTHWEST DEFILE III, 5.8, A2, 5 pitches, 430 feet (131 m)

First Ascent: John Auld, Gary Ziegler, John Kuglin, 1–2 February 1961. First solo and 5th ascent of the spire, Mike Baker, December 1991.

Location and Access: Grand View Spire is northeast of Grand View Point and is climbed by the southwest face.

Paraphernalia: Camalots #0.75 through #3; TCUs (4) small; stoppers small to medium; Lowe Balls (3); medium cams; knifeblades (2); Lost Arrows (2); angles (6) 0.5".

Descent: Double-rope rappels down the route.

71   GRAND VIEW SPIRE—SOUTHWEST DEFILE VARIATION 5.8, A2, 6 pitches

First Ascent: Harvey T. Carter, Art Howells, Don Doucette, Fred Beckey, 23 April 1966.

Location and Access: The variation was made during the second ascent of the spire and adds a new pitch to the bottom of the route. Begin at the base of the spire and climb to the notch, then join the original route.

72   GRAND VIEW SPIRE—RELICS IV, 5.11, A3, 5 pitches, 430 feet (131 m) ★★★★

First Ascent: Mike Baker, Michael Kennedy, Bob Wade, 3rd ascent of the tower, 13 November 1991.

Location and Access: *Relics* climbs the south face of Grand View Spire. Pitch 5 may be climbed at 5.11 or A2 on the left side (protect with a #3 Camalot in a hole) or to the right by a 5.10 offwidth.

Pitch 1: Climb a splitter crack starting with fist to hands thinning to fingers. Where the crack ends, face climb past 2 drilled angles, moving left toward a large right-facing dihedral and a 2-bolt hanging belay, 5.10, 130 feet (40 m).

Pitch 2: Climb a right-facing dihedral to a small roof (crux A3), pass the roof on the left, and continue up the crack system to a 2-bolt drilled anchor at a small stance, 145 feet (44 m).

Pitch 3: Chimney and stem the crack system to a sandy belay ledge, 5.9, 100 feet (30 m). Protect with medium cams and (1) #3 Camalot.

Pitch 4: Continue up, then left around a loose block, and up to a large belay ledge, 40 feet (12 m).

Pitch 5: Continue to the summit, A2 or 5.11 (freed by the second on top-rope), 15 feet (4.5 m). Protect with a #3 Camalot in a hole. There is a possible 5.10 offwidth finish up the crack system at the right edge of the belay ledge.

photo: Mike Baker

Grand View Spire

photo: Mike Baker

Bob Wade leading on the first ascent of *Relics*

Paraphernalia: Camalot (1) #3; TCUs (4) small; stoppers small to medium; knifeblades (2); Lowe Balls (2); Lost Arrows (2); angles (6) 0.5".

Descent: Rappel the original route, then ascend the fixed rope to the rim.

73 GRAND VIEW SPIRE—NORTH FACE IV, Rating unknown

First Ascent: Unknown.

Location and Access: Old bolts are visible on the route.

Paraphernalia: Unknown.

Descent: Rappel the route.

74 DIRTY OLD MAN TOWER III, 5.9, A1, 3 pitches, 300 feet (91 m)

First Ascent: Jon Butler, Luke Laeser, 10–11 December 1995.

Location and Access: Dirty Old Man Tower is between the rimrock and Kissing Couple. The route climbs an obvious crack system on the south face. The original ascent of the tower climbed the north face where old bolts are visible but further information is unknown.

Pitch 1: Begin up a left-facing corner with loose rock to a ledge, then tension traverse right to a thin A1 crack which opens to 3 inches (7.6 cm) and a 2-bolt hanging belay, 5.7, A1, 100 feet (30 m).

Pitch 2: Start with 5.8, then awkward 5.9 to A1 and finally a 5.7 squeeze to a 2-bolt hanging belay, 100 feet (30 m).

Pitch 3: Continue in thin cracks to the soft summit, 5.7, A1, 100 feet (30 m).

Paraphernalia: Friends (3) sets; Camalots (2) #4, (1) #5; stoppers (1) set; long knifeblades (2); Lost Arrows (3); angles (3) 0.5", 5/8", (2) 3/4"; 25 feet (7.6 m) of rope to wrap the summit for the rappel.

Descent: Rappel the route from slings wrapped around the summit.

75 KISSING COUPLE (a.k.a. Bell Tower)—LONG DONG WALL III, 5.11a, 6 pitches, 500 feet (152 m) ★★★★

First Ascent: Layton Kor, Harvey T. Carter, John Auld, 4 May 1960. First free ascent: Andy Petefish, Paul Abott, 1980. First solo ascent: Ron Olesky, 1978.

Location and Access: Kissing Couple is approached by the gully to the northwest of the tower. Fred Knapp: "Follow the Monument Canyon Road until the gully northwest of the tower can be seen. No rappels are required if the approach is done correctly. Getting to the starting crack is probably the crux, involving a boulder problem which gains the starting shelf. Look for a weakness in the notch between the tower and rimrock on the west side. Boulder up this and the start is obvious." *Long Dong Wall* begins at the southwest corner of the rock where it joins the main canyon wall. Approach from the Upper Monument Canyon Trail off Rim Rock Drive at the Coke Ovens Overlook Trailhead. A more direct approach is by rappel from the rim.

Layton Kor: "My first trip to the desert was in part due to the urging of the Colorado Springs climber Harvey T. Carter. He suggested that we spend the entire month of April climbing as many spires as time allowed. In those days quantity was certainly available. Colorado National Monument near Grand Junction was our starting point and the first area to feel the wrath of our steel pitons. . . .Things went well for our little group and three first ascents followed. One of these, the Bell Tower, was an excellent climb . . . one of the few desert first ascents that I later repeated."

photo: Harvey T. Carter

Kissing Couple (Bell Tower)

photo: Harvey T. Carter

Harvey T. Carter (right) and John Auld on the summit of Kissing Couple, 1960

Pitch 1: Climb a crack to a fixed piton, then traverse left (crux) and belay at chain anchors, 5.11a.

Pitch 2: Continue up a chimney to a belay, 5.7.

Pitch 3: Traverse right and climb blocks to a belay at a gully, 4th class.

Pitch 4: Begin with an offwidth, then climb a 5.8 chimney to the "belfry," a window visible from the road. Fred Knapp: "The exposed chimney is perhaps the best 5.8 pitch in the desert."

Pitch 5: Stem past double bolts into guano-coated cracks which lead to a belay ledge beneath the summit, 5.10.

Pitch 6: Tunnel to the summit.

Paraphernalia Standard desert rack.

Descent: Rappel the route.

76   KISSING COUPLE (a.k.a. Bell Tower)—BIG HETTI III, 5.11 R X, 5 pitches, 360 feet (110 m) ★

First Ascent: Unknown. First free ascent: Marco Cornacchione, Bret Ruckman, 31 March 1996.

Location and Access: *Big Hetti* climbs the southeast face of the tower. Pitches 1 and 2 were previously climbed by an unknown party. The first crack system left of *Big Hetti* has probably been climbed by an unknown party. Bret Ruckman: "This route epitomizes high adventure."

Pitch 1: Climb a dirty crack for 30 feet (9 m) to a cleaner hand/fist crack, passing a bolt on the right wall, then belay at old bolts, 5.10, 80 feet (24 m).

Pitch 2: Climb a 12-inch (30 cm) crack past 1/4" bolts, then a 4-inch (10 m) crack to a belay in an intimidating chimney. Climb 20 feet (6 m) higher in the chimney to place belay anchors, 5.11-, 60 feet (18 m).

Pitch 3: Continue up the chimney, setting a #5 Camalot high, then downclimb with overhead protection and move to the outside of the chimney. Climb an offwidth to a belay in a groove protected by #3 Friends, 5.11, 80 feet (24 m).

Pitch 4: Climb a poorly protected chimney and belay on a pedestal with double bolts, 5.8, 80 feet (24 m).

Pitch 5: Traverse up and left with no protection, then stem on dicey rock (or tension traverse) and join *Long Dong Wall* to the summit (protect with TCUs), 5.11 R X, AO, 60 feet (18 m).

Paraphernalia: Friends (2) #3, (3) #3.5, #4; Camalots (1) #3, (4) #4, (1) #5; Big Bros (1) #3; small TCUs for Pitch 5.

Descent: Rappel Long Dong Wall.

77   KISSING COUPLE NORTHEAST OFFWIDTH—EXCELLENT RIDE IV, 5.10, A3, 3 pitches, 380 feet (116 m)

First Ascent: Andy Petefish, Tom Stubbs, 1991.

Location and Access: *Excellent Ride* is the only route that finishes on the outside of the tower. Climb the first crack system right of *Big Hetti*.

Pitch 1: Climb A1, 5.10 up an offwidth crack to a belay from bolts, 110 feet (34 m).

Pitch 2: Make an A2 move right up a steep headwall crack to a small ledge with belay bolts, 140 feet (43 m).

Pitch 3: Crux pitch. Climb a shallow dihedral with hooks and pitons, 5.10, A3, to the shoulder, then up thin broken cracks to the Kayenta caprock and the summit, 130 feet (40 m).

Paraphernalia: Standard desert rack; many pitons and nuts 1" through 1.5" for Pitch 2.

Descent: Rappel *Long Dong Wall.*

78   KISSING COUPLE—DESERT DECEPTION III, 5.10, 5 pitches, 380 feet (116 m)

First Ascent: Joel Arellano et al, mid 1990s

Location and Access: *Desert Deception* climbs a splitter crack on the prow of Kissing Couple, left of *Big Hetti*.

Paraphernalia: Standard desert rack.

Descent: Rappel the route.

79   MONUMENT WALL I, 5.10, 1 pitch, 100 feet (30 m)

First Ascent: Harvey T. Carter, Bill Kurimay, 26 April 1978.

Location and Access: The route climbs an overhanging bulge. No further information is known about the climb.

Paraphernalia: The first ascent party used a medium nut and thin pitons.

Descent: Rappel the route.

80   RAINBOW TOWER III, 5.9, A2, 3 pitches, 220 feet (67 m) ★★

First Ascent: Jon Butler, Jesse Harvey, 27 August 1995.

Location and Access: Rainbow Tower is in Upper Monument Canyon on the west side past Kissing Couple and Pharaoh Point. It is a landform next to the rimrock with its top

100 feet (30 m) freestanding. Jon Butler: "The best approach is from the Upper Monument Canyon Trail. It is the tower on the left before Kissing Couple which is on the right when hiking down the trail." The route ascends the obvious dihedral and chimney on the southeast side of the tower.

Pitch 1: Climb a thin A1 crack to a hanging belay from double anchors, 90 feet (27 m).

Pitch 2: Climb awkward 5.9, A1 past large blocks into a 5.7 chimney, then 5.9 and finally A1 up a left-facing corner past a torpedo block (scary A2) and a double-anchor belay at a saddle, 90 feet (27 m).

Pitch 3: Continue up an A1 seam, then past holes and a final 5.8 mantle to the very soft summit, 40 feet (12 m).

Paraphernalia: Friends (2–3) sets with (1) #3.5 through #5; stoppers (1) set; Lost Arrows (3); baby angles (6) 0.5", (5) 5/8", (3) 3/4"; webbing for summit 25 feet (7.6 m).

Descent: Rappel from the summit to the top of Pitch 2 from 25 feet (7.6 m) of webbing wrapped around the high point, then to the top of Pitch 1, and finally to the ground.

81   EGYPT ROCK III, 5.10-, 3 pitches, 500 feet (152 m)

First Ascent: Gary Ziegler, Gary Boucher, Bob Doane, John Auld, early 1960s. Second ascent: Harvey T. Carter, Steve Mack, 23 May 1966. First free ascent: David Kozak, Eric Boehlke, 1985.

Location and Access: Egypt Rock is at the southeast end of Monument Canyon and is approached from the Upper Monument Canyon Trail. Climb the rock by 3 squeeze chimney/offwidth cracks. The crux is the Kayenta caprock, which is negotiated with face moves.

Paraphernalia: Friends medium through #4 and a large Tri-cam.

Descent: One double-rope rappel down the northwest face, then 3rd-class scrambling to the right.

82   PHARAOH POINT—CHIMNEY WIDE III, 5.9, A1, 3 pitches, 400 feet (122 m)

First Ascent: Harvey T. Carter, Layton Kor, 5 May 1960.

Location and Access: Pharaoh Point is beyond Egypt Rock and is the smaller of the two. Descend from the rimrock by the Upper Monument Canyon Trail. The tower is visible approximately 1 mile (1.6 km) to the east when viewed from the bottom of the canyon. Approach with a 45-minute hike cross-country from the canyon floor. *Chimney Wide* ascends a large chimney system on the north side of the landform.

Paraphernalia: Standard desert rack.

Descent: Double-rope rappels down the route.

83   PHARAOH POINT—CHIMNEY TOWER I, 5.9, 2 pitches, 150 feet (46 m)

First Ascent: Ron Olevsky, solo, spring 1976.

Location and Access: *Chimney Tower* is climbed from the northwest.

Paraphernalia: Standard desert rack.

Descent: Rappel the route.

84   SQUAW FINGERS—PINKIE—MANO A GUANO II, 5.10+, 3 pitches, 200 feet (61 m)

First Ascent: Dave Goldstein, Dougald MacDonald, April 1995.

Location and Access: *Mano a Guano* is the outermost pinnacle of the Squaw Fingers in view from Artists Point on Rim Rock Drive. Approach from the Upper Monument Canyon Trail or rappel into the canyon from Artists Point. *Mano a Guano* climbs the northwest face of the tower.

Pitch 1: Start in a right-facing corner and climb a wide crack at 5.10+ to a 5.9 lieback. Belay in an alcove.

Pitch 2: Climb a 5.9+ handcrack through a roof, then a wide crack to a good ledge.

Pitch 3: Boulder to the summit.

Paraphernalia: Standard desert rack.

Descent: Downclimb to the top of Pitch 2, then make 1 double-rope rappel to the ground.

85   SQUAW FINGERS—RING FINGER—COLD FEET II, 5.10, 2 pitches, 200 feet (61 m)

First Ascent: Dougald MacDonald, Mark Hammond, fall 1995.

Location and Access: Ring Finger is the second Squaw Finger from the end. *Cold Feet* climbs the northwest face of the landform.

Pitch 1: Chimney to a steep handcrack and belay.

Pitch 2: Continue to the top with face and crack climbing.

Paraphernalia: Standard desert rack.

Descent: Rappel the route.

86   COKE BOTTLE—SLOT WITH A VIEW II, 5.10+, 3 pitches, 200 feet (61 m)

First Ascent: Dougald MacDonald, Mark Hammond, fall 1995.

Location and Access: *Slot With a View* climbs the southeast side of the outermost Coke Oven. The route ends at a ledge below a blank overhanging face.

Pitch 1: Begin up a good hand-and-finger crack in a shallow right-facing corner. Belay on a ledge to the left or continue to the alcove above, 5.10+.

Pitch 2: Climb a steep fingercrack to an alcove, then continue up a poorly protected slab, right around a roof, and up a slab to belay below a chimney, 5.9.

Pitch 3: Chimney (with views through the tower in 3 directions) to a large ledge, 5.9+.

Paraphernalia: Standard desert rack.

Descent: Rappel the route.

Liberty Cap Buttress—Ute Canyon

Approach from Liberty Cap Trailhead off Wildwood Drive. Drive west out of Grand Junction on Broadway (State Highway 340) into the Redlands. Drive approximately 3 miles (4.8 km) turning left (south) onto Redlands Parkway. After 0.5 mile (0.8 km), the road curves right (east) and becomes South Broadway at South Camp Road. Continue west on South Broadway for approximately 0.5 mile (0.8 km) to Wildwood Drive, turning left at the Liberty Cap Trailhead sign

photo: Cameron M. Burns

Northwest side of Liberty Cap

and parking lot on the right. A 30- to 40-minute hike, level at first then steep, will bring you to a sign reading "To Rim Rock Drive–Liberty Cap Trail (right), Ute Canyon Trail (left), 1 mile to Trailhead" (indicating back to the parking area). Ute Canyon is about 10 minutes to the left of the sign, a beautiful hike through much ancient black-and-white granite rock. Liberty Cap Buttress routes are listed from right to left. The first eight routes, ending with *KB Traverse*, are east-facing. The next nine routes, beginning with *F/S* and ending with *Notch*, are south-facing. The climbs are most easily approached from the left prow of the Wingate Sandstone buttress, then by traversing along the base of the cliff. Jolly Tower is 800 feet (244 m) west of Liberty Cap Tower. Bush-whack uphill to the shelf below Liberty Cap Tower and proceed west. Jolly Tower is approximately 800 to 1,000 feet (243 m to 305 m) west of Liberty Cap and is an obvious semi-detached thin spire. Oompah Tower lies in an alcove 500 feet (152 m) southwest of Jolly Tower. To reach WalMart Tower and Safeway Spire, hike approximately 1 mile (1.8 km) into Upper Ute Canyon. WalMart Tower is visible first, then Safeway Spire.

87   IRISH PRIDE I, 5.10d/5.11a, 1 pitch, 65 feet (20 m) ★★★

First Ascent: KC Baum, Tom Archibeque, 17 March 1990 (St. Patrick's Day).

Location and Access: *Irish Pride* is behind a large boulder lying on its side, visible above the trail as it traverses right to left beneath the east-facing buttress just before entering Ute Canyon proper. Begin on top of a 6-foot (1.8 m) pillar with a small pine tree at its base. To reach, traverse from the right prow, right to the start of the route.

Paraphernalia: Quickdraws (6).

Descent: Rappel the route.

88   LEPRECHAUN I, 5.10a, 1 pitch, 70 feet (21 m) ★

First Ascent: Tom Archibeque, KC Baum, 17 March 1990.

Location and Access: *Leprechaun* is 20 feet (6 m) left (south) of *Irish Pride* in a left-facing dihedral. Climb fingers to hands and finish at *Irish Pride* rappel anchors.

Paraphernalia: Small- to hand-sized cams.

Descent: Rappel *Irish Pride*.

89   FIRE WITHIN I, 5.10d, 1 pitch, 105 feet (32 m) ★★★

First Ascent: KC Baum, Tom Archibeque, May 1990.

Location and Access: *Fire Within* is approximately 150 feet (46 m) left (south) of *Leprechaun* at a vertical crack leading to a right-facing dihedral. Climb a 20-foot (6 m) section of poorly protected Chinle to the base of the Wingate Sandstone. Continue with small-to-large hands into a shallow chimney with a 2-bolt rappel anchor.

Paraphernalia: Small- to hand-sized cams; Camalots (2–3) #3.

Descent: Rappel the route.

90   STONEHENGE I, 5.10b/c, 1 pitch, 65 feet (20 m) ★★★

First Ascent: KC Baum, Tom Archibeque, April 1990.

Location and Access: *Stonehenge* is approximately 30 feet (9 m) left (south) of *Fire Within* at a left-facing dihedral formed by a large pedestal block sitting against the main wall. Climb the corner with large fingers and tight hands to a rest. Finish the upper section with finger-pocket liebacks on good varnished rock with a final lunge/mantle onto the top of the pedestal block at a 2-bolt rappel anchor.

Paraphernalia: Tri-cams; small to medium cams; wires.

Descent: Rappel the route.

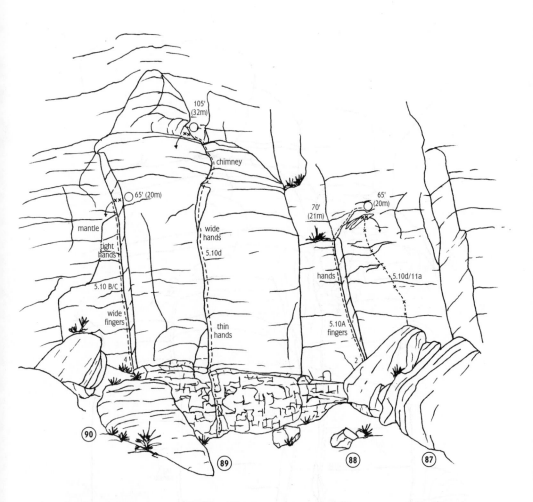

91 KOKOPELLI I, 5.11a (downgrade for small hands), 1 pitch, 75 feet (23 m) ★★

First Ascent: KC Baum, Chris Vickers, May 1990.

Location and Access: *Kokopelli* is reached approximately 175 feet (53 m) left (south) of *Stonehenge* in a shallow right-facing dihedral. Climb a short, poorly protected Chinle section to a small roof at the base of the Wingate. Continue with overhanging tight hands for 20 feet (6 m) to a good rest, then a mellow offwidth section to a good stance and a 2-bolt rappel anchor.

Paraphernalia: Small to large cams; big pieces (1–2).

Descent: Rappel the route.

92 OSIRIS I, 5.12b, 1 pitch, 75 feet (23 m) ★★★★

First Ascent: KC Baum, Tom Archibeque, April 1990.

Location and Access: *Osiris* is 35 feet (11 m) left (south) of *Kokopelli* in a large left-facing dihedral. KC Baum: "Beautiful rock, beautiful crack!" Climb a short section of

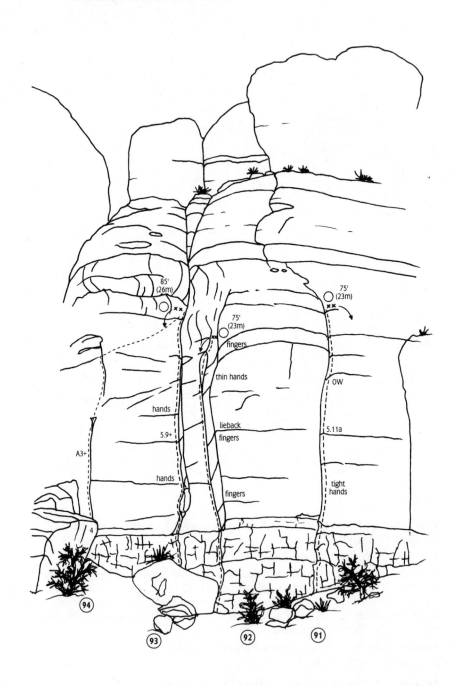

85'
(26m)

75'
(23m)

75'
(23m)

fingers

thin hands

OW

hands

5.9+

lieback
fingers

5.11a

A3+

hands

fingers

tight
hands

94

93

92

91

Chinle to the base of an overhanging, left-facing corner with a good fingercrack. Continue up a strenuous, overhanging lieback for 20 feet (6 m) to a small rest stance. Climb with liebacks to a straight-in fingercrack (crux), then climb thin hands into a large alcove and a good rest. Make a few tricky 5.10+ moves out of the alcove and climb fingers to 2-bolt anchor chains. *Osiris* is a mythical Egyptian hero, king, and educator of his people who is known as god of the dead.

Paraphernalia: Camalot (1) #0.5, #0.75, (2) #1; TCUs; Tri-cam (1) #0.5.

Descent: Rappel the route.

93 STEPPIN' ON IT I, 5.9+, 1 pitch, 85 feet (26 m) ★★★

First Ascent: Tom Blake, Kurt Luhrs, spring 1989.

Location and Access: *Steppin' On It* is 10 feet (3 m) left (south) of *Osiris* in an obvious vertical crack that starts in a right-facing dihedral and ends in a left-facing dihedral. Climb a short section of the lower Chinle Formation to a ledge beneath a good parallel-sided handcrack in a right-facing corner. Continue with perfect hands to a roof, passing it on the left side, then continue into a left-facing corner with a perfect handcrack. The route finishes with a few moves of large hands, climbing to a 2-bolt anchor beneath a large roof.

Paraphernalia: Medium to hand-sized cams; Camalots (3–4) #2, (1) #3.

Descent: Rappel the route.

94 KB TRAVERSE I, A3+, 1 pitch, 85 feet (26 m) ★★

First Ascent: KC Baum, solo, October 1990.

Location and Access: *KB Traverse* is 30 feet (9 m) left (south) of *Steppin' On It*, in a shallow, left-facing corner with a thin vertical flake-crack. Fourth class onto a large ledge, then climb a thin crack for 30 feet (9 m). Traverse right several feet and follow the crack system as it angles up and right to *Steppin' On It*'s rappel anchors.

Paraphernalia: TCUs small to medium; several baby angles, (2–3) 3/4"; medium-thick knifeblades; Lost Arrows (2–3) 0.5".

Descent: Rappel *Steppin' On It*.

95 F/S I, 5.10c, 1 pitch, 140 feet (43 m) ★★

First Ascent: Tom Blake, Kurt Luhrs, spring 1989. First free ascent: KC Baum, Tom Archibeque, April 1990.

Location and Access: *F/S* begins up an obvious splitter crack on the nose of Liberty Cap Buttress. A large rectangular block sits 20 feet (6 m) left (west) of the start. This is a point about 175 feet (53 m) left and around (south then west) the nose of the buttress from the *KB Traverse*. Begin in an obvious double handcrack and climb through 2 bulges to a soft white section with a 2-bolt anchor.

Paraphernalia: Finger- to large hand–sized Friends with mostly hands; Camalots (2) #3.

Descent: Rappel the route.

96 COOL BREEZE I, 5.11a, 1 pitch, 75 feet (23 m) ★★★

First Ascent: Tom Blake, Kurt Luhrs, spring 1989. 5.10, AO. First free ascent: KC Baum, Tom Archibeque, April 1990.

Location and Access: *Cool Breeze* is 40 feet (12 m) left (west) of *F/S* and is directly behind the west end of a large rectangular block. Begin in a varnished, parallel-sided handcrack. Continue with hands through a small bulge and into an offwidth, then lieback a flake to a rappel anchor.

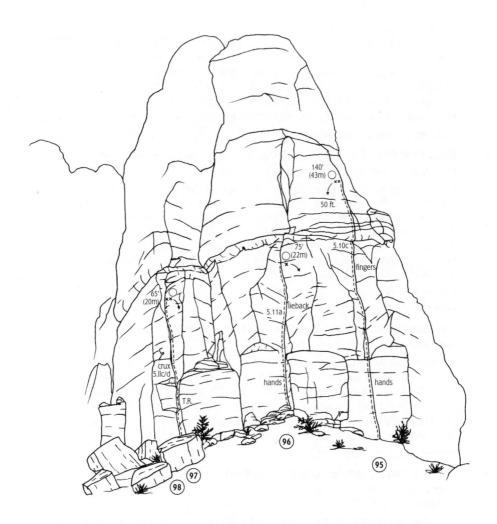

Paraphernalia: Small- to hand-sized cams with (1) big piece.

Descent: Rappel the route from a single bolt.

97 PENNY CRACK VARIATION (Top-rope) I, 5.10a, 1 pitch, 65 feet (20 m) ★

First Ascent: KC Baum, Tom Archibeque, January 1990.

Location and Access: *Penny Crack* is a top-rope variation off the *Never Cry Wolf* rappel anchor. It is 50 feet (15 m) left (west) of *Cool Breeze*, 10 feet (3 m) right of *Never Cry Wolf*.

98 NEVER CRY WOLF I, 5.11c/d, 1 pitch, 65 feet (20 m) ★★★★

First Ascent: KC Baum, Tom Archibeque, January 1990.

Location and Access: *Never Cry Wolf* climbs a classic finger-to-hand crack on excellent rock. It is 60 feet (18 m) left (west) of *Cool Breeze* in an open book. Climb a

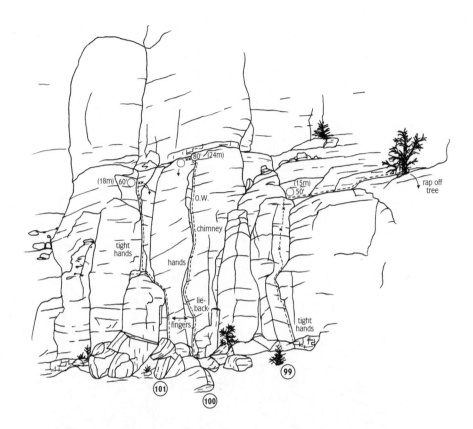

strenuous overhanging finger lieback through a gentle curve (crux) in the crack to a small rest. Continue with hands into a short but uniquely contoured offwidth with a nice knee-lock rest, then gain good hands under a small bulging roof. Pass the roof and finish with hands to a 2-bolt anchor.

Paraphernalia: Camalots (1) #3; Tri-cams; TCUs or Quad Cams through hand-sized.

Descent: Rappel the route.

99 WHIRLING DERVISH I, 5.11a, 1 pitch, 50 feet (15 m) ★

First Ascent: KC Baum, solo, December 1990.

Location and Access: *Whirling Dervish* is 150 feet (46 m) left (west) of *Never Cry Wolf* at an overhanging left-facing dihedral. Climb tight hands through a small roof and gain a large ledge at the base of a black, pocketed, overhanging face. Continue up the face past 3 bolts to a large ledge and belay (2–3 big cams are needed to build a good belay anchor at the back of the ledge).

Paraphernalia: Medium hand-sized cams with (2–3) big cams for an anchor; quickdraws (3).

Descent: Walk east about 50 feet (15 m) to a pine tree with a chain rappel anchor.

100 ST. PATRICK'S DAY MASSACRE I, 5.10d, 1 pitch, 80 feet (24 m) ★

First Ascent: KC Baum, Tom Archibeque, 17 March 1990 (St. Patrick's Day).

Location and Access: *St. Patrick's Day Massacre* is approximately 40 feet (12 m) left (west) of *Whirling Dervish* at a crack with an obvious lightning bolt zig-zag. Lieback a fingercrack into good hands, angling right to a chimney. KC Baum: "Struggle like a man possessed to gain the chimney, then finish with a not-too-bad offwidth up to a 2-bolt rappel anchor."

Paraphernalia: Small- to hand-sized cams with (2) large cams.

Descent: Rappel the route.

101   DOUBLE JEOPARDY I, 5.10c, 1 pitch, 60 feet (18 m) ★★★

First Ascent: KC Baum, Tom Archibeque, January 1990.

Location and Access: *Double Jeopardy* is 15 feet (5 m) left (west) of *St. Patrick's Day Massacre*. Begin on the east side of a large block sitting against the main buttress and climb with fingers into a 7-foot-high (2 m) flaring alcove with a small roof. Pass the roof with hands to a large ledge (top of the block). Walk to the main wall with a splitter crack and climb tight hands to a 2-bolt rappel anchor. KC Baum: "The left side of the block can be top-roped for a nice variation."

Paraphernalia: Finger to hand-sized cams.

Descent: Rappel the route.

102   HUECO ME UP WHEN IT'S OVER (Top-rope) I, 5.11+/5.12-, 1 pitch, 75 feet (23 m)

First Ascent: KC Baum, Tom Archibeque, May 1990.

Location and Access: The route is a top-rope climb 130 feet (40 m) left (west) of *Double Jeopardy* at a hueco-pocketed face with a 6-foot (2 m) roof formed by the base of the Wingate Sandstone. Due to marginal rock quality, there is no rappel anchor at the top of the climb, only a sling around a soft sandstone horn. Approach from *Notch*.

103   NOTCH I, 5.7, A1, 1 pitch, 75 feet (23 m)

First Ascent: KC Baum, solo, April 1990.

Location and Access: *Notch* is 15 feet (5 m) left (west) of *Hueco Me Up When It's Over* at a slightly overhanging hand-and-finger crack below a flaring notch. It is the access route for *Hueco Me Up When It's Over.*

Paraphernalia: Standard desert rack.

Descent: Rappel *Hueco Me Up When It's Over.*

104   BEAUTY AND THE BEAST I, 5.10d, 1 pitch, 135 feet (41 m) ★★

First Ascent: KC Baum, Tom Archibeque, February 1990.

Location and Access: *Beauty and the Beast* is 25 feet (8 m) left (west) of *Notch* in a large right-facing dihedral. Begin up 15 feet (5 m) of Chinle to a small roof at the base of the Wingate. Pass the roof with good hands and continue up a dihedral. Finish with a short offwidth section to a 2-bolt rappel anchor.

Paraphernalia: Protection for small hands through #4 Camalots, including (2) #4s.

Descent: Rappel the route.

105   ANGULAR MOTION IV, 5.8, C2, 6 pitches, 400 feet (122 m)

First Ascent: Ron Olevsky, Andy Petefish, October 1977.

Location and Access: *Angular Motion* is on the north side of Ute Canyon. The route is easily viewed from Upper Ute Canyon Overlook off Rim Rock Drive. Climb the largest buttress that juts into the canyon at the point where the drainage changes directions from a southeasterly to a northeasterly flow. The climb faces southwest and begins approximately 500 feet (152 m) right of Fallen Rock, and ascends the only obvious crack system on the buttress. At the base of the route are hidden the initials "A.M." Fourteen bolts were placed by the first ascent team. Fallen Rock is identified on the map in the monument brochure. The route may also be located north of point 6401 on the Trails Illustrated topo map of Colorado National Monument.

To reach *Angular Motion*, park at the Ute Canyon Trailhead parking lot, about 0.5 mile (0.8 km) east of Fallen Rock View Point and hike the trail to the canyon bottom. Follow the drainage downstream (southeast) for 30 to 45 minutes, approximately 1 mile (1.6 km). The route comes into view on the north side of the canyon.

Pitch 1: Climb C2 to a hanging belay, or continue up a 5.8 lieback to a semi-hanging belay.

Pitch 2: Continue with C1 to a belay stance.

Pitch 3: Climb the headwall to a hanging belay, C1.

Pitch 4: Bolts and empty holes ascend left to a pillar and a C1 crack that ends at a belay on the rubble-covered "Barney's Ledge."

Pitch 5: Continue up a left-sloping lieback/jam to a C1 crack and a belay shelf.

Pitch 6: Climb 5.6 over the Kayenta caprock to the summit.

Paraphernalia: Many pitons were used on the first ascent, but it is now possible to climb the route clean with small cams.

Descent: Hike in a northwesterly direction along the rim of Ute Canyon. Walk 1 mile (1.6 km) to a point where the head of the canyon narrows, which is identified as "Suction Point" on the map in the Monument brochure.

106 PUTTERBUTT I, 5.7+, 1 pitch, 50 feet (15 m) ★

First Ascent: Cameron Burns, Ann Robertson, 5 November 1994.

Location and Access: *Putterbutt* is 1.2 miles (1.9 km) past the West Glade Park road turnoff when driving east on Rim Rock Drive. *Putterbutt* is on a south-facing wall in Upper Ute Canyon on the north side of the park road. Climb to the base of a pillar forming on the upper wall. Begin up easy ground, then 5.7+ to 5.6 up a 1-inch (2.5 cm) crack system. Rappel slings are visible from the road.

Paraphernalia: Friends #0.5 through #1.5; wired stoppers.

Descent: One-rope rappel from fixed anchors.

107 LIBERTY CAP III, 4 pitches, 400 feet (122 m)

First Ascent: Unknown.

Location and Access: The route climbs the northeast face of the tower. Further information is unknown.

Paraphernalia: Unknown.

Descent: Make 4 rappels from double anchors and slings visible from below the route.

108 JOLLY TOWER—MARITAL BLISS II, 5.6, A2, 1 pitch, 160 feet (49 m) ★★

First Ascent: Cameron Burns, Jesse Harvey, 20–21 June 1998.

Location and Access: The route starts up the west side of the tower to the left of a large overhanging flake. Begin free up loose blocks below thin cracks to a drilled hole. Continue up a medium-to-wide crack. The route may be split into 2 pitches by stopping on the obvious ledge with 2 drilled holes directly above. Baby- or 5/8-inch angles are necessary to set a belay here. The second pitch follows the obvious bolt ladder to the summit.

Paraphernalia: Camalots (2) #0.5, #0.75, (1) #1, #2, (2) #3, #4; small to medium stoppers; (8) 3/8-inch angles, (1) 5/8-inch angle.

Descent: Rappel the route.

109 OOMPAH TOWER—ETHAN PUTTERMAN AND THE CHOCOLATE FACTORY III, 5.9, C1, 3 pitches, 240 feet (73 m) ★★★★

First Ascent: Cameron Burns, Jonathan Butler, Jesse Harvey, 25 July–August 1 1998.

Location and Access: The route climbs the northwest face of the tower.

photo: Cameron M. Burns

WalMart Tower

photo: Cameron M. Burns

Safeway Spire

Pitch 1: Scramble up loose rock below a flaring chimney. Climb the crack leading to the top of a pillar right of the chimney. Continue up cracks to drilled angles, then traverse left to a 2–3" (5–7.6 cm) crack, C1 to the first anchor.

Pitch 2: Make a long-arm stretch traverse right to a fixed angle. Continue C1 to a second anchor and belay.

Pitch 3: Follow a 7-bolt ladder past overhanging offwidth to a 5.9 offwidth, then continue up a chimney to the summit, 5.8.

Paraphernalia: Standard desert rack; Camalots (3) #5; wires for the bolt ladder (7).

Descent: Double-rope rappel to the top of Pitch 2, then to the ground.

110   WALMART TOWER—TWELVE PACK OF TUBE SOCKS III, 5.6 A1, 2 pitches, 150 feet (46 m) ★★

First Ascent: Cameron Burns, Jon Butler, 22 April 1995.

Location and Access: *Twelve Pack of Tube Socks* climbs the north face of WalMart Tower.

Pitch 1: Begin at the shoulder, then climb a prominent crack system on the north face to a belay ledge, 5.6, A1.

Pitch 2: Climb empty holes to a bolt, then continue to the summit.

Paraphernalia: Friends (2) sets; angles (5) 5/8", (1) 3/4; hangers (2) 3/8".

Descent: One double-rope rappel down the north face.

111   SAFEWAY SPIRE—FIVE FINGER DISCOUNT IV, 5.10d A1, 5 pitches, 400 feet (122 m) ★★★★★

First Ascent: Jon Butler, Cameron Burns, with Luke Laeser on Pitch 1, 8 April 1995.

Location and Access: *Five Finger Discount* starts on the south face of the tower and follows a prominent crack system to the top.

Pitch 1: Climb a vertical right-facing crack (5.10d) into 2 chimney. Exit of its left to a 2-bolt hanging belay.

Pitch 2: Continue up a bolt ladder (A1), angling left to a 2-bolt hanging belay, 130 feet (40m).

Pitch 3: Climb an A1 seam until it widens to a 2" crack (5 cm) to a 3-bolt hanging belay, 70 feet (21 m).

Pitch 4: Continue following a thin A1 crack to a 3" (7.6 cm) splitter crack through an offwidth pod with a bolt ending at a 2-bolt hanging belay, A1, 70 feet (21 m).

Pitch 5: Climb a 3" crack (7.6 cm), then offwidth crack, A1, 5.7, past a 5.8 offwidth to a short bolt ladder leading to the summit and a 2-bolt anchor, 5.8, A1, 130 feet (40 m).

Paraphernalia: Friends (2) sets with (1) #5, #6, #7; Micro-Friends (2) sets; Hexes (1) set; knifeblades (4); Lost Arrows (9); angles (4) 0.5", 5/8", (2) 3/4".

Descent: Three double-rope rappels down the route, skipping the second belay. All are from hanging stations.

Hueco Buttress

Hueco Buttress is south facing and approximately 0.75 mile (1.2 km) due west of Liberty Cap Buttress in Ute Canyon, at a point where the canyon turns to the southwest. The wall has prominent, dark desert varnish and numerous large-pocketed huecos; same approach as Liberty Cap Buttress.

112　NORTHWEST PASSAGE II, 5.10+, 1 pitch, 80 feet (24 m) ★★

First Ascent: KC Baum, solo, December 1993.

Location and Access: *Northwest Passage* ascends an obvious big hands splitter crack on the main wall. Climb a slightly overhanging crack to a small alcove beneath loose blocks.

Paraphernalia: Medium to large cams; Camalots (3–4) #3, (1) #4.

Descent: Rappel the route.

113　MONUMENTAL CRACKMASTER II, 5.11, 1 pitch, 130 feet (40 m) ★★

First Ascent: John Culberson, Mel Thorson, spring 1993.

Location and Access: *Monumental Crackmaster* is approximately 200 feet (61 m) left of *Northwest Passage* and climbs a good-looking fingercrack with the crux high on the route.

Paraphernalia: Friends (2) sets with extra small sizes.

Descent: Rappel the route.

114　PLAYING HOOKY II, 5.10, 1 pitch, 100 feet (30 m) ★

First Ascent: Mel Thorson, John Culberson, spring 1993.

Location and Access: *Playing Hooky* is approximately 200 feet (61 m) left (west) of *Monumental Crackmaster* in a left-facing dihedral. The first 40 feet (12 m) are up soft rock with poor protection. The upper part of the route climbs good rock up a left-facing dihedral to a ledge with double rappel anchors.

Paraphernalia: Friends (2) sets with extra small sizes.

Descent: Rappel the route.

NO THOROUGHFARE CANYON

Primal Instinct Buttress

The south-facing Primal Instinct Buttress may be approached by a long hike from the Devils Kitchen area south of the East Entrance to the Monument. The preferred approach is by a rappel from the rimrock. From the East Entrance and Rim Rock Drive, turn (left) onto East Glade Park Road and park beyond the monument boundary sign at a large gravel pullout on the right side of the road just before a sign: "Speed Limit 50 mph." Climb the fence by a sign reading "No Hunting or Trapping." Walk due south approximately 100 yards (91 m) to the rim of No Thoroughfare Canyon, then contour left a few yards to a stout pinyon pine a few inches from the edge of the canyon, and rappel 300 feet (91 m) from (two) 165 foot (50 m) ropes tied together. After a vertical rappel to a small ledge, downclimb 30 feet (9 m) to the ground. Walk east approximately 200 yards (183 m) to a shallow indented face with dihedrals on each side, 25 feet (8 m) apart at the base and converging to within 8 feet (2 m) at an anchor. The right-facing dihedral (left side) is the start for *Freedom of Expression* and *Primal Instinct*.

Over the Edge Spire is in the Over the Edge climbing area, so named because the easiest way to get there is by rappeling over the edge. To reach the spire, park at a pullout approximately 1 mile (1.8 km) beyond the intersection of Glade Park and Rim Rock Drive, near the East Entrance of the monument. Hike 0.5 mile (0.8 km) east to the rim (where the spire is in view to the east) and rappel to the canyon floor.

photo: Scott Evens

Over the Edge Spire

115   FREEDOM OF EXPRESSION II, 5.11b/c, 1 pitch, 95 feet (29 m) ★★

First Ascent: KC Baum, John Culberson, January 1993.

Location and Access: *Freedom of Expression* begins in a right-facing dihedral on the east face of Primal Instinct Buttress. Make delicate moves left around an arête onto a bolted face. Climb a varnished face with pockets and sharp edges past a 4-inch (10 cm) horizontal crack to a small bulge (crux). Continue up a bolted face to a 2-bolt rappel anchor.

Paraphernalia: Camalots (1) #4 optional; (1) medium TCU or Quad Cam (above 2nd bolt); quickdraws.

Descent: Rappel the route.

116   PRIMAL INSTINCT II, 5.10a/b, 1 pitch, 85 feet (26 m) ★★★

First Ascent: KC Baum, Tom Archibeque, January 1991.

Location and Access: *Primal Instinct* involves varied climbing on good rock. Begin in the right-facing dihedral on a small pillar of soft rock and climb an offwidth with chockstones past a large, pointed block with good hands. Continue with fingers to a small roof at the base of a jagged flake, then climb with hands and a lieback to a 2-bolt rappel anchor shared with *Desert Fox*.

Paraphernalia: Camalots (1) #4 (at the start), then finger- to hand-sized protection.

Descent: Rappel the route.

117   DESERT FOX II, 5.11a, 1 pitch, 85 feet (26 m) ★★★

First Ascent: KC Baum, Bob Hustava, February 1991.

Location and Access: *Desert Fox* is 25 feet (8 m) right (east) of *Primal Instinct* at a left-facing dihedral. Climb good hands, then lieback as the crack opens into an offwidth with 1 bolt protecting the upper squeeze section. Climb to big hands at the top of a chimney and continue to a small roof and a good rest. Continue with hands, then undercling, then lieback (crux) past 2 small dihedral roofs to *Primal Instinct* rappel anchor.

Paraphernalia: Medium to big cams through 4"; Camalots (2) #4.

Descent: Rappel *Primal Instinct*.

118   DESERT ROSE II, 5.11c/d, 1 pitch, 100 feet (30 m) ★★★★

First Ascent: KC Baum, Tom Archibeque, February 1991.

Location and Access: *Desert Rose* is 30 feet (9 m) right (east) of *Desert Fox* at a varnished left-facing dihedral that arches left. Begin the ascent at a small roof at the base of the Wingate and climb with good hands. Continue into tight hands, then fingers as the corner arches left. Lieback, then mantle onto a hollow flake (soft) and continue with an undercling/lieback into a shallow alcove below the lip of an overhang. Pass the lip (crux) and gain a good handcrack which narrows to small fingers on an exposed flake. Continue to a 2-bolt anchor as the crack begins to seam out.

Paraphernalia: Finger- to hand-sized protection; mostly medium cams.

Descent: Rappel the route.

119   TWO CENTS WORTH II, 5.9+, 1 pitch, 40 feet (12 m) ★★

First Ascent: Bob Hustava, KC Baum, February 1991.

Location and Access: *Two Cent's Worth* is 500 feet (152 m) right (east) of *Desert Rose* at a large rounded block sitting against the main wall. Climb a straight-in fingers to a handcrack with many sharp surface and crack edges. Belay on top of the block. The route may be top-roped.

Paraphernalia: Finger- to hand-sized cams.

Descent: Downclimb to the west.

120 SANDMAN II, 5.10a, 1 pitch, 75 feet (23 m) ★★

First Ascent: KC Baum, Bob Hustava, February 1991.

Location and Access: *Sandman* is approximately 350 feet (107 m) right (east) of *Two Cent's Worth*. KC Baum: "This is an excellent climb except for a soft, sandy section just beneath the summit anchor." The route starts at a shallow, right-facing dihedral on the right side of a very large detached pillar. Begin atop large rectangular blocks of Wingate Sandstone lying on the ground beneath a nice-looking handcrack. Pass a small roof and climb an easy offwidth to a bulge with bomber hand jams. Continue to

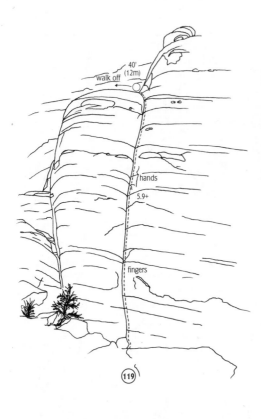

a small roof and offwidth section. Climb a short, soft offwidth (crux) using footholds on the adjoining face.

Paraphernalia: Mostly hand-sized cams with (1) big piece.

Descent: Rappel the route from a 2-bolt anchor.

121 PIRANHA II, 5.12a, 1 pitch, 90 feet (27 m) ★★★★

First Ascent: KC Baum, Bob Hustava, 5.11, A0, May 1991. First free ascent: Jeff Hollenbaugh, KC Baum, February 1992.

Location and Access: *Piranha* is approximately 3/8 mile (0.4 km) right (east) of *Primal Instinct* and 300 yards (91 m) right (east) of *Sandman*. When walking east from *Sandman*, look for prominent white calcite streaks on the main wall with several large boulders below. Continue east and walk down and around the boulders, then back uphill toward the main wall. The splitter crack of *Piranha* is in the center of an indented wall with prominent streaks of calcite over dark brown desert varnish (1 calcite streak forms a perfect right-angle dog leg), and is bounded on the right (east) by a large spire forming a left-facing dihedral and on the left (west) by 2 large blocks, one sitting atop the other. Climb hands into fingers, then make an awkward move into tight hands as the wall begins to overhang slighty and arch to the right. Climb off-balance, strenuous tight hands to a small rest as the crack angles to the vertical again. Finish the route at a large ledge with a 2-bolt rappel anchor.

Paraphernalia: Small hand-sized cams (mostly medium); Camalots several #1.

Descent: Rappel the route.

122 MASTER CHAMBER II, 5.11a, 1 pitch, 90 feet (27 m) ★★★

First Ascent: KC Baum, Bob Hustava, March 1991.

Location and Access: KC Baum: "The most uniquely formed desert crack I have ever seen, not to be missed." *Master Chamber* climbs a crack in the main wall 20 feet (6 m) right (east) of *Piranha*, at the base of a large chimney formed by a spire adjacent to the main wall. KC: "A beautiful calcite streak forms two incredibly perfect right-angle corners just left of the crack, and the crack forms a near perfect right-angle dog leg which angles right on the main wall and into the big chimney (really a wild-looking route)." Climb with hands to where the crack makes a right turn, then traverses horizontally for 8 feet (2 m). Traverse with heel hooks and finger nails until the crack turns left and arches up and right. Make strenuous moves to gain a large handcrack, then continue into good hands through a slightly overhanging bulge and finish on a large ledge.

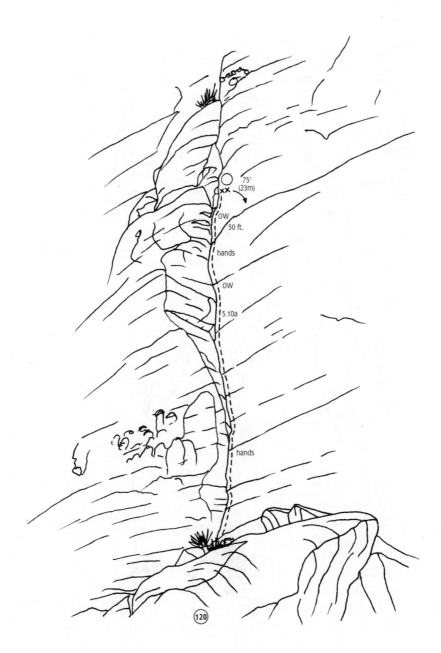

75'
(23m)

OW
50 ft.

hands

OW

5.10a

hands

120

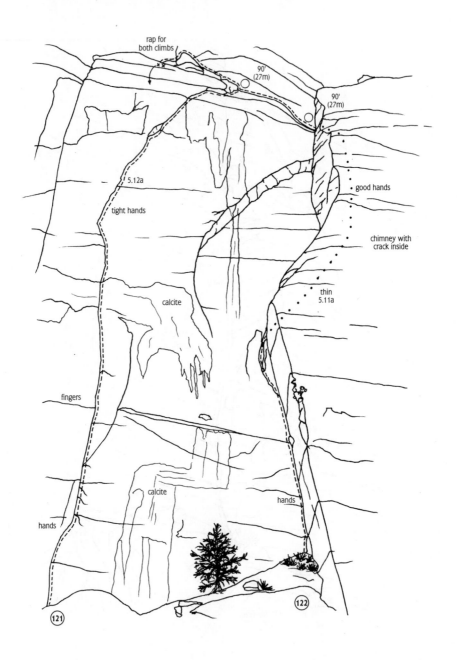

rap for
both climbs

90'
(27m)

90'
(27m)

5.12a

tight hands

good hands

chimney with
crack inside

calcite

thin
5.11a

fingers

calcite

hands

hands

121

122

Paraphernalia: Small through large cams; Camalots (2) #3.

Descent: Walk 40 feet (12 m) west and rappel *Piranha*.

123   OVER THE EDGE SPIRE (a.k.a. Fisher Price Pinnacle)—CHILDS PLAY II, 5.8+ R, 2 pitches, 140 feet (43 m)

First Ascent: Jon Burnham, Bill Duncan, Brent Higgins, March 1996.

Location and Access: *Childs Play* ascends the west face of the spire.

Pitch 1: Begin with 5.7 hands, then 5.8 fists to 5.6 R. Belay at the top of a chimney.

Pitch 2: Continue up the chimney (5.7) using 2 empty baby angle holes for protection. Climb the face above the chimney, passing 1 empty hole to the summit and a 3-bolt anchor, 5.8+ R.

Paraphernalia: Very small to very wide units; baby angles (4).

Descent: One double-rope rappel.

124   OVER THE EDGE SPIRE (a.k.a. Fisher Price Pinnacle)—ONE TOKE OVER THE LINE II, 5.10b, 1 pitch, 140 feet (43 m)

First Ascent: Mike Colacino, Scott Evens, Matt Simpson, March 1996.

Location and Access: *One Toke Over the Line* ascends the east face of Over the Edge Spire, opposite *Childs Play*. Climb 5.9 hands, then 5.10b offwidth until the climbing eases to a 5.6 chimney where the route meets *Childs Play* and climbs to the summit.

Paraphernalia: Hand-sized units through 7"; angle pitons (4) 0.5" for empty holes.

Descent: One double-rope rappel.

Lost Arrow Buttress

Routes in the area of Lost Arrow Buttress are a short distance right (west) of the Primal Instinct Buttress when approached from the parking area. To reach, climb the fence a short distance right of the Primal Instinct Buttress approach and walk approximately 200 yards (183 m) up an obvious old road cut. This overgrown road/trail branches at a 45-degree right angle from the parking area. Turn left at a dead pinyon tree, which is on the right as you face the canyon. From the edge of No Thoroughfare Canyon, at a prominent bowl right of an obvious projecting point of the rimrock, make (two) 165-foot (50 m) rappels to the floor of the canyon. From the canyon rim, rappel a full 165 feet (50 m) from a small pinyon pine down a low-angled slab to a large ledge (leave fixed rope). Walk approximately 50 feet (15 m) southwest on a ledge and rappel another full 165–170 feet (50–52 m) from one lone pine tree down a vertical face to a small ledge about 8 feet (2 m) off the ground (leave a fixed rope for the prusik out), between *Silent Witness*, 25 feet (8 m) east, and *the 22nd Day*, 75 feet (23 m) west. Downclimb 8 feet (2 m) to the ground and walk east for 125 feet (38 m) to the start of *Lost Arrow* crack.

125   LOST ARROW II, 5.12a (downgrade for small to medium hands), 1 pitch, 100 feet (30 m) ★★★★

First Ascent: KC Baum, Bob Hustava, February 1992.

Location and Access: *Lost Arrow* begins at a straight-in handcrack. Climb hands into tight hands (if you have big hands) through a slightly overhanging bulge to a small rest at the base of a flare. Continue tight hands through a flare and make a strenuous and

rap from top
to access buttress

80'
(24m)

crux

5.10 A1

fingers

(126)

awkward move onto a good rest 15 feet (5 m) below an anchor. Continue with a strenuous lieback and fingers to a good ledge and a 2-bolt rappel anchor.

Paraphernalia: Camalots (6–8) #1, (2) #2 (at the start); TCUs (2–3) medium to large.

Descent: Rappel the route.

126   SILENT WITNESS II, 5.10, A1, 1 pitch, 80 feet (24 m) ★★

First Ascent: KC Baum, solo, March 1993.

Location and Access: *Silent Witness* is 100 feet (30 m) left (west) of *Lost Arrow* and 25 feet (8 m) right of the rappel line. Climb a flake fingercrack to a small rounded roof. Pass the roof (crux) and continue with fingers to a 2-bolt anchor.

Paraphernalia: TCUs; many medium size through 2".

Descent: Rappel the route.

127   22nd DAY II, 5.9+, 1 pitch, 85 feet (26 m) ★★

First Ascent: KC Baum, Bob Hustava, Mel Thorson, February 1992.

Location and Access: *22nd Day* is 100 feet (30 m) left (west) of *Silent Witness* and 75 feet (23 m) left of the rappel line. Begin at a detached pillar forming a left-facing

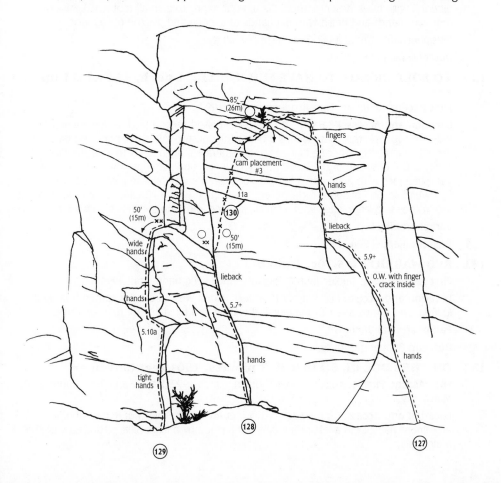

dihedral and climb good hands into an offwidth with a fingercrack on the right face. Pass a ledge and continue up a right-facing dihedral with a lieback, hands, fingers, and finish with an easy offwidth onto a large ledge with a small pinyon tree and a 2-bolt anchor.

Paraphernalia: Medium to large cams; Camalots (2–3) #4.

Descent: Rappel the route.

128   LAYBACK II, 5.7+, 1 pitch, 50 feet (15 m) ★★

First Ascent: KC Baum, Bob Hustava, December 1991.

Location and Access: *Layback* is 20 feet (6 m) left (west) of *22nd Day* at a low-angle handcrack. Climb hands and lieback to a large ledge and a 2-bolt anchor.

Paraphernalia: Hand- to large-sized cams through 4".

Descent: Rappel the route.

129   RED IGUANA II, 5.10a, 1 pitch, 50 feet (15 m) ★★★

First Ascent: Bob Hustava, KC Baum, February 1992.

Location and Access: *Red Iguana* is 25 feet (8 m) left (west) of *Layback* in a left-facing dihedral with black desert varnish. Climb tight hands to a small roof (crux). Pass the roof with hands and finish with big hands to a ledge and the top of *Layback*.

Paraphernalia: Camalots (2–3) #1, (3–4) #2, (2) #3.

Descent: Rappel *Layback*.

130   TO BOLT OR NOT TO HAVE FUN II, 5.11a, 1 pitch, 35 feet (11 m) ★★★

First Ascent: KC Baum, Tom Archibeque, May 1992.

Location and Access: KC Baum: "A not-to-be-missed second pitch to *Red Iguana* or finish to *Layback*, this route climbs a beautifully desert-varnished, pocketed face with three bolts." Climb either *Red Iguana* (recommended) or *Layback* to a large ledge. Move to the east end of the ledge (top of *Layback*) and step right onto a dark brown varnished face with good edges and pockets. Climb a vertical face past 3 bolts to a rest in a white section of softer rock. Protect this section with a #3 Camalot or make runout face moves to a large ledge with a small pine tree and 2-bolt anchor for *22nd Day*.

Paraphernalia: Camalot (1) #3; Quickdraws (3).

Descent: Rappel *22nd Day*.

131   RED WARRIOR I, 5.10c, 1 pitch

First Ascent: Dave Takker, John Culberson, Vince Longmann, April 1994.

Location and Access: *Red Warrior* is 50 feet (15 m) west (around a corner) from *Red Iguana*, and climbs a left-facing dihedral ending at a fixed anchor right of a tree.

Paraphernalia: Unknown.

Descent: Rappel the route.

132   ON THE EDGE III, 5.11b/c R, 3 pitches, 190+ feet (58+m) ★★

First Ascent: Pitch 1: KC Baum, Mel Thorson, March 1992. Pitch 2 and 3: KC Baum, solo, March 1992.

Location and Access: *On the Edge* is 225 feet (69 m) left (west) of *Red Iguana* at a prominent flat roof in a left-facing dihedral formed by a large pillar sitting against the main wall.

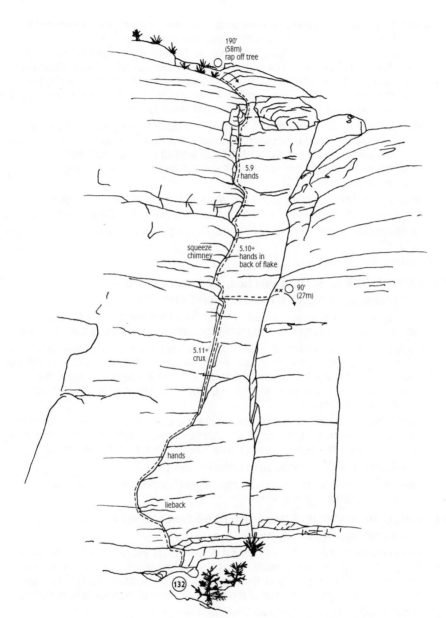

190'
(58m)
rap off tree

5.9
hands

squeeze
chimney

5.10+
hands in
back of flake

×× 90'
(27m)

5.11+
crux

hands

lieback

132

Pitch 1: Traverse left 8 feet (2 m) and pass a roof with a strenuous 5.10 undercling, lieback, and hand jams onto a right-trending, low-angle flake with a sharp edge. Use long runners on the cams through the roof, so the rope will not push the cams out of reach. Follow the flake to 2 blocks that sit in an alcove behind the flake. Climb an offset and overlapped crack (crux) to a large ledge and belay. Protect the pitch with small to large cams, (4–5) #1, #2, and (2) #3, (1) #4 Camalots. Small to medium TCUs or Quad Cams. A 2-bolt anchor is on the east end of the ledge, 5.11b/c, 90 feet (27 m).

Pitch 2: Begin in the overhanging 5.10+ flared squeeze with a good handcrack in the back. Struggle to a good ledge, then climb an easier flare with good hands. Continue with 5.9 hands to a small alcove with a bulge leading to a low-angle slot with loose chockstones. Carefully climb into a low-angle slot and onto a large ledge, 5.10+, 100 feet (30 m).

Pitch 3: Easy 5th class to the top of the Wingate, but it is not recommended due to soft, runout rock. Bring webbing for a rappel from a tree below the slot to avoid pitch 3.

Paraphernalia: Finger- to hand-sized cams; Camalot (4–5) #1, #2, (2) #3, (1) #4; rappel webbing.

Descent: Rappel the route.

133   LAW OF ONE II, 5.10, 2 pitches, 175 feet (53 m) ★★★

First Ascent: KC Baum, Bob Hustava, November 1992.

Location and Access: *Law of One* is 125 feet (38 m) left (west) of *On The Edge* on a flat face with broken cracks leading to a prominent splitter crack at the main wall.

Pitch 1: Make a few unprotected face moves to broken flakes and a small pillar. Gain a dark brown parallel-sided handcrack in the main wall. Climb hands into offwidth and lieback onto a small ledge. Continue through a roof to a belay on a large ledge. Protect with TCUs, cams up to 4", (2–3) #3, and #4 Camalots, (1) #4 for the belay anchor, 5.10, 100 feet (30 m).

Pitch 2: Make awkward moves off the belay ledge through a bulgy roof, then climb into an open chimney. At the top of the chimney, traverse right and move onto the face with a good handcrack. Continue to a 2-bolt anchor, 5.10, 75 feet (23 m).

Paraphernalia: Small- to hand-sized cams; (1) large piece.

Descent: One 165-foot (50 m) double-rope rappel reaches a small pillar from which you can downclimb to the ground.

134   CINCO DE MAYO II, 5.9+, 1 pitch, 60 feet (18 m) ★

First Ascent: Bob Hustava, KC Baum, 5 May 1991.

Location and Access: *Cinco de Mayo* is 175 feet (53 m) left (west) of *Law of One* at a 60-foot-tall (18 m) by 30-foot-wide (9 m) pillar leaning against the main wall. The route begins on the right side of the pillar up a shallow right-facing dihedral. Climb hands through fingers to the top of the pillar and belay off a 2-bolt rappel anchor.

Paraphernalia: Finger- to hand-sized cams.

Descent: Rappel the route.

135   CHOCOLATE CORNER II, 5.10a/b, 1 pitch, 60 feet (18 m) ★★★

First Ascent: KC Baum, Bob Hustava, December 1991.

Location and Access: *Chocolate Corner* is named for the color of the Wingate Sandstone it ascends. Begin 30 feet (9 m) left (west) of *Cinco de Mayo* on the left side of a pillar in a left-facing dihedral. Climb fingers, then hands, and finally lieback a short offwidth section to the top of the pillar and a 2-bolt rappel anchor.

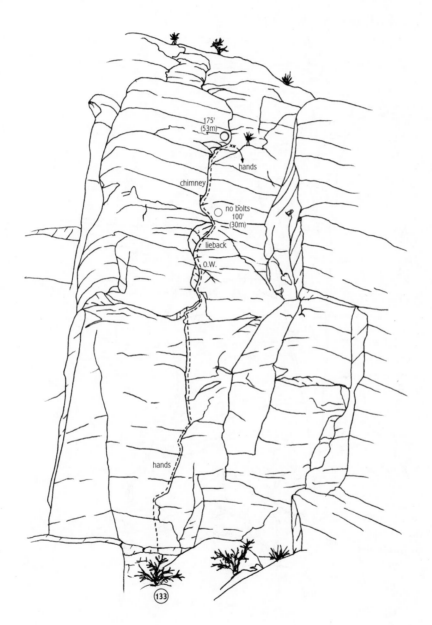

175'
(53m)

hands

chimney

no bolts
100'
(30m)

lieback

O.W.

hands

(133)

60'
(18m)

lieback
O.W.

fingers

5.10a/b

5.9+

hands

hands

fingers

134

135

Paraphernalia: Small- to hand-sized cams; Camalots (1) #3.

Descent: Rappel the route

East Entrance Tunnel

Drive west on Rim Rock Drive toward the East Entrance kiosk. East Entrance Tunnel area is 0.5 mile (0.8 km) past the tunnel.

136 MOTHER'S DAY II, 5.9, 1 pitch, 75 feet (23 m) ★★★

First Ascent: KC Baum, Judy Baum, 9 May 1993.

Location and Access: *Mother's Day* is 1.8 miles (2.9 km) from the East Entrance kiosk or, when driving west to east on the Rim Rock Road, just below the first switchback after exiting the East Entrance tunnel. The route is on the right wall just inside a chimney across (left) from a 20 mph sign with a right-angle, 90-degree arrow indicating a sharp right turn. There is an old piton 20 feet (6 m) up the route.

Paraphernalia: Small- to hand-sized units.

Descent: Rappel the route.

137 SUNKEN CURVE CORNER I, 5.8, 1 pitch, 50 feet (15 m)

First Ascent: Paul Cowen et al, 1984.

Location and Access: *Sunken Curve Corner* is near the first hairpin switchback beyond (downhill) the tunnel. Further information is unknown.

Paraphernalia: Hand-sized Friends.

Descent: Rappel the route.

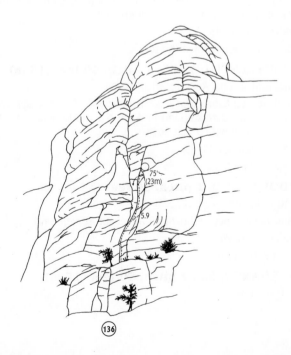

75'
(23m)

5.9

(136)

Devils Kitchen

Devils Kitchen is in No Thoroughfare Canyon near the East Entrance to the monument. To reach, drive approximately 200 yards (183 m) past the East Entrance kiosk and park at the signed Devils Kitchen Trailhead. Hike south into No Thoroughfare Canyon. After crossing a large, rocky wash, work up toward large Wingate rocks (Devils Kitchen), which are in view above the trail.

138 FRESH AS A DAISY I, 5.10, 1 pitch, 50 feet (15 m)

First Ascent: Steve Johnson, Tom Blake, early 1980s.

Location and Access: *Fresh as a Daisy* climbs the west outside face of Devils Kitchen. Ascend an offwidth crack to a right-slanting dihedral. Above a ledge, continue with face climbing, difficult thin crack climbing, and a step around a corner to a flared crack.

Paraphernalia: Standard desert rack..

Descent: One-rope rappel to the ground.

139 TRASH CAN ALLEY I, 5.10, 1 pitch, 50 feet (15 m)

First Ascent: Unknown. *Trash Can Alley* is south of *Fresh as a Daisy,* near an obvious gully.

Paraphernalia: Standard desert rack.

Descent: Rappel the route.

140 LAST TACO I, 5.11-, 1 pitch, 50 feet (15 m)

First Ascent: Tom Stubbs, Andy Petefish, 1970s.

Location and Access: *Last Taco* faces north and is the first route on the first crack on the left as you step inside the Devils Kitchen landform. Climb with difficult stemming, then lieback an overhanging face to a rappel bolt.

Paraphernalia: Large units.

Descent: One-rope rappel down the route.

141 FUTURE REFERENCE I, 5.10b, 1 pitch, 50 feet (15 m)

First Ascent: Tom Stubbs, Andy Petefish, 1970s.

Location and Access: *Future Reference* is right of *Last Taco.* Begin with a 5.7 handcrack in a corner, then step left and climb a short handcrack (10 feet, 3 m) to a 15-foot (5 m) chimney with a bolt at its top.

Paraphernalia: Hand-sized units.

Descent: Rappel the route.

142 BOOGIE DOWN I, 5.9, 1 pitch, 50 feet (15 m)

First Ascent: Unknown.

Location and Access: *Boogie Down* is east of *Future Reference.*

Paraphernalia: Unknown.

Descent: Rappel the route.

143 EASY OVERHANG I, 5.2, 1 pitch, 50 feet (15 m)

First Ascent: Unknown.

Location and Access: *Easy Overhang* is on the northeast side of Devils Kitchen. Climb a wide crack system which winds its way to the top of the north face. The route is obvious when viewed from the drainage below Devils Kitchen.

Paraphernalia: Unknown.

Descent: Rappel the route.

144   BAT GUANO I, 5.5, 1 pitch, 50 feet (15 m)

First Ascent: Unknown.

Location and Access: *Bat Guano* follows an obvious crack system on the northeast corner of the outer face of Devils Kitchen.

Paraphernalia: Unknown.

Descent: Rappel the route.

145   CHIMNEY CLIMB I, 5.9, 1 pitch, 50 feet (15 m)

First Ascent: Unknown.

Location and Access: *Chimney Climb* is on the south face of the northernmost tower of Devils Kitchen, directly opposite and approximately 15 feet (4.5 m) from *Easy Overhang*.

Paraphernalia: Unknown.

Descent: Rappel the route.

146   FRIDAY AFTERNOON CLUB I, 5.10, 1 pitch, 50 feet (15 m)

First Ascent: Tom Stubbs, Andy Petefish, Joe Kaelin, 1980s.

Location and Access: *Friday Afternoon Club* is on a satellite formation northeast of Devils Kitchen.

Paraphernalia: Unknown.

Descent: Rappel the route.

Friction Wall

Several climbs have been established on a large friction wall east and across the canyon from Devils Kitchen. They average approximately 70 feet (21 m) in height. To reach, hike east from the No Thoroughfare Canyon Trail, across the canyon and up to the slabs behind the tallest tree in the area.

147   FORBIDDEN ZONE I, 5.9, 1 pitch

First Ascent: Tom Stubbs, Andy Petefish, late '70s early '80s.

Location and Access: *Forbidden Zone* climbs the friction wall opposite Devils Kitchen. Further information is unknown.

Paraphernalia: Friends medium to large.

Descent: Rappel the route.

148   CAKE WALK I, 5.9, 1 pitch

First Ascent: Tom Stubbs, Andy Petefish, late '70s early '80s.

Location and Access: Same as *Forbidden Zone*. Further information is unknown.

Paraphernalia: Friends, medium to large.

Descent: Rappel the route.

East Entrance–Gypsy Towers

To reach, take Monument Road toward the East Entrance kiosk and turn right (west) on South Camp Road just before entering the monument. A sign reads "Monument Valley." Continue past Fallen Rock Road east to Rim Rock Road, which will be the next left turn. Follow the road until it ends in a cul-de-sac and park. Gypsy Towers are the obvious three fingers at the left end of a butte. The approach from the car is approximately 40 minutes. Hike up a hill from the road and work right into a wash, cross the fence into the park, then traverse the fence line from the inside for about 0.5 miles (0.8 km). When the wash below the towers is reached, hike directly up to them.

149   UPPER GYPSY—MAN-EATER III, 5.10d, 3 pitches, 200 feet (61 m) ★★★

First Ascent: Jon Butler, Luke Laeser, August 1993.

Location and Access: Upper Gypsy is the farthest right of the 3 towers.

Pitch 1: Begin with loose 5.7 climbing to the base of the tower, then continue up 5.10d offwidth at the far-right edge between the tower and the butte behind it.

Pitch 2: Climb 5.9 offwidth.

Pitch 3: Continue to the summit with an unprotected 5.7 mantle.

Paraphernalia: Standard desert rack.

Descent: Rappel the south face.

150   MIDDLE GYPSY—SANDSTONE SANDWICH III, 5.9, AO-A1, 2 pitches, 160 feet (49 m) ★★★

First Ascent: Luke Laeser, Jon Butler, September 1993.

Location and Access: The tower is between the Upper Gypsy and Lower Gypsy. *Sandstone Sandwich* begins up a chimney on the south side and continues up the right side of the north face, emerging on the north side partway up Pitch 2. The summit is reached with 5.8 fingers and hands.

Paraphernalia: Standard desert rack.

Descent: Rappel the south face with double ropes from fixed anchors.

151   EAST CHIMNEY II, 5.8+ R, A1, 3 pitches, 210 feet (64 m)

First Ascent: Luke Laeser, Jon Butler, fall 1993.

Location and Access: *East Chimney* begins directly below the saddle between Middle Gypsy and Upper Gypsy.

Pitch 1: Climb with hands up a left-facing corner and into a 5.6 squeeze chimney ending at the saddle between the 2 towers, 5.8+, 100 feet (30 m).

Pitch 2: Climb 5.5 with no protection to a ledge with double anchors (optional belay) then up holes to a ledge meeting *Sky Pilot* and belay, 80 feet (24 m).

Pitch 3: Continue 5.7 fingers to the summit, 30 feet (9 m).

Paraphernalia: Friends (1) set; angles for empty holes.

Descent: One double-rope rappel down the east face.

152   SKY PILOT II, 5.7, A2, 3 pitches, 210 Feet (64 m) ★★★★

First Ascent: Jon Butler, solo, 6 November 1994.

photo: Melissa MacDonnell

The Gypsy Towers

photo: Luke Laeser

Jon Butler following first pitch of Middle Gypsy

Location and Access: *Sky Pilot* climbs a small splitter crack on the west face of Middle Gypsy.

Pitch 1: Climb up and left past a flake (A1) to a hanging belay, 5.7, A1, 90 feet (27 m).

Pitch 2: Climb past holes up thin A2, then past more holes ending on a belay ledge with double anchors below the summit, A2, 90 feet (27 m).

Pitch 3: Finish to the summit with 5.7 fingers joining the top of *East Chimney*, 5.7, 30 feet (9 m).

Paraphernalia: Small cams; nuts (1) set; Lost Arrows (15); knifeblades (6); angles (6) 0.5", (6) 5/8", (3) 3/8", (2) 1", 1 1/4", (1) 2", 2.5".

Descent: One double rappel down the east face.

153   BABY GYPSY—NORTH FACE I, A1, 1 pitch, 70 feet (21 m) ★

First Ascent: Jon Butler, solo, 1993.

Location and Access: *Baby Gypsy* climbs the center crack system on the west face of the tower next to (left of) Middle Gypsy when viewing from the west face.

Paraphernalia: Friends (1) set.

Descent: Rappel the route.

Super Crack Buttress

Super Crack Buttress is in Red Canyon, faces south, and requires a 20-minute approach hike from Monument Canyon Village. To reach, turn onto South Camp Road from Monument Canyon Road and drive 1.2 miles (1.9 km) to Dakota Street. A sign reads "Monument Valley Estates." Turn left (south) on Dakota and go 0.2 mile (0.3 km) beyond Chinle Street and park. Walk south up the obvious drainage from Red Canyon, which by law must remain open for access. Go past million-dollar homes and pass through the Colorado National Monument access gate. Hike up the ridge directly toward Super Crack Buttress.

There is an excellent view of Super Crack Buttress from Cold Shivers Point, where Super Crack is just in from the right profile of the obvious wall in view 0.75 mile (1.2 km) north. The benchmark at Cold Shivers Point reads "Elevation 6,106 feet."

154   SUPER CRACK OF THE MONUMENT II, 5.10c, 1 pitch, 130 feet (40 m) ★★★★

First Ascent: KC Baum, Tom Archibeque, January 1990.

Location and Access: *Supercrack of the Monument* is approximately 100 yards (91 m) right (east) of *Catch 22*. The climb is very similar to *Super Crack* in Indian Creek. It ascends an obvious splitter crack near the eastern end of the northeastern prow at the mouth of Red Canyon. Begin in the Chinle Formation and climb a low-angle handcrack on the right side of a 15-foot (4.5 m) pillar which leans against and covers the lower portion of the crack. Climb with tight hands through big hands to a 2-bolt rappel anchor.

Paraphernalia: Small to large cams; Camalots (1) #0.75 for just below the rappel anchor, (3–4) #1, (6–7) #2, (1–2) #3.

Descent: Rappel the route.

155   CATCH 22 II, 5.11a, 1 pitch, 145 feet (44 m) ★★

First Ascent: KC Baum, Tom Archibeque, February 1990.

Location and Access: *Catch 22* is approximately 100 yards (91 m) left (west) of *Super Crack of the Monument* at a leaning pillar beneath a large left-facing dihedral, or about 4 crack systems left (west) of *Super Crack*. Start up a ramp on the left side of a low-angle pillar and climb hands-to-fingers to the top of the pillar. Continue with fists into a large left-facing dihedral, then begin a long, strenuous lieback through a parallel-sided offwidth section. The climb ends after pulling into a large alcove with a 2-bolt anchor.

Paraphernalia: Small fingers to large size cams; Camalots (4–5) #4.

Descent: Rappel the route.

Terra Tower–Tiara Rado Buttress

Tiara Rado Buttress is south-facing, approximately 0.5 mile (0.8 km) northwest of Tiara Rado Spire. Begin the 40-minute approach to the buttress from the Tiara Rado golf course home sites. Drive west on Broadway (Colorado Highway 340), then turn left (south) on 20 3/4 Road. Go approximately 1 mile (1.6 km), then turn right (west) onto South Broadway, and continue approximately 0.25 mile (0.4 km) to Tiara Drive. At the intersection of South Broadway and Tiara Drive, turn left (south) and continue approximately 0.75 mile (1.2 km) to Wood Court. Continue 0.1 mile (0.16 km) past Wood Court and park along the street. Walk up the drainage (right of the parking) between houses and cross under the Colorado National Monument fence into the monument. Drainages are legal access. Please avoid the private property in the area. Traverse right through granite rock bands, then west to the buttress.

156   TIARA RADO BUTTRESS—STRAIGHT SHOOTER II, 5.10-, 1 pitch, 140 feet (43 m) ★★★★★

First Ascent: KC Baum, Peter Hollis, October 1989.

Location and Access: Approach is the same as for Tiara Spire–traverse right through granite rock bands, then west to the buttress. *Straight Shooter* is on the south-facing wall near the east end of the buttress. The buttress is approximately 0.5 mile (0.8 km) north of Tiara Rado Spire and is the first buttress across from a shallow canyon. The climb faces south and is near the east end of the buttress.

Paraphernalia: Many hand-sized cams; Camalot (1) #3.

Descent: Rappel the route.

157   TERRA TOWER—BAZAAR III, 5.8, A3, 4 pitches, 220 feet (67 m)

First Ascent: Harvey T. Carter, Tom Merrill, 28 April 1978.

Location and Access: *Bazaar* ascends Terra Tower from the southeast. The 4 pitches are rated 5.8 A3, 5.7, 5.7, and 5.8 A2, respectively.

Paraphernalia: Standard desert rack.

Descent: Two double-rope rappels down the route.

158   TERRA TOWER—SOUTH FACE III, 5.11, 3 pitches, 220 feet (67 m)

First Ascent: Tom Stubbs, Joe Calin, 1980s.

Location and Access: *South Face* climbs offwidth and overhangs on the front side of the tower for 3 pitches before ending below a large roof.

Paraphernalia: Large-sized units.

Descent: Rappel the route.

159   GRANITE CLIFF—NICE GOING II, 5.6, 2 pitches

First Ascent: Harvey T. Carter, Bill Kurimay, 27 April 1978.

Location and Access: *Nice Going* climbs the best-looking crack system below Terra Tower.

Paraphernalia: Friends (1) set.

Descent: Rappel the route.

160   STUDENT AID I, 5.7 C1, 1 pitch, 100 feet (30 m)

First Ascent: Joe Cole, Joe Prescott, 19 October 1997.

Location and Access: *Student Aid* is in the Tiara Rado climbing area 500 yards (457 m) west of Terra Tower. It is 25 yards (23 m) right and around the corner from the Granite Cliff. Approach from the access into Gold Star Canyon along South Broadway 1.8 miles (2.8 km) south of the Monument Canyon Trailhead. There is limited parking at the gate. Upon entering the gate, walk south along the trail following the fence for approximately 0.8 mile (1.2 km). Leave the trail soon after crossing a gulch and climb the steep slope heading for the prominent buttress above. The route is on the northeast facing wall. There are numerous climbs around the corner to the left known as the Tiara Rado climbing area. *Student Aid* climbs a clean thin to hand-sized crack with a pod halfway up. Begin up a rotten 15-foot (4.5 m) corner under a 10-foot (3 m) roof, 5.7 with no protection. Climb the roof with small TCUs and continue on aid 85 feet (26 m) to anchors where the crack disappears.

Paraphernalia: Many cams size #00 ; TCUs to #2 Camalot.

Descent: Rappel the route.

DS Road Buttress

The DS Road (a county road) is reached by driving through Colorado National Monument south to the high land of Glade Park. At the main intersection of the park, turn right (west) on DS Road, which travels for many miles through desolate country to eventually reach the ford across the Dolores River and a few miles farther River Road (Utah Scenic Byway 128) leading west to Moab. The following two routes are approximately 3 miles (4.8 km) into Utah on the Wingate Wall on the right side of the road after crossing the border.

161   REACHING FOR HANGING DIRT SNAKE (Top-rope) I, 5.9, 1 pitch, 35 feet (10 m)

First Ascent: Team Rio de Caca, top-rope solo, April 1993.

Location and Access: *Reaching for Hanging Dirt Snake* faces south and climbs a steep face ending on a wide ledge. Climb a small, right-facing dihedral topped by a small overhang. Pull over the overhang to the left and climb to a ledge. Fixed anchors for top-rope can be reached by walking right until it is possible to scramble up and onto the ledge.

Descent: Walk off to the right.

162   UNFINISHED PUTTERMAN I, 5.7, 1 pitch

First Ascent: Team Rio de Caca, April 1993.

Location and Access: *Unfinished Putterman* is approximately 200 feet (61 m) left of *Reaching for Hanging Dirt Snake* or the first place where the creek and road converge.

Begin on the left side of broken blocks and climb past 2 fixed anchors to a rappel anchor where the crack system flares and juts to the right.

Paraphernalia: Unknown.

Descent: Rappel the route.

Rough Canyon

Tabeguache Tower is in Rough Canyon, east of Colorado National Monument. Turn off Broadway (Colorado Highway 340) onto Rim Rock Drive and go 1 block, then turn left onto D Road, which turns into Rosevale and leads to CS Road (a.k.a. Little Park Road). Follow CS Road for approximately 5 miles (8 km) to the turnoff to Rough and Bangs Canyons at the first left after cresting a hill (trailhead to Tabeguache Trail). Turn east (left) once in the canyon, and follow it 0.5 mile (0.8 km) to where the canyon joins a large valley. Tabeguache Tower is obvious to the south.

Tabeguache Tower is also visible from the rim of Rough Canyon, and is reached by a 0.5-mile (0.8 km) hike from the parking area down Tabeguache Trail to the south-southeast.

163 TABEGUACHE TOWER IV, 5.9 R, A2, 3 pitches, 335 feet (102 m) ★★

First Ascent: Steve Anderton, Bill Duncan, Matt Simpson, 18 February 1996.

Location and Access: The route ascends an obvious crack system on the east face, ending on the west face of the tower.

Pitch 1: Begin up a small crack (A2) until a blocky section can be free climbed at 5.8 to a belay ledge, 120 feet (37 m).

Pitch 2: Climb a 5.8 fistcrack to a large bombay chimney. Continue around a large flake in a chimney and climb with offwidth and squeeze to a small roof, 5.9. Aid the

photo: Bill Duncan

Tabeguache Tower

roof (A1, #4 Camalots) and climb 30 feet (9 m) in a squeeze chimney (The Time Warp), then past loose blocks (5.7) to a 2-bolt belay, 5.9 R.

Pitch 3: Aid climb with gear and 3/8" empty holes with Bird Beaks to the summit and a 2-bolt rappel station, A2.

Paraphernalia: Standard desert rack; Camalots (1) set, (3) #4, (1) #5; wires; Big Bros (2) #4; knifeblades (3); angle pitons (6) 0.5", (2) 5/8"; Bird Beaks (3).

Descent: Rappel 50 feet (15 m) to the saddle, then scramble down to the north. Traverse around to the top of a small gully, then rappel from slings around a large block to the ground, 60 feet (18 m).

Things of Beauty (a.k.a. Interstate 70 Towers)

Things of Beauty Towers are mud and sandstone cobble landforms between Clifton and Palisade on the north side of I-70 between mile markers 39 and 40, approximately 9 miles (9.8 km) east of Grand Junction, Colorado. Take the Palisade exit, then turn right (west) on a rough paved road and continue through an orchard. After approximately 2 miles (3.2 km) turn right (north) on a dirt road, drive under the interstate and park at the Mount Garfield recreational area parking lot. Hike west (paralleling I-70) for approximately 20 minutes to the col of the obvious Fortress. Pete Takeda: "The knobby blob to the right and uphill is the Turkey Neck–the climb goes up the backside. The Mantis is the delicate Cerro Torre–like shaft partly hidden in the cirque just before the Fortress. . . . Their only redeeming qualities were their untouched summits and bizarre geometry."

164 FORTRESS—REGULAR ROUTE I, 5.9, A2, 1 pitch, 120 feet (37 m)

First Ascent: Pete Takeda, Joel Arellano, fall 1992.

Location and Access: *Regular Route* ascends the left edge of the tower (40 feet, 12 m) as viewed from the south. Start on the high point of the ridge connecting the landform to the slope behind.

Paraphernalia: Pitons (3) 5/8" through 1 1/4".

Descent: Rappel 40 feet (12 m) from double anchors on the Dakota Sandstone capstone.

165 FORTRESS—PROW II, 5.8, A3, 1 pitch, 120 feet (37 m) ★★★

First Ascent: Pete Takeda, Tyler Stableford, Duane Raleigh, spring 1993.

Location and Access: *Prow* climbs the back side at the east end of the landform.

Paraphernalia: Spectres; long Leepers; pitons (3) 5/8" through 1 1/4"; hangers 0.5".

Descent: Rappel 40 feet (12 m) from double anchors on the Dakota Sandstone capstone.

166 TURKEY NECK I, 5.7, A3, 1 pitch ★★

First Ascent: Jeff Jackson, Duane Raleigh, Pete Takeda, summer 1993.

Location and Access: *Turkey Neck* is on the east side of the alcove from *Fortress* and closer to the interstate. Climb from the notch at the side of the spire. There is an attempted line with fixed anchors at the left edge of the spire. Pete Takeda: "It rises out of a hillside like a giant raspy gizzard with a house-sized capstone overhanging on all sides."

Paraphernalia: Angle pitons (1) each; ice tool (1); hangers 0.5".

photo: Pete Takeda

Duane Raleigh on *Mantis*

Descent: Rappel from a single-bolt anchor to the notch at the side of the spire.

167 MANTIS II, 5.7, A3, 1 pitch, 180 feet ★★★★

First Ascent: Duane Raleigh, Pete Takeda, summer 1993.

Location and Access: *Mantis* is in the next major drainage right (east) of *Fortress* and *Turkey Neck*. The route is obvious on the west face of the tower. Pete Takeda: "A wedge of mud, the Mantis is a thin rib of clay crested by a precarious series of isolated blocks. The blocks, perched on raised clay mounds, resemble bug eyes, lending an insect-like appearance. The 180-foot formation is split clean through by a crack."

Paraphernalia: Camalots (2) #3 through #4; pitons (5) 1 1/4" through 2"; Bong-Bongs through 4" (10–15); Spectres; 0.5" hangers.

Descent: There are no summit anchors. Lower off the backside. Pete Takeda: "To descend, Duane tied the haul line to the lead rope and rappelled off the opposite side of the tower using my body as a counterweight. To clean, I jumared the lead rope using his body as an anchor, and, for fear of being slingshotted off the tower, didn't dare peek over the summit ridge."

Rim Rock Spire

Rim Rock Spire is approximately 25 miles (40 km) east of the monument, about 18 miles (29 km) northeast of the airport exit from Interstate 70 in Grand Junction. To reach, take I-70 toward Glenwood Springs. Take the Collbran (State Highway 65) and Grand Mesa exit. Before making the exit, the spire will be visible on the cliffs straight ahead of the freeway.

168 NORTHWEST II, 5.10d, 3 pitches, 200 feet (61 m) ★★★

First Ascent: Harvey T. Carter, Bill Kurimay, 5.8, A2, 28 April 1978. First free ascent: Fred Knapp, Bret Ruckman.

Location and Access: *Northwest* ascends the left side of the tower as viewed from the freeway.

Pitch 1: Climb an easy 5.7 chimney to a belay.

Pitch 2: Continue up an overhanging crack system that is offwidth at its top, 5.10d.

Pitch 3: Traverse to the northwest corner and climb to the summit.

Paraphernalia: Friends (1) set. The original ascent used Bong-Bongs, Bugaboos, and medium nuts.

Descent: Rappel the route.

169 BINGBONG (a.k.a. Thin Rock) II, 5.10d, 3 pitches, 200 feet (61 m)

First Ascent: Harvey T. Carter, 5.8, A3, solo, 28 April 1978. First free ascent: Jim Bodenhamer et al.

Location and Access: *Bingbong* ascends the right side of the tower as viewed from the freeway.

Pitch 1: Climb a bolt ladder, 5.10d to a double-bolt anchor.

Pitch 2: Traverse left and join Pitch 2 of *Northwest* route.

Pitch 3: Follow Pitch 3 of *Northwest* route.

Paraphernalia: Friends (1) set.

Descent: Rappel the route.

Afternoon On A Hill

I will be the gladdest thing under the sun!
I will touch a hundred flowers and not pick one.

I will look at cliffs and clouds with quiet eyes,
Watch the wind bow down the grass, and the grass rise.

And when lights begin to show up from the town,
I will mark which must be mine, and then start down!

–Edna St. Vincent Millay

team for eight years, and represented American climbers during the Seattle World's Fair

photo: Mike Baker

Towers in Colorado National Monument

ERIC BJØRNSTAD—A CLIMBING LIFE

BY JEFF WIDEN

Eric Bjørnstad is perhaps best known as a pioneer of desert towers during the incredible early years when those phenomenal spires were first being climbed. Indeed, many of us climbing his routes today would shudder at the idea of doing them in the 1960s and early 1970s with the available gear and lack of information. Certainly, Eric's name is indelibly etched in the rich lore of desert climbing. But a broader look also reveals a life of great variety and interest, both within and outside the climbing world.

From the start, Eric engaged in a wide range of endeavors. Raised in California, his early passions included poetry writing, chess, speed typing, and classical music—playing both piano and oboe. He also sought physical challenges such as boxing, in which he excelled. Eric began camping early, with numerous trips to the High Sierra, and like many climbers then and now, a great love of high places was kindled.

Eric's first job was as a gandy dancer on the narrow-gauge railroad near Lone Pine, California. This began a working life of incredible variety; over the years he worked as a draftsman, piano salesman, photo processor, gardener, bartender, dump truck driver, tree topper, and handyman at a sorority (where he also lived), to mention only a few. His life apart

photo: Cameron M. Burns

from work was no less interesting. He married three times (to a Hungarian beauty queen, an art student, and the daughter of a major American business mogul), divorced three times, and fathered four children (David, Heather, Mara, and Eigerwand). He practiced Theravada Buddhism in Berkeley in the 1950s; partied with the likes of Alan Watts, Jack Kerouac, and Lawrence Ferlinghetti; and took up spelunking. In the late 1950s, he moved to Seattle and began a long career in alpine mountaineering. He amassed an impressive list of climbs and first ascents: Zodiac Wall, the first grade VI on the Squamish Chief, the North Face of Mount Howser in the Bugaboos, first winter ascent of Mount Robson, first ascent of the North Face of Mount Slesse, seventh ascent of Liberty Ridge on Mount Rainier, Mount Seattle in the St. Elias Range in Alaska, second ascent of the West Peak of the Moose's Tooth, and many others. He also taught climbing for the Seattle Mountaineers, served on the Seattle Mountain Rescue team for eight years, and represented American climbers durring the Seattle World's Fair French-American climbing week. It was also during this time that Eric began to write about climbing, in both magazines and books. He co-authored *Climber's Guide to Leavenworth Climbing Areas* with Fred Beckey and wrote the Pitoncraft Chapter for the second edition of the classic text *Mountaineering, Freedom of the Hills*.

From the 1960s on, Eric moved often and lived in cities across the country. He added weaving and three-dimensional stained glass to his professional repertoire, as well as the proprietorship of six restaurant-coffeehouses. He also developed a passion for climbing in the mysterious landscape of the Southwest desert. The routes that he and other desert pioneers established on these spooky towers tested the limits of existing equipment and techniques as well as their nerves. First ascents in the 1960s included Echo Tower in the Fisher Towers, the Beckey Buttress on Shiprock (20 days), Middle Sister and Jacobs Ladder in Monument Valley, Chinle Spire, and the 574th overall ascent of Devil's Tower when he and Fred Beckey put up the popular El Matador Route.

During these years, Eric climbed with such well-known figures as Ed Cooper, Alex Bertulis, Don Claunch, Harvey T. Carter, Yvon Chouinard, and Galen Rowell. He also developed an intense relationship with Fred Beckey–the two would share many first ascents over the years.

In 1970 he opened his famous Teahouse Tamarisk (24-page menu). In 1975 he began a ten-year period as a researcher investigating the effects of air pollution on lung health for the Harvard School of Public Health, which kept him traveling extensively. He returned to the desert time and again during this period, establishing first ascents such as Eagle Rock Spire in Monument Valley (another 16-day marathon), and Zeus and Moses in Canyonlands. He also did the fifth ascent of the incredible Totem Pole in Monument Valley, during the making of the film *The Eiger Sanction*.

In 1985 Eric finally returned to live in Moab and made the 600th ascent of Castleton Tower and the first ascent of the 1,000-foot El Piñon Blanca in Mexico, and participated in the first ascents of such well-known climbs as Zenyatta Entrada in Arches. He also undertook the phenomenal researching and writing task of authoring *Desert Rock*, the only comprehensive guide to the sandstone climbs of the Colorado Plateau.

Eric now gives private tours in little-known regions of the Colorado Plateau, drives four-wheel commercial tours, produces and sells Desert Glass Light Catchers–etched glass window hangings of Anasazi rock art–and is completing an expanded five-volume guide to technical rock climbs on the sandstone walls of the Southwest desert. Eric has truly lived a climbing life–in the high mountains, on rock walls, and in the desert Southwest. He has lived a well-rounded life as well, full of rich and enviable experiences. He loves the company of climbers, and will spend hours telling and listening to stories or pressing for information. His home is like a climbing museum. Yet, just as easily, he will revel in an opera or classical orchestral piece, or spend an evening preparing a fine dinner.

These guides are a tribute to Eric's life as a climber–and to his love for this desert land.

photo: Elaine Frederick

Eric Bjørnstad (right) and Fred Beckey, 1995

INDEX

Route names are set in CAPITAL LETTERS. Page numbers of illustrated routes, formations, areas, and persons are set in **bold** type.

BIRDING GUIDES

Birding Minnesota
Birding Montana
Birding Northern California
Birding Texas
Birding Utah

FIELD GUIDES

Bitterroot: Montana State Flower
Canyon Country Wildflowers
Central Rocky Moutnain
    Wildflowers
Great Lakes Berry Book
New England Berry Book
Pacific Northwest Berry Book
Plants of Arizona
Rare Plants of Colorado
Rocky Mountain Berry Book
Scats & Tracks of the
    Pacific Coast States
Scats & Tracks of the Rocky Mtns.
Tallgrass Prairie Wildflowers
Western Trees
Wildflowers of Southwestern Utah
Willow Bark and Rosehips

WALKING

Walking Colorado Springs
Walking Denver
Walking Portland
Walking St. Louis
Walking Virginia Beach

FISHING GUIDES

Fishing Alaska
Fishing the Beartooths
Fishing Florida
Fishing Glacier National Park
Fishing Maine
Fishing Montana
Fishing Wyoming
Fishing Yellowstone Natl. Park

PADDLING GUIDES

Floater's Guide to Colorado
Paddling Minnesota
Paddling Montana
Paddling Okefenoke
Paddling Oregon
Paddling Yellowstone & Grand
    Teton National Parks

ROCKHOUNDING GUIDES

Rockhounding Arizona
Rockhounding California
Rockhounding Colorado
Rockhounding Montana
Rockhounding Nevada
Rockhound's Guide to
    New Mexico
Rockhounding Texas
Rockhounding Utah
Rockhounding Wyoming

HOW-TO GUIDES

Avalanche Aware
Backpacking Tips
Bear Aware
Desert Hiking Tips
Hiking with Dogs
Leave No Trace
Mountain Lion Alert
Reading Weather
Route Finding
Using GPS
Wild Country Companion
Wilderness First Aid
Wilderness Survival

ROCK CLIMBING GUIDES

Rock Climbing Colorado
Rock Climbing Montana
Rock Climbing New Mexico
    & Texas
Rock Climbing Utah
Rock Climbing Washington

HIKING GUIDES

Best Hikes Along the Continental Divide
Hiking Alaska
Hiking Arizona
Hiking Arizona's Cactus Country
Hiking the Beartooths
Hiking Big Bend National Park
Hiking the Bob Marshall Country
Hiking California
Hiking California's Desert Parks
Hiking Carlsbad Caverns
  and Guadalupe Mtns. National Parks
Hiking Colorado
Hiking Colorado, Vol. II
Hiking Colorado's Summits
Hiking Colorado's Weminuche Wilderness
Hiking the Columbia River Gorge
Hiking Florida
Hiking Georgia
Hiking Glacier & Waterton Lakes National Parks
Hiking Grand Canyon National Park
Hiking Grand Staircase-Escalante/Glen Canyon
Hiking Grand Teton National Park
Hiking Great Basin National Park
Hiking Hot Springs in the Pacific Northwest
Hiking Idaho
Hiking Maine
Hiking Michigan
Hiking Minnesota
Hiking Montana
Hiking Mount Rainier National Park
Hiking Mount St. Helens
Hiking Nevada

Hiking New Hampshire
Hiking New Mexico
Hiking New York
Hiking the North Cascades
Hiking Northern Arizona
Hiking Olympic National Park
Hiking Oregon
Hiking Oregon's Eagle Cap Wilderness
Hiking Oregon's Mount Hood/Badger Creek
Hiking Oregon's Three Sisters Country
Hiking Pennsylvania
Hiking Shenandoah
Hiking the Sierra Nevada
Hiking South Carolina
Hiking South Dakota's Black Hills Country
Hiking Southern New England
Hiking Tennessee
Hiking Texas
Hiking Utah
Hiking Utah's Summits
Hiking Vermont
Hiking Virginia
Hiking Washington
Hiking Wisconsin
Hiking Wyoming
Hiking Wyoming's Cloud Peak Wilderness
Hiking Wyoming's Wind River Range
Hiking Yellowstone National Park
Hiking Zion & Bryce Canyon National Parks
Wild Montana
Wild Country Companion
Wild Utah

■ *To order any of these books, check with your local bookseller*
*or call FALCON ® at **1-800-582-2665**.*
Visit us on the world wide web at:
www.FalconOutdoors.com

FALCON®

FALCON GUIDES ®Leading the Way™

MOUNTAIN BIKING GUIDES

Mountain Biking Arizona
Mountain Biking Colorado
Mountain Biking Georgia
Mountain Biking New Mexico
Mountain Biking New York
Mountain Biking Northern New England
Mountain Biking Oregon
Mountain Biking South Carolina
Mountain Biking Southern California
Mountain Biking Southern New England
Mountain Biking Utah
Mountain Biking Wisconsin
Mountain Biking Wyoming

LOCAL CYCLING SERIES

Fat Trax Bozeman
Mountain Biking Bend
Mountain Biking Boise
Mountain Biking Chequamegon
Mountain Biking Chico
Mountain Biking Colorado Springs
Mountain Biking Denver/Boulder
Mountain Biking Durango
Mountain Biking Flagstaff and Sedona
Mountain Biking Helena
Mountain Biking Moab
Mountain Biking Utah's
  St. George/Cedar City Area
Mountain Biking the White
  Mountains (West)

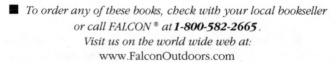

■ *To order any of these books, check with your local bookseller
or call FALCON* ® *at **1-800-582-2665**.
Visit us on the world wide web at:
www.FalconOutdoors.com*

FALCON®